ASPECTS OF TOURISM 18
Series Editors: Chris   ralia),
C. Michael Hall (U
and Dallen Timo

Tourism Marketing
A Collaborative Approach

Alan Fyall and Brian Garrod

CHANNEL VIEW PUBLICATIONS
Clevedon • Buffalo • Toronto

Library of Congress Cataloging in Publication Data
Fyall, Alan.
Tourism Marketing: A Collaborative Approach/by Alan Fyall and Brian Garrod.
Aspects of Tourism: 18
Includes bibliographical references and index.
1. Tourism–Marketing. I. Garrod, B. (Brian) II. Title. III. Series.
G155.A1F93 2004
910'.68'8–dc22   2004014170

British Library Cataloguing in Publication Data
A catalogue entry for this book is available from the British Library.

ISBN 1-873150-90-3 (hbk)
ISBN 1-873150-89-x (pbk)

Channel View Publications
An imprint of Multilingual Matters Ltd

UK: Frankfurt Lodge, Clevedon Hall, Victoria Road, Clevedon BS21 7HH.
USA: 2250 Military Road, Tonawanda, NY 14150, USA.
Canada: 5201 Dufferin Street, North York, Ontario, Canada M3H 5T8.

Typeset by Florence Production Ltd.
Printed and bound in Great Britain by the Cromwell Press.

Contents

Preface

The tourism industry is notoriously interdependent and dynamic, and tourism products are widely acknowledged to be inherently complex to co-ordinate and difficult to manage. The authors therefore find it surprising that there remains such a paucity of literature that explores the dynamics, relationships and outcomes of collaborative strategies within the tourism industry. This paucity is particularly apparent with respect to the domain of tourism marketing. While there is a large number of books that have contributed to our understanding of marketing principles and practice in the tourism and hospitality industries, these books largely fail to acknowledge that collaboration, in its various guises, is now an integral component of tourism marketing strategy.

Indeed, the authors note that the growing number of academic books covering tourism marketing that have been published to date continue to adopt the traditional, competitive marketing paradigm, presumably considering this to be the approach most suitable for the teaching of the subject. While this might be considered understandable in some of the earlier publications, the strength of forces in the external environment is such that alternative approaches to the study of the subject are now required. The fundamental premise on which this book is written is that tourism marketing needs, with some urgency, to embrace the collaborative marketing paradigm. This, indeed, is increasingly the trend in many other applications of marketing. The reason is simple: the collaborative paradigm represents by far the more versatile, penetrating and realistic conceptual basis on which to study (and, for that matter, practice) tourism marketing.

This situation is not, of course, unique to the study and practice of tourism marketing. When analysing competing publications in the area of strategy, for example, de Wit and Meyer (1998) found that almost all of the textbooks available shared four basic characteristics:

- The presentation of a *limited number of perspectives and theories* as accepted knowledge, from which prescriptions can easily be derived.

- The use of a simple *step-by-step strategic planning approach* as the book's basic structure.
- The reworking of original material into the textbook author's own words to create *consistent and easily digestible pieces of text*.
- The choice of perspectives, theories, examples and cases that are heavily biased towards the textbook author's own *national context*.

Although perhaps not evident to the same extent in the field of tourism marketing, there apparently remains a nervous reluctance to escape from the safe confines of the competitive marketing paradigm and enter the rather less familiar territory of collaborative marketing. There is no doubt that the majority of tourism marketing books currently in existence do have considerable strengths and are familiar to scholars of tourism marketing throughout the English-speaking world. In fact, many of the ideas existing within this body of marketing knowledge have been catalytic foci for much of the theoretical work that underpins this book, especially Chapters 3 and 4. However, rather than present yet another extension of the product range, so to speak, this book offers an alternative 'collaborative' way forward for students, academics and practitioners of tourism marketing. It is not strictly the intention of this book to propagate new thoughts and ideas, theories or solutions to age-old problems. In marketing, and in tourism marketing especially, very little can really be classified as new. Indeed, a large number of marketing 'innovations' in travel and tourism, although certainly not all, have been transferred from elsewhere. This is mainly because, unlike travel and tourism, other industries have had far greater exposure to the competitive dynamics of buyers' markets: markets that require customer-driven strategies.

The adoption of a market orientation and the implementation of effective marketing strategies are now almost universally considered to be prerequisites for success in the tourism industry. Although perhaps not carrying the same weight in the corridors of power as tourism policy, or for that matter issues pertaining to the environment and sustainability, the elevation of tourism marketing in the academic literature in recent years is testament to the increasingly competitive arena that is tourism. Tourism academics and professionals are increasingly recognising that there is a need to break away from the perceived superficiality and 'secondary' importance that is so often attached to tourism marketing when compared to tourism marketing's more illustrious and 'holistic' parent body of knowledge, tourism planning. Maybe this is even true of sustainability and sustainable tourism. However, it can be argued that recent additions to the literature have done little to advance the tourism marketing debate, with many authors choosing to adopt the 'tried-and-tested' approach to tourism marketing by merely importing standard marketing theory and practice to the tourism industry context. Although useful to a degree, a shortcoming of these texts is that they fail to acknow-ledge the fundamental importance of collaboration, both currently and in prospect, and its impact on all tourism marketing activity, albeit to varying degrees. Hence, there is a need to move outside existing bound-aries of marketing theory and practice and enter a new collaborative paradigm, a subset perhaps of the emerging bodies of knowledge surrounding relationship marketing, network marketing, stakeholder theory and inter-organisational collaboration.

The growing body of literature on inter-organisational collaboration in many ways represents the innovative core of this book. Inter-organ-isational collaboration is not a new area of academic research. What is new, however, is its emergence as a potential paradigm upon which to structure marketing thinking and practice in the tourism industry. Much has been written about inter-organisational collaboration, in a variety of contexts – as will become apparent throughout this book. There is, however, a very real dearth of applications of inter-organisational collaboration theory to past and existing tourism contexts of a marketing nature. The text *Tourism Collaboration and Partnerships: Politics, Practice and Sustainability*, edited by Bramwell and Lane (2000), and the text *Quality Management in Urban Tourism*, edited by Murphy (1997), are two of the very few published works that explore the role of collaboration in the effective management of tourism resources. Although there is rather more evidence of academic papers in refereed journals on the subject of collaboration, only recently have journal editors deemed it to be of sufficient importance to warrant the allocation of special issues to the subject. Recent volumes of the *Journal of Sustainable Tourism* (7 (3)) and the *International Journal of Hospitality & Tourism Administration* (1 (1)) have done much to raise the profile of collaboration in tourism.

In the words of Huxham (1996: 1–2) collaboration is 'happening', 'valuable' and 'difficult'. It is happening in a variety of forms and is finding a place in the lexicon of management where collaborative terms such as 'strategic alliance', 'joint venture' and 'partnership' are used on a daily basis. Its value comes in the form of economies of scale, the sharing of resources and enabling organisations to establish a foothold in new markets: all benefits that can be acquired through working with others. At the same time, collaboration should not be seen as a magic elixir or curer of all ills. The fact is that many collaborative arrange-ments are considered to have failed by the participants within a relatively short space of time. This high failure rate is testament to the fact that inter-organisational collaboration is never easy and offers no simple recipe for the achievement of competitive or collaborative advantage. Collaboration does, however, represent an alternative approach to solving problems: problems that are frequently considered outside the scope of resolution by individual organisations acting alone.

The aim of this book is, therefore, to provide the reader with a thorough and detailed understanding of tourism marketing principles and practice within the context of inter-organisational collaboration. The book will:

- provide an overview of existing strategic tourism marketing theory and practice;
- introduce the concepts, theories and issues central to inter-organisational collaboration; and
- include detailed sector-based chapters with contemporary tourism marketing case study material that sets out to explore the myriad of collaborative marketing strategies undertaken by tourism and hospitality organisations across the world.

Particular attention will be accorded to providing the reader with a critical understanding of the above, with a focus throughout on inter-organisational collaborative marketing strategies. Issues for discussion include: the benefits and drawbacks of collaborative marketing strategy; the internal processes, resource implications and external impacts of collaborative marketing action; issues relating to managerial power and resource imbalance; and the challenge of managing parallel competitive and collaborative tourism marketing strategies.

The book aims to offer readers an alternative 'collaborative' perspective on tourism marketing, as well as to provide an insight into the dynamics of collaborative marketing and the considerable challenges it faces. In short, this book attempts to redress the paucity of literature that investigates the difficulties posed by collaboration activity in the extant marketing and tourism marketing literature.

The book is arranged in five parts. Part 1, which comprises Chapters 1 and 2, sets the contextual background for the book with an explanation of the rationale for increasing levels of collaboration in the tourism industry. This is supported in Chapter 1 by an analysis of the factors that drive collaboration in the tourism industry and the anticipated future impacts of such forces. Chapter 2 then presents a detailed discussion on the corpus of theory which underpins collaborative or 'symbiotic' marketing behaviour (Robson & Dunk, 1999) across the tourism and hospitality industries. The chapter introduces the origins of market orientation, discusses the migration to a relational orientation perspective, and provides an overview of the existing 'standardised' approach to the study of tourism marketing adopted by the majority of authors of tourism marketing texts. In so doing, the book will sow the seeds for an alternative 'collaborative' way forward for tourism marketing. Chapter 2 will also introduce the underlying drivers of marketing change and explain the rationale behind the emerging influence of collaboration on contemporary tourism marketing thinking and practice.

Part 2 of the book, which comprises Chapters 3 and 4, begins with a critical overview of the existing standardised approach to tourism marketing strategy. Rather than investigate the nature of each individual impact of collaboration on the existing models of tourism marketing strategy in depth, this chapter will discuss the fundamental nature of the impacts of collaboration on tourism marketing strategy and identify issues for discussion in the sector-based chapters that follow in Part 3 of the book. This discussion is intended to serve as a catalyst for change for practitioners, academics and students of tourism marketing in considering the future adoption of collaborative marketing strategies in tourism.

Similar in style to the previous chapter, Chapter 4 will examine the potential impact of collaboration on the more specific elements of the marketing mix when brought together under collaborative tourism marketing programmes. As in Chapter 3, discussion is intended to serve as the catalyst for practitioners, academics and students of tourism marketing in considering the future implementation of collaborative tourism marketing programmes. This chapter will demonstrate to readers the inappropriateness of much of the current tourism marketing literature in explaining the tourism marketing domain.

Part 3 of the book, which comprises Chapters 5 to 7 and which we believe represents the innovative core of the book, includes detailed discussion on inter-organisational exchange theory. Chapter 5 will introduce readers to the theories, concepts, issues and perspectives of inter-organisational collaboration and highlight the advantages and disadvantages of collaborative activity. A number of seminal studies will be used to provide the reader with the necessary theoretical underpinning to the area of inter-organisational collaboration.

Chapter 6 will introduce readers to the variety of collaborative forms in existence, with particular reference to tourism marketing forms of inter-organisational collaboration. Seminal work by Palmer and Bejou (1995), Selin (1993) and Selin and Chavez (1995), will be utilised to provide the necessary theoretical underpinning.

Chapter 7 will conclude Part 3 of the book with a detailed discussion of the organisational and governance criteria necessary for the effective management of inter-organisational forms. Work by a variety of authors, including ground-breaking studies by Bucklin and Sengupta (1993), Palmer (1998b) and Waddock and Bannister (1991), will be used to underpin discussion of the organisational forms and governance structures in this chapter.

Part 4 of the book, which comprises Chapters 8 to 10, will critically discuss the application of many of the theoretical perspectives outlined in Chapters 2 to 7 to the specific collaborative tourism marketing challenges in three of the principal sectors of the tourism industry. Various examples will be used throughout, with discussion points and issues for future research highlighted at the end of each chapter. First, Chapter 8 focuses on transportation, undertaking an examination of the dynamics of marketing collaboration in global airline alliances. Chapter 9 follows with an investigation into the application of collaborative marketing strategies in the accommodation sector, namely hotel consortia. Thereafter, Chapter 10 investigates the innovative use of inter-destination collaboration initiatives among tourist destinations.

Part 5, which comprises Chapter 11, concludes the book as a whole by bringing together the key issues raised in the book and presenting the reader with a strategic marketing framework suitable for use in inter-organisational collaborative marketing situations in the tourism industry. Part 5 will close with an examination of the appropriateness of the existing marketing paradigm in an industry where in 'so few situations does one company or organisation control all the components, or all the stages in the decision-making processes in the creation and delivery of the tourism product' (Bramwell & Lane, 2000: 1).

Upon reading this book, it is our hope that the reader feels challenged and provoked to consider the wider rationale, dynamics and implications of collaborative marketing strategies in tourism. Strategies of collaboration are now widespread across all sectors of the tourism industry. Many are, however, still in their early stages of development, with a large number – airline alliances included – still as yet to prove their robustness as strategies able to accommodate the enormous pressures and environmental changes apparent in the highly dynamic and turbulent market conditions of today. It is hoped that this book will play a small part in offering a critique of the developments that have taken place, and are continuing to take place, in the domain of tourism marketing. It is also our aspiration that this book will serve as a catalyst for questioning the suitability of an alternative collaborative 'relational' orientation for the application of marketing in what is now being called the world's largest industry.

Alan Fyall,
Bournemouth

Brian Garrod,
Aberystwyth

Acknowledgements

In writing this book, both authors acknowledge the unstinting support of their families, particularly during April 2003. This is because on 8 April 2003, Brian and Alison welcomed Andrew Brian George into the Garrod family, a brother for Lydia. Meanwhile on 14 April 2003, Alan and Lise, not wishing to be left out, welcomed Alix Rose into the Fyall household. Needless to say, the expansion of both the Garrod and Fyall dynasties has not exactly been conducive to writing a book, and we would therefore like to thank Mike and Marjukka Grover for their patience while awaiting the long-overdue final draft of this book. We would also like to thank Cicely Carimbocas for her contribution to Chapter 9 and Athanasios Spyriadis for some excellent ideas in the early stages of the book. Thanks are also due to Denise Hewlett for her unique brand of research assistance in the latter stages of the project. Most importantly, however, although writing this book has been a very interesting and enjoyable journey for us both, it is fair to say that the arrival of Andrew and Alix has taught us both that sometimes, just sometimes, other things in life are more important than writing books. For obvious reasons, this book is dedicated to Andrew and Alix.

Copyright material

We are grateful to the following for permission to reproduce copyright material:

Figure 1.1 reproduced from Yip, G. (1995) *Total Global Strategy* with permission from Prentice Hall. Figure 2.1 reproduced from Donaldson, B. and O'Toole, T. (2002) © *Strategic Market Relationships: From Strategy to Implementation* and Figure 3.4 reproduced from Doyle, P. (2000) © *Value-based Marketing: Marketing Strategies for Corporate Growth and Shareholder Value* with permission from John Wiley & Sons Limited. Figure 2.2 reproduced from Helfert, G., Ritter, T. and Walter, A. (2002) © Redefining market orientation from a relational perspective: Theoretical considerations and empirical results, *European Journal of Marketing* 36 (9&10) with permission from Emerald Insight, 1119–1139; Figure 2.3 reprinted from McDonald, N. and Payne, A. (1996) © *Marketing Planning for Services* with permission from Elsevier, Oxford. Figure 2.4 reprinted from Middleton, V.T.C. (1998) © *Sustainable Tourism: A Marketing Perspective* with permission from Elsevier, Oxford. Figure 3.2 reprinted from Drummond, G. and Ensor, J. (1999) © *Strategic Marketing: Planning and Control* with permission from Elsevier, Oxford. Figure 3.3, Figure 4.1, Figure 4.2 and Figure 4.3 reprinted from Evans, N., Campbell, D. and Stonehouse, G. (2003) © *Strategic Management for Travel and Tourism* with permission from Elsevier, Oxford. Figure 3.9 reproduced from Lumsdon, L. (1997) © *Tourism Marketing* with permission from International Thomson Business Press, London. Figure 3.10 reproduced from McKercher, B. (1995) © The destination-market matrix: A tourism market portfolio analysis model, *Journal of Travel and Tourism Marketing* 4 (2), 23–40 with permission from The Haworth Press, New York. Figure 3.11 reprinted from Piercy, N. (1997) © *Market-led Strategic Change* (2nd edn) with permission from Elsevier, Oxford. Table 5.1 reproduced from Chaston, I. (1999) © *New Marketing Strategies*, Table 6.1 reproduced from Himmelman, A.T. (1996) © On the theory and practice of transformational collaboration: From social service to social justice, in C. Huxham (ed.) *Creating Collaborative Advantage*, 19–43, Figure 6.3 reproduced from Huxham, C. (1996) © Dimensions of collaboration rationale and relationship between them, in C. Huxham *Creating Collaborative Advantage* and Box 7.2 reproduced from Gray, B. (1996) © Cross-sectoral partners: Collaborative alliances among businesses, government and communities, in C. Huxham (ed.) *Creating Collaborative Advantage*, 57–79, with permission from Sage Publications, London. Figure 6.1 reproduced from Walker, D.H.T. and Johannes, D.S. (2003) © Construction industry joint venture behaviour in Hong King: Designed for collaborative results, *International Journal of Project Management* 21 (1), 39–49, Table 8.2 reproduced from Rhoades, D.L. and Lush, H. (1997) © A typology of strategic alliances in the airline industry: Propositions for stability and duration, *Journal of Air Transport Management* 3 (3), 109–114, and Figure 8.2 reproduced from Evans, N. (2001) © Collaborative strategy: An analysis of the changing world of airline alliances, *Tourism Management* 22 (3), 229–243 with permission from Elsevier Science. Figure 6.2 reproduced from Child, J. and Faulkner, D. (1998) © *Strategies of Co-operation: Managing Alliances, Networks and Joint Ventures* with permission from Oxford University Press, Oxford. Figures 6.4, 6.5, 6.6 and 6.7 reproduced from Selin, S. (1999) © Developing a typology of sustainable tourism partnerships, *Journal of Sustainable Tourism* 7 (3&4), 260–273, and Figure 6.10 reproduced from Caffyn, A. (2000) © Is there a tourism partnership life cycle? In B. Bramwell and B. Lane (eds) *Tourism Collaboration and Partnerships: Politics, Practice and Sustainability,*

200–229 with permission from Channel View Publi-cations, Clevedon. Figure 6.8 reproduced from Waddock, S.A. (1989) © Understanding social partnerships: An evolutionary model of partnership organizations, *Administration & Society* 21 (1), 78–100 and Table 7.1 reproduced from Wood, D.J. and Gray, B. (1991) © Toward a comprehensive theory of collaboration, *Journal of Applied Behavioral Science* 27 (2), 139–162, with permission from Sage Publications Limited. Figure 10.1 reproduced from Prideaux, B. and Cooper, C. (2002) © Marketing and destination growth: A symbiotic relationship or simple coincidence?, *Journal of Vacation Marketing* 9 (1), 40 with permission from Henry Stewart Publications.

In some instances we have been unable to trace the owners of copyright material, and we would therefore appreciate any information that would enable us to do so.

Acronyms

ADB	Asian Development Bank
AMB	Alliance Management Board
AMTA	Agency for Coordinating Mekong Tourism Activities
ASEAN	Association of Southeast Asian Nations
ASP	application service provider
ATC	Australian Tourist Commission
BA	British Airways
BCG	Boston Consulting Group
bmi	British Midland International
B2B	business-to-business
B2C	business-to-consumer
CRO	central reservation office
CRS	computerised reservation system
DMO	destination marketing organisation
ECA	European Cooperation Agreement
EEA	European Economic Area
ETB	English Tourist Board
EU	European Union
EWEC	East–West Economic Corridor
FFP	frequent-flier programme
GCCC	Gold Coast City Council
GCITC	Gold Coast International Tourism Committee
GCTB	Gold Coast Tourism Bureau
GDP	Gross Domestic Product
GDS	global distribution system
GE	General Electric
GMS	Greater Mekong Subregion
GNP	Gross National Product
GSP	Gross State Product
ICT	information and communication technology
LGA	local government authority
MGC	Museums and Galleries Commission

MICE	meetings, incentives, conventions and exhibitions
MNC	multinational company
NAFTA	North American Free Trade Agreement
NATO	North Atlantic Treaty Organisation
NTO	national tourism organisation
OLS	ordinary least squares
OPEC	Organization of Petroleum Exporting Countries
PATA	Pacific Area Tourism Association
P3	public–private partnership
RAS	Redemption Availability and Sell
SARS	Severe Acute Respiratory Syndrome
SBU	strategic business unit
SIS	Stockholm Information Service
SLH	Small Luxury Hotels (of the World)
STO	state tourism organisation
SWOT	strengths, weaknesses, opportunities and threats
TAT	Tourism Authority of Thailand
TDAP	Tourism Development Action Plan
TSC	Tourism Sunshine Coast
TWG	Tourism Working Group
UNESCO	United Nations Educational, Scientific and Cultural Organization
VCB	Visitor and Convention Bureau
WTO	World Tourism Organization

Part 1: Collaboration and Tourism

Chapter 1
Collaboration and Tourism

Introduction

In most industrial sectors it has become commonplace for organisations to collaborate in order to achieve the goals they have established for themselves. With the accelerating pace of technological innovation and the ever hastening trend towards globalisation, traditional adversarial relationships among business organisations are increasingly being swept away and replaced by enduring collaborative arrangements. This trend is particularly apparent in the tourism industry, where the fragmented, multi-sectoral and interdependent nature of tourism provides a powerful catalytic focus for inter-organisational co-ordination and collective decision-making. Tourism is a notoriously difficult industry in which to manage an organisation, and the increasingly competitive nature of the market relationships in which tourism organisations typically now find themselves does not make this management task any easier. Both at an international scale and locally, therefore, 'tourism planners and operators are discovering the power of collaborative action' (Selin, 1993: 218) and are moving away from the traditional 'adversarial model' of conducting business (Telfer, 2000: 72).

In few stages of the tourism 'assembly process' does any one company or organisation control all the components or all the stages of the decision-making process involved in the creation and delivery of the final product. As such, organisational performance is critically dependent on establishing and maintaining effective relationships, with organisations working collaboratively to serve the consumer. Indeed, some commentators even go so far as to suggest that successful collaborative relationships are an essential ingredient of organisational longevity in the tourism industry (Crotts et al., 2000; Haywood, 1992; Murphy, 1997).

A key reason for the growing interest in collaboration in tourism is the belief that organisations and destination areas may be able to gain competitive advantage by bringing together and sharing their combined knowledge, expertise, capital and other resources (Kotler et al., 1999b).

3

If this is true, then the implication is that the more widespread adoption of collaborative working will be critical to the future of the tourism industry: firms and organisations will increasingly need to work together in order to meet the needs of the customer, in this instance the tourist. Meanwhile, rapid economic, social and political change also provides powerful incentives for tourism organisations to concede their independence and collaborate with one another. Osborne and Gaebler (1992), for example, argue that the divide between the public and private sectors is becoming increasingly nebulous, encouraging organisations that were previously isolated from one another to begin working collaboratively. They also point to tightening budgetary constraints, combined with political and public pressure for greater accountability, as key incentives for collaboration in the tourism industry.

Interest in collaboration in tourism has arisen at a time of increasing environmental turbulence and operational complexity for organisations of all kinds, particularly since the terrorist atrocities committed in New York and Washington, DC on 11 September 2001 (now widely referred to as '9/11'). The transition to alternative forms of collaboration, in particular strategic alliances, has been recognised by organisational theorists and practitioners alike, and has intensified scrutiny on all issues 'collaborative' (Long, 1997). For example, collaboration is now widespread in many public tourism initiatives, especially in the European Union (EU) where funding for many urban and regional regeneration projects demands collaboration as a precondition. Collaboration also represents a ready 'bridge' between the traditional 'bureaucratic' production culture of the public sector and the 'marketing culture' of the private tourism sector (Palmer, 1996). Arguably, in many instances it is the lack of a marketing culture in the public sector that has motivated collaboration with private-sector organisations, the aim being to gain access to core competencies in marketing and related activities. Waddock (1989) supports this viewpoint by stating that the private sector generally has a much greater commitment to a market orientation, which it can exchange for access to the public sector's political and economic resources, which cannot be obtained on the open market.

In spite of the above rationale, and regardless of the existence of considerable environmental pressures, the intrinsically competitive nature of tourism has not always assisted in the development of effective collaboration among tourism organisations. This tendency has been particularly evident at the local level. Unsophisticated communication systems, endemic geographical and organisational fragmentation, issues pertaining to jurisdictional boundaries and the ideological divide between public and private sectors have often inhibited the adoption and implementation of effective collaborative tourism initiatives.

It may therefore be considered surprising that, although the subject of collaboration has been researched in depth in the fields of health, organisational behaviour, corporate strategy and public policy, its emergence on the tourism research agenda is still relatively recent. Publications by Crotts *et al.* (2000), Palmer (1998b), Palmer and Bejou (1995) and Selin (1993) have contributed much to greater understanding of the issues, actions and implications of collaborative behaviour in tourism. However, the study of collaboration in the tourism context nevertheless remains in its academic infancy, both in respect of tourism generally and applied to tourism marketing in particular. Long (1996), for example, claims that there is a distinct lack of studies that employ theoretical frameworks and methods associated with the analysis of collaboration in tourism, while Pearce (1992) suggests that limited research has been conducted on tourist organisations per se. In a more recent publication, Bramwell and Lane (2000: 3) argue that 'despite increasing interest in tourism partnerships, until recently there has been little systematic research on the internal processes and external impacts of these organisational forms'.

A central argument being put forward in the present text is that questions directed at co-ordination and inter-organisational interaction are critical, indeed fundamental, to the future analysis of tourism and tourist organisations. Moreover, Jamal and Getz (1995) suggest that, in view of the interdependencies and the simultaneous use of competitive and collaborative strategies in tourism, the various stages and actual implementation of the collaboration process require investigation. The time has truly arrived where a paradigm shift is required in the study of tourism and, in particular, the study of tourism marketing. It is clear that the focus of academic concern now needs to shift from the individual 'competitive' organisation to the inter-organisational 'collaborative' domain (meaning the configuration of organisations linked to a particular shared problem). This shift is likely to be hastened by the considerable economic, social and political pressures that are encouraging tourism organisations to relinquish their autonomy and to participate in collaborative decision-making. Indeed, as Go and Appelman (2001) note, collaboration is now widespread in the tourism domain. The number and variety of inter-organisational collaborative relationships and networks has grown significantly over the past two decades, and the pace of change is clearly increasing. Those interested in the management and marketing of the tourism industry misunderstand the dynamics of collaboration at their peril. Collaboration, in all its many forms, is not only integral to the management of tourism; it is arguably the single most important aspect of management in determining the success, or indeed the failure, of tourism marketing strategies and programmes. What is more, collaboration looks set to maintain such primacy for many years to come.

Drivers of Collaboration

The foregoing discussion has highlighted the increasing tendency for organisations to adopt collaborative strategies to address problems that have traditionally been considered to be 'competitive' in nature. The purpose of this section is to consider the major forces that have driven the emergence and acceptance of collaborative strategies both in the tourism context and in business more generally.

Globalisation

Many writers propose that the predominant force acting on the world's economic systems at the present time is that of globalisation (for example, Levitt, 1983; Ohmae, 1989; Yip, 1993). Indeed, it is rapidly becoming untenable even to speak of more than one economic system in the world. The process of globalisation has broken down the barriers between economic systems and encouraged them to become progressively more integrated with one another. The result has been the emergence of what can increasingly only be described as a single global economy.

Globalisation has been, and continues to be, driven by an array of converging forces. Figure 1.1 identifies those forces identified by Yip (1995) as some of those central to the emergence of globalisation as the world's predominant economic order. Advances in information technology, communication methods and distribution systems, along with continued economic growth in the developing world, have all contributed greatly. Likewise, policy changes in many countries around the world and the emergence of transnational corporations – the so-called new vistas of competition (Ohmae, 1991) – are also reinforcing the trend towards globalisation.

There can be little doubt that globalisation has substantially raised the level of competition in many markets, many business organisations now having to compete in a much more complex and multi-faceted economic environment. Indeed, Wahab and Cooper (2001: 4) suggest that globalisation has now become an all-embracing term that denotes a world which 'due to many political, economic, technological and informational advancements and developments is on its way to becoming borderless and an interdependent whole'. In the specific context of tourism, Wahab and Cooper go on to suggest that the continuing growth in demand for tourism, the expansion and diversification of travel motivations and the enlarged expectations of tourists are all contributing to the increasing global presence and significance of tourism in the world economy. Fierce competition between an increasing number of tourist destinations and a trend towards increasing deregulation in many of the world's tourism industries are also contributing to a more globalised environment in which the business of tourism is conducted.

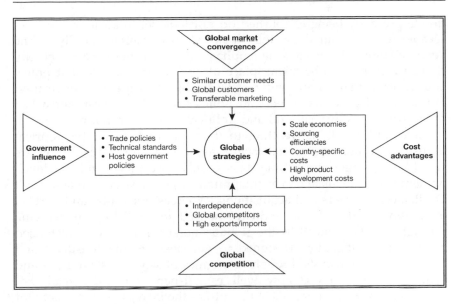

Figure 1.1 Drivers of globalisation

Source: Based on Yip, 1995

Globalisation is leading to an increasingly borderless and interdependent world, and this serves as the catalytic focus for much collaborative activity, both within the tourism industry and outside it. Magun (1996) argues that across all industrial sectors there is growing acceptance that competition itself does not necessarily promote optimum, innovation-led growth. The realisation is that both competition and collaboration between organisations is now needed to ensure survival and growth in an increasingly uncertain and dynamic world. Armed with new strategies, both competitive and collaborative in nature, business organisations are now able to penetrate formerly inaccessible markets and take advantage of the opportunities afforded to them by globalisation. This is true for industries as diverse as pharmaceuticals and petrochemicals, automotive and semi-conductor manufacturing, financial services and the provision of health and educational services. Magun's explanation for this trend is that the need for complementary specialised inputs has forced organisations to change their business strategies by embracing collaboration. This has enabled them to create added organisational flexibility in their value chain activities, such as research and development, and in logistics and channels of distribution.

The socio-economic, cultural and political forces of globalisation are such that one can argue that an international 'global society' is not just in the making, it is already with us. Moreover, for many writers, the trends presently being established do not look set to abate in the foreseeable future. If anything, they look set to accelerate rapidly in the years to come. This is an issue emphasised by Gartner (1996), whereby change is argued to be taking place at such a prolific rate that policy and decision makers are under considerable pressure to change their attitudes and previous beliefs and policies in order to keep abreast of basic socio-economic, cultural and political values and norms.

Forces are one thing; reacting to them is another. For the tourism industry, the most influential factors associated with globalisation are significant changes in consumer tastes and expectations, and the development and adjustment of new integrated corporate structures as a result of alliances, mergers and acquisitions. Whereas horizontal and vertical integration in the tourism industry started in the 1960s, intensifying through the 1960s and 1970s, the globalisation era is mainly characterised by diagonal integration. Designed to get closer to the consumer and reduce transaction costs through economies of scope, system gains and synergies, this trend is now well established and widespread. For example, Domke-Damonte (2000) identifies the increasing propensity for diagonal collaborative relationships to be established between airlines, hotels, restaurants, mortgage companies, rental car companies and credit card providers, all of which are important constituent elements of the tourism product.

Given the enormous power and reach of globalisation as a driving force in the business environment, Kanter (1995) argues that the criteria of success for tourism organisations in a globalised society are changing. Kanter suggests that in the future tourism organisations will be judged increasingly on the quality of their concepts (leading-edge ideas, designs and product formulations), on their competencies (their ability to deliver products and to transform ideas into services) and, above all, on their connections. The notion of 'connections' relates to the organisation's collaborative networks, that is, the alliances and relationships that lever core capabilities, create value for customers and remove boundaries. Global airline alliances are just one example of such new inter-organisational forms in the era of globalisation.

International political and trade agreements

An important factor contributing to globalisation, and clearly also to the emergence and accelerated growth of inter-organisational collaboration, is the proliferation of trade agreements and new inter-nation forms of political integration. The recent accession of 10 new member states into the EU, and the entry of former Eastern Bloc countries such as Hungary and Romania into the North Atlantic Treaty Organisation (NATO), are both witness to the success of these new political forms. This having been said, the current debate on the suitability of existing structures, frameworks and the wider constitution of the EU is such that observers believe that the collaborative form and governance structure for 15 member states is not necessarily that most suited to its enlarged existence. It is not only in Europe, however, where political and trade agreements have proliferated. Such agreements have multiplied steadily on every continent, which in turn has opened up the global economy. The North American Free Trade Agreement (NAFTA) has promoted trade throughout the western hemisphere, with recent expansion beyond the original participants (the US, Canada and Mexico) into Chile. Other political collaborations across the world include the MERCOSUR grouping between Argentina, Brazil, Uruguay and Paraguay, the Association of Southeast Asian Nations (ASEAN) and the Organization of the Petroleum Exporting Countries (OPEC). Although each has contrasting missions and objectives, they are all testimony to the emergence and impact of collaborative political forms in contemporary global politics.

Such international groupings of nations demonstrate the energies of collaboration in delivering outcomes deemed unachievable by nations in isolation. While it is clear that these agreements have significance beyond tourism, it can nevertheless be argued that they have had an enormous impact on the growth of tourism at the international level. Within the EU alone, the lack of border controls, a single currency in the majority of member states and the harmonisation of many legal and financial statutes facilitating the free movement of people have all contributed greatly to the growth of the tourism industry.

Another major driver of collaboration specific to the facilitation of travel and tourism is the deregulation in North America and Europe of international air transportation. The policy of liberalisation has resulted in the emergence of numerous bilateral 'open skies' agreements between international airlines. These agreements determine the cities to be served, the number of airline carriers that can fly the routes, the frequency of flights and approved pricing schedules. Some routes are very restrictive and competition is regulated tightly by the agreements in place. On other routes, control is less severe. This policy has undoubtedly contributed to the emergence of 'collaborative' international airline alliances in recent years and has served as the catalyst for the development of airline hubs (WTO, 2002). Although specific to airlines, the impact of deregulation of international air transportation and, more importantly, the collaborative response on the part of international airlines, has brought to life an inter-organisational form that the entire tourism industry is watching with interest. Its high-profile nature, expansive global reach, cross-cultural dynamics and interdependence with so many other facets of the tourism product all add to its potential to impact significantly on the wider travel and tourism industry.

One cautionary note with regard to the influence of international trade agreements is the emergence of a trend towards consolidation and concentration in the global economy. Most global trade is now conducted by some 40,000 business organisations, most of which belong to some form of international network. A third of this trade takes place between subsidiaries and parent companies. Another third of global trade is conducted by multinational companies (MNCs). Thus, although much of the literature refers to the globalisation of free and open markets, an alternative viewpoint suggests that many markets are in fact 'closed' and therefore out of reach to many business organisations. This is especially the case in the developing world, where the costs of establishing such relationships can often be prohibitive. Although this is not an issue for debate in this chapter, it does highlight the need for organisations to achieve connectivity with 'active' participants in the world economy. Such connectivity is at a premium, with many smaller firms jostling with one another to win the privilege of collaborating with the 'world-class players'. As such, one fear is that the strategy of collaboration may be beyond the capabilities of organisations that have not already made their move.

Shareholding restrictions

Alternative forms of inter-organisational collaboration also arise in response to restrictions in international shareholdings. For example, in Canada and the US legislation is such that foreign ownership of a domestic airline is restricted to 25% of voting shares. In contrast, this figure is 49.9% in Europe. Thus, whereas a North American airline can own almost half a European airline, the same European airline can only own 25% of a North American airline (WTO, 2002). Although government restrictions on the foreign ownership of national carriers vary across the world, restrictions are nevertheless easing gradually. For example, in Thailand the percentage of foreign ownership allowed has risen from 10% to 30% in recent years (WTO, 2002).

While the above discussion relates specifically to international airlines, similar restrictive trade practices impact on all other aspects of the tourism industry, most notably among hotels and tour operations. Inter-organisational collaboration represents a potential solution to such constraints, serving as a mechanism to confront the inequalities and inconsistencies of international shareholding restrictions.

Integration and networks

Regardless of whether one refers to 'synergy', 'synthesis' or 'symbiosis', the benefits of obtaining 'added value' through the creation of integrated networks or alliances can be considerable. Drawing on Porter's (1980) concept of the value chain, Ashkenas *et al.* (1995) argue that, in a globalised society, the value chain has come to represent the single most significant concept by which organisations and enterprises are linked together. By integrating the activities along their value chain, organisations can work together to create products and services that have more value combined than separately. The increasingly competitive nature of global markets suggests that co-operation between firms, especially among smaller players, will continue to expand. However, the aforementioned rise of MNCs that base their competitive advantage partly on economies of scale and scope is likely to impact significantly on these smaller operators. Smaller operators are likely to become niche players and, where appropriate, complement the major players in the travel and tourism industry. To do this, smaller players will need to develop suitable organisational structures to enable them to function effectively within the 'collaborative' value network and fiercely competitive markets. This collaborative imperative is of particular importance in tourism, where the value chain is central to the creation of products by intermediaries. In this instance, globalisation provides the environment for a new way of thinking in the tourism distribution channel as individual tourism businesses, intermediaries and tourists cease to be adversarial in the channel and move to a more co-operative model (Crotts & Wilson, 1995).

The recognition that added value is often created through inter-organisational collaborative forms highlights the current and future importance of the network concept. This is particularly significant for tourism in that information flows largely consist of a complex network of business organisations engaged in providing entertainment, accommodation, food, transportation, communication and other products to the tourist, and where the tourism system exists to deliver an enjoyable and satisfactory experience to the tourist. Go and Appelman (2001) build further on this by introducing the concept of the consumer-driven value chain, that generates capability within organisations to deliver added value for stakeholders. The application of this approach enables small players to capitalise on the challenges and opportunities presented to them in newly emerging markets. The central thesis of the consumer-driven value chain is that horizontal and vertical harmonisation and co-operation are essential when one seeks to provide consumers with the quality and variety of products they demand in an efficient way. Clearly, the ideas central to the concept are equally valid to strategic alliances among larger corporations. This would suggest that the principal issue for the future, both for smaller and large business organisations, will be how best to manage parallel competitive and collaborative strategies, the firm competing with its rivals in some contexts and collaborating with its colleagues in others.

Consolidation and concentration of economic power

Much of the growth of MNCs in recent years can be attributed to the explosion in the number of mergers and acquisitions across the globe. This trend, which is evident across the entire spectrum of industries, has contributed in recent years to the emergence of numerous 'mega' multinationals. The creation of AOL/Time Warner, Philip Morris/ Nabisco and Viacom/CBS is testament to the increasing consolidation and concentration of market power in the world economy. Where some lead others inevitably follow, with mergers and acquisitions becoming an increasingly popular strategic option for firms eager to strengthen their competitive position in the global marketplace. The consequence of such developments is the emergence of numerous alternative types of collaborative relationships, uniting a variety of sectors and activities. The rationale, form, governance, coverage and longevity of such relationships will all vary depending on the environmental context and factors specific to the organisation in question.

One possible outcome of the current economic slowdown in the US and across the globe is that the growth of merger and acquisition activity will slow down. This having been said, mergers and acquisitions are still likely to remain a formidable economic force in the years to come. This is particularly so for the tourism industry. Indeed, according to Wahab and Cooper (2001) it is the development of new integrated corporate structures as a result of alliances, mergers and acquisitions that is likely to cause the greatest structural impact on the tourism industry.

Advances in technology

Bradley *et al.* (1993: 33) argue that 'globalisation and technology are mutually reinforcing drivers of change'. They go on to suggest that advances in information technology oblige firms 'to act local and think global', while fundamentally transforming existing patterns of production and consumption. With in excess of 450 million users around the world, the expansion of the Internet is central to this scenario, and its development has undoubtedly contributed much to the emergence of collaboration strategies in a multitude of industry sectors. Although more prevalent in business-to-business (B2B), rather than business-to-consumer (B2C) situations, electronic commerce remains an inescapable reality for business organisations, with exponential growth forecast. This is despite widespread concerns among consumers about security and confidentiality, especially with regard to the transmission of personal data. The Internet is highly affordable and user-friendly. It has global market reach, immense flexibility and is particularly popular with younger target markets. It is also highly suitable for the marketing and distribution of service-based products, especially tourism. Although there is a number of legal issues outstanding, especially pertaining to legal liability, the growth of Internet-driven commerce is substantial.

Considerable disparities and inequalities exist in the world, however, with regard to the adoption and application of Internet technologies. With growth most prominent in Europe, Africa and the Middle East demonstrate minimal Internet usage in comparison, showing a much lower level of growth. Despite all the benefits that the Internet offers, it is clear that not every corner of the world is benefiting equally from the phenomenon. This then reopens the issue as to which firms, organisations, or even countries, are able to participate in collaboration in an effective manner. In short, are the benefits to be derived from collaboration and 'connectivity' with the globalising world on offer to all?

In addition to the exponential growth of the Internet, mobile technologies are expanding fast, both in their design and in their application. Although the jury remains out on their real impact on consumer purchasing behaviour, 'm-commerce' combines mobile technology with wireless application technology, and offers the consumer a freedom of movement hitherto not available due to the need to be in close proximity to a personal computer.

The purchase of travel and tourism products 'online' has recorded dramatic growth in recent years, with brands such as Expedia, Travelocity and, more recently, Opodo becoming established household names. Opodo is an interesting example in that it represents a collaborative venture between British Airways, Air France, Alitalia, Iberia, KLM, Lufthansa, Aer Lingus, Austrian Airlines Finnair and Amadeus, and is testimony to the driving force of technological advances in furthering the scope and potential for collaborative advantage among traditionally competitive organisations. Not only does this reflect the power of technology, but it also reflects the changing philosophy among business leaders in the new economic order.

Growth in tourism demand

While the aforementioned drivers have contributed much to the emergence of inter-organisational collaboration strategies, so too has the unprecedented boom in demand for travel, despite the events of 9/11. Current growth predictions from the World Tourism Organization (WTO) are that the number of international tourists will increase from 664 million each year to more than one billion by the year 2010 to 1.6 billion by the year 2020 of which 1.18 billion will be intra-regional and 377 million will be long-haul travellers (WTO, 2003). The consequences of such large-scale expansion are considerable, both for the tourist and for the tourism industry. For the tourist, there can be no doubt such a vast expansion will bring considerable pressure on the already fragile natural and cultural environments upon which tourism relies. If this pressure is not managed in a sustainable manner it has the potential to have a massive negative impact on levels of tourist satisfaction. Likewise, the global tourism industry will be under considerable political and market pressure to manage growth in a sustainable manner. Managing such large and rapid growth will be a challenge for all component parts of the tourism industry. The interdependent nature of the tourism product, combined with the aforementioned growth in tourist arrivals, serves as a major driver for the adoption of collaborative 'coping' strategies. The recent work by Bramwell and Lane (2000) suggests that in most instances it is only through sustainable 'collaborative' relationships that this growth can be met.

Strategic alliances

In order to serve the increasing growth in tourism demand worldwide, emerging collaborative forms of strategy have been forced to evolve. One of the tourism industry's prominent responses in recent years has been to create strategic alliances, many of which are on an international scale. Although by no means the only form of collaboration active in the tourism industry, strategic alliances have grown spectacularly across all tourism sectors, rising from 1000 in 1989 to 7000 in 1999 (WTO, 2002).

Strategic alliances offer business organisations the flexibility they need to 'deal with globalisation, increased consolidation of economic power, the high cost of keeping up with constantly changing technologies and a highly competitive business environment' (WTO, 2002: 3). Participants in the strategic alliance are able to share resources and risks in a relatively cost-efficient manner, thereby combining their strengths and enhancing their ability to achieve economies of scale. With nearly 70% of all strategic alliances between 1989 and 1999 international in nature, it is fair to assume that many in the wider tourism industry support their role as a powerful strategy for responding to the challenges of globalisation. Of particular relevance to this book, however, is that the majority of alliance forms are in existence for purposes of sales and marketing, and research and development (WTO, 2002).

Heightened competition

Despite the increasing consolidation and concentration in many industry sectors, especially tourism, there remains one constant throughout: heightened competition. Although this can result in positive benefits for the tourist in the form of lower prices, often driven by reactionary promotional discounting, the competitive environment is such that the margin for profit for many operators of transport, accommodation and tour operations has become very tight indeed. For a variety of reasons, an ever greater number of destinations continues to appear in the 'tourism supermarket', so that the range of choice for the tourist continues to grow year on year. The allure of tourism as a generator of quick economic gains, as a catalyst for urban regeneration and as a means of generating much-needed foreign exchange is just one of the reasons for the continued focus on tourism as a development option in many countries around the world. Although providing a vast array of choice for the tourist, such intense competition for 'leisure-time spend' creates an environment where traditional adversarial competitive behaviour becomes prohibitive in terms of cost and impossible to conduct for many smaller destination players.

Increasing customer expectations

Much is said about increasing levels of customer expectation in all market areas in many countries around the world. In many instances it provides a somewhat simplistic response to explain away a variety of changing patterns of customer behaviour. In the developed world, it is clear that customers are becoming more experienced and more discerning. At the same time, evidence suggests that customers are becoming more susceptible to the trickery of marketing and its offshoots of advertising, promotion and public relations. This having been said, the maturing of many capitalist systems in Western economies guarantees a large supply of customers familiar with the rules of engagement and wary of sub-standard practice and delivery, especially in respect of their encounters with service. This has important implications for tourism due to the intangible and 'experiential' nature of the product, as well as the considerable array of products now available, be they airlines, tour operators, hotels and, perhaps most noticeably, destinations.

One factor driving up expectation levels is time, or rather 'free time'. Buhalis (2001: 70) makes the point that increasingly 'people are becoming more aware of their limited time and are looking for both value for time and value for money'. Moreover, the challenge is to provide tourism products and services that meet the needs, wants and expectations of tourists, and especially 'new tourists' as characterised by Poon (1993). Rather than simply to 'bundle' the component parts of the tourism product into a mass-market product, tourist trends are such that suppliers of transport, accommodation, attractions and destinations are now having to seek alternative 'collaborative' means by which tourism products can be co-ordinated so as to deliver real value and quality to more discerning, independent tourists. Increasing sophistication and specialisation are just two of the trends tourism marketers will need to address in the coming years. The question for many operators and destinations is how they can deliver satisfaction to more discerning tourists, when the competitive pressures are such that budget constraints and resource limitations render individual competitive action no longer viable.

Sustainable development

An increasingly important driver of broad-based collaboration among organisations across the public, private and voluntary sectors is the growing awareness that a collaborative approach is required in order to build effective responses to the challenges of sustainable development. Indeed, this is probably the most important driver behind the widespread development of public–private sector collaboration (sometimes known as public–private partnerships, or 'P3s'). Organisations of all kinds are realising that making significant steps towards achieving the objectives of sustainable development requires the adoption of an integrated, 'stakeholder' approach to policy-making.

As Selin (1999) points out, there has been considerable debate among academics and practitioners about what 'sustainable development' might mean in principle and in practice. It is not the intention of this chapter to enter into this debate, which is both extensive and complex (for a review of some of the major issues in the tourism context, see Butler, 1999). Suffice it at this stage to say that sustainable development is about managing the planet's resource stocks equitably. This means ensuring that the needs and wants of today's generation are met without impacting adversely on their potential to meet the needs and wants of future generations. It also implies a concern of equity, or fairness, in terms of access to the resources that are needed to meet the needs and wants of the present generation (Garrod & Fyall, 1998).

Of more direct relevance to the present discussion is that the integration of stakeholders into the policy-making and decision-making processes involved is often considered fundamental to their potential success (Hall, 1999; Timothy, 1998). The basis of this view is that the natural, manufactured, socio-cultural and human assets (or 'capital') on which human well-being is fundamentally based must be managed in a holistic manner in order for sustainable development to be effectively pursued. If the needs, intentions or actions of any one stakeholder group are ignored in the management process, the likelihood is that the policies and programmes designed to maintain the assets concerned for the benefit of future generations will fail. In the tourism context, the most common form of organisation that has been developed to address the need to integrate stakeholders into sustainable development policies and programmes has been the P3. Most of these are cross-sectoral initiatives that bring together the interests of the tourism industry, local resident groups, community interest groups and public-sector organisations across a number of levels.

This is not to suggest that cross-sectoral collaboration is the only means of pursuing sustainable development. As Selin (1999) points out, cases of collaboration oriented towards attaining sustainable development objectives taking place within a single tourism sector abound. Recent initiatives among hotels and restaurant associations in terms of recycling and energy efficiency measures are good examples. It is also relevant to point out, as does Hall (1999), that most versions of the concept of sustainable development include a concern for maintaining and/or enhancing 'social capital' – meaning the rich social relationships and networks that underpin and connect the activities of the wider socio-economic system. Collaboration might therefore be seen as both one of the means to and an important end of sustainable development.

Public funding

Another important driver of public–private sector collaboration, particularly in the context of the growing importance of the EU as a source of funding for tourism development projects and programmes, is the tendency for such funds to require a collaborative approach (Long, 1996). In the EU context, regional development funding from programmes such as LEADER requires collaboration on the part of participating organisations (Hall, 1999). Collaboration can also be the objective of projects eligible for EU funding. For example, the development of transnational research and information exchange networks is also an important theme of the Interreg spatial planning programme. In Britain, various urban regeneration schemes and National Lottery funding also require the participants to adopt a partnership approach (Fyall *et al.*, 2000).

More specifically in the tourism context, Palmer (1996) argues that collaboration may often represent a vital bridge between the competencies of public- and private-sector organisations, allowing them to gain access to high-level funding. By successfully combining the 'bureaucratic production culture' of the public sector and the 'marketing culture' of the private sector, funding bids based on cross-sectoral collaboration will be better able to demonstrate the broad-based competencies required for successful (and sustainable) tourism development.

Conclusion

Although collaboration has prospered in the domain of tourism policy and planning, instances in which collaborative marketing strategies have come under critical scrutiny are few and far between. As was historically the case with tourism policy and planning, many collaborative marketing strategies have to date only been subject to 'restricted accounts by practitioners' (Bramwell & Lane, 2000: 3). Similarly, one has witnessed the 'tendency to condense complex processes into simple description, to avoid analysis and criticism, and to gloss over points of conflict in order to present a project in the best possible light' (Bramwell & Lane, 2000: 3). The drivers of collaboration discussed in this chapter represent significant forces in the global market environment and serve to drive the momentum for the adoption of collaborative marketing strategies across all sectors of the tourism industry. The time is now ripe, therefore, to raise questions as to how successful collaboration in the tourism industry proves to be in the long term, and how collaboration impacts on marketing issues such as branding, service quality and product consistency. Further questions might be how collaborating partners are able to coexist with their 'collaborating' competitors, what the new rules of engagement and competition might be, and to what extent collaborative forms might be seen as seamless products by the tourist. There also remains the question of how appropriate the variety of forms of inter-organisational collaboration may be in each of the sectors of the tourism industry. To what extent can airlines, hotels and destinations seek collaborative advantage from similar models of business organisation? The remainder of this book will go a considerable way in addressing many of these questions and conclude with a collaborative 'road map' for future adoption by tourism marketers, irrespective of their sector of interest.

Chapter 2
Collaborative Marketing: A New Marketing Paradigm

Introduction

The essence of the marketing concept is that organisations achieve their objectives by satisfying customers (Houston, 1986). With competition a fundamental aspect of market-driven economies, the marketing perspective also asserts that the key to achieving organisational goals is for organisations to determine the needs and wants of target markets and to deliver the desired satisfactions more efficiently and effectively than competitors. This notion has been debated at great length in the academic literature, where it has been examined from a multitude of often sharply contrasting perspectives. What is common throughout this ongoing debate, however, is that marketing is a fundamental aspect of competitive behaviour and represents the modus operandi for a significant majority of organisations of all shapes and sizes around the world, albeit to varying degrees and in a range of different guises. Work by a number of authors, including Hunt (1970), Kohli and Jaworski (1990), Kotler and Levy (1969) and Levitt (1960), has done much to develop the philosophical and theoretical underpinnings for the application of the marketing concept in practice. This process of application continually finds itself under the research spotlight and is for ever evolving and reconfiguring itself in the face of considerable pressures both internal and external to the organisations involved. It is, in fact, the accelerating rate of change in today's business environment, most notably with the development of mass-production techniques, the onset of oversupply and the emergence of saturation in many markets, that explains marketing's rapid evolution in recent years. It has also reconfirmed the status of marketing in many organisations. This has not always, however, been the case.

In the late 19th and early 20th centuries, goods were sufficiently scarce and competition sufficiently underdeveloped that, for the clear majority of producer organisations, marketing as described above was deemed to be unnecessary. The primary goal of most businesses was to increase

production to meet demand. The focus of this inward-looking orientation, commonly referred to as the 'production era' of marketing, was on
satisfying demand as efficiently and cost-effectively as possible. The
'production era' of marketing prospered in an age of buoyant demand
and strong and rising growth, with its philosophy of 'what is for sale is
of such quality and appeal that it will sell itself' (Morgan, 1996: 24). As
competition grew and supply began to exceed demand, businesses developed increasingly larger and more proactive sales forces and adopted
ever more aggressive approaches to advertising. At this point in time,
marketing moved into what is commonly referred to as the 'selling era'.
This orientation created a form of 'marketing myopia', in that undue
focus and concentration was on selling products rather than meeting the
needs and wants of customers. Like the 'production era' before it, the
'selling era' was effectively another inward-looking orientation, the situation being one of growing surplus capacity and hence the need to increase
sales at almost any cost. Indeed, according to Middleton (2001), increased
expenditure on advertising, distribution channels and sales promotion,
and the use of price discounts, is simply a rational response on the part
of producers needing to capture higher levels of demand in order to
make use of their existing production capacity. Buttle (1986) has described
the sales orientation as being synonymous with the hotel industry, particularly in view of the immobile nature of hotels and the high cost of
structural alterations. As such, a sales orientation can represent a valid
approach to business if market share is the ultimate goal. However, as
Morgan (1996) points out, such a strategy can also have serious consequences in so far as that price wars, declining product quality as prices
are held down and poor public perceptions of product quality can occur.
These are likely to cause longer-term problems for producers.

It is widely considered, however, that marketing's migration from having a heavy emphasis of post-production selling and advertising to
becoming a more comprehensive and integrated field, earning its place as
a major driver of corporate strategy, took place in the 1960s and 1970s.
With consumer demand growing more slowly than production capacity
and productivity, the emergence of greater levels of consumer affluence
and the transition from mass markets to multiple sub-markets, the marketing era was clearly on the ascendancy in this time period (Cooper
et al., 1998). This period is also acknowledged as being that which witnessed the introduction of 'market orientation': a business culture focused
on the continuous creation of customer value (Narver & Slater, 1990; see
also Gray & Hooley, 2002). Slater and Narver (1994), meanwhile, identify
three core components of market orientation, namely customer orientation, competitor orientation and interfunctional coordination. For an
organisation to exhibit customer orientation, a sufficient understanding of its target buyers is required in order to facilitate the creation of

superior value for them. In a similar vein, competitor orientation involves the organisation demonstrating an understanding of the short-term strengths and weaknesses and of the long-term capabilities and strategies of current and potential competitors. Finally, interfunctional coordination refers to the manner in which an organisation uses its resources in creating superior value for target customers. Many groups within an organisation are responsible for creating 'value', especially in service organisations where production and consumption are effectively inseparable.

The fact that many organisations in the 1960s and 1970s were beginning to move away from a 'sell what we can make' mindset, in which marketing was a peripheral activity, towards a 'make what we can sell' philosophy, where marketing takes on a greater prominence, is testament to the increasing importance of a market-oriented approach to business. Unlike the inward-looking product and sales orientations, marketing is demonstrably an outward-looking orientation, whereby business operations are continually adapted to meet the changing needs and expectations of their customers. It is also worth noting that, while this may at first sight appear to be a new approach, the concepts of market orientation, and specifically customer orientation, were not so much a major new discovery as they were a 'rediscovery' of principles as old as commerce itself. What was deemed to be new was their 'systematic application to mass markets supported by a developing range of procedures, concepts and data gathering methods' (Seaton & Bennett, 1996: 22).

Components of Marketing

Opinion as to what marketing really consists of varies among authors, and it can be argued that this variety may sometimes contribute to a perceived lack of robustness in the domain of marketing theory and its worthiness as a discipline in its own right. In reality, however, while there are alternative positions on what does and does not constitute marketing, there are also remarkable similarities in what those positions hold to be important.

In attempting to break marketing down into its component parts, Middleton (2001) proposed five components or propositions of marketing, as can be seen in Box 2.1. The first component, that marketing is a management orientation or philosophy, finds favour with a number of authors and is consistent with the views expressed by Lumsdon (1997), Narver and Slater (1990) and Seaton and Bennett (1996). Lumsdon, for example, suggests that marketing can be considered as a way of thinking, a set of guiding principles, a culture that pervades an entire organisation, a personal philosophy or a form of ideology. He validates this viewpoint, however, by suggesting that marketing is essentially a collection of strategic and tactical management tools that are embraced by a set of guiding principles. As such, marketing is not deemed to constitute fully a management philosophy per se. A similar approach is adopted by Seaton and Bennett (1996), who support their view of marketing as a management orientation by pointing out that a set of analytical procedures and concepts are in existence that can be used to develop the philosophy. The marketing audit is proposed as that vehicle by which organisations attempt to appraise their current performance and future potential in relation to their existing and predicted capacity, their current and potential future customers, and various predicted economic, socio-cultural, political and technological trends. Consisting of a market and consumer analysis, an organisational audit and an environmental scan, the sequential implementation of these analytical procedures is intended to further an organisation's ability to achieve market orientation.

Box 2.1 Components of marketing

Marketing is a management orientation or philosophy

- A positive, outward-looking, innovative and highly competitive attitude towards the conduct of exchange transactions.
- Recognition that the conduct of business operations must revolve around the long-run interests and satisfaction of customers, rather than one-off exchanges, and, where possible, the selective development of relationships with loyal buyers.
- Understanding that the achievement of profits and other organisational goals result from customer satisfaction and customer retention.
- An outward-looking, responsive attitude to events and conditions in the external business environment within which an organisation operates, especially the actions of competitors.
- An understanding of the strategic balance to be achieved between the need to earn profits from existing assets and the equally important need to adapt an organisation to achieve future profits, recognising social and environmental resource constraints.

Marketing comprises three main elements linked within a system of exchange transactions

- The attitudes and decisions of target customers concerning the perceived utility and value of available goods and services, in terms of their needs, wants, interests and ability to pay.

- The attitudes and decisions of producers concerning production of goods and services for sale, in the context of their long-term business objectives and the wider environment in which they operate.
- The ways in which producers communicate with consumers before, during and after the point of sale, and distribute or provide access to their products.

Marketing is concerned with the long term (strategy) and short term (tactics)

- The short term may be defined as the period of time in which an organisation is able to make only marginal alterations to its product specifications, production capacity and published prices.
- In the long term, organisations may decide to alter product specifications and production capacity, introduce new products or phase out old ones, alter its pricing strategy or change its position within a market.

Marketing is especially relevant to analysing 21st-century market conditions and can make a contribution to sustainable development

- A relatively small number of large, still growing, highly competitive businesses with standardised products and brands, and relatively large shares of the markets they serve, operating on a national, international and increasingly global scale.
- A massive number of small enterprises.
- Revolutionary development of information and communication technologies (ICT) that simultaneously facilitates the growth and management control of large corporations and offers a networking collaborative route for small businesses to compete.
- Capacity of supply considerably in excess of what markets can absorb naturally.
- A growing number of consumers in developed countries with sufficient disposable income and leisure time to indulge in non-essential purchases, many of them choosing to engage in frequent travel for leisure purposes.
- Sustainable development requirements epitomised in the post-1992 Agenda 21 process that will increasingly have to be embraced and reflected in marketing decisions.

Marketing facilitates the efficient and effective control of business

Source: Middleton, 2001

The second conceptual component, that marketing comprises three main elements linked within a system of exchange transactions, represents a 'transactional' process-driven view of marketing. The ideal 'system' situation is one where balance between producer and customer is achieved. In this instance the producer delivers what the customer wants, at a price they are prepared to pay and at a suitable outlet of distribution.

The 'process' aspect of marketing relates to the analysis of market opportunities, researching and selecting target markets, developing marketing strategies, planning marketing tactics and implementing and controlling the marketing effort (Kotler, 1983). The marketing process can also be said to represent a body of data-gathering techniques, which act as the tools for operationalising the procedures and concepts, as well as a sequence of strategic decision areas and planning functions (Seaton & Bennett, 1996). Box 2.2 represents the strategic tourism marketing planning process advocated for this book. Implied in this process is reference to Middleton's (2001) third and fifth components of marketing: that marketing is concerned with both the long and short term, and that marketing facilitates the efficient and effective control of business. The long-term strategic aspects of marketing are to be explored in more depth in Chapter 3 of this book, while the short-term operational aspects of marketing feature in Chapter 4. Briefly, in the longer term, marketing implies an ability to make decisions with regard to capacity, design, performance, pricing and strategic positioning. In the shorter term, marginal changes to marketing decisions take precedent. This is best exemplified by Middleton (2001: 28) who suggests that:

> what always distinguishes the marketing-led organisation in the short term is not the objectives of its tactics, but the speed and the way in which it uses and exploits its deep knowledge of customers to achieve its specified targets, while at the same time holding firm to its longer-term vision and strategy developed around long-run customer orientation and satisfaction.

Although perhaps appearing as a process to be adopted for mass consumption by organisations, in reality the marketing process represents a systematic process which marketing-oriented companies are likely to adopt in some form depending upon organisational size, resources, expertise, market sector and time scale.

The fourth proposition is that marketing is especially relevant to analysing 21st-century market conditions and can make a contribution to sustainable development. Across many industries, market saturation, increased competition and increasing customer choice provide the competitive conditions upon which marketing strategies are based today. Perhaps the condition most prevalent in the world is that of production

---

**Box 2.2 The strategic tourism marketing planning
          process**

Strategic tourism marketing planning	Components of the strategic tourism marketing planning process
Strategic context	• Corporate vision • Corporate mission • Corporate goals and objectives
Marketing audit	• Analysis of the macro-environment • Analysis of the micro-environment • Analysis of the market environment • Analysis of the internal resource environment • Portfolio analysis • Analysis of strengths, weaknesses, opportunities and threats
Marketing strategy formulation and planning	• Generic strategy options • Market position • Push or pull approaches to marketing strategy • Marketing objectives • Segmentation, targeting and positioning
Implementation: the tourism marketing mix	• Product • Price • Place • Promotion • Extended marketing mix
Marketing control	• Evaluation and monitoring • Control

---

excess, insofar as the world is able to manufacture considerably more goods and services than its citizens are able to consume. With the slow-down of most large Western economies at the current moment in time, the economic climate is likely to become even more competitive in years to come, with an even greater need for organisations to meet the needs and wants of an ever more discerning clientele.

The fifth, and final, proposition is that marketing facilitates the efficient and effective control of business. It is clear that both current and future market conditions are likely to be such that the adoption of a market orientation is a necessary condition for survival. Indeed, according to Middleton (2001: 31):

> marketing-oriented businesses are characterised by the systematic organisation of their planning processes, their knowledge of the effects of their actions on their customers, the precision with which they state their targets and the speed at which they can act in relation to competitors. Identifying, responding and adapting to market changes ahead of competitors is the essence of the modern marketing approach.

Clear and effective objectives, and a sense of mission and direction within the organisation, ultimately determine the success of this approach. There is also the need to understand the necessary strategic balance between the need to earn profits from existing assets and the equally important need to adapt an organisation to achieve future profits while at the same time recognising social and environmental resource constraints.

In concluding this discussion of the components of marketing, although the emergence of the marketing concept suggests a progressive evolution, this is perhaps an illusion, since organisations confront the challenges of market orientation on a continual basis. Changes in environmental conditions, often combined with a variety of resource constraints (be they of a human resource or funding nature), can impact on the degree to which a truly market-oriented approach is adopted. For market orientation to succeed, all organisational activities need to be focused upon the provision of customer satisfaction. Furthermore, all staff need to accept the responsibility for creating customer satisfaction in an environment where the belief is that organisational goals can only be achieved through satisfying customer needs and wants (Jobber, 1998).

Definitions of Marketing

When it comes to defining marketing, the five components of marketing outlined in the section above serve as a useful touchstone for understanding the diversity of definitions that exist. Perhaps unsurprisingly, definitions of marketing tend to fall into two principal camps: for some the central focus is on processes and/or systems, while for others it is on philosophy and/or the consumer. Process-centric definitions tend to originate from professional bodies such as the American Marketing Association and the Chartered Institute of Marketing in the UK, while philosophy-centric definitions traditionally have their origins in academia.

Process-centric definitions of marketing

The process of planning and executing the conception, pricing, promotion and distribution of ideas, goods and services to create exchange and satisfy individual and organizational objectives.

American Marketing Association, in Gilligan and
Wilson (2003: 3)

The management process responsible for identifying, anticipating and satisfying customer requirements profitably.

Chartered Institute of Marketing, in Gilligan and
Wilson (2003: 3)

The marketing concept holds that the key to achieving organizational goals consists in determining the needs and wants of target markets and delivering the desired satisfactions more effectively and efficiently than competitors.

Kotler, in Middleton (2001: 23)

Philosophy-centric definitions of marketing

It is the customer who determines what a business is. It is the customer alone whose willingness to pay for a good or service converts it into wealth, things into goods. What the customer thinks he is buying, what he considers value is decisive – it determines what a business is, what it produces, and whether it will prosper.

Drucker (1973: 61)

Management must think of itself not as producing products, but as providing customer-creating value satisfactions. It must push this idea into the entire organisation. It has to do this continuously and with a kind of flair that excites and stimulates the people in it.

A truly marketing-minded firm tries to create value-satisfying goods and services that consumers will want to buy. What it offers for sale includes not only the generic product or service, but also how it is made available to the customer, in what form, when, under what conditions, and at what terms of trade. Most important, what it offers for sale is determined not by the seller but by the buyer.

Levitt (1960: 3/13)

Marketing is about customers. It is about how to find them, how to satisfy them, and how to keep them. Without customers, there will be no money to pay staff, creditors and shareholders. Without customers, there can be no reason for the organisation to exist.

Morgan (1996: 13)

The latter definitions are based on the view that marketing is as much a philosophy of doing business as it is a business function or process in its own right (Brassington & Pettit, 1997). The debate as to whether marketing is an art or a science continues. Indeed, a recently published compendium of marketing classics by Baker (2001) provides a forum for many of the seminal studies in the early 1960s and 1970s to spark renewed debate. Many of these early studies laid the foundations for modern marketing thought and a reorientation of business priorities.

As is evident in the definition provided by the American Marketing Association, process-centric definitions often refer to marketing as involving anticipation, management and satisfaction through the process of exchange (Kitchen, 1993). Reflecting worries about global warming and environmental damage in the 1980s, a greater emphasis on the wider societal aspects of marketing began to impact on marketing thinking and practice. Recognition of wider societal and ethical issues and marketing's responsibilities towards these, and growing reference to other stakeholder groups, led to the emergence of societal-centric definitions of marketing, expanding upon the remit implied by earlier process-centric definitions.

Societal-centric definition of marketing

> The organisation's task is to determine the needs, wants and interests of target markets and to deliver the desired satisfactions more effectively and efficiently than competitors in a way that preserves or enhances the customers' and the society's well being.
>
> Kotler, in Middleton (2001: 23)

In addition to demands for a more societal and environment-friendly form of marketing, there have also been calls for definitions of marketing to include longer-term 'relational' aspects. For example, authors such as Grönroos (1989) and Morgan and Hunt (1994) suggest that the aim of marketing is to establish, maintain and enhance relationships with customers, and other stakeholders, at a profit, so that the objectives of the parties involved are met. This is to be achieved by mutual exchange and the fulfilment of promises.

Relational-centric definitions of marketing

> Marketing is to establish, develop and commercialise long-term customer relationships so that objectives are met. This is done by a mutual exchange and keeping of promises.
>
> Grönroos (1989: 57)

> Relationship marketing refers to all marketing activities directed towards establishing, developing, and maintaining successful relational exchanges.
>
> Morgan and Hunt (1994: 22)

Although no standard definition exists, most definitions of marketing include the criteria of being market-driven and customer-led, with the premise that customers need to and can be satisfied more effectively than by the competition. What is not in doubt, however, is the extent to which marketing is, more than ever before, the primary focus for management in today's globally competitive marketplace (Middleton, 2001). While raising a number of new issues, recent work by McDonald and Wilson (2002) confirms the important role to be played by marketing in the future. With reference to the term 'new marketing', the writers go on to suggest that marketing in the new millennium will represent a process of:

- defining markets;
- quantifying the needs of the customer groups (segments) within these markets;
- determining the value propositions to meet these needs;
- communicating these value propositions to all those people in the organisation responsible for delivering them and getting them to 'buy in' to their role;
- playing an appropriate part in delivering these value propositions to the chosen market segments; and
- monitoring the value actually delivered.

The first four aspects of the process relate to developing marketing strategies, while the final two refer to delivery and measurement. The overriding proposition, however, refers to the nature of the offer from the organisation to the market, while at the same time accepting that not everything is under the control of the marketing department, even factors internal to the organisation. This is an important point inasmuch as the suggestion is that a single department or single organisation cannot always unilaterally be in control of the destiny of its output. For a variety of reasons, which will be addressed in the following pages, there is a growing belief that the unilateral 'competitive orientation' of marketing that has dominated marketing theory to date may in fact be facing a paradigmatic challenge in the form of multi-party relational marketing.

Emerging Relational Perspectives on Marketing

Although an understanding of the origins and meaning of the marketing concept provides the context for this book, it is arguably incomplete and of limited value in its ability to accommodate the driving forces of collaboration as discussed in Chapter 1. Talk of the marketing concept and of a market orientation (or, sometimes, 'marketing orientation') has served the management and marketing literature well for the past 40 years. However, the driving forces of collaboration are now such that, as Donaldson and O'Toole (2002) argue, considerable change is taking place in the world of business and management. Change, in this context, refers to the means by which an organisation interacts and deals with the demands of its stakeholders. Donaldson and O'Toole (2002) suggest that the traditional orientation of marketing is now insufficient to meet the demands of a more dynamic and complex marketplace, and that the manipulation of former marketing tools is deficient as a vehicle for an organisation to compete effectively in the marketplace. The consequences of such a dynamic are that marketing conducted at the organisational level in the future that does not make explicit reference to the organisation's relationship with other key stakeholders is unlikely to meet the objectives set for it. If the collaborative dimension is overlooked, or ignored, marketing strategies of the future will lack relevance and potency. The suggestion is that the marketing domain is intrinsically one in which collaboration is not just desirable but indispensable.

The winds of collaborative change are such that an alternative view of business – one that encompasses exchange and relationships, and that focuses on collaboration and the needs of different stakeholders – is widely seen as the way forward. Change is seen as vital in that organisations need to:

- reconfigure in terms of philosophy, organisation and management;
- develop and maintain partnerships with a range of stakeholders; and
- find ways to secure competitive advantage and deliver superior added value.

Although not applicable to all organisations at all times, collaboration is increasingly becoming the modus operandi for many. The question thus arises as to the extent to which this emerging 'relational' or 'collaborative' orientation to business may be considered consistent with the notion of the marketing concept discussed in the first part of this chapter. The traditional understanding of the marketing concept was based on the notion of business as a system of exchange. A comparison with the emerging relational approach to business can be viewed in Box 2.3.

Box 2.3 represents the two polar extremes of the transaction and relational approaches to business. Figure 2.1, however, shows that, more realistically, a continuum is likely to exist between the two extreme approaches to business identified in Box 2.3. On the one hand, the extreme transaction-based approach indicates that little or no joint

---

Box 2.3 A comparison between the traditional 'transactional' and emerging 'relational' approach to business

Transactional approach	Relational approach
• Transaction focus	• Partnership focus
• Competition	• Collaboration
• Organisation-induced	• Co-operation
• Value to the organisation	• Value in partnership
• Buyer passive	• Buyer as an active participant
• Organisation as a focus for control	• Organisation as part of the process
• Organisation as a boundary	• Boundaryless
• Short-term focus	• Long-term focus
• Independent	• Dependence- and network-led

---

involvement is necessary or desirable, while, at the other extreme, the more significant relationships existing between organisations may be formalised into various forms of collaboration, such as partnerships, joint ventures and strategic alliances. In between these two extremes exist two other approaches to business. The first, the repeat transaction scenario, is where some evidence of repetition is in existence (and possibly opportunities for the development of relationships). The second scenario, meanwhile, focuses on relationships of minor importance, which are

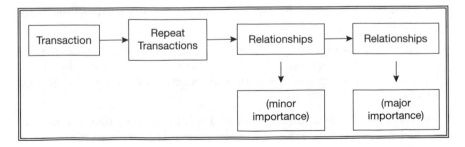

Figure 2.1 A continuum of business relationships

Source: Donaldson and O'Toole, 2002, adapted from Jackson, 1985

more typical of many business-to-business and service situations. Of more importance in the context of this discussion is the extent to which the traditional view of market orientation is able to incorporate the emerging relational approach to business. Indeed, this relational view of markets questions the very appropriateness of the existing notion of the marketing concept. In reality, there is a considerable paucity of work that connects the literature of market orientation with that of inter-organisational behavioural theory. Therefore, if relationships are to be viewed as an organisation's most valuable asset, as indicated by Donaldson and O'Toole (2002), the question arises as to how these two bodies of literature can be synthesised to bring about a 'relational' market orientation more suited to the turbulent environment of the new millennium.

Recent work by Helfert *et al.* (2002) has, however, begun to grasp this particular nettle. They argue that, in most cases, the organisation's 'surroundings' should be seen as a network of inter-organisational relationships, rather than as an anonymous market. The primary conclusion drawn from the study is that the existing formulation of the marketing concept needs to be translated to a relationship level in order to be effective. The study also concludes that market orientation on a relationship level can be interpreted in terms of the resources the organisation employs and the activities it undertakes further to the process of relational exchange. For market orientation to be relevant in the relational sense, Helfert *et al.* (2002) argue that four main relationship management 'task bundles' need to be performed. These are:

- *Exchange activities*, in that exchange can involve either product/service-, problem- or person-related activities.
- *Inter-organisational co-ordination*, which refers to the synchronisation of the relationship partners' actions and comprises the establishment, use and control of formal rules and procedures and the exertion of informal influence.
- *Conflict resolution mechanisms*, in that non-standard situations are bound to occur in every long-term relationship.
- *Adaptation*, in order to meet the special needs or capabilities of a partner.

Figure 2.2 provides an overview of this conceptualisation of market orientation at the 'relational' level. The connection between the above four tasks and the dimensions of market orientation can be summarised as follows:

- With the desire to understand and meet customer needs, a market orientation can serve as an enabler for relational activities.
- With customer satisfaction measures in place, employees can be motivated to fulfil the relationship management tasks in order to satisfy the customer.

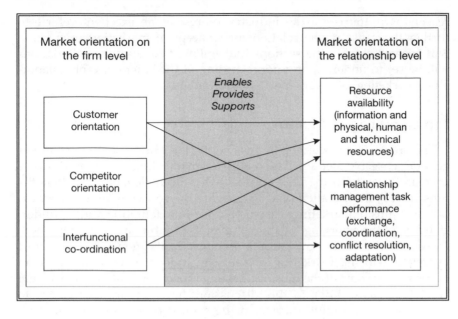

Figure 2.2 A relationship concept of marketing orientation
Source: Helfert *et al.*, 2002

- An understanding of competitors and their movements can serve as a basis upon which to build mechanisms to resolve conflict.
- Finally, as most relationships are handled by more than one individual and frequently require complex exchange, interfunctional co-ordination is the key to serving customers.

For the above to be achieved, Helfert *et al.* (2002) note that informational, physical, human and financial resources will be required for relationship management to be present in market-oriented firms. In Part 4 of this book, this conceptualisation will be put to the test in that the application of 'relational' collaborative marketing strategies and tactics will be critically explored and examined with regard to their adherence or otherwise to the principles of the 'collaborative' relational concept of market orientation.

This emerging 'relational' view of market orientation, which retains a focus on being market-driven and customer-led, has begun to appear in the definitional lexicon of marketing and forms the theoretical underpinning for collaborative marketing. However, before taking this debate further, it is timely to introduce the thematic focus of this book, in that, rather than talking generally about industries and markets, the book focuses solely on issues pertaining to the marketing of tourism. The reasons why tourism as an industry represents an excellent vehicle to further the cause of the relationship concept of marketing orientation will become clear in the sections that follow. Likewise, the foundations will be set to underpin an understanding of the emergence of collaborative marketing as a new marketing paradigm.

The Marketing of Tourism

The proceeding discussion in this chapter talks of marketing in a rather general sense. No mention has so far been made of marketing as it relates specifically to tourism. This approach has been deliberate in that the present chapter has attempted to provide the reader with an overview of the origins of marketing, various facets of its definition and an understanding of the emerging 'relational' aspects of future market orientation. However, the book now adopts a more application-specific context by relating to the marketing of tourism. Indeed, it is in the tourism industry that some of the most interesting aspects of relational marketing are taking place. Prior to this discussion, however, it is necessary to locate the marketing of tourism in the context of services and services marketing, its industrial sector and the theoretical family in which it is located.

The service context

A service is defined as any 'activity that one party can offer to another which is essentially intangible and does not result in the ownership of anything. Its production may or may not be tied to a physical product' (Kotler *et al.*, in Palmer, 1998a: 2). Although the theory of marketing has been argued to have universal value, in the sense that the same core concerns and principles apply whatever the nature of the business, it is widely accepted that there exist certain differences in marketing approaches for products and services (McDonald & Payne, 1996). Much of this is attributed to the four distinct characteristics of services, namely: intangibility (Hoffman & Bateson, 1997); perishability (Bateson, 1977); variability (Berry, 1980); and inseparability of production and consumption where the act of production and consumption is simultaneous (Palmer, 1998a).

The frequently cited service characteristics of intangibility, heterogeneity, inseparability and perishability highlight both the reduced emphasis on tangibles and the increased role that a consumer plays in the service process. The integral involvement of the consumer within the service process suggests the need to develop close and trusting relationships in order to increase customer perceived value. Arguably, such relationships are most strongly fostered by market orientation.

In the context of marketing's historical evolution, Figure 2.3 demonstrates the emerging contribution of relational aspects as a focus of marketing activity. As was the case for 'product' marketing, service-based organisations also alter their marketing focus as they evolve and develop. Seeking to reach the final stage requires the service company to (McDonald & Payne, 1996):

- integrate all marketing activities;
- develop a realistic and focused approach to marketing planning;
- develop a market-oriented culture;
- recognise the importance of quality transactions both inside the company and with customers; and
- increase profitability through improved customer retention.

Helfert *et al.* (2002) go further, however, to suggest that the relationship concept of market orientation is even more important for service providers because they are more likely to interact intensively with their customers. For this reason, service organisations need to embrace the relationship level as well as the corporate level of market orientation.

Cravens and Piercy (1994: 39) contend that 'rapidly changing markets, a complex array of technologies, shortages of skills and resources and

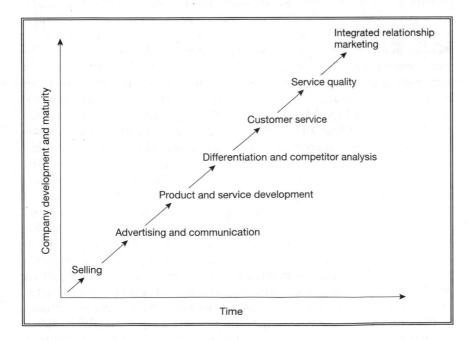

Figure 2.3 General development pattern of marketing approaches

Source: McDonald and Payne, 1996

more demanding customers present services organisations with an unprecedented set of challenges'. A central feature of these challenges is the recognition that building relationships with other stakeholders is essential to compete effectively in the turbulent and rapidly changing post-industrial era that is presently confronting developed world economies (Huber, 1984).

Tourism marketing and the marketing of tourism

The service context is important in that tourism, which is continually lauded as the world's largest industry, represents a significant component of the service economy. What is open to question here, however, is the extent to which the lessons of services marketing can be applied equally well to tourism as they can be to other service sectors such as financial services and retailing. Tourism shares a number of characteristics with much of the service sector, albeit to varying extents. For example, the tourism product is clearly intangible in nature in that the core offering is often a performance rather than an object. Krippendorf (1987) argues that much of tourism is about the marketing of dreams – an intangible if ever there was one. Likewise, tourism products are often perishable in nature because production is fixed in time and space. For example, the perishability of hotel rooms, airline seats and cruise cabins has, over the years, served as a catalyst for the effective management of demand and capacity, and has led to the development of yield-management systems. Tourism also shares issues of high product variability and inseparability of production and consumption. Tourism is more often than not heterogeneous (or variable) in that standardisation, although achievable in some instances, is frequently impossible. The high level of human involvement in much tourism activity, especially at the service encounter, makes standardisation of service quality difficult. The inseparable nature of the producer and consumer of the tourism product merely adds to the problem. The lack of real ownership is also an issue. As was outlined in Chapter 1, the tourism product is an amalgam or 'bundle' of different products and services, often owned by a variety of different parties. Tourism is also subject to considerable market turbulence, particularly since the terrorist atrocities of 9/11. It can also be highly sensitive to a general economic slowdown in tourism-generating economies, the threat of war in sensitive areas and further attacks from a myriad of terrorist organisations. The tourism product is also said to evolve over time in that it does not simply become a variant of the original but a totally different product over time (Ryan, 1991). The question to be asked now, therefore, is to what extent is tourism marketing, or the marketing of tourism products and services, different to the marketing of services in general.

In the late 1980s and early 1990s, tourism marketing was viewed as the application of marketing in tourism management situations (for example Gilbert, 1989; Holloway & Plant, 1988; Middleton, 1988). More recent debate suggests that there are important common characteristics of travel and tourism service products that require particular forms of marketing response (Middleton, 2001). But it is perhaps the volume of activity, the scale of the tourism industry on a global perspective and the integral role marketing now takes with planning in tourism that gives it greater importance. With a range of established academic journals in the field (for example, the *Journal of Travel and Tourism Marketing*, the *Journal of Vacation Marketing*, and the *Journal of Hospitality and Leisure Marketing*), tourism marketing is gradually forming an identity of its own: one that is distinct from services marketing. Notwithstanding this, much of the cutting-edge debate in marketing academia remains in the marketing-specific journals such as the *European Journal of Marketing*, the *Journal of Marketing* and the *Journal of Marketing Management*, among others.

However, unlike traditional product marketing, and unlike the rest of the service sector, one can argue that tourism is unique and worthy of individual academic attention. Tourism is a highly complex, multisectoral industry where no single organisation provides or has control over the entire tourism product. As is apparent from the tourism marketing system exhibited in Figure 2.4, successful delivery of the wider tourism product is dependent on close working relationships, interdependencies and interactions with numerous other stakeholders, enabling the tourism organisation to provide a seamless experience for its customers.

Tourism organisations often have to deal with multi-stakeholder scenarios, demonstrate responsibilities to the environment and ethical considerations, and be receptive to social and cultural pressures, frequently from central, regional and local government (Bramwell & Lane, 2000; Robson & Robson, 1996; Wheeler, 1993, 1995). The dependency upon public goods like beaches and areas of natural beauty for the success of many tourism organisations, such as tour operators, transport companies and accommodation providers, is such that any one component part of the tourism system is dependent on the others for the system as a whole to work. One further difference between tourism and other sectors within the wider service economy is the need to take into account the needs and wants of the local or 'host' community when determining strategy. This point is highlighted by Mill and Morrison in Haywood (1990: 200) who emphasised the uniqueness of tourism by suggesting that:

A philosophy that concentrates solely on the needs of the market is not the best orientation, even for the market itself. Tourism supply

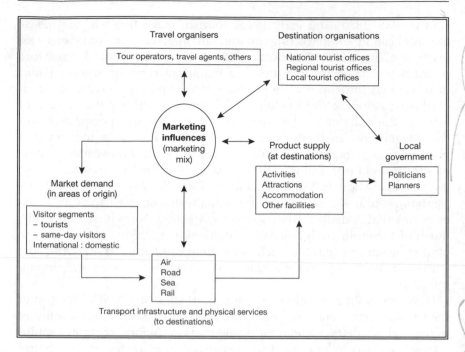

Figure 2.4 The systematic links between demand and supply, and the influence of marketing

Source: Middleton, 1998

is oriented toward the resources of a community. To become totally marketing oriented, all aspects of the community would have to be oriented toward satisfying the needs and wants of the tourist. The risk for the community as well as for the tourist ultimately is that by orienting strictly and totally for the tourists' needs, the needs and integrity of the community may be abused. Destination areas that have attempted to adapt their resources to satisfy tourist needs may have lost the very thing that has made them attractive and unique in the first place.

This suggests that putting the customer, visitor or tourist at the centre of the organisation, so as to meet the demands of market orientation, is not always practical or desirable in particular situations. This said, Kotler's aforementioned definition of societal marketing makes inroads into addressing this issue.

While perhaps not technically unique to tourism, a number of characteristics are clearly important in setting the context for tourism marketing and are fundamental in explaining the emergence of the relationship concept of market orientation and collaborative forms of marketing within the tourism industry. All of the issues mentioned below are worthy of a mention, some more so than others, in facilitating an understanding of the challenges involved in the marketing of tourism rather than services more generally.

Tourism is more product-driven/supply-led than other services

Recognised as being one of the last industries to experience the change from a seller's to a buyer's market, much of the tourism industry has been slow to apply the principles of marketing theory. March (1994) contends that the adoption of marketing principles within the tourism industry, compared to other service industries, has been poor. He goes on to argue that marketing has been universally undervalued and misrepresented by tourism practitioners and policy-makers alike. The management literature has encouraged many business executives to develop an appropriate marketing culture to enhance their marketing effectiveness and, consequently, to achieve superior customer satisfaction levels, profit maximisation, competitive advantage and organisational co-ordination. The tourism industry, however, has been plagued by a general misconception with regard to the nature and value of marketing (Appiah-Adu *et al.*, 2000). Much of this historical misunderstanding can best be explained by the interchangeable use of the terms 'marketing' and 'promotion', as well as the evidently disparate priorities implicit to the amalgam of products and services that constitute the tourism product (March, 1994).

Some may argue that the above context is now a little dated, these viewpoints being perhaps a fair representation of the situation a decade ago. Indeed, the service revolution that took place throughout the 1990s suggests that many players within the tourism industry have been at the cutting edge of marketing, with innovative strategies being designed to increase levels of customer retention and loyalty (Fyall *et al.*, 2003). For example, international airlines, hotel groups and car hire companies have been at the forefront of relationship-building activities over the past decade. This having been said, there still remain many tourism organisations, most notably museums and galleries, visitor attractions and destination marketing organisations, that have failed to migrate from their product-driven origins to a more customer-driven approach to business (Leask *et al.*, 2002). With such a large number of smaller businesses, many owned by families, there remains the danger of an overly product-centric focus resulting in market myopia and the changing needs and wants of the market being either ignored or simply missed.

In justifying the imbalance of promotional to marketing effort taking place, March (1994) states that there remain considerable economies of scale in promoting a 'generic' destination rather than the individual components of the 'amalgam' tourism product. He adds that marketing is often perceived to be the least influential of the demand variables. Given the significant role played by intermediaries in the tourism system, a lack of focus on repeat visitation on the part of many tourism organisations and the alleged failure of marketing scholars to provide valuable insights into the tourism marketing domain, the historical reliance on promotional forms of marketing is perhaps understandable (Frechtling, 1987). Although likely to remain a feature of future marketing activity, it is anticipated that a greater balance of marketing activity will represent the way forward, particularly given that many tourism organisations are likely to become less supply-led as time passes. While achieving greater balance in marketing activity may well represent a significant challenge to the tourism industry, it may also represent a much needed release in that, post-9/11, many airlines, hotel operators and tourism service providers have adopted an aggressive discount culture. Although perhaps understandable in the circumstances, worries are being expressed about the longer-term damage if the resulting changes in tourist buying behaviour were to persist.

Tourism is often driven by short-term need rather than longer-term objectives

The aforementioned example is testament to the volatility of many tourism markets, whereby short-run profitability and cash flow become the focal points for marketing strategy. As such, the strategic focus of tourism is often on the short term. The conflict between short-term and long-term financial goals, an overemphasis on short-term measures of senior management performance, and senior management's own values and priorities concerning the relative importance of customers and the organisation's other stakeholders, have also been said to contribute to and reinforce this trend (Webster, 1988). Meanwhile, the turbulent nature of the market environment contributes nothing to helping tourism businesses with longer-term forecasting, budgeting and financial planning.

Arguably, the issue of temporary ownership – in that the tourist, in most instances, displays no permanent ownership of a hotel room, a destination, an airline seat or a car hired while at the destination – often contributes to the short-term orientation of many managers of tourism products. The seasonal and cyclical nature of tourism can also be said to contribute to the short-term orientation of much of the tourism industry.

Tourism is frequently susceptible to fixed capacity constraints

There are frequently issues pertaining to the high fixed cost and inelastic nature of supply to consider in tourism. In particular, it is relevant to note that physical structures and infrastructure such as hotels and airports cannot be changed at short notice to meet the changing trends in the marketplace. This, at least in part, explains the historical over-dependence of promotional marketing activity in the wider domain of tourism marketing. In contrast, whereas supply is more often than not inelastic, demand is frequently price-elastic. As such, a sudden change in the cost of supply can have a highly detrimental impact on sales. Tourists, especially those of a leisure orientation, are highly susceptible to changes in product price, and they are notoriously fickle in terms of purchasing behaviour.

The fixed capacity constraints of many players in the tourism industry, especially airlines and hotels, have contributed in no small part to the emergence of yield management and yield-management systems in the tourism industry. This is one area where the tourism industry is at the forefront of developments, driven largely by its susceptibility to fixed capacity constraints.

Tourism is a high-involvement, high-risk purchase

More often than not, tourism represents a high-involvement purchase, thereby carrying a higher than normal level of risk for customers. Most tourism products are experienced after the point of purchase, thereby contributing to certain levels of unease and uncertainty in the purchasing process. They can often be expensive (airline flights, hotel rooms, package holidays) and as such carry a significant degree of purchase risk. On the other hand, recent developments, such as the commodification of many tourism destinations, growth in the cheap package tours market and the emergence of discount airlines, suggest that the tourism industry also has its fair share of low-involvement purchase activity. In such instances, the point of sale, outlet of distribution and promotional activity represent important aspects of marketing programmes.

The tourism product is impacted on both positively and negatively by customer perceptions and is highly susceptible to external influences beyond its control

Related to the issue of high-involvement purchase activity in tourism is the role played by customer perceptions in the purchase process. Tourism is more often than not a product that is partly constituted by the dreams and fantasies of its customers (Krippendorf, 1987), where perception can be highly favourable or detrimental to marketing efforts. The instrumental role played by brochures in the marketing efforts of tour operators, tourism destinations and travel companies has done much to create positive images in the minds of customers and create powerful perceptive benchmarks. However, the ability of tourism businesses, organisations and destinations to meet the very high level of expectation frequently generated by their own marketing material has sometimes hindered the potential to develop loyalty among customers.

In a world of 24-hour media, any event of a negative nature can impact significantly on tourist demand. The maxim that 'perception is everything' is so true in the world of tourism. Tourism is clearly a fragile product which is particularly disposed to external forces beyond the control of its suppliers. This is most noticeable at times of war, civil unrest and political instability in destinations where tourism is either present or close by. Examples over the years, be it the Gulf War, terrorist attacks in Luxor or political instability in Zimbabwe, have all caused a substantial decrease in visitor numbers, with tourists often selecting perceived 'safer' destinations. The increase in intra-regional travel in view of the perceived danger of long-haul travel post-9/11 is another example. Events in Bali and, more recently, in Iraq have clearly contributed to perceptions of insecurity among tourists. Although danger may be at a considerable distance, the volume of choice and variety of destination or alternative supplier are such that the environment is conducive to substantial switching behaviour. This, unfortunately, tends to impact on the short-term mindset of players in the industry and results in the dominance, at certain times, of heavy discounting activity to reactivate and regenerate demand.

The tourism product is highly complex and multi-faceted

There can be little doubt that tourism is a highly complex, extended product experience, with identification of the critical evaluation point not always straightforward. For example, the fact that the tourism product is frequently one of multiple ownership, where no one organisation or business controls all aspects of the tourism product, can prove problematic when identifying the true cause of a problem and the identity of the culpable party. Control over the tourism product and the tourism brand is more often than not dispersed, so that the shortcomings of one organisation can easily affect the reputation of others adversely. Co-ordination of all the components of the tourism product is necessary in being able to present a product that can be easily selected, consumed and appreciated by consumers. Related to this is the fact that many tourism products are complementary in nature, in that a large variety of sub-products is essential to the purchase. This fact alone highlights the interdependent nature of tourism and the unavoidable need for contact with a number of other partners and stakeholders, often across the public–private sector divide.

The tourism product is also often intensive in its use of labour. Not only does this have implications with regard to costs but it also impacts on the service encounter and the achievement of suitable levels of service quality and consistency of the tourism product.

Defining tourism marketing

To date, no universal theory of tourism marketing exists. In many ways, the lack of consensus is of little consequence, as there is no reason why unanimity should exist in what is still a relatively new domain. The modern tourism industry is still in its infancy compared to most and in many aspects of management remains a follower rather than setting the agenda itself. Does tourism marketing thus represent a separate discipline? Middleton (2001) believes that ultimately the answer has to be in the negative: tourism marketing merely represents an adaptation of basic principles that have been developed and practised for many decades across a wide spectrum of predominantly consumer products. However, in view of tourism's particular characteristics – tourism being a highly complex and interdependent domain, and one that is highly susceptibility to external forces – it might be argued that tourism marketing is worthy of special status from a marketing standpoint. Lumsdon (1997: 25) suggests that:

> Tourism marketing is the managerial process of anticipating and satisfying existing and potential visitor wants more effectively than competitive suppliers or destinations. The management of exchange is driven by profit, community gain, or both; either way long-term success depends on a satisfactory interaction between consumer and supplier. It also means securing environmental and societal needs as well as core consumer satisfaction. They can no longer be regarded as mutually exclusive.

While this may well be true, the extent to which the above definition is workable in competitive isolation represents the crux of the future direction of tourism marketing. Based on work previously undertaken by Fayos-Sola (1996) and Poon (1993), Lumsdon (1997) summarises some of the future challenges for the marketing of tourism, these being:

- New consumers (fragmentation, greater segmentation, experiences and quality of life).
- New technologies (reduction in number and type of intermediaries).
- Limits to growth (managing tourism impacts, environmental sensitivity, sustainability).
- Flexibility in provision (super-segmentation of demand, flexibility of supply and distribution, diagonal integration, system economies and integrated values rather than economies of scale).

Given the particular characteristics of tourism as a product, it can be argued that these issues collectively serve as stimuli for the development of a more relational, collaborative approach to the marketing of tourism. Indeed, it is clear that the vast majority of the industry is no longer able to meet the future needs and demands of customers by working independently. By adopting the relational principles advocated by Helfert *et al.* (2002), an alternative notion of the marketing concept is therefore proposed as a viable solution to handle, manage and develop tourism to its full potential. In reality, relational activity has been a key feature of the marketing of tourism for some time. For example, airlines, hotels and local authorities have been working together for many years. Whether these inter-organisational relationships are called alliances, consortia or partnerships, they are all forms of working together for the achievement of a mutual goal, that is, forms of collaboration. However, rather than be viewed as aspects of tourism marketing or vehicles to achieve marketing ends, the authors propose that the philosophical underpinning of the notion of market orientation, the marketing strategy process and the implementation of marketing programmes themselves require scrutiny and revalidation from a relational-collaborative perspective.

Discussion earlier in the chapter has suggested that the traditional orientation of marketing is now insufficient to meet the demands of a more dynamic and complex marketplace, and that the manipulation of former marketing tools is deficient as a vehicle for organisations to compete effectively in the global marketplace. The consequences are that, in the future, marketing that is conducted at the organisational level, without explicit relevance to the organisation's relationship with other key stakeholders, will be unlikely to meet its objectives fully. If the collaborative dimensions are overlooked or ignored, marketing strategies in the future will lack potency and relevance. The suggestion is that, in many industrial sectors across the developed world, the marketing domain is intrinsically one in which collaboration is not just desirable but indispensable. What is proposed in this book is that it is exactly the way forward for the tourism industry and those responsible for marketing the tourism product.

Collaboration: A New Marketing Paradigm?

It has been said that much of the literature on competitive strategy has focused on how firms seek to develop advantage over their competitors by maintaining secrecy of their actions in order to pre-empt competitive actions taken by competitors (Domke-Damonte, 2000). More recent work has identified the importance of considering inter-organisational collaboration as a useful tool to understand strategic action, with work by Gulati (1998), Jarillo (1988) and Nielsen (1988), to name but a few, providing evidence to support its emergence as a suitable strategic approach for growth. The intention of the debate here is not to rubbish previous discussion on marketing theory and practice but to add to it, to offer a collaborative insight into the dynamics of marketing in the tourism industry and to provide a foundation for the emergence of a new collaborative paradigm for those practising and studying the management and marketing of tourism. A few initial questions emerge:

- Are there more appropriate models for interaction and effective delivery of joint public- and private-sector initiatives?
- To what extent can individual organisations and businesses cope with natural and human-made disasters?
- How are individual enterprises able to cope with the impacts of globalisation and the increasing consolidation and concentration of power in the tourism industry?
- Are organisations unilaterally able to source and access funds?
- Are traditional 'transactional' models of marketing able to accommodate the complexity of problems and demands facing markets of tourism products and services?

According to a recent publication by the WTO (2002: 53):

> it is increasingly difficult for businesses to survive alone. Regardless of the strategy adopted to respond to an increasingly competitive business environment, it is important to develop local partnerships to bring in complementary strengths and thereby offer an attractive product representative of the location.

This reinforces some of the issues raised above and adds weight to the belief that alternative approaches to existing 'competitive' marketing theory and practice are required for the future development of tourism. Before any definition is offered or new paradigm proposed, the next two chapters will critically examine the existing authority on tourism marketing strategy and the implementation of tourism marketing programmes and assess their suitability for the relational concept of market orientation proposed by Helfert *et al.* (2002) and the 'collaborating' ideas of the two authors. It is our belief that the foundations upon which existing tourism marketing theory and practice are based are set to be tested and reconfigured in light of the drivers of collaboration discussed in Chapter 1, and which are making such a profound impact on the world we live in and the ways in which we manage ourselves to accommodate them.

Part 2: Strategic Tourism Marketing Planning

Part 2 Introduction
Strategic Tourism Marketing Planning

A widely-held maxim among academics and practitioners of marketing is that, in order to compete effectively, businesses need to achieve a dynamic fit between their internal resources and capabilities and their external market environments (Drummond & Ensor, 1999; Evans *et al.*, 2003; Faulkner, 1998; Sharma, 1999). This viewpoint is reflected in the definition of strategic marketing planning by Kotler *et al.* (2003) which considers market-oriented planning to be a managerial process of developing and maintaining a feasible fit between the organisation's objectives, skills and resources and its changing market opportunities.

Faulkner (1998) goes further to suggest that the future of tourism as a dynamic and viable industry is dependent on the adoption of a strategic approach to planning and marketing. He suggests that:

> [the] hallmark of such an approach is the inclusion of a systematic and structured analysis of broader environmental factors affecting tourism demand as an integral part of the planning process. Equally, as an adjunct to this approach, the ongoing evaluation of the strategies adopted is essential to ensure programmes that become ineffective or counter-productive are identified and replaced. (Faulkner, 1998: 297)

Strategic marketing planning undoubtedly provides a sense of direction, organisational leadership and an agreed framework for the conduct of business in ever changing and competitive market environments (Middleton, 2001). Although tourism as an industry has in recent decades been on a continued growth trajectory, growing uncertainties in the world make for a greater need for planning: unpredictable market behaviour, greater regionalisation, market shifts and changing consumer priorities, and economic slowdown contributing to the greater need for forward planning. The fact that so much of the wider tourism industry is experiencing pressures of consolidation, concentration and integration (be it vertical, horizontal or diagonal) merely reinforces the need for greater scrutiny of market environments and the need for detailed strategic planning.

Marketing represents a holistic, competitive orientation for business. The 'strategic' dimension to marketing reflects its growing impingement on traditional 'strategic management' territory and is in response to criticisms that marketing has historically failed to consider adequately the development of long-term competitive advantage (Sharma, 1999). As will become evident throughout Chapter 3 and Chapter 4, strategic marketing planning clearly involves the matching of an organisation's resources with environmental opportunities and constraints in its efforts to achieve long-term 'strategic' competitive advantage. It is true that the domain of strategic marketing is usually associated closely with the field of strategic management, as can be seen in the recent work by Evans *et al.* (2003). Although there is clearly an overlap between the two domains, Sharma (1999) suggests that the prefix 'marketing' should normally precede the term 'strategy' when identifying functional product-market strategies.

According to Faulkner (1998), the strategic approach to marketing involves:

- A comprehensive and integrated plan of action for an enterprise organisation.
- A clearly enunciated set of goals and objectives that provide the focus for the plan of action. These will reflect the corporate view of what is essential for the long-term effectiveness and survival of the organisation and its products.
- The establishment of systems for monitoring and evaluating progress towards goals, objectives and targets specified in action plans.
- An approach to planning that explicitly reconciles the inherent competitive advantage and limitations of the organisation (or its products) with the challenges (opportunities and threats) of the environment.

Earlier studies by Papadopoulos (1989a, b) identified the fact that strategic marketing planning in the tourism domain is, however, multifaceted and requires an interdisciplinary and integrated approach that must be supplemented by continuous and systematic research into all aspects of tourism. Strategic marketing planning needs to be a dynamic and continuous process with related and interacting variables. Marketing decision-making activities, however original and exciting, have to be compatible with the organisation's own resources, constraints and objectives.

Although opinion will always vary with regard to the precise formula for the process of strategic marketing planning, the framework offered by Lumsdon (1997) is typical of many (including that of Faulkner discussed above) in that it:

- Sits within the broader domain of corporate strategy and is consistent with the wider vision, mission, goals and objectives of the organisation.
- Includes detailed analysis of both external and internal environments.
- Involves the detailed application of strategy concepts to marketing planning, in this instance in tourism.
- Sees product and market decisions as central to the entire process of marketing planning.
- Has both short-term (tactical) and longer-term (strategic) dimensions.
- Concludes with programmes for implementation, evaluation and control.

In support of the above, Cooper *et al.* (1998) suggest that, as the most important activity of marketing management, planning provides a common structure and focus for all of the organisation's management activities. For example, marketing planning:

- Provides clear direction to the marketing operation based upon a systematic, written approach to planning and action.
- Co-ordinates the resources of the organisation.
- Sets targets against which progress can be measured.
- Minimises risk through analysis of the internal and external environment.
- Examines the various ways of targeting different market segments.
- Provides a record of the organisation's marketing policies and plans.
- Thinks about the long-term business objectives so that the organisation plans to be in the best position to achieve its future aims.

In addition to the above, Drummond and Ensor (1999) state that strategic marketing planning requires consistency, integration, communication, motivation and control. Consistency is important in that, by providing a common base to work from, the overall decision-making process should be enhanced. Likewise, integration should engender co-ordination of the marketing mix elements of the plan and, ideally, serve as a catalyst for synergy among the individual components of the mix. The plan should also be communicated to both external and internal stakeholder groups, in turn generating a sense of 'ownership' among stakeholders, and, finally, be under some form of control in that the criteria by which success is to be determined are defined. These points are also emphasised by Cooper *et al.* (1998), who argue that the marketing plan requires control over the changes that have to be made, needs to allow for the exploitation of any short-term advantages and improvement on weaknesses, and has to promote the use of analysis, reason and evaluation as an integral part of planning procedure.

Although there are no guarantees to success, the consequences of no or inadequate planning are significant in that new market opportunities in growth markets may be missed: demand may be poorly managed, with longer-term damage on product and service quality arising as a consequence. Although it is never easy to pinpoint exactly the origins of poor planning, it is usually some combination of lack of support from senior management, inappropriate planning procedures, the occurrence of unexpected and unpredictable external events, organisational bureaucracy and incompetence. In addition, the prevailing culture of the organisation may not be amenable to planning, in that the internal power and political struggles are such that the development of planning becomes a battlefield among vested interests and inaction becomes the outcome.

The above introduction to strategic marketing planning is highly significant in the context of this book, however, in that it relates to, and originates from, theories and concepts of strategic management and strategic marketing planning in the domain of competition theory. For, in competition theory, the individual firm or organisation is the primary focus of inquiry. The central question to be addressed in the following two chapters, therefore, is the extent to which existing 'competitive' frameworks and models of strategic marketing planning are in fact compatible with the emerging 'relational' approach to marketing advocated by Helfert *et al.* (2002), as outlined in Chapter 2, and the drivers of collaboration introduced in Chapter 1. In the past one could perhaps have criticised the focus of theory on marketing as a pure system of exchange, with a preoccupation with making short-term transactions rather than developing long-term relationships. However, there is evidence in the literature to suggest that, in the late 1980s and throughout the 1990s, strategic marketing began to draw from the inter-organisational relationships literature to explain a shift from marketing transaction and customer-centred views of strategy (Berthon *et al.*, 1997; Hulbert & Pitt, 1996) to an increasing emphasis on relationship-building internally within a firm and collaborations and networks outside the firm (Webster, 1992). Webster goes further to suggest that, as organisations travelled up a continuum of increasing integration with other organisations, market control would be replaced by administrative and managerial control. Thus, emphasis would shift away from customer focus to mutual dependence through networks based on skills and resources that the partners could bring to the relationship. This perspective goes beyond the narrow function-based concept of marketing in a product-market domain.

The discussion presented above is consistent with the views put forward by Donaldson and O'Toole (2002) in Chapter 1, in that new organisational forms are beginning to dissolve functional boundaries.

Work by Badaracco (1991), Piercy (1997), and Webster (1992) among others, suggests that clear distinctions between firms and markets, and between the company and its external environment, are disappearing. The onset of collaboration, in all its forms, offers a scenario where it is feasible for a customer also to be a competitor, supplier, partner and regulator. This realisation is a central tenet of this book and serves as the catalytic focus for trying to understand and explain why the existing strategic marketing planning literature base remains so loyal to the neo-classical economic paradigm. It also raises the question as to why academia has been so slow to address the emerging emphasis, and need, to work in collaboration with others in search of longer-term relational marketing strategies.

Sharma (1999) openly suggests that greater integration of academic disciplines is required to help understand, explain and act upon these emerging trends. He continues by arguing that:

> The new business realities of team building, close partnerships with customers, boundaryless organisations, organisational learning and adaptation, internal innovation, the need to manage alliances and co-operative networks, social responsiveness and ethics, indicate that multi-disciplinary research approaches and theoretical frameworks will have to be dealt with by multi-disciplinary teams of managers trained by multi-disciplinary teams of educators. (Sharma, 1999: 84)

It is now the purpose of the following two chapters to explore, in depth, the existing 'standardised' approach to strategic marketing planning found in the literature and to investigate its appropriateness to the new collaborative environment discussed in the first two chapters of this book. The aim is not to dismiss the frameworks and models that have served the marketing domain so well, but to explore their suitability in facilitating the underpinning of strategic marketing planning for collaborating firms and organisations in the tourism industry.

Chapter 3
Situation Analysis

Strategic Context

The strategic tourism marketing planning process can be subdivided into three key sections: first, strategic or situational analysis; second, strategic choice; and, third, strategic implementation, evaluation and control. The purpose of this chapter is to explore the first dimension of the strategic planning process, namely the analysis of the situational context. Chapter 4 will investigate the models, frameworks and issues pertaining to the second and third dimensions: strategic choice and strategic implementation, evaluation and control. In looking at the first dimension of the strategic marketing planning process, it is important from the outset to establish that it sits within the domain of the corporate strategic plan and as such should be consistent with the overriding vision, mission, goals and objectives of the organisation. It is at this stage, prior to the marketing planning phase, that the question 'what is our business?' needs to be addressed. Clearly this question does not relate entirely to the domain of marketing, since marketing is just one element of the corporate equation and therefore requires full integration with other aspects of the organisation. This is particularly important when considering the overall desired direction of the organisation, and in particular when establishing the corporate vision, mission, goals and objectives. These items will thus be introduced prior to discussion of the situational analysis as applied to the strategic tourism marketing planning process.

Corporate vision

The corporate vision defines the basic need the organisation aims to fulfil and establishes the generic direction of the business (Drummond & Ensor, 1999). It represents a picture of the organisation at an indeterminate time in the future when it has materially achieved its purpose. This will enable the organisation to establish the size, scope and activities of its business, and will provide a model towards which stakeholders can strive. Marketing strategy reflects and at the same time informs corporate vision and leadership. It is related to the external business environment, the organisation's view of customer needs and its competitors' actions. It is also concerned with the overall values that a business seeks to develop and communicate to customers, shareholders and its wider stakeholder base.

The central issue for organisations in situations of collaborative behaviour is one of consistency and compatibility. For example, to what degree, and with what consequences (either positive or negative), are individual competitive and joint collaborative visions compatible with each other, consistent with stakeholder expectations and in accord with employees' or participants' understanding of the overriding direction of the organisation? If organisational visions contrast strongly at the outset, there is tremendous scope for conflict further down the strategic marketing planning process. This will also be the case for the corporate mission and objectives. For international airlines, many of which have chosen to compete and collaborate with each other at various junctures, the advent of international airline alliances has introduced a new dimension into the strategy equation. International airlines of all shapes and sizes are represented in alliances, each one having both an individual and collaborative sense of purpose. Although still relatively immature forms of collaboration, it will be interesting to see how inter-organisational dynamics within alliances impact on future individual organisational behaviour and strategy setting. The question also arises as to the extent to which these inter-organisational forms are a precursor to eventual strategies of merger and acquisition.

Corporate mission

The corporate mission represents the combination of purpose, strategy, values and behaviour standards of an organisation and incorporates the core tasks an organisation intends to carry out in order to achieve the corporate purpose within the constraints of the corporate vision. More often than not, the corporate mission will be articulated in a mission statement: an enduring statement of purpose that provides an animated vision of the organisation's current and future business activities, in service and market terms, together with its values and beliefs and its points of differentiation from competitors (McDonald & Payne, 1996). The corporate mission helps determine the organisation's relationships with each of the key markets with which it interacts and provides a sense of direction and purpose which leads to better independent decisions being made at all levels of the organisation. According to Kotler *et al.* (2003), an organisation's mission statement ought to include reference to industry scope, its breadth of products and applications, its core competencies and market segments. The mission statement is also expected to include reference to channel scope, the number of channel levels from raw materials to final product and the channel of distribution and choice of intermediaries in which the organisation will engage, along with the organisation's geographic scope.

A properly constructed mission statement, developed by a broad base of industry and community leaders, presents a clear sense of direction to all stakeholders. The mission statement fosters common business goals, serving as a basis for both internal and external communication, and, ultimately, the effective evaluation of actual efforts. Once a common direction and purpose have been agreed upon, managers may then establish goals and objectives whereby progress towards the common mission can be measured (Evans *et al.*, 1995).

Intended to be motivating, inclusive, challenging and achievable, mission statements are not always easy to write or easy to achieve consensus on. They are, however, the bedrock of organisational strategy and the foundation for the organisation's *raison d'être*, both to external and internal stakeholders. This has important implications for inter-organisational collaboration. As with the corporate vision itself, there are clearly going to be instances where conflict can arise among organisations collaborating with one another because of their differing visions and missions. For example, not only will the individual organisational ideals, culture, structure and objectives impact on the collaborating organisation's vision and mission, but so too will the ideals, culture, structure and objectives of the collaborative form impact on the participating organisations' visions and missions. While the institutional forms of inter-organisational collaboration are often less permanent than those of participating organisations, there is an important set of questions relating to which ideals, cultures and structures take precedence, on what occasions and for how long. The question then arises as to what mechanisms are in place to co-ordinate the activity between the competing and collaborating organisations, thereby ensuring delivery of the corporate vision and mission. Developing suitable mechanisms will be fundamental to nurturing a sense of organisational identity, motivating staff working within and between the organisations involved, and achieving commitment to meeting both organisational and collaborative goals and objectives.

Corporate goals and objectives

A corporate goal can be defined as a major target that organisations will adopt for long-range purposes, and more often than not is represented in the organisation's mission statement. Such goals are not usually quantified or limited to a specific time period (Heath & Wall, 1992). The goals of an organisation do, however, reflect the reason for its existence, and the activities of the organisation should be directed to the attainment of its goals (Mullins, 2002). Corporate goals are translated into objectives in order to provide guidelines for the operation and management of the organisation. Objectives set out more specifically the goals of the organisation, the aims to be achieved and the desired results, and have more defined areas of application and time limits (Mullins, 2002). According to Cooper *et al.* (1998), objectives need to be 'SMART', which means they are:

- Specific, in that they should be focused on the results required.
- Measurable for each objective set.
- Achievable, in that they are set against trends and market position constraints and are assessed fully.
- Realistic, by taking into consideration given resource constraints of time, money and personnel.
- Time-specific, in that targets are set as to when the objectives should be met.

Strategic objectives are frequently set for the longer term, usually beyond the period of the current corporate plan but often short of achieving the competitive or market postures targeted in the mission statement.

As was the case for the corporate vision and mission, the principal question for those organisations conducting both competitive and collaborative strategies centres on issues of compatibility and consistency. For example, how compatible are the individual organisation's goals and objectives with those of the collaboration domain and how compatible are the collaboration goals and objectives with the participating organisation's goals and objectives? Answers to these questions will have implications for the perceived and actual degree of strategic marketing independence and flexibility for organisations participating in collaborative marketing and will to the greater extent determine what control individual participants in collaboration settings have over strategic marketing. There is, however, no particular reason why organisational objectives should be compatible in the context of collaboration. For example, Kanter (1994) argues that, for inter-organisational collaboration to succeed, partners' strategic goals should converge while their competitive goals diverge. In this situation, collaborating organisations, although clearly benefiting from collaboration, are not hindering each other's competitive domain. In their study of collaboration among visitor attractions in Scotland, Fyall *et al.* (2001: 224) argued that 'the focus should be on trying to counter the threat of external competition from outside of the visitor attractions sector, rather than concentrating on petty competition from within the sector'. The external threat of competition being viewed as more pressing than the local threat posed by competing attractions, the development of the destination domain was the ultimate prize in this instance. In a further study by Fyall and Leask (2002), collaboration among a number of attractions in close proximity to the South Bank of the Thames, including Shakespeare's Globe, the Tate Modern and Vinopolis, was deemed instrumental in raising the profile of the South Bank as a destination in its own right. While the individual attractions will continue to act independently in an operational sense, the collective benefits of collaboration in developing the wider destination, especially in competing against the more traditional tourist sites north of the Thames, is likely to lead to a higher visitor profile and an increase in visitor numbers in a cost-effective manner.

Marketing Audit

Once the corporate vision, mission, goals and objectives have been established it is then appropriate for the individual functional planning process to proceed – in this instance, the strategic marketing planning process. The first hurdle involves analysis of the external and internal environments. The complex and constantly changing environment in which an organisation operates can be divided into three major components, namely the macro-environment, the micro-environment and the market environment. Analysis of each will now take place in the following sections in the specific context of tourism.

Analysis of the macro-environment

Analysis of the macro-environment examines the wide range of environmental factors that create opportunities and pose threats to the destination or to the organisation. These are forces that the tourism organisation cannot control and to which it has to adapt. They include a wide variety of social, political, technological, economic and demographic factors, and are often analysed within a PEST framework as set out and illustrated in Box 3.1.

In addition to the PEST analysis, Butler's life-cycle model (Butler, 1980) facilitates understanding of the evolution of tourist products and destinations and provides guidance for strategic decision-taking (Buhalis, 2000). The basic hypothesis of the model, as shown in Figure 3.1, is that a destination or a tourism product goes through five basic phases of development – introduction, growth, maturity, saturation and decline – each of which has implications for corporate strategy. McKercher (1995), however, argues that the applicability of Butler's model to strategic marketing is limited by its perspective, which looks at only the macro-view of a destination's evolution. The model cannot, nor was it designed to, reflect the subtleties of market shifts, the changing appeal of a

---

Box 3.1 PEST analysis of influences in the external environment

Political/legal factors

- Employment law
- Environmental legislation
- Foreign trade agreements
- Political and governmental stability
- War and terrorism

Economic factors

- Monetary and fiscal policy
- Unemployment and labour force issues
- GDP and GNP growth rates
- Economic and business cycles
- Exchange rates
- Inflation

Socio-cultural factors

- Age profiles
- Social mobility
- Population growth
- Lifestyle trends and changes
- Family structures
- Educational patterns and levels of achievement
- Income distribution
- Social class
- Attitudes and values
- Consumerism

Technological factors

- Technological developments
- Internet and e-technologies
- Government research and development
- Computerised reservation systems
- Development cycles
- Production technology

Source: Adapted from Drummond and Ensor, 1999; Tribe, 1997

---

destination to different types of tourists seeking different experiences, the evolving nature of development to attract new clients and the rise and fall of individual markets that occurs within a destination. However, in spite of these criticisms of the model, the wider lessons to be drawn from the model can nevertheless be helpful to marketers when contemplating strategy decisions.

The models have important implications for collaborating organisations. With regard to the PEST analysis, there are important questions relating to how the individual factors impact upon parallel competitive and collaborative marketing practice, and about the extent to which the PEST analysis may be equally valid to both competitive and collaborative market environments. There is also the issue as to whether certain factors carry

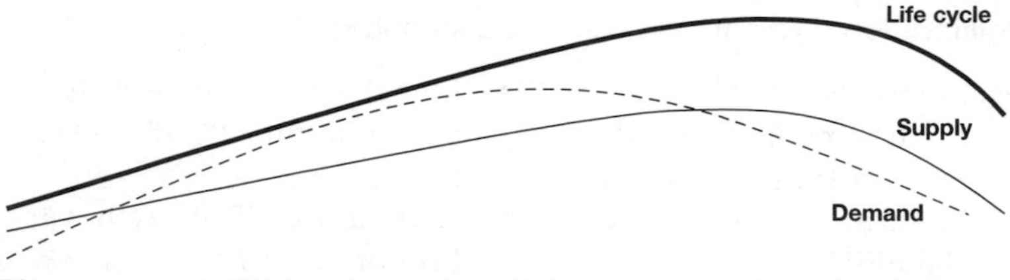

Impact analysis	Introduction	Growth	Maturity	Saturation	Decline

| SITUATION | New trendy destination | More people interested Investment in accommodation and facilities | Maximum visitation Increasing facilities | Oversupply Original demand moves | Reduction of demand Special offers to boost visitation |

Destination characteristics					
Visitor numbers	Few	Many	Too many	Many	Many
Growth rate	Low	Fast	Fast	Very high	Decline
Accommodation capacity	Very low	Low	High	Very high	Very high
Occupancy levels	Low	Very high	Very high	High	Low
Prices of services	High	Very high	High	Low	Very low
Expenditure per capita	High	Very high	Very high	Low	Very low
Visitor types	Drifters	Innovators	Innovators	Followers	Cheap mass market
Image and attractions	Low	Very high	High	Low	Very low
Tourists are perceived as	Guests	Guests	Customers	Customers	Foreigners
Marketing response					
Marketing target	Awareness	Information	Persuasion	Persuasion	Loyalty/new market
Strategic focus	Expansion	Penetration	Defence	Defence	Reintroduction
Marketing expenditure	Growing	High	High	Falling	Consolidating
Product	Basic	Improved	Good	Deteriorating	Decaying
Promotion	Introduction	Advertising	Travel trade	Travel trade	Travel trade
Price	High	High	Lower	Low	Below cost
Distribution	Independent	Independent	Travel trade	Travel trade	Travel trade
Economic impacts					
Dependency on intermediaries	Negligible	Low	High	Over-dependent	Over-dependent

Figure 3.1 Destination life cycle

Source: Adapted from Buhalis, 2000

more weight in the context of collaboration, and the overriding question as to how valid an understanding of PEST factors are when determining strategy in collaborative environments. While such issues are discussed in greater detail in Part 4 of this book, it would certainly seem reasonable to suggest that events, trends, issues and circumstances in the wider macro-environment that are relevant to competing organisations are equally applicable to collaborating ones. However, the various impacts of each factor, and the extent to which an individual or collaborating organisation is able to accommodate or respond to them, will tend to vary. For example, the recent war in Iraq and the outbreak of a new strand of pneumonia (SARS) in Hong Kong have had significant impacts on many international airlines based in these regions. This said, the geographical reach and scope of international airline alliances offers many airlines a certain degree of protection from external threats. The recent filing for bankruptcy by United Airlines does, however, highlight that, in extreme cases, even being protected by collaborating partners is insufficient for survival. The examination of hotel consortia in Chapter 9 and collaborative destination marketing in Chapter 10 also offers examples of the differing impacts of external opportunities and threats on both individual and collaborating organisations.

With respect to life-cycle analysis, there is also a number of questions that need to be answered in the context of collaboration. For example, are the five life-cycle stages of equal importance to competitive and collaborative marketing? Is the duration of each stage and the marketing responses deemed appropriate in situations of competitive marketing equally valid in the context of collaborative marketing? Are situations of parallel competitive and collaborative marketing by organisations reflected in the model as it stands? In a study by Henderson (2001), attempts to market the Greater Mekong Subregion (GMS) as a tourist destination are explored with specific attention given to the strategic alliances between the countries and agencies involved that would be needed for success. Although this will be discussed in greater depth in Chapter 10, the example is significant in that it is likely to impact on the life cycle of Thailand as a destination. For example, as a mature destination, does this opportunity for international collaboration serve as a form of product repositioning, market development or even new-product development? On the one hand, it could expand Thailand's sphere of influence in the area as the dominant partner, both financially and experientially. On the other hand, collaborating countries could benefit from an advanced tourism infrastructure in developing their own propositions. One of the problems in accurately applying life-cycle analysis is the availability of longitudinal data for the destination (Wanhill & Lundtorp, 2001), something that is likely to be even more problematic in cases of collaborative destination development.

Analysis of the micro-environment

The most common framework adopted to serve as a base upon which to examine the micro-environment is the Five Forces model of establishing industry attractiveness for an organisation. According to Porter (1980), there are five forces that typically shape the industry structure and the state of competition in it: intensity of rivalry among competitors, threat of new entrants, threat of substitutes, bargaining power of buyers and bargaining power of suppliers. These five forces delimit prices, costs and long-term profitability prospects. These factors in turn determine industry attractiveness, which provides the groundwork for a strategic plan of action.

Box 3.2 outlines the basic principles of this model. Once the model has been applied to the situation in hand, two key questions need to be addressed. First, what is the likelihood that the nature of the relationships identified in the model will change given the trends in the wider macro-environment? Second, what actions can the organisation undertake to improve its position against the current forces in the industry?

According to Lynch (2003), it can be argued that Porter's model is static and fails to recognise the dynamic forces of the external environment. There also exists a number of questions specific to its application in a collaborative context. For example, is the model suitable for situations of collaborative marketing, are amendments required to the model to represent the collaboration context more accurately, and how may relationships vary between suppliers, buyers and competitors in contrasting competitive and collaborative environments? Conducting a review of the model, Thurlby (1998) noted that a competitive forces model should be seen as a framework rather than as a definitive model. In view of emerging trends and collaborative developments, albeit in a non-tourism environment, Thurlby forwards six alternative forces to the Porter model. Using the example of the tour operations industry, Dale (2000) shows that these six competitive forces – regulation, new entrants, customer expectation, improved digital information, synergistic alliances and organisation reinvention, together with the threat of alternatives – can easily be applied in the tourism industry. Thurlby's alternative model therefore serves as a very useful vehicle with which to evaluate the impact of collaborative marketing on individual organisational behaviour.

Two further tools for examining the micro-environment are the analysis of strategic groups, as advocated by Drummond and Ensor (1999) and highlighted in Figure 3.2, and the Four Links model advocated by Lynch (2003). Drummond and Ensor argue that, more often than not, the notion of 'an industry' is too broad to facilitate a useful understanding of an organisation's real competitive position. In such circumstances, strategic group analysis can be used to focus on defined business units which compete on similar territory. A number of characteristics can be used to define the axes upon which strategic groups can be clustered. For example, Figure 3.2 identifies a strategic group analysis for the airline industry based on price and geographic reach. Alternative axes could be company size, operational scope, breadth of product range, relative product quality, market segments served and/or brand image.

The key questions arising with strategic group analysis are, first, the extent to which, if at all, an amended version of the model is necessary to accommodate more accurately the relational networks that exist in the collaboration domain and, second, the degree to which the model is of equal value to both competitive and collaborative situations. The model can perhaps serve as a useful vehicle to analyse competing collaborative alliances in the same manner as is demonstrated in Figure 3.2. Axes may vary but the central premise to the model remains the same. A more thorny issue, however, is the extent to which competing and collaborating organisations may be successfully represented on the same model.

It is increasingly being recognised that, as well as competitors, the considerations of other stakeholder groups are also crucial in developing a successful marketing strategy. Today's businesses are now recognising that, unless the needs, wants and views of stakeholders are taken into consideration, it is unlikely that shareholders, hitherto the dominant stakeholder group in the development of corporate strategies, will be satisfied. This is consistent with the viewpoint expressed by Helfert *et al.* (2002) in their discussion of relational marketing. Stakeholders are often large in number and diverse in nature, especially in the context of the tourism destination. Work by Haywood (1990) highlighted the importance of host communities in implementing the marketing concept in tourism destinations, while Fyall *et al.* (2003) stressed the role played by stakeholders in developing relationship marketing programmes at the destination level. Meanwhile Kotler *et al.* (2003) argue that a dynamic relationship can, if applied properly, connect stakeholder groups and result in higher quality products and services, the result being to create high levels of customer and stakeholder satisfaction. The Four Links model, advocated by Lynch (2003) goes some way towards serving as a useful medium upon which to scrutinise the collaborative relationships between an organisation and others in its environment. The four links identified in the model comprise:

- *Government links and networks*: relationships that many organisations have with local, regional, national and international government bodies.

Box 3.2 The Five Forces model

Suppliers
The power of suppliers
is liable to be strong
where:

- Control over suppliers is
  concentrated into the
  hands of a few players.
- Costs of switching to a
  new source of supply
  are high.
- The supplier has a
  strong brand.
- The supplier is in an
  industry with a large
  number of smaller
  disparate customers.

Buyers
The power of buyers
is liable to be strong
when:

- A few buyers control a
  large percentage of a
  volume market.
- There is a large number of
  small suppliers.
- The costs of switching to
  a new supplier are low.
- The supplier's product is
  relatively undifferentiated,
  effectively lowering barriers
  to alternative sources of
  supply.

Potential entrants
The threat of potential
entrants will be determined
by a number of barriers to
entry that may exist in any
given industry where:

- The capital investment
  necessary to enter the
  industry is high.
- A well-entrenched
  competitor who moved
  into the industry early
  has been able to establish
  cost advantages irrespective
  of the size of their
  operation.
- Gaining access to
  appropriate distribution
  channels is difficult.

Substitutes
Substitution can arise in a
number of ways:

- A new product or service
  may eradicate the need for a
  previous process.
- A new product replaces an
  existing product or service.
- All products and services, to
  some extent, suffer from
  generic substitution.

Competitive rivalry
The intensity of competition in
the industry will be determined
by a range of factors:

- The stage of the industry
  life cycle.

- Government legislation and policies, such as patent protection, trade relations with other states and state-owned monopolies can all act to restrict the entry of competitors.
- The prospect of a well-established organisation's hostile reactions to a new entrant is sufficient to act as a deterrent.

- The relative size of competitors. In an industry where rivals are of similar size, competition is likely to be intense as they strive for a dominant position. Industries that already have a clear dominant player tend to be less competitive
- In industries that suffer from high fixed costs, businesses will try to gain as much volume throughput as possible. This may create competition based on price discounting. There may be barriers that prevent businesses withdrawing from an industry.

Source: Adapted from Drummond and Ensor, 1999

- *Complementors*: those organisations whose products and services add more value to the products and services of the base organisation than they would derive by themselves.
- *Informal co-operative links and networks*: occasions when organisations link together for a mutual or common purpose without a legally binding contractual relationship.
- *Formal co-operative links*: more formal and permanent versions of the above, often bound by some form of legal contract. Strengths and weaknesses of such relationships can be measured in terms of their depth, longevity and degree of mutual trust.

Lynch (2003: 112) suggests that, although the Four Links model 'may not have the precision and clarity of the Five Forces model and other competitor analyses', its focus on the collaborative relationships between organisations is most suited to the emerging relational paradigm of marketing advocated by Helfert *et al.* (2002). Lynch goes further to suggest that the Four Links approach is typical of an emergent approach to strategy development in that the links provide the organisation with opportunities to experiment and develop new and original strategies. In conclusion, the four links of the model, although often less structured and formalised than those involving competitor analysis, may

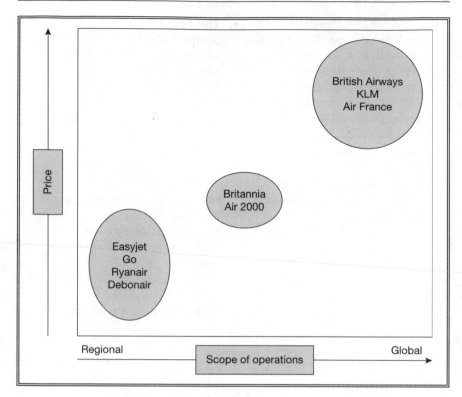

Figure 3.2 Strategic groups in the airline industry
Source: Drummond and Ensor, 1999

in fact represent greater potential with respect to long-term competitive advantage.

Analysis of the market environment

A marketing audit involves an examination of the marketing function as it currently exists within an organisation. It may include a study of the marketing objectives, current marketing plans, activities, positioning, target markets, sales channels, media utilised, customer data being collected and a comparison of the results of the marketing efforts with the budget and marketing goals (Edgell *et al.*, 1999). A marketing audit provides the means to enable an organisation to understand how it relates to the environment in which it operates. The audit should be a systematic, critical and unbiased review and appraisal of the company's marketing operations (McDonald & Payne, 1996). In short, the marketing audit represents a diagnostic approach to understanding the dynamics driving an organisation. A detailed marketing audit checklist is illustrated in Box 3.3.

A number of important questions surface with regard to the application of such an audit in the context of collaboration. First, are the various components of the audit of equal value to both competitive and collaborative environments? Second, how are issues of confidentiality, trust and proprietary skills accommodated in such a framework? Third, are there likely to be significant information gaps in the collaboration context? The issue of information is explored by Papadopoulos (1989b), who argues the need for an effective tourism marketing information system as part of the strategic tourism marketing planning process. This may include, among other things:

- A *tourism accounting system* in which data on costs from points of origin and within the tourist destination country, as well as tourist receipts by region, country and per capita, are kept.
- A *tourism marketing intelligence system* to gather up-to-date, relevant data from each major tourist-generating market and the local tourist services sector in the country concerned.
- A *tourism marketing research system* in which specific market research studies can be carried out, either by specialist organisations at home or abroad, or by the national tourist organisations themselves.

Detailed analysis of visitor profiles, visitor behaviour, the volume and value of visitors and the benefits sought by visitors is an essential ingredient for the pursuit of market segmentation, targeting and positioning (to be discussed in the latter part of this chapter). In addition, the marketing audit provides detailed insight into the degree of market orientation evident within the organisation, a view of the level of specific marketing organisation and an insight into issues pertaining to implementation and control of the strategic marketing plan. The marketing audit will also help introduce those variables considered crucial in achieving sustainable competitive advantage in the marketplace.

However, a number of questions specific to the development of a marketing information system arises in the context of collaboration. First, how are issues of confidentiality, trust and proprietary skills accommodated in such a system? Second, how readily are collaborating organisations prepared to contribute equitable amounts and quality of information in such a system? Third, are there likely to be significant information gaps in the collaboration context and is a marketing information system a realistic proposition in a collaborative domain? Fourth, what may be some of the system and organisational dynamics of developing such a tool for information and research in the context of collaboration? Outlined as an issue of collaborative significance in Fyall (2003), the benefits to be accrued from collaborative research efforts

---

Box 3.3 Marketing audit checklist

External audit

The market
- Total market, size, growth and trends (value/volume)
- Market characteristics, developments and trends
- Products
- Prices
- Distribution channels
- Customers/consumers
- Communication
- Industry practices

Competition
- Major competitors
- Size
- Market share/coverage
- Market standing/reputation
- Production capabilities
- Distribution policies
- Marketing methods
- Extent of diversification
- Personnel issues
- International links
- Profitability
- Key strengths and weaknesses

Internal audit

- Marketing operational variables
- Own company
- Sales (total, by geographical location, industrial type, customer and product)
- Market shares
- Profit margins/costs
- Marketing information/ research
- Product management
- Price distribution
- Promotion
- Operations and resources

Source: Adapted from McDonald and Christopher, 2003

---

are significant. This is especially true in the visitor attractions sector where 'although attractions can individually monitor aspects of quality control and conduct customer tracking studies, more in-depth research programmes are normally either too expensive to undertake or too time-consuming for staff to conduct' (Fyall, 2003: 244).

Analysis of the internal resource environment

The purpose of resource analysis is to identify the strengths and weaknesses of the tourism organisations, the destination at large and the tourism business units in the region (Heath & Wall, 1992). An important aspect of this type of analysis is the identification of distinctive competences. Having a distinctive competitive advantage in a specific area can provide a clear foundation and direction for the strategic marketing planning process (Hrebiniak & Joyce, 1984). One of the most useful models for analysis of the internal resource base of organisations is the Value Chain model, advocated by Porter (1980). Outlined in Figure 3.3, the Value Chain model is built on the premise that every organisation is a collection of activities that are performed to design, produce, market, deliver and support its product. They are split into primary activities of production and the support activities that give the necessary foundation. The value chain links the value of the activities of an organisation with its main functional parts. It is the organisation's task to examine the value chain and look for ways to improve its costs and performance in each value-creating activity. It should also estimate its costs and performances as benchmarks against which to compare its own costs and performances. To the extent that it can perform certain activities better than its competitors, it can achieve a competitive advantage.

The appropriateness of the value chain in an individual competitive scenario is not in question. The extent to which it is possible to construct a collaborative version of the value chain is, however, an issue. For example, what are the necessary linkages and sources of 'added value' for collaborative marketing activities and organisations? What are the likely sources of friction of analysing such organisational competences and attributes in a collaborative setting? Most importantly, perhaps, how is 'value added' measured in the context of collaborative marketing? Doyle (2000) highlights the role the value chain can play in such settings, with reference to the organisation's value chain system, as can be seen in Figure 3.4. Doyle acknowledges that organisational competitiveness is no longer dependent on the effectiveness of internal and cross-functional networks, but points out that the competitiveness of an organisation is increasingly dependent on its external networks and collaborative relationships. In many cases, the individual organisation's value chain is merely part of a myriad of value chains that interlink to form an extensive system for delivering solutions to customers. Doyle concludes that it is the effectiveness with which managers handle the entire supply chain and network of collaborating partners that will determine the future competitiveness of the firm. This point was also raised by Johnson and Scholes (1997) in their analysis of future uses of the value chain.

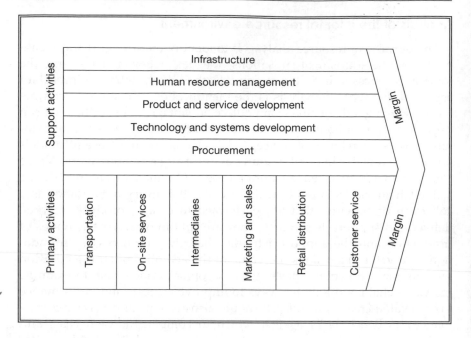

Figure 3.3 The value chain

Source: Adapted from Evans *et al.*, 2003, based on Porter, 1980

Three further models serve as useful vehicles upon which to analyse the internal resources of the organisation. The Hierarchy of Resources model (Figure 3.5), which was adapted from work undertaken by Chaharbaghi and Lynch, as featured in Lynch (2003), is similar to the value chain in that it identifies key resources within the organisation. Normally categorised as tangible, intangible or organisational in nature, the hierarchy of resources identifies four levels of resource that are internal to the organisation:

- *Peripheral resources,* which are often brought in but can occasionally give competitive advantage.
- *Base resources,* which are common to many organisations but useful to keep inside the organisation.
- *Core resources,* which are unique to the organisation and the basis of its sustainable competitive advantage.
- *Breakthrough resources,* which will bring a major strategic shift in an industry.

Lynch argues that the resource-based view of strategy has as its central premise that the individual resources of an organisation provide a stronger basis for strategy development than industry analysis. The

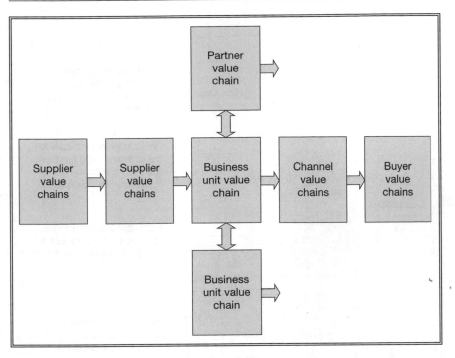

Figure 3.4 The firm's value chain system
Source: Adapted from Doyle, 2000

rationale behind this is that the resource-based view identifies those resources that are exceptional and have sustainable competitive advantage. With seven suggested elements – those being prior or acquired resources, innovative ability, being truly competitive, substitutability, appropriability, durability and imitability – it is not suggested that an organisation possess all of them prior to having some competitive advantage. Each organisation will have a particular combination of resources. The opportunity to collaborate with others serves as a vehicle to obtain, share or have access to resources necessary to achieve sustainable competitive advantage in the marketplace. For example, within global airline alliances this may be a case of acquiring access to new route networks, maintenance capabilities and service operational procedures. For hotel consortia, meanwhile, benefits may be in the form of new market development and access to global distribution systems. Questions pertaining to instances of collaboration include the means by which resources are funded, allocated and used for competitive and collaborative marketing activity, and the degree to which resources are used equitably between competitive and collaborative marketing. There is also

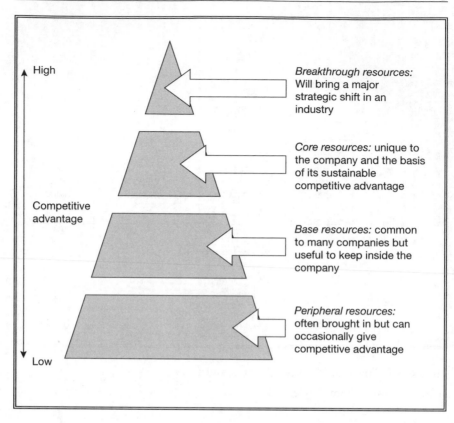

Figure 3.5 The hierarchy of resources
Source: Lynch, 2003

the issue as to how resource use is monitored in each situation. The theoretical background and underpinning to this debate is explored in Chapter 7 and represents the debate central to the entire rationale behind opportunities for collaborative marketing initiatives.

The two final models in this section relate to brands and branding. The first, the Brand Pyramid (Figure 3.6) represents a useful model for identifying the variables constituting a brand and the relationships between the variables, and predicts the effects of changes on consumer response (Doyle, 2000). Initially conceptualised by Kapferer (1997), the brand pyramid identifies six dimensions of the brand, each requiring management to influence the customer's image of it. These are identified as follows:

- *Physical*: the appearance of the brand in terms of its chosen name, colours, logo and packaging.

- *Reflection*: the image of the target audience as reflected in the brand's communication.
- *Relationship*: how the brand seeks to relate to the customer.
- *Personality*: the individual character of the brand.
- *Culture*: the background and values of the brand.
- *Self-image*: how the customer sees himself or herself in relation to the brand.

In addition to the above is the brand core, which represents the guiding principles of the brand. Doyle argues that this element should be permanent and guide the consistent evolution of the brand's style and themes.

As a key internal resource of the organisation, the brand is central to the organisation's overriding vision, mission, goals and objectives. The degree to which brands work in collaboration with others, be it in a formal or informal sense, is thus highly significant, as there are likely to be significant impacts 'by association'. Referred to as 'co-branding' (Blackett & Boad, 1999; Boone, 1998; Grossman, 1997; Prince & Davies, 2002), strategies of brand collaboration are becoming increasingly commonplace

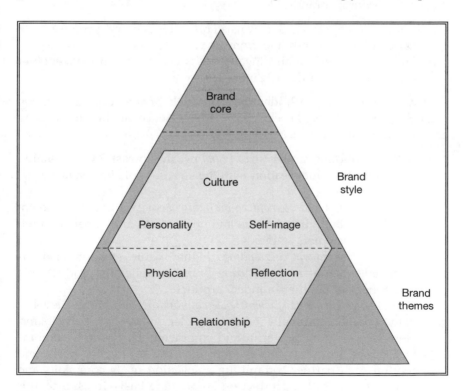

Figure 3.6 Brand identity and the brand pyramid

Source: Kapferer, 1997, in Doyle, 2000

among airline alliances, hotel consortia, visitor attraction partnerships and instances of collaboration involving diagonal integration. The fact that the brand is the aspect of an organisation's internal resource that is most visible to the customer ensures its status as a highly significant and powerful element in the marketer's arsenal of strategic options. In their seminal publication, *Co-Branding: The Science of Alliance*, Blackett and Boad (1999) argue that eventually co-branding will inevitably alter customers' perceptions of the constituent brands. When this does occur, one key question for all collaborative marketing forms is how they are to manage their own brand and their association with the collaborative co-brand. Clearly there are disadvantages that can accrue from such action. For example, there will always be the inherent danger of combining incompatible corporate personalities, the effect on one or more partners of repositioning their brand(s), the dilution or loss of distinctive features of one of the ingredient brands and possible failure to meet collaborative co-branding targets. In contrast, however, considerable benefits can accrue. For example, co-branding can result in transferring the three virtues of corporate brands:

- Communicate clearly and consistently the co-brand promise.
- Differentiate the co-brand from its competitors.
- Enhance the esteem and loyalty of its customers and stakeholder groups and networks. (Balmer, 2001)

Blackett and Boad (1999) identify four levels of shared value creation – the higher the level the closer the true essence of the co-branding concept. The four levels are as follows:

- *Level 1 – reaching awareness co-branding*: the lowest level of shared involvement/value creation with the largest pool of possible participants.
- *Level 2 – values endorsement co-branding*: achieved by endorsement of either (or both) brand value and positioning, and aimed at brand values in customers' minds.
- *Level 3 – ingredient co-branding*: higher value creation again is achieved when a market-leading brand supplies its product as a component of another branded product.
- *Level 4 – complementary competence co-branding*: the highest level of value creation, normally with a smaller number of participants. Here two or more powerful and complementary brands combine to produce a product that is more than the sum of the parts, and rely on each partner committing a selection of its core skills and competencies to that product on an ongoing basis. In essence, this last level represents the achievement of collaborative advantage through brand collaboration.

Benefits appear particularly strong for the smaller partners who gain significant benefits of association from collaboration with the market leaders. Although the true value of collaborative co-branding to airlines, hotels and destinations may not as yet have been empirically proven, current developments are such that it appears an irreversible trend. Nonetheless, Blackett and Boad (1999) suggest that future collaborative co-branding requires careful management to achieve the desired exchange of values and reputation between brands so that each partner is perceived to be better as a result of the collaboration. Clearly, as collaborative co-branding activity increases, a more systematic process is required for identifying potential partners and for developing strategies for mutual brand enhancement. To help marketers understand the characteristics of their own brand prior to searching for co-branding partners, Blackett and Boad (1999) propose a 'brand blueprint' which includes two important steps. First, they suggest that collaborating partners need to identify their individual brand values and sort them into *core* (the key emotional and rational brand ingredients and differentiators), *absentee* (lacking but desirable), *peripheral* (values that are inappropriate or negative) and *generic* (needed to enter and compete in brand category) categories. Thereafter, they suggest that the key diagnostic information for developing the brand be selected which would include key *brand supports* (the emotional and functional elements that underpin core brand values), the *core brand proposition* and *brand personality*. On completion of these two steps, suitable partners can be found by:

- Combining the brand's strategic objectives with assumptions about which market category, territory and/or premium level the co-branding initiative should involve so as to yield the best results.
- Using the brand blueprint to create a separate list of reasons why the brand might be desirable within these hypothesised scenarios.
- Generating a list of third-party brands that should thrive in these desirable contexts, then removing all those that do not match the original brand's strategic objective requirements.

Suitable partners should then be found. For the future, therefore, collaborating partners need to question the value of retaining their brand independence and have suitable systems in place to monitor and measure customer reaction and behaviour as ultimately success will be determined by what customers think they are buying in to.

One further branding model is the Branding Iceberg, which is advocated by Davidson (1997). Figure 3.7 shows that the Branding Iceberg features elements of the brand both 'above' and 'below' the line – more accurately explained as what the customer 'can' and 'can't' see. As stated by Davidson, the exact elements of the model will differ by market, although many of those featured in the figure are common to most.

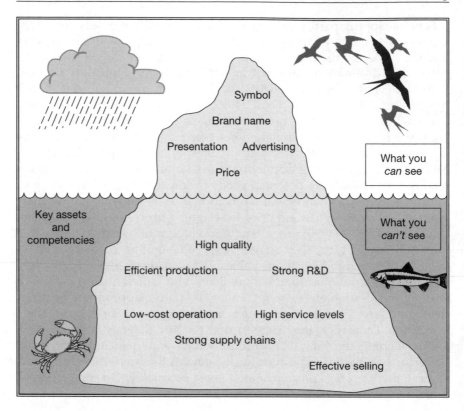

Figure 3.7 The Branding Iceberg

Source: Adapted from Davidson, 1997

In situations of co-branding, many of the key assets and competencies of the brand will be shared by collaborating partners and, in most cases, will be outside the vision of customers. This is especially the case for many hotels in consortia, airlines in alliances and destinations in partnerships. For example, computerised reservation systems (CRSs), e-ticketing, extranets and intranets are commonly developed in collaboration with others, while each individual organisation retains its own visible brand independence. Specific questions pertaining to the use of the Branding Iceberg in collaborative marketing initiatives are important however. For example, how valuable is this model in situations of co-branding and to what extent do the competitive and collaborative brands 'above' and 'below' the line compete with or complement each other? In a similar vein, what evidence is there of conflict and friction in the 'below'-the-line management of co-brands and how compatible are organisational attributes and competencies in situations of co-branding?

Portfolio analysis

One further approach to analysing the internal resource base of an organisation is that of portfolio analysis. Although this relates to strategic decisions about what products and services to develop and in what markets, one outcome of such an analysis is the impact resulting decisions have on the internal resources of the organisation. The two most popular models of this genre are the Boston Consulting Group Growth-Share Matrix (BCG matrix) and the General Electric Market Attractiveness–Competitive Position Matrix (GE matrix). The first, the BCG matrix, recommends that organisations appraise each of their products on the basis of market growth rate and the organisation's share of the market relative to its largest competitor. As shown in Figure 3.8, the BCG matrix is divided into four cells, each indicating a different type of business:

- *Problem children*: businesses that operate in high-growth markets but have low relative market shares and require a high investment (cash negative). Most businesses start off as problem children as the company tries to enter a high-growth market in which there is already a market leader.
- *Stars*: market leaders in a high-growth market, although not necessarily producing a positive cash flow (cash neutral). The business must still spend to keep up with the high market growth and fight off competition. Stars are usually profitable and often become future cash cows.
- *Cash cows*: former stars with the largest relative market share in a slow-growth market (where growth rates fall to less than 10%). A cash cow produces a lot of cash for the company and supports its other businesses (cash positive).
- *Dogs*: businesses with weak market shares in low-growth markets and that usually generate low profits or even losses (cash negative or neutral).

The BCG matrix is useful in that it provides an overview of the organisation's product or strategic business unit (SBU) portfolio and the financial resources likely to be required both now and in the future. This can provide a sound basis upon which to plan future developments and can contribute to the effective management of the portfolio with respect to decisions to build, hold, harvest or divest. Most organisations seek a balanced portfolio.

While it is generally held to be a useful vehicle for portfolio planning, a number of criticisms have been levelled at the BCG matrix. For example, McDonald and Payne (1996) argue that it is often difficult to measure market share with accuracy or to be confident about market growth

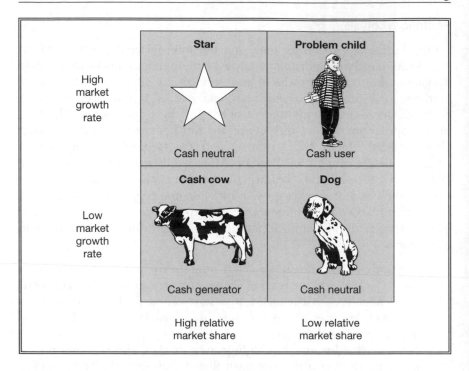

Figure 3.8 The BCG Growth-Share Matrix

Source: Based on ten Have *et al.*, 2003

rates. Calantone and Mazanec (1991) and Nicholls (1995) have also demonstrated that the BCG matrix is constrained by the limited number of evaluation criteria utilised and by its inability to incorporate qualitative data. The model is also oriented to a firm's product mix, rather than its market mix. A useful list of criticisms is also provided by Lumsdon (1997), whereby the BCG matrix is said to:

- Ignore the dynamism of markets.
- Omit the true level of competitor activity. Competitor reaction is not embraced in the model and the related concept of market share does not substitute for the strategic dimension known as sustainable competitive advantage.
- Refer only to one dimension of market attractiveness (market growth) and omits other valuable dimensions such as nature of competitors, potential size, company capability and barriers to market entry.
- Exclude the interrelationships between tourism offerings which are so important in building strategy.

- Be essentially deterministic in nature, in that the service position within one of the quadrants demands a strategic direction which is well rehearsed from previous experiences.
- Fails to recognise that strategic direction also relies on marketing acumen and creativity which might suggest a risk strategy in given circumstances rather than the predictable route.

In situations of collaborative marketing, the application of the BCG matrix raises a number of issues. On a general level, how appropriate is such a model in the context of collaborative marketing? More specifically, what are the likely resource implications for alternative forms of collaborative marketing and how suitable are the existing market growth and relative market share axis as bases for analysis?

The above questions are also of relevance to the second portfolio analysis model, the GE matrix. The GE matrix was in fact developed to remedy some of the problems of the BCG matrix. The GE matrix, as outlined in Figure 3.9, adds more variables to aid investment decision appraisal. It uses two principal dimensions: sector attractiveness and competitive position. Within the matrix, there are three zones, each implying a different marketing and management strategy (Brassington & Pettit, 1997):

- *High attractiveness, strong position*: the strategy should be investment for further growth.
- *Medium attractiveness*: because there is a weakness on one dimension, the strategy should be one of selective investment, without high commitment.
- *Least attractive*: either make short-term gains or pull out.

As Abell and Hammond (1979) argue, the development of the GE matrix approach may face certain difficulties, with the main areas of concern being linked to methodology and the lack of clear guidelines for implementing strategies. The major difficulty that may occur in the tourism context is that of identifying the relevant factors, relating the factors to sector attractiveness and competitive position, and weighting the factors. According to Lumsdon (1997), the model is more sophisticated than the BCG matrix in that the concept of attractiveness incorporates the findings of a PEST analysis, an assessment of the size and growth rate of the market, the strength of competitors and profitability potential, rather than just one factor – market growth. The factors incorporated into competitive strength include differential advantage, cost maintenance advantages, distribution power and company standing. The principal difficulty of this model comes in the weightings of the different variables. Although on the surface quite straightforward, the impact of subjective interpretation is always likely to be a problem for

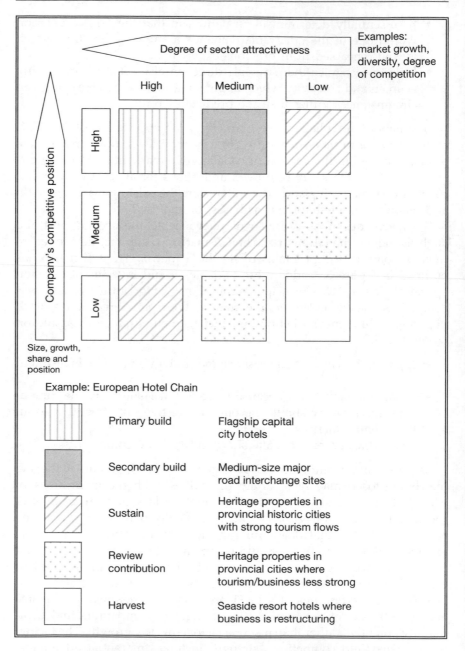

Figure 3.9 The GE Market Attractiveness–Competitive Position Matrix
Source: Lumsdon, 1997

accurate decision-making. When used in instances of collaborative marketing, the nature and scope of networks, partnership activity and potential for collaboration, and the strength of value chain systems could easily represent viable alternative variables for inclusion in the model.

Arguing that most of the portfolio analysis models are product oriented rather than market oriented, McKercher (1995) offers the Destination Marketing Matrix (Figure 3.10). This is a qualitative market portfolio analysis model that combines a range of statistical and subjective measures when locating a market within a cell of the matrix that is specific to tourism destinations.

The four cells of the Destination Marketing Matrix represent the four life-cycle stages, where markets would normally progress through during their effective life. Circle size represents the size of the market in relation to the other markets drawn to the area. The vertical axis reflects the likely future performance of each market, ranging from high growth, through stability, to rapid decline. A market's position along this axis is determined by an assessment of its likely future performance based on current marketing efforts. The horizontal axis represents the age of a market in any given life cycle cell.

The Destination Marketing Matrix displays six relationships that exist between a destination area and the many markets it serves:

- The relative importance of each market.
- The life-cycle stage of each market.
- The age of each market in each life-cycle stage.
- A prediction of the future performance of the market, if current marketing efforts remain unchanged.
- The total number of markets attracted to an area.
- The relationship that exists among these markets.

This model enables strategic tourism planners to portray the relationship between a destination and its markets when insufficient data are available. However, it is a subjective model and there is a greater risk of error being introduced by individuals who may lack objectivity when conducting their analyses. In the regional tourism context, for example, tourism products will vary in their importance and contribution to the regional mission. It is also not always possible to give equal financial, promotional and developmental attention to all tourism products in the region. Therefore, it is important to view the tourism products in the region as a portfolio that periodically should be critically reviewed and evaluated (Heath & Wall, 1992). In a similar vein to the BCG matrix and GE matrix, when it is to be used in a collaborative situation two key questions arise in respect of its applicability and appropriateness. First, how suitable is this matrix to multiple destination collaborative marketing strategies? Second, are the four life-cycle stages of equal

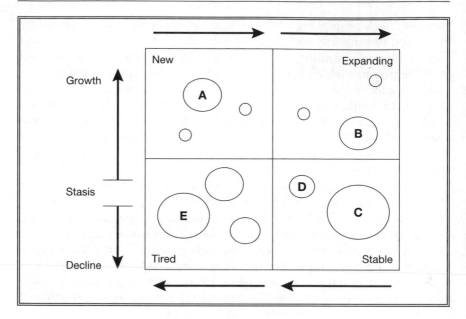

Figure 3.10 The Destination Marketing Matrix
Source: McKercher, 1995

validity to multiple destination collaboration situations? Third, what are
the most appropriate criteria for analysis along each axis?

It must be noted that within any portfolio situation there will always
be some products or business units that will be growing while others
remain in declining markets. According to Middleton (2001), portfolios
are therefore continuously evaluated according to a set of key variables:

- Shares of current markets held by own and competing organisa-
  tions and trend patterns.
- Perceived market size, growth prospects and product life cycles –
  including assessment of emerging and predicted markets.
- Cash flow generation.
- Return on investment compared with other major competitors.
- Strength of competition and profitability of others entering markets
  under consideration.
- Knowledge and core competencies developed within an entity that
  might be utilised in additional directions.

Summarising the usefulness of portfolio models in general, it is clear
that they can help marketers establish an overview of the organisation's
existing product portfolio strengths and weaknesses, as well as their

relationships with the markets, prior to the formulation of future marketing strategy. In particular, they can be useful to:

- Evaluate the organisation's current product-market portfolio.
- Evaluate the competitor's current product-market portfolio.
- Generate conditional projections of the organisation's future competitive position.
- Guide the development of a strategic marketing intelligence system.
- Determine strategy options.

Similarly, Aaker (1992) states that portfolio analysis can be used to assess the strength of a business position in a market in three important ways:

- It permits an organisation to evaluate its products or services in relation to their market attractiveness.
- It enables strategic assessments to be made concerning multiple strategic business units and in particular, their future resourcing requirements.
- Finally, baseline recommendations concerning the investment strategies for each business unit based on an assessment of business position and market attractiveness can be made.

It is important to stress, however, that the alternative approaches to product-market portfolio analysis do not provide instant formulation of strategy. In fact, they frequently involve a considerable research effort in terms of data gathering and analysis. Notwithstanding this, there is little doubt that they can, if prepared and applied properly, provide a powerful analytical framework for the review of organisational strengths, weaknesses, opportunities and threats, as well as contribute to the formulation of strategic options (Cox & McGinnis, 1982). This would appear to apply equally to both competitive and collaborative situations, the only differences perhaps being the nature of the variables along the axes and the accuracy and reliability of the data used in developing the matrices.

Analysis of strengths, weaknesses, opportunities and threats (SWOT)

Any organisation undertaking strategic marketing planning will at some point reach a stage where its internal strengths and weaknesses will need to be assessed. When set against its external opportunities and threats, which more often than not are beyond its sphere of influence, the organisation is effectively conducting a SWOT analysis (ten Have *et al.*, 2003). Cravens and Woodruff (1986) argue that this periodic assessment of the organisation represents the very heart of marketing planning, while Piercy (1997) adds that the SWOT analysis can be turned into a very dynamic tool for strategy generation and testing, with the outcome often helping to identify a robust basis upon which to evaluate future strategic options. Piercy (1997) goes further to suggest that the popularity of the SWOT is due to:

- The technique being simple enough in concept to be immediately and readily accessible to managers.
- The model being able to be used without extensive market information systems, although flexible enough to incorporate them where appropriate.
- It providing a device to structure the vast array and mix of information which characterises strategic planning.

One of the problems of SWOT analysis is that it is frequently used in too broad a context. The more focused the issue at hand, the more productive the analysis is likely to be. Piercy argues that, by focusing on a specific product market, a specific customer segment or a specific issue related to the organisation's marketing programmes, a more defined outcome is likely to arise. Piercy (1997) goes on to suggest that the SWOT takes on an even more powerful role in strategic marketing planning if the analysis only includes those resources or capabilities which would be recognised and valued by the customer with whom the organisation is concerned. As shown in Figure 3.11, this approach serves as a vehicle to summarise the critical success factors of a business, customers' needs and, therefore, the factors influencing customer satisfaction.

In concluding discussion of the SWOT analysis, it has to be remembered that it does not provide any real answers and gives no indication as to what choices are likely to be the most suited to the organisation. As such, it merely represents:

> [a] position statement, stating where the organisation is at the time of the analysis in relation to its environment. It is not the strategy itself and should not involve making statements about what should be done next. Instead it provides a firm platform for planning for the future of the organisation, i.e. formulating the strategy which is the next stage in the strategic marketing process. (Evans *et al.*, 2003: 197)

As with the majority of the models discussed in this chapter, two key questions arise when considering the application of the SWOT analysis to instances of collaborative marketing. First, are the fundamentals of a competitive SWOT analysis equally valid to collaborative marketing situations? Although this issue is explored in greater depth in Part 4, it is probably fair to conclude that the SWOT can be applied equally well to virtually all marketing scenarios, irrespective of the degree to which the

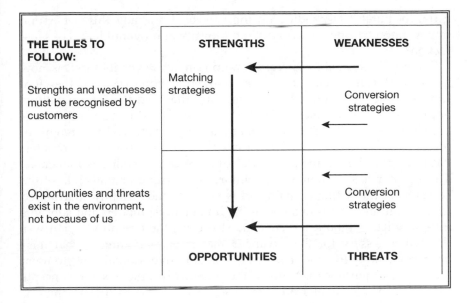

Figure 3.11 Customer-oriented SWOT

Source: Piercy, 1997

context is competitive or collaborative. The second question relates to the extent to which customers are able to distinguish sufficiently the critical success factors of a collaborative marketing initiative to make the consumer-oriented SWOT a worthwhile model to enhance effective 'collaborative' strategic marketing planning.

Conclusion

This chapter has sought to bring together many of the frameworks, models and concepts common to the literature of strategic analysis and analysis of the situational context in an attempt to evaluate their use when organisations are in collaboration with others and where collaboration, in whatever its form, is the modus operandi. For example, to what extent can an international airline determine future marketing strategy in isolation from its alliance partners, what conflicts are likely to emerge and from where are collective benefits likely to be derived? Likewise, once in a hotel consortium, how does the independent hotel conduct a situational analysis of its business – in isolation or across the collaborative domain that is the consortium? To what extent are its organisational vision, mission, goals and objectives compatible with the consortium group? How is the hotel 'brand' perceived by customers – as an independent hotel or as a member of a domestic or international consortium group of hotels? Depending on the answer, how may this perception impact upon buying behaviour, brand loyalty and overall levels of satisfaction?

There is little doubt that collaboration, in whatever its form, is now an integral component of tourism marketing strategy. It is therefore unreasonable to continue to propagate the traditional competitive approach to strategic marketing planning without due care and consideration to the implications for collaborative marketing. The strength of forces in the external environment is such that the introduction of alternative approaches to the study and practice of marketing is inevitable. This chapter has in some ways reinforced the traditional agenda of the competitive marketing domain and may have inadvertently contributed to the 'icon'-like status of some of the frameworks, models and concepts introduced throughout the chapter. However, their reintroduction was deemed necessary for the advanced reader of marketing in that their appropriateness for the emerging collaborative domain of tourism marketing is questioned. Many of the frameworks, models and concepts discussed in this chapter are well over 40 years old. Although there is nothing inherently wrong with this, the market environment has changed significantly in the last 10 years, let alone the past 40. As suggested by Donaldson and O'Toole (2002), the traditional orientation of marketing is now insufficient to meet the demands of a more dynamic and complex marketplace. The theme of this chapter, therefore, has been to examine the degree to which the manipulation of the standard marketing tools are now deficient as a vehicle for an organisation to compete effectively in the marketplace of the future. If the collaborative dimension is overlooked or ignored, marketing strategies of the future will clearly lack relevance and potency. The airline industry is typical of the developing trend in that future competition is no longer likely to be with individual airlines but between alliances of airline groupings (Piercy, 1997).

Although we would not wish to go so far as Donaldson and O'Toole in rejecting the current standardised tools of strategic marketing analysis, the questions raised throughout this chapter do require answers. It is probably fair to say that, despite the negative views spread by some, many of the concepts, frameworks and models outlined in this chapter do in fact remain viable in situations of collaborative marketing. What they require, however, are imaginative approaches to their usage, more applicable axis variables and more thought and application of relational concepts and inter-organisational dynamics. This chapter will hopefully serve as a catalyst for moving the tourism marketing debate forward and for encouraging practitioners, academics and students of marketing to question the existing status quo. In turn, it is hoped that eventually new frameworks, new models and new concepts will be developed. New structures that are compatible with the emerging collaborative tourism marketing paradigm – a subset perhaps of the emerging bodies of knowledge surrounding relationship marketing, stakeholder theory and inter-organisational collaboration – will eventually become the future 'establishment' of strategic tourism marketing planning. In the future, the organisation's surroundings will need to be viewed as a network of inter-organisational relationships, rather than as an anonymous, unilaterally competitive market.

Chapter 4

Tourism Marketing Planning, Implementation and Control

Marketing Strategy Formulation and Planning

All of the components of the strategic tourism marketing planning process discussed in Chapter 3 involve the gathering of internal and external information to provide an overview of the current situation facing the organisation. Culminating in a SWOT analysis, the need to establish the existing status quo is a necessary prerequisite to the consideration of the strategic options facing the organisation. According to Evans *et al.* (2003) there are three key facets of strategic choice:

- Formulating options for future development.
- Evaluating the available options.
- Selecting which options should be chosen.

The first task, however, is to establish the basis upon which the organisation wishes to compete, commonly referred to as an organisation's competitive strategy.

Generic strategy options

According to Porter (1980), competitive strategies can be condensed into three generic types that can be applied equally to any industry. These are:

- *Overall low-cost leadership*: by achieving the lowest costs of production among competitors.
- *Differentiation*: through achieving superior performance in an important customer benefit area.
- *Focusing*: on the needs of one or more small market segments and achieving either cost leadership (cost focus) or product differentiation (focused differentiation).

Although the above viewpoint has its critics, the original ideas of Porter still carry currency in modern business environments. For example, according to Lumsdon (1997: 89), cost leadership remains a 'common strategy among major tour operators and travel agents vying for market share and leadership'. Alternatively, and especially among destinations, a more common strategic option is that of differentiation, which involves the organisation deciding to concentrate on those variables that give it a competitive edge in the marketplace. The third and final option – that of focus – involves total immersion in one market segment by developing strong relationships with existing and potential customers. This may be achieved through strength in focus, excellence and market concentration. The thrust of Porter's ideas in this context is that organisations should avoid being 'stuck in the middle' between the three generic options. While this view is widely accepted, however, a number of instances do exist wherein organisations have been able to pursue a low-cost differentiation strategy which combines two of the three generic options. Indeed a variation on the Porter model is advocated by Evans *et al.* (2003) in which it is recognised that, in certain circumstances, a 'hybrid' strategy can be successful.

In most instances, the strategic option chosen is a reflection of the market environment in which the organisation finds itself (see Figure 4.1). For example, cost leadership is likely to be particularly valuable where markets are sensitive to changes in price. Via cost-leadership strategies, organisations are likely to benefit from earning higher profits by charging a price equal to, or even below, that of competition because of a lower cost base. This, in turn, enables them to gain higher market share. A low cost base can also serve as a significant barrier to entry for others wishing to enter the market in question. In supporting this strategic choice Evans *et al.* (2003) provide a range of means by which cost savings can be made. These comprise:

- Using less expensive resource inputs.
- Producing products with 'no frills', thus reducing labour costs and increasing labour productivity.
- Achieving economies of scale by high volume sales.
- Gaining volume purchasing discounts.
- Locating activities in areas where costs are low.
- Obtaining 'experience' curve benefits.
- Standardising products or resource inputs.

In contrast, a differentiation strategy, which will often command a higher price, be less susceptible to elastic demand and, at the same time, create barriers to entry, can be achieved by:

- Superior product performance (whether through superior product quality, durability or performance).
- Superiority of product perception (achieved through marketing communications and the direct experience of customer groups).

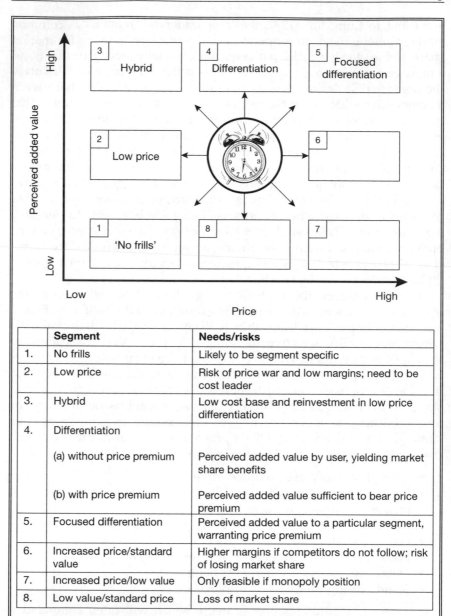

Figure 4.1 The strategy clock

Source: Evans *et al.*, 2003

- Augmentation of the product through higher service levels, better after-sales support and more affordable financing.

Finally, a focus strategy might be based on a particular geographic area, adopt a focus on the end user, or specialise on a single product or product line (Drummond & Ensor, 1999).

Porter's generic strategy options are, however, not immune to criticism. Drummond and Ensor (1999) argue that effective differentiation or absolute cost leadership is rarely achieved, especially in the long term, with all levels of management being concerned with cost when setting the strategic direction of the organisation. Indeed, Evans *et al.* (2003) suggest that:

- Cost leadership does not in itself sell products.
- Differentiation strategies can be used to increase sales volume rather than to charge a premium price.
- Price can in itself be used to differentiate.
- A 'generic' strategy cannot give competitive advantage.

Drummond and Ensor (1999) conclude the debate by stating that, in reality, many successful organisations are stuck in the middle within their competitive environments. This is not to decry the importance of establishing competitive advantage and consistency of approach. It merely serves to illustrate the competitive nature of modern business and the importance of uncovering and optimising all available sources of competitive advantage. It is a question of how best to add value within the context of the strategic business environment.

Collaboration and the nature, scope and breadth of strategic market relationships may in fact serve as the basis for an organisation's competitive advantage. However, as with many of the models introduced in Chapter 3, Porter's generic strategy options were intended for individual usage in analysing the strategic options for organisations rather than for organisations in collaboration with each other. This said, there are perhaps arguments in favour of such an approach for collaborative forms of marketing alliances, consortia and partnerships. For example, Fyall and Spyriadis (2003) argue that hotel consortia such as Best Western and The Luxury Hotels of the World clearly offer a differential advantage in the marketplace while the two major global airline alliances, Star Alliance and Oneworld, are increasingly pursuing collective means of differentiating their proposition in the marketplace. The more pressing question, perhaps, is the extent to which the generic strategy option of the collaborative domain sits comfortably alongside the generic strategies of the participant organisations and how organisations conducting parallel competing and collaborating marketing strategies reconcile their generic strategies. Likewise, in what circumstances does an organisation's selected generic strategy contribute to its choice of collaborating partner? Furthermore, are hybrid strategies more or less likely in a collaborative marketing context?

Market position

When determining strategic options, organisations need to take full consideration of their position in the marketplace as this will in itself influence the strategic options available. Four principal categories of market position are commonplace within the literature, namely market leaders, market challengers, market followers and market nichers. A brief description of the characteristics of each is given in Box 4.1.

A number of questions arise as a consequence of these characteristics in relation to instances of collaborative marketing activity. For example, how does an organisation's market position impact on its choice of partner(s) in collaborative marketing situations and on the effectiveness of its relationship with other collaborating partners? In a similar vein, how does an organisation's market position impact on the structure, governance and outcome of a collaborative form?

Related to the above are strategies that are either 'offensive' or 'defensive' in nature. Originally identified by Kotler *et al.* (1999a), offensive and defensive strategies are often used in combination by organisations in order to attack or repel competitive forces. A summary of the most common offensive and defensive strategies is presented in Box 4.2.

For organisations wishing to pursue, or already pursuing, collaborative marketing strategies, an important question is how might offensive and defensive strategies vary in competitive and collaborative situations? Likewise, are offensive and defensive strategies more suited to one situation than another, and is it possible to implement offensive and defensive strategies at the same time in parallel competitive and collaborative environments?

Push and pull approaches to marketing strategy

When discussing strategy as applied to the tourism-marketing context it is important to distinguish between two contrasting approaches to strategy: *pull* strategy and *push* strategy. *Pull*, or consumer-oriented, strategy, tends to concentrate on two core marketing strategies. These are:

- *Undifferentiated marketing strategy*, which focuses on the average expectations of target markets. Marketing efforts centre on the common interests of the target segments' needs rather than their variances.
- *Differentiated marketing strategy*, which aims to identify the characteristics of diverse consumer groups and suit their particular needs and expectations.

Box 4.1 Market position framework

Market leadership
This is where the organisation holds a dominant position within a given industry or segment, normally through market share. Common strategies include:

- Expanding the market by finding new users of or new uses for the product or service.
- Adopting an offensive strategy by aggressively pursuing market share where the fight is taken to the principal competitor.
- Instigating a defensive strategy in that the existing customer base is protected and market share is retained.

Market challenger
This is where the organisation seeks market leadership and a long-term sustained challenge to the current market leader is initiated. Common strategies include:

- Selective targeting where upon under-financed or under-resourced competitors become vulnerable.
- A direct attack on the market leader's dominant position using offensive techniques. Often very costly, market share will not erode immediately.

Market follower
This is where the organisation tends to 'shadow' the market leader as opposed to confronting them outright. Common strategies include:

- Duplication or 'me-tooism'.
- Slight product or service product line specialisation.

Market nicher
This is where the organisation pays particular attention to specific market segments and seeks to gain competitive advantage by adding value in a manner consistent with the demands of the target group. Common strategies include:

- Geographic, end-user or adaptation.

Source: Adapted from Drummond and Ensor, 1999

Box 4.2 Offensive and defensive strategies

Offensive strategies

Frontal attack
An all-out attack on a well-established competitor, which normally requires substantial resources, a sustained effort and a clearly defined advantage.

Flank attack
Achieved by attacking selective market segments where the competition is deemed to be weak. Resources are concentrated on narrow areas where superiority is achievable.

Encirclement attack
By encircling the competitor with a wide range of products, competition is effectively 'squeezed out' of the marketplace by a range of very focused rivals.

Bypass attack
Slightly defensive in nature, this approach involves the attacker moving into areas where the competition is deemed to be weak or inactive. Bypass attacks frequently involve movements into new geographic areas, the adoption of new technologies or the selection of alternative channels of distribution.

Guerrilla attack
Achieved by implementing tactical, short-term marketing initiatives to gradually weaken the competition. The key to

Defensive strategies

Position defence
This approach aims to strengthen the current position and shut out competition. By using its distinct assets and competencies, the organisation sets out to build an unassailable position in the marketplace. Position defence can be enhanced by offering a differentiated, value-added product to customers.

Flank defence
The onus is on the organisation to identify its weak flanks and protect them, in turn monitoring the impact of an attack on its flank on its core business areas.

Pre-emptive defence
This approach adopts the philosophy that you attack your competitors before they attack you, the organisation therefore adopting many of the attack strategies opposite.

Counter defence
This reactive strategy represents a form of counter attack whereby either an immediate or more considered response is likely.

Mobile defence
This involves a flexible and adaptive response, allowing the defending organisation to switch into new areas of interest

success is the unpredictability of such attacks and their ability to destroy morale and deplete competitor resources.	as threats or opportunities materialise. *Contraction defence* On occasions where a defensive response is deemed to be impossible, strategic withdrawal is likely to take place from certain market areas. In this case, resources are often freed up to concentrate on more productive product groups.

Source: Adapted from Drummond and Ensor, 1999

On the other hand, *push*, or trade-oriented, approaches to strategy, focus on intermediaries and are particularly pertinent to the tourism industry. According to Poon (1993), the distribution of tourism products is the most important activity along the tourism chain. In this instance, there are two primary considerations which need to be distinguished: first, the degree to which organisations become involved in organising and structuring the distribution channel; second, the organisation's reactions and responses to the marketing and distribution strategies of intermediaries. As a result of the organisation's activeness or passiveness with regard to these two considerations, four trade-oriented strategies are possible: *bypassing, co-operation, conflict* and *adaptation*. First, a *bypassing* strategy takes place in instances where an organisation relinquishes all collaboration with the distribution channel (Riege & Perry, 2000). Second, a *co-operation* strategy is adopted widely in instances of vertical marketing. These interactive forms of strategy vary on a continuum from very loose co-operative forms with fairly unrestrained degrees of binding force or commitment, through to very strictly regulated distribution systems (Webster, 1992). Third, a *conflict* strategy involves a situation where organisational bodies attempt to bring about or enforce their own interests against the resistance of the trade in order to gain marketing leadership in the distribution system (Riege & Perry, 2000). Fourth, *adaptation* strategy is characterised by a passive reaction of public and private tourism organisations to the marketing strategies of intermediaries in terms of organising and structuring the distribution channel. In instances where collaborative marketing is taking place, two key questions arise. First, how may the application and implementation of these two approaches to strategy vary in competitive and collaborative market conditions? Second, to what extent is strategic overlap likely to occur in contrasting competitive and collaborative situations?

Marketing objectives

Once decisions relating to the organisation's overall generic strategy and market position have been made, and having determined the extent to which push and pull approaches to strategy are to be adopted, it is then necessary to establish the exact marketing objectives to be pursued. Whereas objectives at the corporate level relate to the organisation's overall direction in terms of its general attitude towards growth, marketing objectives relate specifically to product-market decisions and the means by which such decisions will contribute to the overall achievement of corporate objectives. This 'hierarchical' approach to objective setting is complete when operational objectives are then set for each component of the marketing mix.

The model first advocated by Ansoff in the mid-1960s remains the one most commonly referred to in the marketing literature in respect of analysing strategic choice options. Outlined in Figure 4.2, the Ansoff Matrix, which contains two variables (products and markets), demonstrates the potential areas in which core competencies and generic strategies may be deployed: market penetration, product development, market development and diversification (Evans *et al.*, 2003).

The primary aim of market penetration is to increase market share in existing markets by using existing products. In the short term, margins and prices may be reduced. In the longer term, cost reductions or differentiation strategies are required for sustainable market penetration to be achieved. According to Evans *et al.* (2003), market penetration strategies are most likely to be appropriate when:

- Existing markets exhibit growth potential.
- Competitors are exiting the market.
- The organisation is able to maximise benefit from its acquired experience and market knowledge.
- The organisation is unable to enter new markets.

In contrast, market development involves attempts by organisations to take their existing product range into new market areas, which can include new geographical areas and new market segments. The extent to which the product range is easily transferable into other market segments is the key to success. Situations where market development strategies are likely to be effective include:

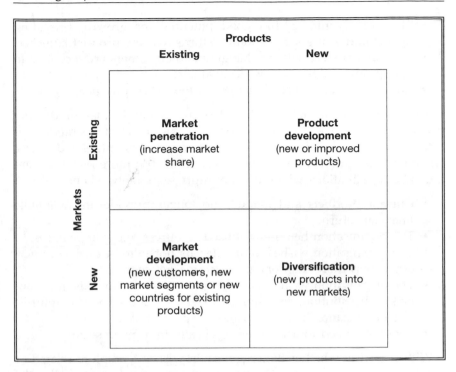

Figure 4.2 Ansoff Matrix

Source: Evans *et al.*, 2003, adapted from Ansoff, 1987

- Where the existing market shows little or no potential for growth.
- Where other market segments or geographic markets exhibit better potential for growth.
- Where regulatory or other restrictions prevent an increase in an organisation's market share in its current market.

Product development contrasts with the above in that it involves the development of new products in existing markets. According to Tribe (1997) the continuing development of products is almost an essential strategy in the dynamic environment within which organisations now find themselves. This approach is particularly applicable for those organisations pursuing differentiation strategies, as is it also for those pursuing cost strategies. In this instance, price-based strategies require product development so as to maintain low production costs. According to Evans *et al.* (2003), product development strategies are likely to be appropriate when:

- An organisation already holds a high share of the market and could strengthen its position by the launch of new products.

- The existing market has good potential for growth, providing opportunities of good economic returns for new product launches.
- Customer preferences are changing and customers are receptive to new product ideas or new destinations.
- Competitors have already launched their own products.

The final strategic option advocated by Ansoff is that of diversification. This involves moving beyond existing areas of operation and actively seeking involvement in either related or unrelated areas. Although this option almost certainly carries with it more risk, there are a number of situations where it is appropriate, notably when:

- Current products and markets no longer provide an acceptable financial return.
- The organisation has underutilised resources and competences.
- The organisation wishes to broaden its portfolio of business interests across more than one product/market segment.
- The organisation wishes to make greater use of any existing channels of distribution, thus diluting fixed costs and increasing returns.
- The organisation actively wishes to spread risks.
- There is a need to act counter-cyclically in a given sector.

With regard to whether the organisation wishes to explore related or unrelated avenues for growth, the organisation needs to consider the potential for either vertical (backwards or forwards), horizontal or diagonal of integration. A useful model of this choice is provided in Figure 4.3.

When applying the Ansoff Matrix to collaborative marketing situations, one needs to consider the balance of its value to both competitive and collaborative market situations, as well as the extent to which organisations are able to reconcile their product-market decisions in parallel competitive and collaborative market situations.

When setting the marketing objectives for the individual business unit or organisation in its entirety, the strategic options of market penetration, product development, market development and diversification are instrumental in providing a sense of direction. Thereafter, it is imperative that the marketing objectives set meet the widely accepted SMART criteria for objectives, in that they are specific, measurable, achievable, realistic and timed (see Chapter 3). Marketing objectives not only serve as the principal means by which marketing's contribution to the overall strategy of the organisation may be evaluated, but they also set the tone for the launch and implementation of the marketing programmes.

When applied to collaborative marketing contexts, a number of questions are of significance. For example, how compatible are the marketing objectives determined for the individual organisation and those of

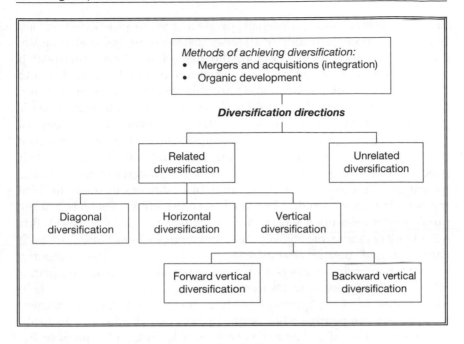

Figure 4.3 Directions and methods of diversification

Source: Evans *et al.*, 2003

collaborating partners, and how likely are the marketing objectives of the collaborative form to satisfy the marketing objectives of the individual organisation? There is also the question as to who determines the marketing objectives of the collaborative marketing form and what the resource implications may be for individual partners in meeting the requirements of the collaborative marketing objectives.

Segmentation, targeting and positioning

The issue at the very core of the strategic marketing planning process is that of segmentation, targeting and positioning. Technically separate items within the strategic marketing plan, the three are closely interrelated and serve as the foundation upon which marketing objectives are achieved. Each one will be addressed in turn with a summary provided of the overall process at the end of this section.

Segmentation

Very few products or services are able to satisfy all customers in a market. Therefore, to implement the marketing concept and successfully satisfy customer needs, different product and service offerings are required to meet the needs of diverse customer groups that typically comprise a market. Segmentation, the first of the three inter-related steps, is the name given to the subdivision of the total market into discrete and identifiable segments in accordance with a number of clearly defined characteristics. McDonald and Wilson (2002) state that the basic premise of market segmentation is that a heterogeneous group of customers can be grouped into homogeneous clusters or segments, each requiring different applications of the marketing mix to service their needs. Market segmentation is, thus, the art of discerning and defining meaningful differences between groups of customers in order to form the foundations of a more focused marketing effort. There is a large number of criteria upon which market segmentation can be based. Box 4.3 identifies some of the key segmentation variables used in both consumer and business-to-business markets. If conducted properly, segmentation arguably offers a number of benefits to marketers: first, it allows customer needs to be met more precisely; second, it can help identify new market opportunities; third, it can enable the organisation to achieve a competitive edge. Segmentation can also be said to facilitate the retention of customers as well as help focus all aspects of the marketing mix.

Market segmentation provides the basis for the selection of target markets. It allows marketers to develop differential marketing strategies and customise marketing programmes so as to meet the requirements of different segments (Jobber, 2001). To be effective, Kotler (2001) argues that market segments need to be:

- *Measurable*: the size, purchasing power and characteristics of the segments must be measurable.
- *Substantial*: the segments are large and profitable enough to serve.
- *Accessible*: the segments can be effectively reached and served.
- *Differentiable*: the segments are conceptually distinguishable and respond differently to different marketing mixes.
- *Actionable*: effective programmes can be formulated for attracting and serving the segments.

It has also been suggested that segments need to be 'defendable' in the face of eventual competition in the short, medium and long term. Furthermore, in evaluating different market segments, the organisation is recommended to consider two further factors: the segment's overall attractiveness and the organisation's objectives and resources. Having evaluated different market segments, Kotler (2001) suggests that the organisation can then consider five patterns of target market selection:

Box 4.3 Bases of segmentation

Consumer bases of segmentation bases of segmentation		Business-to-business
Social bases	*Personal bases*	*Macro bases*
• Culture	• Age	• Organisation size
• Subculture	• Life cycle	• Geographic
• Social class	• Occupation	location
• References groups	• Industrial sector	• End market served
• Family	• Educational	
• Roles and status	attainment	*Micro-bases*
	• Lifestyle	• Choice criteria
Psychological bases	• Personality	• Structure of
• Motivation	• Self-concept	decision-making
• Perception	• Household	unit
• Learning	income	• Importance of
• Beliefs and values	• Geographic	purchasing
	location	• Type of purchasing
		organisation
	Behavioural bases	• Innovation level of
	• Purchase	organisation
	occasion	• Purchasing
	• Situational	strategy
	context	• Personal attributes
	• User benefits	
	• Usage levels	

Source: Adapted from Drummond and Ensor, 1999

- *Single-segment concentration.*
- *Selective specialisation*: selecting a number of segments.
- *Product specialisation*: specialising in making a certain product for several segments.
- *Market specialisation*: concentrating on serving many needs of a particular customer group.
- *Full market coverage*: serving all customer groups with all of the products they might need.

Only very large organisations can undertake a full market coverage strategy, doing so in two broad ways: through undifferentiated marketing or differentiated marketing.

This leads on to the second stage of the process – that of targeting. This refers to the way in which an organisation assesses the attractiveness of each segment which subsequently might warrant selection and the application of resources.

Targeting

Target marketing is the common term used to describe the selection of market segments to be served by the various elements of the marketing mix. Drummond and Ensor (1999) suggest that, to evaluate different market segments effectively, it is necessary to undertake a systematic review of two issues: first, the market attractiveness of the competing segments and, second, the organisation's comparative ability to address the needs of that segment. A number of criteria can be used in order to the evaluate a segment's overall attractiveness, including market factors, the nature of competition and wider environmental factors. These are outlined in Box 4.4.

In addressing the criteria, it is necessary for the organisation to compare and contrast the ideal segments to be targeted with the organisation's overall capability to meet the segments' needs. A review of the organisation's key assets and competencies, along with analysis conducted as part of the internal resource component of the situational analysis, particularly in respect of the value chain, will help determine organisational capability. Ultimately, the choice of which market segment or segments to pursue boils down to one of four options:

- *Undifferentiated marketing*: where no rationale for market segmentation exists, such as when the market is deemed to be homogenous, and a marketing programme to the entire market with a single proposition is delivered.
- *Differentiated marketing*: where several market segments are delineated and the product or service offering is embellished accordingly to suit the requirements of each specific segment.
- *Focused marketing*: where one core segment is selected and deemed worthy of particular attention.
- *Customised* or *one-to-one marketing*: where the entire market is broken down to its maximum in that each individual customer is satisfied by a unique marketing proposition.

For the tourism destination, it is probably fair to say that each destination can only match certain types of demand and hence tourism marketers need to appreciate travel motivations in order to develop appropriate offerings and brand destinations for the right target markets. In addition, destinations should be aware not only of the needs and wants of the active demand but also of the potential markets they can

Box 4.4 Market segment attractiveness

Market factors	Nature of competition	Environmental factors
• Segment size • Segment's rate of growth • Segment's profitability • Customers' price sensitivity • Stage of industry life cycle • Predictability • Pattern of demand • Potential for substitution	• Quality of competition • Potential to create a differentiated position • Likelihood of new entrants • Bargaining power of suppliers • Bargaining power of customers • Barriers to entry in the market segment • Barriers to exiting the market segment	• Social change • Political change • Economic trends • Technological developments • Environmental factors

attract. They can then develop a product portfolio, which will enable them to optimise the available benefits and adapt their marketing mix to their target markets (Tribe, 1997). Heath and Wall (1992), on the other hand, argue that, although destination tourism organisations and tourism business units may have considerable discretion in selecting target markets, there may be factors that limit this choice. For example, if a destination has limited resources it may not be feasible to target the whole market or to tailor special offerings to each segment. Likewise, if the destination's market is fairly homogeneous in its needs and desires, an undifferentiated approach would probably be the most acceptable, as little would be gained by having a differentiated offering. Finally, if competitors have already established dominance in several segments of the market, it may be more sensible to concentrate on one of the remaining segments.

Positioning

The final stage in the process, positioning, involves an organisation positioning itself to meet the expectations of its customers, or potential customers, better than its competitors. According to Lumsdon (1997), positioning lies ultimately in the eyes of the consumer and represents the way in which an organisation locates itself in the marketplace through its service offering and the communication of this to various market segments. Positioning, therefore, is about detecting or developing product attributes that are expected to establish a competitive advantage and may therefore be transformed into valuable arguments and appeals in advertising (Calantone & Mazanec, 1991). Thus a product's position is the result of a complex set of perceptions, impressions and feelings that tourists as consumers have for the product as compared with competing products (Zafar, 1991). Positioning can be broken down into three key stages, those being:

- Identification of a set of competitive advantages to choose from (differentiation).
- Prioritising these advantages in order to select an optimum set.
- Communicating and delivering the selected position to target segments.

It can be argued that perceptions are probably more important to positioning than attributes. Positioning involves determining how consumers perceive the marketer's product, as well as developing and implementing marketing strategies to achieve the desired market position. By managing the marketing planning process, it is possible for a tourist destination to move towards a position of status rather than low price. Positioning can alter the perception of the destination to that of a special attraction, which cannot be found elsewhere. Once a destination builds an image through effective positioning of having a special attraction, the tourist perceives added value for the product (Zafar, 1991). This can result in a destination being perceived as fashionable because tourists want to be associated with the status the destination has developed by virtue of the different positioning of its image.

For the interrelated aspects of segmentation, targeting and positioning a number of questions are significant in the collaborative marketing context. For example, how are organisations able to reconcile their segmentation, targeting and positioning decisions in parallel competitive and collaborative market situations, and who determines the segmentation, targeting and positioning strategies for the collaborative marketing form? In addition, what are the resource implications for individual partners in meeting the requirements of the collaborative decision on segmentation, targeting and positioning?

Once the segmentation, targeting and positioning process is complete, the strategic marketing planning process enters the implementation phase. This phase is significant in that it is where individual marketing programmes are developed and implemented in an attempt, first, to meet the marketing objectives set earlier in the planning process and, ultimately, to contribute to the overall goals and objectives of the organisation set at the very start. Thereafter, the onus is on the marketer to evaluate, monitor and control the outcomes of the marketing planning process.

Implementation: The Tourism Marketing Mix

Identified by Cooper *et al.* (1998: 391) as a set of controllable 'tools that may be manipulated to meet specific objectives and attract predefined target markets', opinion varies as to which elements fully constitute the marketing mix as applied to tourism. Agreement is universal, however, in respect of the four main elements: *product, price, place* and *promotion*. These are commonly referred to as the 'Four Ps' and represent the elements of the marketing mix that must be managed continuously to meet the conditions of the marketplace and the actions of competitors. The term 'product' refers to the means by which the tourism product is adapted to the changing needs of the market, while 'price' refers to the amount to be charged for product usage or consumption. Meanwhile, 'place' represents the outlets of distribution to be used in establishing access to the marketplace for the tourism product, and 'promotion' represents the means by which those in the market are made aware of the product and are favourably disposed towards buying it. Originally described by McCarthy in 1960, the 'Four Ps' were deemed to be distinctly producer-oriented by Kotler *et al.* (1999a), who recast the 'Four Ps' into 'Four Cs' to reflect the consumer orientation that is central to modern services marketing thinking in an era of growing competition. This reclassification of the 'Four Ps' into the 'Four Cs' was as follows:

- Product means *customer value*: the perceived benefits provided to meet needs and wants, quality of service received and the value for money delivered assessed against the competition.
- Price means *cost*: price is a supply-side decision, cost is the consumer-focused equivalent also assessed against the competition.
- Place means *convenience*: in terms of consumer access to the products they buy.
- Promotion means *communication*: embracing all forms of producer/customer dialogue, including information and two-way interactive relationship marketing, not just sales persuasion.

Although the 'Four Cs' perhaps more accurately reflect the intended consumer orientation of marketing, in the lexicon of marketing the 'Four

Ps' have remained a formidable platform for marketing theory and practice over a number of decades, so it is the 'P' terminology that the remainder of this book will retain. More significant perhaps is the extent to which the 'Four Ps' may or may not be sufficient for purposes of tourism marketing. In the context of services marketing in particular, the 'Four Ps' are often said to fail to describe fully the marketing activities that are taking place. To fill this void, Booms and Bitner (1981) introduced three additional 'Ps' into the equation, notably: *people*, *processes* and *physical evidence*. For tourism in particular, Goeldner *et al.* (2000) recommend that *partnership* be added to the marketing mix.

The particular combination of the tourism marketing mix (which could now be said to stand at 'Eight Ps') used by any organisation needs to offer it a competitive edge or differential advantage in the marketplace. This means that the marketer is creating something unique that the potential customer will recognise and value, and something that is distinguishable from competition. The edge or advantage may be created mainly through one element of the mix, or through a combination of them (Brassington & Pettit, 1997). Each of the 'Eight Ps' will now be discussed with specific reference to the context of tourism.

Product

There can be little doubt that the formulation of the tourism product is a crucial aspect of the marketing mix with product-related decisions being central to all marketing mix-related decisions. Middleton (2001: 121) goes further to suggest that 'product decisions, with all their implications for the management of service operations and profitability, influence not only the marketing mix but a firm's long-term growth strategy and policies for investment and human resources'. In the domain of tourism, the product can encompass a multitude of factors. For example, in the context of the tourism destination, the product is said to include the destination's attractions and its environment, the destination's facilities and services, accessibility to the destination and its imagery and price as perceived and paid for by the consumer. Although each of these components can be managed unilaterally in the pursuit of strategy, for tourism destinations to succeed the separate components need to be managed in collaboration with each other – the central tenet of this book. In a truly marketing or customer-centric perspective, the product is an amalgam of benefits, utilities and satisfactions. This is particularly so in the destination context, where the consumer is buying into a seamless experience in that no boundaries are obvious to them between their accommodation, transportation and overall holiday experience. Buhalis (2000: 99) states quite categorically that failure to ensure and maintain an effective balance between all partners in the development and management of the destination will threaten 'the achievement of the strategic objectives and the long-term competitiveness and prosperity of destinations'. With specific regard to relationship marketing activity, Buhalis (2000: 104) adds that destinations clearly need to 'bring all individual partners together to cooperate rather than compete and to pool resources towards developing an integrated marketing mix and delivery system'.

This represents a considerable challenge for tourism marketers, particularly in that between many components of the tourism product there is no natural or automatic harmony. In addition, there is often a conflict of interest and objectives between parties, as well as historical fragmentation and considerable pressures from stakeholders. Furthermore, many of the individual components are purchased autonomously on a frequent basis.

This represents an appropriate juncture to introduce the framework adopted by Kotler *et al.* (2003) with respect to the categorisation of the product. Four levels of the product are proposed, each identifying particular functions and attributes of the generic product. The four levels comprise:

- *Core product*: this represents the essential benefit designed to satisfy the identified needs of target customer segments.
- *Facilitating product*: the products that are necessary for the core product to be consumed.
- *Supporting products*: extra products offered to add value to the core product and which help to differentiate it from the competition.
- *Augmented product*: all the forms of the added value producers may build into their formal product offers to make them more attractive than competitors' offers to their intended customers. Elements of the augmented product concept might include the physical environment and service delivery systems.

Related to the above, Lumsdon (1997) introduces an alternative model postulated by Smith (1994). With emphasis on the 'generic tourism product', Smith's model comprises elements of the product and the process by which those elements are assembled. The model includes six components, the idea being that the tourism product represents a synergistic interaction among all the components. The six elements introduced by Smith are: physical plant, service, hospitality, freedom of choice (where the notion is that the visitor has some degree of choice in order for the experience to be satisfactory), involvement between employees, host and visitors, and the tourism product process.

One further aspect of the product that warrants attention is branding. Outlined initially in Chapter 3, the brand is a key component of the product, with the Brand Pyramid and Branding Iceberg popular vehicles for analysing its core values and attributes. According to Middleton (2001), the advantages of branding are considerable. For example, brands:

- Reduce medium- and long-term vulnerability to unforeseen external events.
- Reduce risk at the point of purchase for consumers by signalling the expected quality and performance of an intangible product.
- Facilitate accurate marketing segmentation by attracting some and repelling other market segments.
- Provide the focus for the integration of stakeholder effort.
- Represent a strategic weapon for long-range planning in tourism.
- Are an essential attribute for effective use by organisations of communication and distribution on the Internet.

In the context of collaboration, one crucial aspect is that of co-branding, as introduced in Chapter 3. For example, with the advent of alliances and consortia in the airline and hotel sectors, the issue of co-branding is coming to the fore. Questions arising from this include: in what situations is the individual or co-brand used, how do organisations manage the convergence or divergence of brand values in the context of collaboration, what values do customers attach to co-brands, and how are financial values attached to co-brands when they have no corporate home?

A brief introduction also should be given to the concept of the product life cycle and the diffusion of innovation – two concepts that are highly familiar in the marketing and management literature, but for whatever reasons are under-explored in the tourism domain. The concept of the product life cycle served as the catalyst for the destination life cycle introduced by Butler in his seminal study of the early 1980s (as outlined in Chapter 3). The concept of the diffusion of innovation runs parallel to the concept of the product life cycle in that different groups of people are said to have a propensity to consume a product or service at different stages of its development. Although very little empirical work has been conducted in the tourism field, one can assume that the pattern of development will vary according to each offering. Both concepts are, however, useful vehicles upon which to determine future marketing strategies. Lumsdon (1997), meanwhile, provides some useful criticisms of the concept of the product life cycle, which are noted below:

- The curve is never inevitable in that many tourism offerings do not fit neatly into the established framework.
- Used in isolation the product life cycle can be of limited value and demonstrate a misunderstanding of the characteristics of tourism and its wider environment.

- Unlike traditional products or services, when at the maturity stage, destinations are seldom encouraged to be 'withdrawn' due to the extensive social and environmental implications of such a decision.
- The 'product' focus of the model takes the attention away from 'market' factors which are the very essence of the marketing concept.
- Its value as a predictive tool is limited.

For further reading in this area readers are directed to work by Palmer (1998a).

Of significance to all of the above discussion, particularly in the context of tourism, is the distinction to be made between the terms 'product' and 'service' in the literature. The tourism 'product' is arguably inclusive of the 'service' offering. Yet the assumption is often implicitly made that products and services are virtually synonymous with each other. In this regard, Lumsdon (1997) provides a very useful summary of the contemporary debate, indicating that the so-called 'service product' matches the five defining and distinguishing characteristics of services, namely intangibility, perishability, heterogeneity, inseparability and lack of ownership. Seaton and Bennett (1996) go further to suggest 'offering' as an alternative 'composite' and all-encompassing term. Although this debate will not be advanced further here, the authors are in agreement with Lumsdon that, in the context of tourism marketing, the use of the term 'product' should remain. Lumsdon (1997: 142) concludes that there is 'invariably a balance between intangible–tangible benefits dependent on each specific offering', although in tourism specifically, 'the core benefits and service interaction almost always dominate'. What is significant is the extent to which all elements of the tourism 'product' work in harmony with each other and collaborate to produce a composite package of benefits to the tourist. Future success is clearly dependent upon co-ordination and recognition of mutual interests between all the components of the overall tourism product, a rationale in itself for this book. Hence, for the remainder of this book the term 'product' will be used in its generic sense to encompass the terms 'service' and 'offering'.

Price

Although management of the tourism product is often argued to be a crucial aspect of the marketing mix, Doyle (2000: 257) suggests that pricing decisions are 'becoming more critical due to the increasing complexity of markets'. Indeed, price is the element of the marketing mix that directly produces revenue for the organisation. Doyle adds that not only is pricing the single most important determinant of shareholder value but also that in today's dynamic markets more sophisticated methods of pricing are called for. Pricing is particularly important in the tourism context in that the high degree of product intangibility often reduces the number of alternative bases for comparison by customers. Cooper *et al.* (1998: 397) argue that the pricing of tourism products also has to take into account the 'complexity created by seasonality of demand and the inherent perishability of the product'. When it comes to the setting of prices, however, Davidson (1997) argues that success is largely determined by the availability of accurate information upon which to base decision-making, which is not something instantly available in all sectors of the tourism industry (Leask *et al.*, 2002). With regard to the customer perspective, never before have customers exerted so much power and influence on the setting of prices. Middleton (2001) attributes this to the increasing ability of customers, in some sectors of tourism, to compare and contrast prices via the tremendous growth in use of the Internet and interactive television systems, among others.

Pricing has both strategic and tactical dimensions (Middleton, 2001). For example, from a strategic (long-term) standpoint pricing can:

- Reflect overall corporate strategies such as maximum growth, maximum revenue or new market growth objectives.
- Communicate chosen positioning, image and branding for products among target segments.
- Communicate expectations of product quality, status and value to prospective customers.
- Reflect stages in the product life cycle.
- Determine long-run revenue flows and return on investment.
- Determine the level of advance bookings achieved.
- Be used as part of the process for building long-term relationships with customers by offering special price arrangements to frequent repeat buyers.

Alternatively, from a tactical (short-term) standpoint pricing can:

- Manipulate last-minute/late-booking demand through price incentives.
- Determine short-run cash flow.
- Determine daily revenue yield.
- Match competition by the quickest available method and send warning signals of aggressive action.
- Promote brand or product trial for first-time buyers.
- Provide a vital short-run tool for crisis management.

Irrespective of the industrial sector concerned, there is always a large number of variables that impact on the final price to the customer. With regard to pricing of the tourism product, Box 4.5 highlights a number of the key determining variables.

Box 4.5 Factors influencing the price of the tourism product

- Wider organisational goals and objectives.
- Ownership characteristics, i.e. public, private, charity, etc.
- Organisational marketing policy and objectives.
- Uniqueness of the tourism offering and strength of brand.
- Perishable nature of the tourism product.
- High price elasticity of demand in the discretionary segments of leisure, recreation and vacation travel markets.
- Relationship between pricing and customer perception and the perceived quality and status of products and services.
- Ability to reduce costs through effective use of the value chain within the organisation and in terms of suppliers.
- Structure of the market and the organisation's position in the marketplace.
- Degree of competition.
- Ease of switching and product substitutability.
- High fixed operational cost nature of much of the tourism industry, most of which requires high load factors and strict cost control.
- Interrelated and interdependent nature of the pricing of the various elements that constitute the tourism product.
- Seasonal demand that leads to peak and low-season periods, which require demand management pricing to cope with short-run capacity problems.
- Near certainty of tactical price cutting by competition whenever supply exceeds demand.
- Long lead times in holiday markets between price decisions and product sales.
- Government involvement in the market.
- High vulnerability to demand changes due to volatility of the external macro-environment and currency exchange rate fluctuations.
- Pricing of separate elements of the tourism product, which can have detrimental impacts on the demand for other components of the tourism product, i.e. cost of travel.
- Extent to which tourism product is considered to be a luxury or a necessity and the amount of trips taken in a year.

Sources: Adapted from Cooper *et al.*, 1998; Lumsdon, 1997; McIntosh *et al.*, 1995; Middleton, 2001

Unlike many other organisations, it is not unusual for tourism organisations to pursue a number of pricing objectives simultaneously. Multi-objective pricing in tourism is attributed to the characteristics of ownership, in that maximisation of profit, market share, social pricing or pricing for survival can vary considerably depending upon the degree to which an organisation is publicly or privately owned. Prices set will also vary according to the short-, medium- or long-term nature of organisational objectives. For example, with the joint pressures of political instability in the Middle East and the outbreak of SARS in the Far East, many international airlines reduced fares as an essential component of their strategy to minimise the slump in air travel. The maintenance of cash flow is widely viewed as a prerequisite for survival in difficult trading conditions. Alternatively, in instances where social inclusion is a political objective, for example in encouraging lower economic groups to visit a nation's heritage, free access to museums and galleries may be a strategic imperative for local, regional or national governments.

When it comes to determining the pricing strategy to be adopted, a number of options exist. A summary of the key approaches to pricing in the tourism industry is identified below:

- *Cost-plus pricing*: involves a fixed-percentage mark-up on fixed and variable costs. It represents a relatively simplistic form of pricing, as prices are easy to calculate. It also allows for the delegation of price decisions for services which have to be tailored to the individual needs of customers. On the other hand, the nature of the demand curve and competitors' actions are not always taken into consideration, and consumers' value of a service may vary over a period of time. Finally, calculating the actual cost of a service is often difficult, as is it always difficult to predict costs in the future.

- *Marginal pricing*: the high fixed cost and low variable cost of operating airlines, hotels and visitor attractions often serve as the rationale for the adoption of marginal-pricing techniques and yield-management strategies. Middleton (2001: 150) states that 'in an era of excess capacity the concept of yield-management on a daily and hourly basis is increasingly relevant in all sectors of travel and tourism'. Furthermore, care needs to be taken that the marketplace does not become accustomed to discounted prices as this can cause serious longer-term damage in the marketplace and to the organisation's ability to raise prices again. Low prices may also devalue the perceived quality of the product and lead to negative consumer reaction.

- *Demand-based (differential) pricing*: this approach assumes that different market segments will pay different prices for a similar bundle of core benefits. Demand-based pricing is dependent upon the organisation's ability to segment its markets as price differences, or the desired degree of 'price discrimination', can vary between different groups of users, different points of use and different types of use, and by time of service production (Palmer, 1998a). This approach is determined ultimately by the consumers' ability to pay.

- *Price skimming*: when market 'innovators' are being targeted, price skimming is frequently adopted as a strategic imperative. To begin with the highest possible price is set for a niche segment. When saturation point is achieved, the price is reduced so as to accommodate the next segment of the market. This process continues until the mass market is reached with a price that suits. Doyle (2000) argues that skimming may be the best strategy for creating shareholder value under conditions of high barriers to entry, where demand is price inelastic, where there are clearly defined market segments, where there is a short product life cycle and where few economies of scale or experience exist.
- *Penetration pricing*: this is a frequent strategy when imitation is a key objective. Palmer (1998a) suggests that, in the absence of unique product features, a low initial price can be used to encourage people who show little brand loyalty to switch service suppliers. In this situation, understanding the buying behaviour of the market is essential. For example, what is the level of price awareness among consumer groups, to what extent can the service provider increase prices on the basis of perceived added value, and to what extent can a casually gained relationship be turned into a long-term committed relationship? Doyle (2000) argues that penetration pricing may be the best strategy for creating shareholder value under conditions of low barriers to entry, where demand is price inelastic, where there is evidence of network effects and critical mass, where there is a long product life cycle and where there are opportunities for economies of scale and experience.
- *Product-line (portfolio) pricing*: pricing along a product line or across a portfolio of products warrants attention in that product substitution and cannibalisation is to be avoided. This is valid for many tourism sectors where major tour operators, airlines and hotel conglomerates are frequently managing large product lines and a vast array of related, and sometimes unrelated, products in their product portfolio.
- *Price-bundling*: this is a typical pricing approach adopted in the tour operations sector in that the holiday 'package' includes a 'bundle' of products (normally transport and accommodation) where one 'combined' price is charged to the customer.

- *Tactical pricing*: this is often adopted in extreme short-term situations. Tactical pricing measures include a multitude of techniques such as periodic price reductions, early booking discounts, group discounts to secure high volume and loyalty packages. More often than not, tactical approaches are adopted to alleviate excess supply, to remove low-margin items from product portfolios (routes, destinations and rooms) and to protect markets against new entrants.
- *Business-to-business (supplier) pricing*: this is where tour operators will often purchase blocks of seats on aircraft and blocks of rooms in hotels in advance. In this situation, considerable knowledge is required on the state of the market and the possible fluctuations, both positive and negative, that can occur.

In most instances, a variety of pricing strategies will be applied at any one time. To succeed, Davidson (1997) advises that organisations need to understand the dynamics of the 'pricing' marketplace: frequency of purchase, degree of necessity, unit price, degree of comparability and degree of fashion or status associated with the purchase of a product. In turn, organisations need to be aware of alternatives to changing prices, and to avoid profit cannibalisation when pricing new products in the portfolio.

In the context of collaboration, a number of significant questions surface in respect of pricing. For example, how do competing and collaborating organisations reconcile pricing decisions, customer perceived value and brand consistency in addition to achieving differential advantage in the marketplace when operating in unilateral or multilateral environments? To what extent are collaborative forms influential in seasonal pricing strategies, payments made throughout the channels of distribution and in situations where multiple objectives exist, various stakeholder demands need to be met and the collaborating partners demonstrate significantly different patterns of ownership? Any form of marketing collaboration will impact upon prices set and revenues gained, be it in the short or longer term. In turn, in their pursuit of higher yield through the effective delivery of yield-management systems, what efforts are being made to integrate existing yield-management systems across the collaborative domain?

Place

(In the tourism context, Godfrey and Clarke (2000) define the 'place' element of the marketing mix as 'routes of exchange' through which a tourist accesses, books, confirms and pays for a tourism product) Most channels of distribution relate to some method of allocating capacity and creating reservations, these frequently being integrated with yield-management systems. Intermediaries in service channels of distribution arguably perform a number of distinct roles. According to Palmer (1998a) these include:

- As a co-producer of a service, an intermediary assists in making a service available locally to consumers at a place and time that is convenient to them.
- Intermediaries usually provide sales support at the point of sale.
- Consumers may prefer to buy services from an intermediary who offers a wide choice, including the services offered by competing service principals.
- Consumers may enjoy trusting relationships with intermediaries and prefer to choose between competing alternatives on the basis of the intermediary's advice.
- An intermediary as co-producer of a service often shares some of the risk of providing a service.
- The use of independent intermediaries can free up capital which a service principal can reinvest in its core service-production facilities.
- Once the initial service act is completed, there may be a requirement for the provision of 'after-sales' services.

Lumsdon (1997) makes the point that the distribution channel in tourism is different to most other services in that it enables the customer to be enticed to the destination. It is also true to say that the special nature of the tourism product gives particular prominence to the role of intermediaries in the system of tourism distribution. Tourism is special in that no ownership takes place and that no actual product is being distributed. Lumsdon goes on to identify a number of channel facets specific to tourism. For example, tourism distribution channels:

- Present a wide range of travel opportunities to the customer.
- Provide information on crucial aspects at the pre-purchase stage such as price, availability and other dimensions.
- Offer a comprehensive range of ancillary services.
- Allow easy access to the supplier.
- Enable speedy reaction to market conditions given the perishable nature of the tourism product.
- Bring economies of scale for the supply chain.
- Offer feedback to the supplier of tourism products which would not otherwise be feasible from distant markets.

The two most common forms of intermediary in the tourism industry are the tour operator and the travel agent. Tour operators bring together the essential components of a holiday and make those holiday products available through various outlets of distribution. One of those outlets of distribution is the 'traditional' retail travel agent. However, developments

The most common

in technology, in particular ICT, has greatly increased the speed and convenience of purchasing for customers, and has reduced significantly the cost at which access can be provided (Middleton, 2001). This has resulted in an electronic revolution in tourism distribution, with tourism now widely regarded as being one of the few 'pure' global information industries. Expedia, Travelocity, Lastminute.com and, more recently, Opodo are all established e-players within the tourism distribution system, and to various degrees they are beginning to challenge the traditional intermediaries. If anything, with the onset of electronic forms of distribution and 'ticketless travel', distribution is the element of the marketing mix most affected by change. The continuing growth in use of the Internet, computerised reservation systems (CRSs) and global distribution systems (GDSs) have led to increasing volumes of direct bookings and have, in part, begun to challenge the historical dominance of tourism intermediaries in the channels of tourism distribution. Global distribution systems in this context refer to computerised reservation systems that serve as a product catalogue for travel agents and other distributors of hospitality products (Kotler *et al.*, 2003).

In determining the most suitable strategy with respect to place, a number of factors need to be considered, including the nature and particular characteristics of the market, the commitment of resources necessary to service the strategy, the nature and intensity of competitor activity and the balance to be achieved between cost and control. One also needs to consider the overall portfolio of distribution channels being used by the organisation, especially with regard to number, type, cost of servicing and potential for channel conflict. There is also an issue of balance of power, in that any imbalance can have serious impacts on overall performance and ability to determine one's own destiny. Furthermore, Davidson (1997) offers some useful insights with regard to the choice of distribution channels:

- *Channels exist to serve consumers*: their purpose is similar to that of brands, whereby both exist to build superior customer value very efficiently for above-average profits.
- *Channels are segmented, just like markets*: they are segmented to achieve differentiation and to serve different customer needs.
- *Channels can add value to a brand's consumer proposition*: by offering image, services and point of sale impact.
- *Influence over the final consumer affects allocation of industry profitability.*
- *Brand organisations have the option of owning their own marketing channels*: and are showing increasing interest in doing so.
- *Producers and distributors compete within and across channels.*
- *For producers, channel marketing requires business-to-business marketing skills.*

Davidson (1997) also offers some key principles for what he refers to as 'offensive channel marketing':

- Establish clear channel requirements for brands.
- Ensure alignment between channel and market strategies and plans.
- Find ways to exercise influence over channels.
- Tailor products and services to channel needs.
- Ensure consistent presentation of core brand proposition across channels.
- Seek to develop new channels.

In the tourism context, two main strategic choices exist. The former is to adopt an intensive, selective or exclusive distribution strategy regarding outlet types and numbers, while the latter is to adopt a push or pull strategy. The latter choice is that which is fundamental to all tourism-related organisations. The distinction between the two is that a push strategy focuses on distribution outlets, urging them to sell to the tourist, while a pull strategy is directed at generating tourism demand, which is then sucked through the appropriate distribution outlets. The choice is closely related to the promotion element of the marketing mix, with most producers adopting a combination of the two, especially at the destination level. According to Palmer, a traditional push channel of distribution involves a service principal aggressively promoting its service to intermediaries by means of personal selling, trade advertising and the use of trade incentives. The onus is then on the intermediary to push the service through the system to the final consumer, generating a balance between 'maximising the customer's benefit and maximising the incentives offered to the intermediary by the service principal' (Palmer, 1998a: 218). For a pull strategy, the intermediary's role is reduced to one of dispensing pre-sold branded services.

Quite clearly, the increasing trend across the entire industry is to go 'direct'. Advances in technology are encouraging suppliers and operators of the tourism product to reduce wherever possible the number of intermediaries en route to the final customer. Direct booking is now commonplace in the tourism industry, the principal driver being the application of information technology.

In the context of collaborative marketing, place is one element of the marketing mix where collaboration activity has been, and continues to be, widespread. For example, reservation systems frequently provide a cost-effective vehicle for smaller hotels to reach a larger prospective audience when operated in collaboration with others. Fyall and Spyriadis (2003) identify Supranational, Logis de France and Leading Hotels of the World as three examples of collaboration success. In the case of Logis de France, over 4000 small one-, two- and three-star hotels identify themselves as members of the organisation through signage on the hotel and road signs. This form of collaboration (which is further discussed in Chapter 9) serves as the collective booking agent for all the hotels and offers access to markets otherwise unreachable by acting in isolation. The challenge for existing consortia is to expand the marketing potential of what are essentially booking systems.

Collaboration is not, however, without its problems. Channel conflict arises at both the vertical level, where it exists between different levels of the same channel, or at the horizontal level, where it occurs among organisations at the same level of the channel. The latter is significant in that there is considerable growth in the number of horizontal marketing systems in which two or more organisations at one level join in the pursuit of a new marketing opportunity. In such instances there is frequently some form of communication overlap and conflict within the wider value-chain system. However, with considerable advances in electronic distribution, numerous opportunities exist for future co-operation, and for expansion of existing individual and already integrated value chain systems. Numerous hurdles nevertheless exist to synchronise many organisational systems, frequently of a legacy genre in that they do not interact with each other because they were designed for unique purposes, before becoming truly collaborative. The ultimate goal is clearly to develop as much interactivity as possible, and to enhance benefits and reduce costs accordingly. The fact that channel intermediaries are now at the very forefront of tourism marketing activity, and modern marketing thinking, is testament to the means by which many have capitalised on the collaborative and electronic agendas. Once the poor cousin of the tourism marketing mix, place is that element of the marketing mix where innovative collaborative marketing opportunities are most evident.

Promotion

There can be little doubt that, among the elements of the marketing mix, it is the role played by promotion that has been instrumental to the growth of modern mass tourism. The reasons were outlined in Chapter 2. However, while promotion remains an active element of the marketing mix, the current market environment suggests that, for the time being at least, decisions relating to pricing and distribution activity are perhaps higher profile in attempting to establish and maintain competitive advantage in the marketplace.

As with all elements of the marketing mix, however, integration with the other elements is imperative for success. This is no more so than in the case of marketing communications, which represents the promotional element of the marketing mix. Whereas promotion has often been misinterpreted and restricted in meaning, marketing communications is a much broader term that now tends to be the accepted generic term for 'communicating' between producer, intermediary and consumer.

As is the case with place, marketing communications can be either 'push' or 'pull' in nature. The 'pull' elements of marketing communications refer predominantly to instances of business-to-consumer (B2C) marketing where close attention needs to be given to the patterns of buying behaviour demonstrated by selected target markets and the marketing communication messages they are likely to be most responsive towards. When referring to 'push' elements of marketing communications, the focus is more frequently on business-to-business (B2B) marketing situations, where suppliers are using the array of communication methods at their disposal to 'push' the product through the necessary channels of distribution to reach the desired target markets.

As with all elements of the mix, the aforementioned characteristics of services have an important impact when it comes to the development of communication strategies. For example, Palmer (1998a) highlights that:

- The intangible nature of the service offer often results in consumers perceiving a high level of risk in the buying process.
- Promotion of the service offer cannot generally be isolated from promotion of the service provider.
- Visible production processes, especially service personnel, become an important element of the promotion effort.
- The intangible nature of services and the heightened possibilities for fraud result in their promotion being generally more constrained by legal and voluntary controls than is the case with goods.

Of course, all aspects of communication need to be consistent with the overriding marketing objectives and be set with a realistic and achievable budget in mind. Likewise, all aspects of the communication process need to be adhered to. For example, to whom is the message being addressed, in what form and with what message, from what source and channel, and what is the desired response from the communication target? In all aspects of B2C marketing, the role of the buyer, their background, experience and availability and usage of information sources need also to be understood in respect to their influence on buying patterns (Doyle, 2000). Objectives of communication may include:

- Increasing awareness, interest, desire or action in the target audience, or moving the target audience from one stage to the next.
- Strengthening or changing destination image or positioning.
- Changing the relative importance of buying criteria.
- Generating prospects and new business opportunities.
- Shifting buyer behaviour patterns according to seasonality or by time lag between purchase and use.

- Encouraging trial use in the target audience.
- Stimulating additional purchase.
- Prompting repeat usage.
- Developing word-of-mouth recommendation to increase referred business.

When it comes to selecting the most appropriate techniques to convey the desired message and induce a response from target markets, a variety of choices are at the disposal of tourism marketers. The traditional choices are as follows:

- *Public relations*: the planned and sustained effort to establish and maintain goodwill and mutual understanding between an organisation, its products or services and its publics. Although public relations, when conducted professionally, can be highly credible and of low cost, its implementation is often imprecise, with considerable difficulty often encountered when trying to target specific markets accurately. Media relations, crisis management, product placement, sponsorship and attendance at exhibitions and travel fairs are public relations activities common to tourism.
- *Advertising*: non-personal, paid-for mass communication by an identified sponsor in a commercially available medium. Advertising is increasingly convincing to many publics and is highly appropriate for long-term image-building. Effective advertising often legitimises the brand and can be very economical in terms of 'cost per thousand'. On the other hand, it is frequently very costly and remains prohibitive for large sections of the tourism industry.
- *Sales promotions*: these are temporary, short-term incentives designed to stimulate some kind of action in the target audience. They are very popular when it comes to inducing brand trial and increasing the frequency of purchase.
- *Direct marketing and database marketing*: instances where an organisation promotes to and deals directly with the customer. Driven by database technology, direct marketing frequently uses intranets (within an organisation), extranets (networks of suppliers and key customers) and the Internet. Growth in direct marketing is attributed to its ability to target precisely and personalise communications and in its ability to induce a behavioural response.
- *Personal selling*: verbal communication between one or more prospective purchasers and a salesperson for the purpose of making a sale. Predominantly used in B2B settings, personal selling involves personal interaction which can be very costly. On the other hand, personal selling can be highly beneficial when attempting to build relationships in the trade.

Other emerging forms of communication include telemarketing, e-mail and the creation and distribution of CDs, videos and DVDs. These are particularly popular at the destination level.

Each of the above elements of communication has the capacity to achieve a different communication objective. However, prior to selecting the most appropriate vehicle, one needs to consider the wider objectives of the organisation, the nature of the product or service, the characteristics of the marketplace, the need for either a push or pull approach to communication strategy, the readiness stage of the buyer, the stage of the product's life cycle and the evolutionary stage of the market (Doyle, 2000). With regard to actual choice of media, a number of further factors need to be considered, including audience size and type, audience mood, cost of production, reach frequency and impact and the availability of media space.

It is not, however, the purpose of this book to explore the variations between the different components of the communications mix. The agenda here is simply to introduce them briefly and to explore the impact of collaborative marketing on the communication process.

While there exist numerous reasons why collaborative forms of marketing communication are initiated, market reach and cost are perhaps the two most important. A number of issues are, however, significant in the context of collaboration. What level of representation and coverage is warranted to the individual and collaborative messages, brands and associated values? How do the communication objectives vary in parallel competing and collaborating environments, and who ultimately determines and pays for the wider collaborative marketing communications strategy? What structures are put in place to minimise duplication of communication and how are all the collaborating partners' interests accommodated while at the same time maximising the benefit of the collaborative message?

The extended marketing mix

Although the 'Four Ps' provide an adequate framework for future planning in the domain of marketing, and in the context of services marketing of which tourism marketing is a subset, the extended marketing mix advocated by Booms and Bitner (1981) offers some valuable implementation insights. In the 'Seven Ps', 'people', 'process' and 'physical evidence' are added to the original mix. For example, the people element of the marketing mix is significant in that it is that aspect of marketing that contributes most to the variability of the tourism product from a service-encounter context. This applies to interaction and relationships between visitors or tourists, employees of tourism organisations and, more often than not at the destination level, the host community.

07886692478

Interactions and relationships between these three key 'people' groups will impact significantly on the level of product satisfaction experienced by the visitor, the satisfaction of the employees and the degree to which tourism is either accepted or rejected in the host destination. The people element, more than any other, provides evidence of the link between marketing and human resources as functional areas, and highlights the necessity for intra-organisational co-operation and synergy between the two. Indeed, value chain linkages between these two functional areas are instrumental to the delivery of value added in an organisational sense. This is also true across value chain systems as discussed in Chapter 3, and thus has particular ramifications for inter-organisational collaborative marketing.

In addition to people, the process element is frequently instrumental in the final delivery of the service encounter. Other essential components of the value chain such as booking systems, payment systems, queue management and visitor-flow techniques and the area of interpretation are all examples of the process component of marketing in a tourism context. As mentioned by Middleton (2001: 98), the tourism experience is more often than not 'highly dependent on the quality of service delivery as perceived by the user'. In most instances, this will involve the process element of the marketing mix. Instrumental to the effective delivery of the service encounter, marketers need to identify those incidents critical in engendering a positive 'experiential' outcome for tourists, described by Middleton (2001) as service blueprinting. Middleton goes further to suggest that any service blueprinting would include:

- All relevant points of contact between the consumer and the service encounter.
- A dividing line between activity that is visible to customers and the support activity that is not (see the discussion on the Branding Iceberg presented in Chapter 3).
- Activities of participants, both customers and employees, directionally linked in a flow chart.
- Support processes involved in the service delivery.
- Standard length of time for individual activities and time targets based on consumer expectations.
- Bottlenecks or points in the process where consumers are obliged to wait the longest period of time.
- Points in the process where service failure might occur that is both rated as significant and observed by the consumer.
- Evidence of service that aids positioning and consumer evaluation of quality.

Not only is the process element of the marketing mix fundamental to systems of customer-relationship management, complaints and service recovery but it also represents the element that is integral to the success of international airline alliances over the past decade. This aspect of collaborative marketing, although very successful in the context of international airlines, raises a number of issues pertinent to the wider context of collaborative marketing.

The final element of the extended marketing mix advocated by Booms and Bitner (1981) is represented by 'physical evidence'. In many aspects of tourism, the physical environment is a core component of the tourism product. This is especially valid in the context of destinations. In the context of the marketing mix, however, physical evidence refers to the design of the built environment owned and controlled by an organisation. Middleton also argues that, due to the intangible nature of tourism products, the physical evidence aspect of the marketing mix is more often than not used to 'tangibilise' the offer away from the place of consumption 'especially at the point of sale, to influence purchasing' (Middleton, 2001: 102). Lumsdon (1997: 203) adds that physical evidence is significant 'because of the underlying principle of simultaneous provision and consumption'. The physical evidence component of the mix in the context of tourism is used to meet a variety of objectives. For example, it contributes to the communication of messages about quality, positioning and differentiation, facilitates the process of service delivery, helps facilitate desired emotional states of behaviour among employees and communicates values relating to the organisation, brand and product. Often referred to as 'retail theatre', marketers in a service setting are searching to create a 'sense of place' and find the most suitable trade-off between functionality and aesthetics.

One further component of the marketing mix to be added to the above seven is that of 'partnership', as proposed by Goeldner *et al.* (2000). Linked to the wider ideas of collaboration and network development, the foundation of this book is that most aspects of implementation of the marketing mix in tourism involve some form of collaboration activity. Hence, rather than be viewed as a separate item, the authors propose that partnership is consistent with the collaborative paradigm proposed in Chapter 2 and thus warrants special emphasis throughout the entire text. Before closing this chapter, however, there is a particular need to highlight issues pertaining to evaluation, monitoring and control aspects of the marketing planning process and identify those issues of a collaborative genre and their impacts on the traditional planning process.

Marketing Control

Two core components of marketing control, broken down into, first, evaluation and monitoring and, second, control, each have a specific role to play and are instrumental to the achievement of marketing objectives and the implementation of marketing strategies.

Evaluation and monitoring

Described by Godfrey and Clarke (2000: 156) as the 'periodic assessment at the end of a marketing plan to check whether objectives were indeed achieved', evaluation of the marketing plan represents a periodic, often annual, process or 'check' to verify performance of the longer-term strategic marketing plan. Evaluation and monitoring should be proactive initiatives and occur habitually throughout and at the end of the marketing planning process. However, according to Faulkner (1998), the evaluation and monitoring of plans has been distorted by the tendency for it to be carried out largely as a response to external demands for accountability, rather than as a consequence of any recognition of its importance as an integral part of the planning process. In some parts of the tourism industry, therefore, a somewhat piecemeal and fragmented approach to evaluation has prevailed. Faulkner goes on to suggest that, particularly at the destination level, the full potential of evaluation and monitoring as an integral part of the marketing planning process has yet to be realised. In the same study, Faulkner provides a 'four-layer' framework for the comprehensive evaluation of destination marketing programmes. The four stages are referred to as the programme review stage, the performance monitoring stage, the causal analysis stage and the cost-benefit analysis stage. These four stages and their contributions to the evaluation process are illustrated in Box 4.6.

Control

Related to the above, marketing control is said to refer to 'tactical marketing management actions taken continuously in response to the information provided by monitoring' (Middleton, 2001: 226). Godfrey and Clarke (2000: 156), meanwhile, add that control refers to the 'tactical activity carried out to close the gaps between actual performance and daily, weekly or monthly targets identified by monitoring'. Marketing control is in many ways considered as the natural sequel to marketing planning, organisation and implementation. Middleton (2001) identifies five key reasons why marketers should pay particular regard to issues of marketing control. He argues that performance measurement provides the vital information for marketers to:

- Respond quickly and effectively if actual sales and other indicators vary significantly from targets.
- Learn from current experience in ways that will make the subsequent year's campaign targets and budgets more cost-efficient.
- Adjust strategic objectives in the light of current results.

Box 4.6 The evaluation and monitoring of destination marketing plans

Programme review
This stage is where the appropriateness of organisational objectives is assessed and the key strategies are identified. Associated targets around which the marketing programme is structured are also noted as benchmarks for considering outcomes.

Performance monitoring
This stage involves the measurement of the output of each element of the programme in terms of various performance indicators.

Causal analysis
This stage attempts to establish linkages between outputs and responses in the market place. At one level, techniques like tracking studies and conversion studies may be employed to quantify immediate impacts, while market share analyses might be used to map longer-term market trends with a view to identifying longer-term effects. At another level, multivariable analysis or experimental methods might be applied in an effort to distinguish market reactions specifically attributable to the programme from those associated with the effects of broader environmental factors.

Cost-benefit analysis
This stage is essentially concerned with establishing whether or not the costs incurred in implementing the programme are outweighed by the benefits derived from any increase in visitor arrivals that is achieved.

Source: Adapted from Faulkner, 1998

- Integrate marketing decisions with those of other key business functions, especially accounting and finance and operations management.
- Make the vital marginal adjustments to campaigns, which in high-fixed cost businesses will always have a major impact on profit or loss.

Although performance measures and standards will always vary between organisations and market conditions, Drummond and Ensor

(1999: 159) suggest that 'a control system detecting and pre-empting the inevitable problems that accompany implementation is a valuable asset'. Drummond and Ensor highlight a number of facets that contribute to the creation of an effective control system:

- *Involvement*: ensure process is participative in nature, which in turn should contribute to morale, staff motivation and a sense of ownership.
- *Target setting*: target criteria should be objective and measurable, achievable but challenging.
- *Focus*: ability to separate between the symptoms and the source of the problem.
- *Effectiveness*: the temptation is to measure efficiency as opposed to effectiveness.
- *Management by exception*: attention should be given to areas of specific need. This should be driven by predetermined limits and a series of benchmarks.
- *Action*: effective control systems promote action.

Control does not, however, operate in a vacuum and numerous problems can arise that can impair progress. For example, the balance between cost and control is sometimes uneven, while there is always the fear that too much control can lead to a stifling of effort and creativity. There is also the fear that too much control will lead to a culture of inspection as opposed to development, with systems frequently dealing with the symptoms rather than the root causes of the problem. However, in the current climate of market uncertainty and market turbulence, the controlling of marketing performance can be considered a very necessary and worthwhile task. This is particularly the case in situations of collaborative marketing whereby 'boundaryless' multilateral co-operative environments are coming under increasing 'control scrutiny'. Issues of responsibility and accountability are perhaps even more important in collaborative marketing situations, where outcomes are difficult to monitor due to unclear reporting structures, different reporting timescales and measurement inconsistencies between collaborating partners. Notwithstanding this, the complexity and dynamism of the market environment is such that every effort to control annual planning, such as sales and market share, revenues and profitability (disaggregated as much as possible), efficiency (gaining optimum value from marketing assets) and strategic direction (ensuring that marketing activities are being directed towards strategic goals and that marketing is an integral part of the overall process of delivering value) needs to be made.

Conclusion

The complexity of the tourism industry, the fast pace of change, the rapid growth in volume of more experienced, demanding and sophisticated customers, and the growing role of information and communications technology underline the necessity of strategic marketing planning and the evaluation and exploitation of future trends for any tourism organisation that wishes to compete in today's dynamic market environment. In conjunction with Chapter 3, this chapter has sought to shed light on the traditional approach to strategic tourism marketing planning and has identified, in the form of a series of questions, those issues and challenges pertinent to situations where collaborative marketing is either in operation or is being considered as a viable strategic vehicle for the achievement of organisational and collaborating goals. As with all aspects of marketing theory and practice, much of the focus of these two chapters has been on the existing models, theories, concepts and principles of competitive marketing. With so few instances of purely unilateral competitive action evident in the tourism domain, the remainder of this book seeks to address the extent to which this body of literature is sufficient to take the industry forward. In the age of consolidation and collaboration, the authors ask a very simple question: to what extent can existing models, theories, concepts and principles of competitive marketing advance the adoption and effective practice of collaborative marketing in tourism?

Part 3: Inter-organisational Collaboration

Chapter 5

Inter-organisational Collaboration: Concepts and Theories

Introduction

Chapter 2 considered the 'standardised' approach to marketing and identified how collaboration between stakeholder organisations (termed 'inter-organisational collaboration') might be viewed simultaneously as both a challenge and an opportunity for tourism marketing. The chapter argued that, in view of the highly complex and interrelated nature of the tourism product, tourism marketing conducted at the organisational level without explicit relevance to the organisation's relationship with other key stakeholders is unlikely to meet its objectives fully. In this respect, Chapter 2 presents a challenge to the standardised marketing approach in so far as its application in the tourism context may lack potency because the collaborative dimension is overlooked or ignored. The opportunity, meanwhile, is for tourism marketing organisations to recognise that the industry is intrinsically one in which collaboration is not just desirable as a strategy for maximising the potential of marketing, but indispensable if the tourism organisation is to survive in the long term. Chapters 3 and 4, meanwhile, extended this argument by examining in more detail the implications of inter-organisational collaboration for tourism marketing strategy and management.

The primary purpose of this chapter is to introduce the concept of inter-organisational collaboration and to highlight the advantages and disadvantages of pursuing a strategy of inter-organisational collaboration, both for the individual organisation and for the industry as a whole. The chapter then goes on to consider a number of theoretical perspectives on why organisations might, and often do, engage in collaborative strategies.

In beginning to unpack what collaboration means and how it may contribute to tourism marketing, however, a problem immediately arises – collaboration does not present itself in the literature as a single, tightly defined concept, but as a series of concepts that are apparently distinct from one another. Hence, terms such as 'co-operation', 'networking' and 'joint ventures' all appear in the literature, often without more than a sketchy definition of each being given. There is also a tendency for certain terms to be used in certain contexts, so that the airline industry is said to form 'alliances', while hotels join together in 'consortia'. When public-sector organisations are involved, the term 'partnership' is often preferred. Adding to the confusion, such terms are often used interchangeably, so that an alliance among airlines is described as collaboration, while members of a hotel consortium are said to co-operate with one another.

Spyriadis (2002) presents a useful compilation of such terms (see Box 5.1), illustrating the wide range of terminology that presently exists across the collaboration literature to describe positive and negative relationships among organisations. However, the view taken in this book, which is explored more fully in Chapter 6, is that, while such distinctions may be helpful in attaining a better understanding of collaboration, the terms are not used consistently. Indeed, it is clear that even the term 'collaboration' has a number of different and potentially conflicting interpretations. Making fine distinctions between different forms of collaboration may therefore compound the problems of understanding various aspects of the phenomenon, rather than solve them. The approach taken by this book is therefore to treat the various terms listed in Box 5.1 as being for the most part synonymous and, wherever possible, to use the term 'collaboration' as a catch-all term.

Defining Collaboration

The problem of how best to encapsulate the concept of collaboration in a single, comprehensible definition is one that has long troubled those interested in better understanding it. Many writers have attempted to provide a definition that succinctly summarises the key features of collaboration while remaining applicable to the diverse range of contexts in which collaboration occurs.

Eminent among writers on the subject of inter-organisational collaboration over the past two decades has been Barbara Gray. In considering how best to define inter-organisational collaboration, Gray (1989) identifies five key characteristics of the collaboration process, which are that:

- the stakeholders are independent;
- solutions emerge by dealing constructively with differences;
- joint ownership of decisions is involved;
- the stakeholders assume collective responsibility for the ongoing direction of the domain; and
- collaboration is an emergent process, where collaborative initiatives can be understood as emergent organizational arrangements

---

Box 5.1 Terminology used to describe inter-organisational relationships

Positive forms of inter-organisational relationship

Co-operation	Co-ordination	Coalition	Network
Alliance	Partnership	(Joint) venture	Bridge
Minority	Cross holdings	Compact	Cross
holdings	Syndicates	Collaboration	licensing
Agreements			

Negative forms of inter-organisational relationship

Conflict	Competition	Co-option	Collusion

Source: Spyriadis, 2002

---

through which organizations collectively cope with the growing complexity of their environments.

Wood and Gray's definition

Perhaps, however, the best justified and elaborated definition of inter-organisational collaboration is offered by Wood and Gray (1991). Their concern was to develop a comprehensive theory of collaboration. Recognising that the effective theorisation of collaboration would require the adoption of a robust working definition from the outset, the researchers attempted to synthesise one by deconstructing seven definitions of collaboration appearing in a special issue of the *Journal of Applied Behavioral Science* on the subject. By identifying and considering the key elements of each, Wood and Gray then attempted to create a composite definition of the concept of collaboration. Their selection of the key components necessary for such a definition was as follows:

- stakeholders/parties (voluntary membership) with common interests/shared goals;
- seeing different aspects of a problem/having differences;
- acting/deciding/managing/exploring/addressing constructively;
- via shared institutions/rules/norms,
- a temporary structure, and
- an (interactive) process;
- with respect to a problem domain/issue;
- to search for solutions/to produce change;
- beyond their limited visions and abilities;
- to decide the future of a shared domain.

These key elements were then collapsed together into the following definition of collaboration:

> Collaboration occurs when a group of autonomous stakeholders of a problem domain engage in an interactive process, using shared rules, norms, and structures, to act or decide on issues related to that domain. (Wood & Gray, 1991: 146)

Wood and Gray justified their choice of the above key components of their definition of collaboration as follows:

Stakeholders of a problem domain

Stakeholders are defined by Wood and Gray as groups or organisations with an interest in the problem that is to be addressed through a collaborative process. Stakeholders may have both common and differing interests at the start of a collaborative venture, but these may change or be redefined as the collaboration proceeds. This is not intended to imply that all of the stakeholders in the problem domain will necessarily be involved in the collaboration, either at the outset or as it evolves, leaving open the potential for different outcomes to arise as the result of full or partial stakeholder representation.

Autonomy

This element is considered by Wood and Gray to be crucial to the concept of collaboration. Indeed, collaboration must surely involve stakeholders retaining at least some of their independent decision-making powers, even when they agree to abide by the rules of the collaboration. In some cases, participants in the collaboration will retain full autonomy, while in others they may relinquish a great deal. If, however, participants were to relinquish all their autonomy, a very different organisational form would be created (perhaps a merger). Indeed, it has been argued (Bleeke & Ernst, 1995) that the entry of relatively weak and strong organisations into a collaborative relationship can often be a precursor to the stronger acquiring the weaker. This is particularly likely if the weaker organisation was to declare too much sensitive information or failed to keep sufficiently tight control of its core competencies.

Interactive process

Wood and Gray argue that collaboration is an interactive process, indicating a change-centred relationship that takes place over a period of time and involves the participation of stakeholders. Without this dimension, collaboration would simply imply a form of relationship, with no dynamic and hence no explicit purpose.

Shared rules, norms and structures

According to Wood and Gray, shared rules, norms and structures must be agreed in order to provide a framework within which mutually beneficial forms of behaviour can be negotiated among participants and made operational. The structures involved in collaboration are most often of a temporary nature, but to insist on this might exclude more permanent forms of collaboration, such as joint ventures, federations and international associations, from the definition. Wood and Gray argue against this, indicating that, while such inter-organisational relationships may be intended to be permanent, they are also quite capable of suffering collapse or being realigned. Hence, Wood and Gray consider it better to view collaboration simply as involving 'shared structures', and use the duration of such structures as a way of defining different forms of collaboration.

Action or decision

Given that it has already been established that collaboration is fundamentally a process that is deliberately initiated by its participant stakeholders, it would seem reasonable to conclude that collaboration must be directed towards some form of shared objective. For some authors, then, the 'success' or otherwise of a collaboration depends critically on the achievement of predetermined objectives. Several possible target outcomes have been suggested in the literature, including the achievement of change (a 'transmutational' purpose), social change, achieving a broader vision, increasing systematic capacity to respond to environmental change and so forth.

Wood and Gray, however, argue that the stated objectives do not have to be reached for collaboration to be considered to have taken place. Indeed, a collaboration that fails to meet its stated objectives may involve a virtually identical set of actors and processes to one that succeeds – in which case the former could hardly be dismissed as not being true collaboration. It is also possible that collaboration can have unintended consequences, either desirable or undesirable. To exclude inter-organisational relationships that result in tangible outcomes, albeit unintentional ones, would seem highly illogical. Finally, Wood and Gray argue that given the substantial disagreement even as to what the objective of collaboration should be, 'a more general definition of collaboration thus should leave the consequences of collaboration unspecified and open to empirical investigation' (Wood & Gray, 1991: 149).

Domain orientation

Finally, Wood and Gray argue that the participants in a collaboration must have a shared predicament (a 'problem domain') that requires them to come together and seek a solution through a process of collaboration. The problem domain can be as narrow as seeking a joint solution to traffic congestion around a visitor attraction site, or as broad as determining the content of a national tourism promotion strategy. Indeed, it is to be expected that the problem domain will vary a great deal from case to case, depending on the scope of the decisions that need to be made and their likely impact on the future relationship among stakeholders. The problem domain must, nevertheless, have a forward-looking orientation, giving participants in the collaboration an opportunity to impact on the future of their shared domain.

Expanding the definition

Wood and Gray do not concern themselves with developing additional terms to enable them to distinguish between the various forms of collaboration, such as co-operation, alliances and consortia. Indeed, it would seem that Wood and Gray are content to define collaboration broadly enough to enable such variants to be subsumed within their overall definition of collaboration, which assumes a generic status. Other writers, however, have sought to separate out 'collaboration' conceptually from other forms of inter-organisational relationship.

Jamal and Getz (1995), for example, suggest that, while the terms 'co-operation' and 'collaboration' are typically used synonymously, 'co-operation' – which literally means 'working together towards some end' – does not sufficiently capture several major dimensions that are felt to be critical to 'collaboration'. In particular, the nature of collaboration as a necessary response to the complexity of problem domains is felt to be underemphasised by the term 'co-operation'. The authors therefore go on to suggest that the term collaboration should be reserved for those circumstances in which stakeholders recognise the conflicts inherent to a complex problem domain and wish to harness the potential of a shared response to them.

In view of conflicting interpretations associated with the term, Jamal and Getz adopt the following definition for their study of collaboration in community-based tourism planning, which is adapted from that of Gray (1989):

> Collaboration for community-based tourism planning is a process of joint decision-making among autonomous, key stakeholders of an inter-organizational, community tourism domain to resolve planning problems of the domain and/or manage issues related to the planning and development of the domain. (Jamal & Getz, 1995: 188)

The key elements of Jamal and Getz's (1995: 188) definition of collaboration are thus:

- the 'community', which is further defined as a 'body of people living in the same locality';
- which includes 'stakeholders' who are said to be 'actors with an interest in a common problem', including individuals, groups and organisations;
- who retain 'autonomy', and hence 'retain their independent decision-making powers while abiding by shared rules within the collaborative alliance'; and
- who work in a 'problem domain', which is in turn defined as 'a situation where the problems are complex and require an inter- or multi-organizational response, since they are beyond the capability of any single individual or group to solve single-handedly'.

'Co-operation' might therefore be viewed as a subdivision of 'collaboration', which focuses on the notion of organisations working together without presupposing why participants might consider such joint working arrangements to be desirable. For the purposes of this book, however, such terminological distinctions will not be made, and the term 'collaboration' will be used in a generic manner to denote all major instances of joint working between organisations, without necessarily specifying the reasons the organisations involved might have for doing so. This is not to suggest that the reasons why organisations might choose to enter into joint working (i.e. collaborative) arrangements is not itself important. Indeed, this is the subject of the next section of this chapter.

Collaborative advantage

The above definitions (Gray, 1989; Jamal & Getz, 1995) are clearly based on the *process* of collaboration: they focus on the method of working and the objectives adopted. In contrast, Huxham (1993, 1996) introduces the term 'collaborative advantage', which he defines as:

> when something unusually creative is produced – perhaps an objective is met – which no organization could have produced on its own and when each organization, through the collaboration, is able to achieve its own objectives better than it could alone. (Huxham, 1993: 603)

This concept focuses on the *outcomes* of collaboration, which Huxham argues can (but need not necessarily) create synergy between the participating organisations. This means that the joint outcomes of collaboration are in some sense greater than the sum of individual outcomes that could be achieved in the absence of collaboration. For example, the objectives of the participating organisations might be more fully met as a result of the collaboration, or the collaborative process might generate spin-offs for the domain more generally.

The notion of collaborative advantage has enormous implications for the concept of relational marketing, as introduced in Chapter 2. Through collaboration, organisations that do not have any significant competitive advantage in a given market environment independently might be able to achieve sufficient collaborative advantage to compensate for this and thereby enable them to out-perform longer-established organisations. In an industry where the existence of a large number of relative small organisations is the norm, the scope for achieving such collaborative advantage can be considerable. Similarly, seeking collaborative advantage rather than competitive advantage might be a particularly effective market-entry strategy where the product is a composite one and the industry highly fragmented, as is often the case in the context of tourism. Such outcomes simply cannot be achieved in a market environment where organisations are operating independently from one another.

Indeed, Huxham argues that the concept of collaborative advantage is in some ways more important than that of collaboration. In particular, the notion of collaborative advantage has enormous potential value in legitimising collaboration as an activity that is worth investing in. Given that it is often necessary to invest substantial organisational and financial resources in order to collaborate, the potential for benefits to be achieved through collaboration – benefits, moreover, that would otherwise not be captured by the organisation – must form the cornerstone of the rationale for collaboration. The term is, of course, designed to contrast with the more familiar 'competitive advantage'.

Motives for Collaboration

The literature is replete with examples of why organisations come together to form joint-working, or collaborative, arrangements. Even the most cursory review will reveal that these motives are many and varied. A sensible starting point for any discussion of the motives for collaboration might therefore be to sort them into broad types. Indeed, this is the approach taken by Beverland and Brotherton (2001), who divide the motivations for inter-organisational collaboration into eight main groups (see Box 5.2).

Hanlon (1999), meanwhile, reports the findings of an empirical study by Hagedoorn (1993) of some 10,000 collaborative agreements between firms. Hagedoorn's study identified two broad sets of motives for why firms join strategic alliances: first, motives associated with technology (e.g. research) and, second, motives concerned with market access and/or influencing the structure of the market. Further, the study found that, even with a data set aimed specifically at firms likely to have technological motives for joining alliances, market-related motives dominated by far. Meanwhile collaboration was found to be most likely in mature

Box 5.2: Potential motives for collaboration

Market entry and market position-related motives
- Gain access to new international markets.
- Circumvent barriers to entering international markets posed by legal, regulatory or political factors.
- Defend market position in present markets.
- Enhance market position in present markets.

Product-related motives
- Fill gaps in present product line.
- Broaden present product line.
- Differentiate or add value to the product.

Product/market-related motives
- Enter new product/market domains.
- Enter or maintain the option to enter into evolving industries whose product offerings may emerge as either substitutes for, or complements to, the firm's product offerings.

Market structure modification-related motives
- Reduce potential threat of future competition.
- Raise/erect barriers to entry.
- Alter the technological base of competition.

Market entry timing-related motives
- Accelerate pace of entry into new product/market domains by accelerating pace of research and product development and/or market entry.

Resource use efficiency-related motives
- Lower production costs.
- Lower marketing costs.

Resource extension- and risk reduction-related motives
- Pool resources in light of large outlays required.
- Lower risk in the face of large resource outlays required, and technological, market or other uncertainties.

Skills enhancement-related motives
- Learn new skills from alliance partners.
- Enhance present skills by working with alliance partners.

Source: Beverland and Brotherton, 2001

industries, such as food and drink, automobiles, chemicals and – perhaps surprisingly – high-technology industries.

Hanlon goes on to argue that technological motives for collaborating would be more unusual in the service industries, such as the airline industry and, presumably, most other industries that together contribute to the composite tourism sector of the global economy. This would be the case even when such industries make extensive use of new technologies, because issues more immediately related to markets normally dominate the strategic concerns of organisations operating in the service sector. Thus motivations related to issues such as building the customer base, gaining access to new markets, defending existing markets and conducting marketing strategies more generally might be seen to dominate in the tourism context. Table 5.1 (based on Chaston, 1999) illustrates the range of market-related outcomes that may be sought by organisations collaborating with one another. The table takes the form of a three-by-three matrix, with the types of markets in which collaboration is expected to prove a beneficial strategy taking the columns and the types of product expected to be placed in those markets taking the rows. As can be seen from Table 5.1, different combinations of product and market imply different motivations for collaborations, depending on the context in which collaboration is expected to take place.

The study by Hagedoorn found that market motivations tended to dominate empirically the reasons why organisations choose to collaborate, but this is not to suggest that technological motivations cannot explain the formation of some collaborative alliances in the tourism industry. For example, there have been some instances in which technological motivations have been behind the formation of collaborative alliances. In the context of the airline industries, for example, the need to develop common technology so as to achieve efficiencies in aircraft maintenance has emerged as a primary motivation for collaboration (Hanlon, 1999). Hanlon also identifies a lone instance in which both technological and market motivations have been important in the airline industry: the development of computerised reservation systems (CRSs). In the case of CRSs, few airlines would have been able to muster the financial resources necessary to develop such highly complex systems on their own. However, airlines have been able to cluster together and share the cost of developing them. In doing so, they have developed highly sophisticated CRSs, which have not only led to efficiencies in booking and the reduction of operational costs, but have also enabled valuable marketing links to be developed between organisations.

Arguably, the focus on the market benefits of inter-organisational collaboration are in no small part due to the increasing globalisation of economic activities in the last quarter of the 20th century – a phenomenon that has been felt particularly strongly in service industries. Organisations

Table 5.1 Market-related motivations for collaboration

	Existing market(s)		*New market(s)*
	Existing customers	*New customers*	*New customers*
Existing product	Sharing of market management resources to increase existing customer sales	Sharing resources to achieve scale effect to gain access to new customers	Sharing market management resources to execute new market entry strategy
Merged product line to enhance product position	Increased sales to existing customers by offering an enhanced product proposition	Access to new customers through offering an enhanced product proposition	Gaining access to new markets through offering an enhanced product proposition
New product	New sales to existing customers through launching new product	Gaining access to new customers by launching new product	Gaining access to new markets through offering new product

Source: Chaston, 1999

have typically found need to collaborate in order to take up better strategic positions in the emerging global marketplace. Internal growth strategies are often impeded by short-term funding constraints, while the conventional external growth strategies, which are based on mergers and takeovers, have tended to prove unwieldy and drawn out, given the speed of change implied by the globalisation of markets. Collaboration, meanwhile, represents an alternative market access strategy which, given the right conditions, steal the march on other external growth strategies. Thus, to continue with the example of the global airline industry, market-motivated forms of collaboration have included code-sharing arrangements, block-space agreements, franchising and reciprocity between frequent-flier programmes (Hanlon, 1999). The principal motive behind all of these forms of collaboration was to enable the airline companies to step outside their predominantly *national* spheres of activity and establish footholds in an increasingly *global* marketplace. This motivation is especially well demonstrated in the development of inter-airline hubbing arrangements, where restrictions on cabotage prevent the international carrier from serving domestic routes while the domestic carrier has no access to international routes. By collaborating, both airlines can expand the geographical boundaries of their markets, implying a two-way process of market extension.

This line of argument would seem to suggest that globalisation has been a major impetus to the proliferation of collaborative arrangements; yet this can only be part of the explanation. Indeed, the growth in interest in collaboration preceded the recognition of the importance of globalisation, or even that it was taking place, by some time. What, then, can explain the increased imperative that has been placed on collaboration in the tourism industry in recent times?

Part of the answer to this conundrum would seem to lie in the nature of the tourism industry itself, which has long been recognised as exhibiting a number of features that at the same time make collaboration both highly desirable and difficult to achieve. These features might be said to include the complexity of tourism, the fragmented nature of tourism and the turbulence within the tourism environment. As identified in Chapter 2, the context for tourism is clearly very different to that of a typical manufacturing industry or, for that matter, many other service-based industries. For example, tourism is more supply-driven than other services, with the tourism product being a complex, extended product with no clear evaluation point. Tourism is also a high-involvement, high-risk activity for its consumers, while it is partly constituted on the dreams and fantasies of tourists. Finally, the tourism product is frequently a composite one, while tourism is both fragile and highly susceptible to external forces that are beyond its control. These two latter points are expanded upon below.

The fragmented nature of tourism

As well as being highly complex, the tourism environment also tends to be highly fragmented, comprising a large number of organisations from a wide variety of contexts and with a wide variety of organisational characteristics: from non-government organisations to huge multinational companies to public-sector authorities to tiny micro-businesses. Further, as Seaton and Bennett (1996) point out, tourism is a composite product, involving input from a wide range of economic sectors, including transport, accommodation, catering, entertainment, retail, insurance and many others. This implies a high degree of interdependence among tourism organisations; yet the fragmented nature of the tourism product tends to make cohesion very difficult for stakeholders in the domain. Indeed, Jamal and Getz (1995: 187) argue that 'achieving co-ordination among the government agencies, between the public and the private sector, and among private enterprises is a challenging task . . . and requires the development of new mechanisms and processes for incorporating the diverse elements of the tourism system'.

One potential vehicle for combating this fragmentation is collaboration, and the fragmented nature of the tourism industry represents both an opportunity and a challenge for key tourism stakeholders wishing to engage in such a process. The opportunity is that collaboration can assist in bringing together all of the various fragments and enabling them to work effectively together. This may make it possible for stakeholders to achieve outcomes that were unattainable by any one organisation working on its own. Equally, a process of collaboration may enable stakeholders to achieve goals that they could not have achieved individually. The challenge, of course, is that collaboration in a highly fragmented industry context is never going to be easy. Indeed, the conventional wisdom is that the challenges of collaboration tend to rise as the number of participants in the collaboration rise. In a highly fragmented tourism industry, effective collaboration will typically need to involve a considerable number and range of stakeholders.

The turbulence of the tourism environment

We have already noted above that the tourism environment tends to be susceptible to external forces that are beyond the control of the key stakeholders operating within it. However, Jamal and Getz (1995) go even further to argue that the tourism environment is essentially a turbulent one. This, they state, requires tourism organisations to develop a new managerial mindset: one that rejects the notion of business relationships shaped by constraints, choice and competition, and embraces the potential of collaboration to counteract the turbulence that tends to intensify as their industry develops.

The notion of the 'turbulent environment' was developed by Emery and Trist (1965), who posit a spectrum of 'causal textures' – interdependencies that belong to the environment itself – ranging from 'placid' at one extreme, to 'turbulent' at the other. According to Emery and Trist, in turbulent fields – whose dynamic properties arise from the interaction of the constituent organisations and from the field itself – competing organisations, by acting independently and in many different directions, produce unanticipated and dissonant consequences in the environment in which they all share. These dissonant implications generally increase as the field becomes more densely populated, leading to ever greater uncertainty for stakeholders operating within it.

As this turbulence grows and begins to affect more and more organisations in the field, adaptation on the part of individual organisations to the challenges presented to them becomes increasingly difficult for them to achieve on their own. Individual organisations have neither the perspective to perceive and understand domain-level problems sufficiently well to deal with them, nor the managerial capabilities needed to address them effectively. Attempts by individual organisations working autonomously to address this turbulence are thus 'maladaptive' (Gray, 1985) – meaning that they are uncoordinated and can create further problems for other stakeholders in the domain. Hence writers such as Trist (1977) have argued that organisations should reject the independent strategies that have traditionally been formulated at the individual level and focus their efforts on working in the 'inter-organisational domain'.

This discussion leads on to a consideration of theories of collaboration, which is the subject of the next section of this chapter.

Theories of Collaboration

In discussing various theories of inter-organisational collaboration, Wood and Gray (1991: 155) argue that:

> virtually all organizational theories acknowledge that environmental complexity, uncertainty, and turbulence are among the central problems facing organizations, and that a chief task of organizations is to reduce this complexity, uncertainty, and turbulence to manageable proportions. Some have suggested that organizations ... collaborate to reduce and control environmental uncertainty and turbulence.

As we have seen in the section above, the tourism industry would appear to be replete in the characteristics that Wood and Gray suggest are important motivators of collaboration. One might, therefore, expect tourism to be a particularly good testing ground for theories of collaboration.

Researchers have identified a wider range of theories that can be mobilised to explain why organisations choose to establish some form of collaborative relationship. Palmer and Bejou (1995), for example, identify three main theoretical perspectives on inter-organisational collaboration: resource dependency theory, relational (or 'social') exchange theory (Macneil, 1980) and transaction cost theory (Williamson, 1975, 1985). The remainder of this section discusses each of these theoretical approaches in turn.

Resource dependency theory

Resource dependency theory is based fundamentally on the view that interdependencies exist among organisations because individual stakeholders in the domain own or have control over vital resources (be these material, human, political, structural or symbolic). These, in turn, represent sources of environmental pressure for other firms, in that lack of access to these resources may seriously impede the individual organisation in meeting its strategic goals. As such, resource dependency and access to resources may introduce significant uncertainties to the environment in which the organisation is operating.

Under resource dependency theory, organisations seek to reduce these external pressures by gaining control over crucial resource supplies. Traditionally, this is achieved through a process of competition, with those organisations most willing and able to pay the highest price for the resources concerned being the most likely to secure access to them. In this way, organisations hope to reduce the uncertainty they experience for themselves, although in many cases this will actually increase it for others operating in the same domain.

Donaldson and O'Toole (2002) summarise the main features of resource dependency theory as follows:

- The basis of exchange is to gain control over resources upon which the strategy of the organisation is dependent, which the individual organisation may lack or to which it may have only partial access. The conventional response to the lack of access to resources is to invest in increasingly complex internal hierarchies that will produce the resource internally. In recent years, however, this strategy has increasingly been viewed as too risky, particularly because of the ever more turbulent environment in which organisations find they must operate. This, in turn, increases the need for resources to be gained from other parties, and collaboration is one possible means to this end.
- Collaboration is inherently bound up in issues of power, since by collaborating the organisation is essentially trying to gain control over collaborative partners upon which it is at the same time also partly dependent. For resource dependency theorists, increased dependency is not a desirable outcome of collaboration, as it is for relational exchange theorists (see next section), but an obligation or commitment that organisations should only enter into with extreme care.
- For resource dependency theorists, therefore, the key process driving collaboration is power–conflict assessment. Collaboration is fundamentally about balancing the loss of autonomy involved in the collaboration process with the opportunity to gain access to resources through such arrangements.

- Resource dependency theory views collaboration as a response to the uncertainties inherent in a turbulent environment. This view contrasts sharply with relational exchange theory, which posits the development of reciprocal relationships based on the opportunities for mutual gain.
- Because of this focus on reducing uncertainty, switching costs are considered to be a key consideration in assessing collaborative relationships according to resource dependency theory. Switching costs must either be built in to the collaborative arrangements, so that they can be minimised, or, if possible, completely avoided.

A key feature of resource dependency theory is the recognition that collaboration can itself be a valuable resource. Indeed, Wood and Gray (1991) point out that collaboration may actually *increase* environmental complexity insofar as it involves establishing a range of new inter-organisational relationships and dependencies. Yet a critical understanding of resource dependency theory is that this complexity can itself be a resource capable of being wielded against environmental uncertainty. A complex environment need not necessarily be a random or disorganised one (a three-dimensional maze being an example of an environment that is highly complex and yet also highly organised). Thus, complex environments often contain many prime opportunities for organisations to address common issues arising in the turbulent problem domain, even if doing so also presents them with major organisational challenges.

It is in this last observation that resource dependency theory and relational exchange theory meet. The former is to be found where such resources are seen from an individual organisation's perspective; the latter view prevails where such resources are instead seen in terms of their inter-organisational potential.

Relational exchange theory

Relational (or 'social') exchange theory also begins with the assumption that problem domains tend to become more turbulent as they develop and become more densely populated. In this way, organisations become increasingly mutually dependent, so that their central task, which is to solve such problems and reduce the uncertainties encountered in the domain, becomes ever more difficult to achieve if they operate in isolation from one another. Thus, organisations operating within an increasingly complex problem domain are expected to develop inter-organisational relationships that will help them solve their problems by working together, i.e. engage in a process of collaboration.

There is, therefore, a sharp contrast between relational exchange theory and resource dependency theory. For resource dependency theory, the task for organisations is to enter into such relationships in order to make use of other parties' resources, which would otherwise be unavailable to them, thereby helping them to achieve their own objectives more fully. For relational exchange theory, however, collaboration is the result of organisations recognising the interdependence of problems in their domain and the benefits of developing reciprocal relationships aimed at solving them.

According to Donaldson and O'Toole (2002), the main features of relational exchange theory are as follows:

- Relational exchange theory accepts self-interest as the underlying motivation for an organisation to become involved in collaborating with others, but argues that collaboration typically involves cases in which this self-interest is best served by the adoption of joint working strategies. Resource dependency theory, on the other hand, argues that collaboration is typically against the self-interest of the organisation (because it involves surrendering autonomy), but is necessary in order to acquire the critical resources needed by the organisation in order for it to survive and prosper.
- Relational exchange theory focuses on relationships rather than transactions. Hence the exchange approach attempts to study the relational structures that are created by organisations in order to facilitate collaboration. These structures are inherently social, involving interaction among key personnel in the organisations involved, and are intended to achieve a two-way positive social exchange.
- This exchange is achieved through a process of relational contracting, involving a bilateral mechanism for co-ordinating the activities of the organisations involved. This forms a management structure where mutuality, rather than competition, is at the core. Consequently, the boundaries between organisations become blurred, so that organisations progressively become linked to others in the form of a network
- Unlike resource dependency theory, which focuses on power and control, the key forces driving exchanges under relational exchange theory are trust and commitment. These forces serve to moderate the impact of power within the network of organisations and establish a perception of fairness in the exchange relationship.

Transaction cost theory

Transaction cost theory (Williamson, 1975, 1985) is based on the central assumption that exchange takes the form of a series of transactions. For a typical business organisation these would include purchasing inputs, contracting and dismissing staff, selling products, financing investment and so forth. Such activities imply transaction costs to the organisations concerned. For example, organisations will incur search costs in attempting to find buyers and sellers with whom to transact, and striking a deal will typically involve contracting costs.

Transaction cost theorists argue that organisations attempt to minimise such costs by assigning them to suitable governance structures (Douma & Schreuder, 1991). Some transactions will therefore be assigned to the market, while others will be assigned to the organisation. Others again might be assigned to an intermediate governance structure, such as a merger between the organisation or some form of inter-organisational collaboration. Collaboration is thus chosen as a transactional structure because it implies lower costs to the organisation than do other possible structures.

Transaction cost theory is based on two central behavioural assumptions, those being:

- That individuals operate with *bounded rationality*, meaning that the capacity for the human beings to make complex decisions is inherently constrained. This constraint may be due to many possible factors, for example a lack of information relevant to making a particular decision or a critical lack of time to collect and/or process all of the information needed. Bounded rationality will only be a problem in an environment that is complex and/or uncertain, in that the decision maker in such environments will be unable to evaluate fully all of the information relevant to a decision prior to making it.

- That individuals sometimes act *opportunistically*, meaning that they act guilefully so as to exploit a situation (such as a transaction) to their own advantage. This does not mean that individuals will *always* act opportunistically, only that they may sometimes do so. As a result, individuals cannot enter into a transaction being sure that nobody they are transacting with is acting in an opportunistic manner. Opportunism is considered to be a problem particularly in situations where there is a small number of trading partners. This is because, if the transacting partner has a monopoly or monopsony position in the market, they will not be concerned about maintaining their reputation (because losing it will not necessarily cause them to forego opportunities to transact with other partners).

According to the theory, the transaction costs associated with a particular activity will depend on three particular dimensions:

- *Asset specificity*, which refers to the degree to which the transaction needs to be supported by transaction-specific assets, and which is considered to be the most important (Donaldson & O'Toole, 2002). A highly specific asset cannot easily be transferred to another use if one of the participants in the transaction attempts to act opportunistically to renegotiate the contract, knowing that the other is committed to the transaction once the asset has been deployed. For example, a hotel owner might agree to build a hotel near to an airport for the benefit of customers of a tour operator. Knowing that the hotel cannot easily be transferred to another use, the tour operator might seek to renegotiate the agreement once the hotel has been built (perhaps the tour operator will demand lower room rates). The tour operator can do this knowing that the hotel owners have little choice but to accept. Transactions involving transaction-specific assets are therefore unlikely to be assigned to the market. The potential for opportunistic behaviour to assert itself is simply too great. Some alternative structure, such as a merger between the companies – or perhaps some form of collaborative arrangement – will need to be employed instead.

- *Uncertainty* (and/or complexity), which will also make it less likely that a given transaction will be assigned to the market. This is because bounded rationality becomes more of a problem as the level of uncertainty/complexity associated with a transaction rises, the decision maker being less able to detect opportunistic behaviour on the part of a potential business partner.
- *Frequency*, which refers to how often the relevant transactions will be made. Establishing complex transaction structures, such as a vertically integrated firm or an inter-organisational collaborative relationship, will inevitably entail costs, which are more likely to be justified if the frequency of transactions is high. When the frequency of transactions is low they are more likely to be assigned to the market.

For transaction cost theorists, therefore, collaboration is readily explained as a structure that minimises transaction costs for a given combination of asset specificity, level of uncertainty/complexity and frequency of transactions. Collaboration might be seen as particularly appropriate in so far as the ongoing relationships involved enable the partners to be more confident in committing transaction-specific assets to the transaction. At the same time, the transaction costs involved in a collaborative relationship might be less than those implied by establishing an internal hierarchy to substitute for the transaction. As such, collaboration may be thought of as representing a form of 'quasi-hierarchy' (Osborn & Baughn, 1990).

Gulati (1998), meanwhile, identifies the following points in a critique of the transactions economic approach:

- The theory lacks a temporal dimension in that it treats each transaction as being independent from all other previous transactions.
  Yet organisations often have long-standing relationships with one
  another, the nature of which can be critical in determining the likely
  success or failure of the transaction.
- Transaction cost theory tends to focus on the choice of an individual organisation. Yet most collaborative forms are inherently
  dyadic, raising the question of *whose* transaction costs are being
  minimised. Similarly, collaboration is usually not just about cost
  minimisation but also benefits maximisation. Arguably, transaction
  cost theory places too much emphasis on the potential costs of
  collaboration and too little on the potential benefits.
- The structural emphasis of transaction cost economics leads to a
  neglect of issues relating to the *processes* involved in collaboration.
  Collaboration is rarely a one-off event and normally involves a
  continuing exchange and adjustment: the process of collaboration
  is fundamentally dynamic.
- Finally, transaction costs, which arise out of contracting hazards
  and the behavioural uncertainty in the organisation's external environment, are not the only costs an organisation must consider in
  deciding whether or not to collaborate. Co-ordination costs are also
  relevant, and these may be considerable, particularly when the
  collaboration is large and complex.

Conclusion

Collaboration is clearly a complex issue, not least because it is often
a response to the growth of complexity, fragmentation and turbulence
of the tourism field as it develops and becomes more densely populated.
The theories of collaboration developed in this chapter all start from the
premise of an environment that has become so complex, fragmented and
turbulent that the incumbent organisation finds it increasingly difficult
to act independently in addressing the problems that it encounters in
that environment. Where the major theories of collaboration differ is in
how they perceive of organisations responding to this challenge. Hence,
resource dependency theory views the reaction as one of organisations
attempting to achieve *competitive advantage* by accessing resources that
lie out of their individual control. Relational exchange theory, in contrast,
perceives of the reaction as basically one of recognising the mutual
advantages to be gained through collaboration, that is, *collaborative advantage*. Transaction cost theory, meanwhile, depicts collaboration as being
a rational response to the need to control the growth of transaction costs
under such conditions.

At its most basic level, collaboration involves organisations working together in a particular problem domain. As we have seen in this chapter, this collaboration can be the result of many different motivations. For almost every example of collaborative working, each individual organisation will have its own particular motives for joining the collaboration and remaining in it. It is, nevertheless, possible to discern various collaboration-wide objectives in most cases, which enables some kind of distinction to be drawn between different forms of collaboration. Instances will also differ in a number of other critical ways, such as their geographical coverage and organisational structure. Chapter 6 of this book investigates these distinctions and considers where it is possible – and, if so, desirable – to construct from these a generic typology of collaborative forms.

Chapter 6
Types and Stages of Inter-organisational Collaboration

Introduction

The academic literature is replete with terms that have been proposed to describe various manifestations of collaboration. These include 'partnerships', 'alliances' and 'consortia' – all of which are becoming increasingly common in the literature of tourism and tourism marketing. Often, a particular term is preferred in dealing with a given sector of the industry. Hence collaborative relationships among hotels are often described as 'consortia', while in the airline industry they are usually called 'alliances'. In the context of tourism destinations the term 'partnership' is typically preferred.

Yet there is by no means universal agreement regarding when and how to use these terms. The basic problem would seem to be that it is actually rather difficult to distinguish conceptually between these proposed types of collaboration. Some writers, for example, define their preferred term on the basis of the characteristics they perceive to be associated with that particular type of collaboration. Such definitions are, however, often so similar to one another that it would seem unreasonable to draw sharp distinctions between them. Hence, while one writer will define 'partnership' in a particular way, another will use a strikingly similar definition to describe an 'alliance'. At the same time, much of the literature uses two or more of the above terms synonymously, often without particular regard for the context in which each of them is to be used. Such writers typically pay little attention to implied differences of meaning between such terms. Other writers mix the terms, using hybrid language such as 'collaborative partnerships' or 'partners of an alliance'. Meanwhile, definitions of any given term can vary considerably from one writer to the next. One writer will stress a particular characteristic while another will ignore it. Sometimes reference to a particular condition may even be replaced with another that has virtually opposite connotations.

Empirically, it is also difficult to draw consistent distinctions between the terms that tend to be proposed to denote different types of collaboration. For example, it would seem that, in practice, some instances of an 'alliance' share more of their proposed distinguishing characteristics with 'partnerships' in other sectors of the industry than they do with other 'alliances' in their own.

These conceptual difficulties are best illustrated with reference to some proposed definitions, along with the rationale provided for drawing distinctions between them, if indeed any is given.

Himmelman (1996), for example, suggests the continuum of definitions shown in Table 6.1. This starts at networking, which simply involves the exchange of information between participants at one end of the continuum. Next comes co-ordination, which involves information exchange and altering activities, and then co-operation, which involves both of the above plus sharing resources for mutual benefit. At the far end of the continuum is collaboration, which involves all of the above plus the intention to enhance one another's capacity.

Long (1997: 237), meanwhile, suggests that co-operation should be defined simply as 'working together towards some common end'. Co-ordination, meanwhile, is said to be 'the process whereby two or more organizations create and/or use existing decision rules that have been established to deal collectively with their shared task environment' (Long, 1997: 237). Collaboration, meaning 'to work in association', is defined by Wood and Gray (as already discussed in Chapter 5) as:

> when a group of autonomous stakeholders of a problem domain engage in an interactive process, using shared rules, norms, and structures, to act or decide on issues related to that domain. (Wood & Gray, 1991: 146)

Partnership, meanwhile, is considered by Long to imply collaboration, but with the added requirements of cross-sectoral representation and defined geographical boundaries. Thus, he defines partnership as:

> the collaborative efforts of autonomous stakeholders from organizations in two or more sectors with interests in tourism development who emerge in an interactive process using shared rules, norms and structures at an agreed organizational level and over a defined geographical area to act or decide on issues related to tourism development. (Long, 1997: 239)

Selin and Chavez, however, suggest a rather different definition of a partnership:

> a voluntary pooling of resources (labor, money, information, etc) between two or more parties to accomplish collaborative goals. (Selin & Chavez, 1995: 845)

This definition includes neither the additional requirement for cross-sectoral representation nor a well-defined set of geographical boundaries

Table 6.1 Spectrum of definitions of collaboration

	Definition	*Example*
Networking	'Exchanging information for mutual benefit'	Two (or more) organisations meet to share information about their missions, goals, etc.
Co-ordination	'Exchanging information for mutual benefit and altering activities for mutual benefit and to achieve a common purpose'	Two (or more) organisations share information about their respective activities and then decide to change these in order to better serve their common client or customer base
Co-operation	'Exchanging information for mutual benefit and altering activities and sharing resources for mutual benefit and to achieve a common purpose'	Two (or more) organisations share information about their respective activities, decide to change these in order better to serve their common client or customer base, and share physical space and transportation resources
Collaboration	'Exchanging information for mutual benefit and altering activities and sharing resources and enhancing capacity of one another for mutual benefit and to achieve a common purpose'	Two (or more) organisations share information about their respective activities, decide to change these in order better to serve their common client or customer base, share physical space and transportation resources, and offer a series of staff training workshops to one another in areas in which the organisation has special expertise related to their common purpose

Source: Himmelman, 1996

as proposed by Long. In fact, as the authors point out, their definition has been adapted from Gray (1985), who uses it to denote collaboration. Indeed, the goals of a *partnership* are said to be *collaborative*. For Selin and Chavez, therefore, it would seem that collaboration and partnership are essentially one and the same thing.

Cateora and Ghauri, meanwhile, present a definition of an alliance that appears quite similar to Selin and Chavez's definition of a partnership:

> [An alliance is] a business relationship established by two or more companies to co-operate out of a mutual need and to share in achieving a common objective. (Cateora & Ghauri, 2000: 250)

Both definitions stipulate that two or more organisations should be involved (thereby excluding intra-organisational collaboration) and that the organisations should be working together towards a common end. However, it is notable that Selin and Chavez talk of 'collaborative goals', while Cateora and Ghauri state the need for organisations to 'co-operate' with one another. In contrast, Long (1997) draws a sharp distinction between 'co-operation' and 'collaboration', the former not involving many of the complex considerations, such as turbulence in the shared problem domain, which are said to be implied by the latter. Jamal and Getz (1995) make a similar point.

Evans (2001: 229–230), meanwhile, defines a strategic alliance as:

> a particular 'horizontal' form of inter-organisational relationship in which two or more organisations collaborate, without the formation of a separate independent organisation, in order to achieve one or more common strategic objectives.

This contrasts sharply with Cateora and Ghauri's definition, which includes neither the condition that alliances refer only to 'horizontal' relationships nor the need for the organisations to remain independent.

Elmuti and Kathawala (2001), on the other hand, appear to view alliances and partnerships as being essentially the same thing, both of these terms describing instances of two or more organisations working together to achieve strategically significant and mutually beneficial objectives. Meanwhile, Genrekidan and Awuah cite a definition of strategic alliances that appears also to incorporate the concepts of co-operation and partnership:

> Strategic *alliances* are seen as a manifestation of interorganizational *cooperative* strategies that entail the pooling of skills and resources by the alliance *partners* in order to achieve one or more goals linked to the strategic objectives of the cooperating firms. (Czinkota & Ronlainen, in Gebrekidan & Awuah, 2002: 679, emphasis added)

Separating out these terms through the use of explicit definitions is evidently not a straightforward task. Indeed, as Gebrekidan and Awuah (2002: 679–680) go on to suggest:

the definition of strategic alliances is not coherent in the existing literature. . . . Apparently, the various ways that strategic alliances have been defined may have the effect that each proponent . . . may tend to concentrate on particular characteristics of the phenomenon that best suit his/her view of 'reality'.

A gallery of proposed definitions of various types of collaboration is presented in the appendix to this chapter. Inspection will confirm the tendency for definitions of collaboration to compound rather than resolve the many conceptual difficulties bound up in understanding what it involves and what it implies. The approach taken in this book, as outlined in Chapter 5, is therefore to use the term 'collaboration' wherever possible to encompass all of these instances, making distinctions between related terms, such as alliances and partnerships, only when absolutely necessary.

The above discussion is not intended to imply, however, that there are no significant or substantive differences to be noted between different instances of inter-organisational collaboration. Indeed, such distinctions can be very helpful in analysing such issues as collaborative effectiveness, which is the major subject of Chapter 7 of this book. The problem is rather that such distinctions tend to be highly complex and multi-dimensional, with considerable blurring of the boundaries between the groupings they imply. This means that assigning simple labels to particular 'types' of collaboration becomes an impossible task – and one that is not really necessary, as we shall shortly see.

Typologies of Collaboration

Many writers have attempted to draw up typologies of collaboration. Some are fairly simple, drawing upon some readily observable characteristic or combination of characteristics associated with the collaborative relationship. For example, one widely used typology distinguishes between different types of collaboration on the basis of the *direction* of the relationship. Hence collaborations may be *horizontal* (between companies that are in other respects in competition with one another), *vertical* (between suppliers of a product and its buyers) or *diagonal* (between companies in different sectors or industries). Hanlon (1999) presents a similar typology in the context of airline alliances, the main difference being that he refers to 'diagonal' alliances as 'external' collaboration.

Others have compared alliances to personal relationships (Dev & Klein, 1993). Hence, 'one night stands' are characterised as being short-term, opportunistic, one-off relationships with a strictly limited focus, while 'affairs' are said to be medium-term, tactical and are thought to involve a strong sense of self-protection. 'Marriages', meanwhile, are seen as long-term relationships, involving continuity and a high degree of commitment.

Bleeke and Ernst (1995), meanwhile, identify six types of collaboration, using the *outcome* of the collaboration as the major discriminating factor. These are summarised in Box 6.1. Other, more complex typologies are designed to take the form of a continuum or hierarchy, with 'simpler' forms of collaboration at one end of the scale and more 'complex' types at the other.

Kanter (1994), for example, presents a continuum of collaboration, ranging from *weak* and *distant* at one end to *strong* and *close* at the other. Mutual service consortia are said to lie at the former end of the spectrum, involving similar organisations pooling their resources in order to gain a benefit too expensive to acquire alone, for example access to a new technology. The organisations remain at arm's length from one another and do not make any other mutual ties. Joint ventures, meanwhile, sit in the middle of the continuum. This form of collaboration involves each participant accessing the capabilities of the other. For example, one organisation might bring access to a market while the other might bring the technology required to exploit it. The joint venture might operate independently or it might link the organisations' operations, in which case a closer relationship might be inferred. At the other end of the scale are buyer–seller relationships, where companies link different but complementary capabilities to provide value for ultimate users. Commitment to this type of collaboration tends to be high, with participants linking their operations so that substantial change may be generated within each organisation, this implying a 'close' relationship between them.

In contrast, Walker and Johannes (2003), drawing on the work of Segil (1996), focus on risk as the predominant distinguishing feature of different types of collaborative relationship (Figure 6.1). At one end of the continuum or hierarchy is the takeover or merger of organisations, which is considered to be high-risk, high-cost and making the maximum use of human resources. At the other end is the joint marketing/distribution arrangement, which is considered to be low-risk, low-cost and making the minimum use of human resources. Between these two extremes lie a variety of other collaborative relationships, including joint-venture and other equity arrangements, technology transfer and licensing.

Child and Faulkner (1998), meanwhile, present a simple typology of collaborative 'alliances' based on three dimensions: scope (whether it is 'complex' or 'focused'); the number of participants (whether there are two or several partners in the collaboration); and the legal nature of collaboration (whether it is a 'joint venture' or simply a 'collaboration') (Figure 6.2).

Box 6.1 Bleeke and Ernst's six types of collaboration

Collisions between competitors

Two strong companies in direct competition with one another join their core competencies. These collaborative relationships are normally short-lived and often fail to meet their objectives, ending in either dissolution, acquisition by one or other of the participants, or merger.

Alliances of the weak

Two or more weak companies join forces with a view to improving their positions. The weak usually grow weaker and the collaboration eventually dissolves or is taken over by a third party.

Disguised sales

A weak company collaborates with a strong company, often one that is already or will become directly competitive. The weaker player remains weak and is acquired by the stronger player.

Bootstrap alliances

A weak company collaborates with a stronger company in order to improve its capabilities and compete in its own right. These collaborative relationships usually do not last long, with the stronger participant often acquiring the weaker one.

Evolution to a sale

These collaborations start out with two strong companies joining forces, but competitive tensions later develop, bargaining power shifts and one partner ends up selling out to the other. However, these collaborative relationships can be quite long-lived, often exceeding the typical seven-year life span of such arrangements.

Alliances of complementary equals

These instances of collaborations involve two strong companies with complementary capabilities joining together. They are normally robust and can last much longer than the average collaboration.

Source: Bleeke and Ernst, 1995

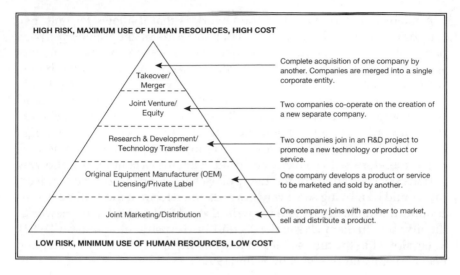

Figure 6.1 Collaboration continuum from a risk perspective

Source: Walker and Johannes, 2003

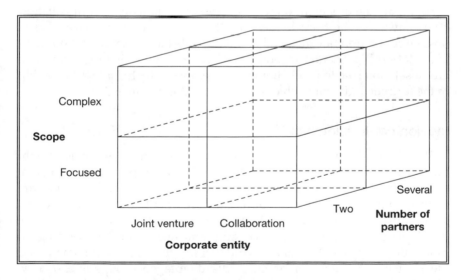

Figure 6.2 A typology of alliance forms

Source: Child and Faulkner, 1998

A major limitation with this framework is that it allows for only two categories along each dimension. Thus in terms of the number of partners, collaboration can involve either two or several partners, but not specifically three or four. Arguably this weakens the value of the framework as an analytical tool, since there might well be important substantive differences between alliances involving two partners (a 'dyadic' relationship) and three partners (a 'triadic' relationship), which classification according to this framework would not uncover. The same might be said of the other two dimensions. An improvement to this framework might therefore be to convert each dimension into a continuum, allowing various concentrations of the two polar characteristics to occur. Indeed, this would be moving some way towards some form of multi-dimensional continuum framework. Here we will discuss three possible frameworks: the first by Huxham (1996); the second by Terpstra and Simonin (1993), as employed in the tourism destination marketing context by Palmer and Bejou (1995); and the third by Selin (1999).

Huxham's Dimensions of the Rationale for Collaboration

Huxham suggests eight dimensions or continua along which collaboration may vary. These are divided into three main groups, which are based on degrees of ambitiousness; relationship/substantive rationale contrasts; and relationship-orientated contrasts. Huxham argues that these continua are closely interrelated and attempts to demonstrate this interrelationship in the form of a diagram, which is reproduced in Figure 6.3.

Ideological-instrumental

This dimension focuses on the purpose of collaboration, which might range from purely ideological on the one hand, to purely instrumental on the other. Huxham argues that most instances of collaboration are instrumental in practice, in so far as they are oriented towards achieving some substantive outcome (in the tourism marketing case, this might be developing a new product or accessing a particular market). Ideological motivations, on the other hand, would imply the pursuit of some moral ideal, such as the empowerment of disadvantaged groups in a society. This introduces the issue of participation, which forms the basis of Huxham's next dimension.

Organisations working together-participation

Here the distinction is made between participation at one end of the spectrum, to organisations working together at the other. The intention

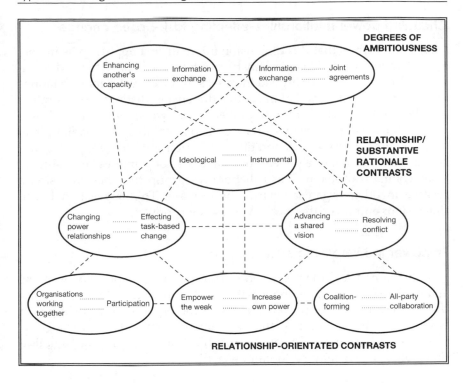

Figure 6.3 Dimensions of collaboration rationale and relationship
between them

Source: Huxham, 1996

of 'participation' is to include various stakeholder groups in the decision-making relating to issues that affect them and are important to
them, and in which otherwise they would have no say. Often, ideological reasoning underpins this approach. Stakeholders should be
included in the decision-making because it is the right thing to do.
However, instrumental reasoning could equally be applied on the
basis that collaboration is likely to be more effective if stakeholder groups
are included in the process. At the other end of the spectrum is joint
working among organisations, which implies the full integration of stakeholder groups in the collaboration process. Many writers have, however,
questioned the extent to which such integration merely represents a
contrived process of consultation with stakeholders, with the organisation that 'owns' the collaborative process retaining the bulk of the
decision-making power (e.g. Pretty, 1995). This leads on to Huxham's
next dimension, which relates to power relationships within the
collaboration.

Changing power relationships–effecting task-based change

Huxham argues that this dimension might at first appear to be merely a restatement of the ideological–instrumental dimension discussed previously. However, it can be argued there exist more complex interpretations of 'power relationships' that make this dimension distinct. Collaboration may be used as a vehicle for empowering the weak, but it may also be used to increase the organisation's own power, thereby enabling it to meet its aims. Indeed, collaborations are often initiated among organisations that are relatively weak but have a strong interest in resolving some common problem. This collaborative group then becomes strong relative to other organisations in the domain. This suggests a fourth dimension: empower the weak–increase own power.

Empower the weak–increase own power

In this dimension, the perceived purpose of the collaboration is at one end of the spectrum to empower the weak and at the other to increase the organisation's own power. Increasing the organisation's own power would seem to be closer to the 'instrumental' end of the ideological–instrumental spectrum. Of course, a spin-off of increasing the organisation's own power may be to empower the weak.

Advancing a shared vision–resolving conflict

Following Gray (1996), this dimension focuses on how conflict is addressed through the collaboration. Typically, participants in collaboration are motivated either by a desire to resolve a mutual conflict or to advance a shared vision for their domain, although it might be considered possible for some collaborations to be motivated by both.

Coalition-forming–all-party collaboration

At one of this dimension lies the view that conflict can be resolved if all parties to the conflict work together on solving it. In contrast, at the other end of the dimension, the view is that a subset of the parties might form a coalition that raises their power relative to other organisations in the domain, thereby leading to conflict resolution through changed power relationships.

Information exchange–joint agreements

According to Huxham, the final two dimensions cut across all of the others. Both are related to the ambitiousness of the collaboration. The first, which is suggested by Gray (1996) as an orthogonal dimension to her 'resolving conflict–advancing a shared vision' dimension, contrasts the exchange of information and reaching joint agreements as the primary motivations for collaboration. Hence, resolving conflict can be achieved either through information exchange (a 'dialogue') or by joint agreement (a 'negotiated settlement'). Meanwhile advancing a shared vision could be achieved through information exchange ('appreciative planning') or joint agreement (a 'collective strategy'). Information exchange is clearly a less ambitious aim than joint agreement, and hence less powerful in addressing the problem domain shared by the participants in the collaboration.

Enhancing another's capacity-information exchange

The second dimension identified by Huxham in relation to the ambitiousness of collaboration has information exchange at one end and enhancing another's capacity at the other. Both are aimed at achieving mutual benefit, but they differ in the means. The former implies the organisation enhancing its own capabilities through the acquisition of information held by other collaborators. The latter implies the development of an inter-organisational domain in which collaborators aim to achieve common benefit by enhancing one another's capacities.

Terpstra and Simonin's Coverage-Form-Mode-Motive Typology

Terpstra and Simonin (1993) identify four principal features that can be used to distinguish conceptually between different types of collaboration: coverage, form, mode and motive. Palmer and Bejou (1995) adopt this model and demonstrate its value in making a comparative analysis of two samples of tourism marketing collaborations: one in the UK and the other in the US. They go on to suggest, however, that these major features of collaboration depend substantially upon the environmental context in which the collaboration is taking place.

Coverage

The 'coverage' of a collaborative form refers to its extensiveness in terms of the markets, marketing functions or geographical areas with which it is concerned (Bleeke & Ernst, 1991). Simpler forms of collaboration are therefore likely to be restricted in their activities to specific products or markets, specific components of the marketing mix and/or specific geographical areas. The most basic coverage of a collaboration is thus represented by single-sector collaborations (for example, among hotels), whose purpose is narrowly defined (for example, the joint production of promotional brochures).

More mature forms of collaboration, on the other hand, will have a more complete coverage in terms of competitive product areas and components of the marketing mix. They may also have a more extensive geographical coverage. By extending its coverage, members of the collaboration will be able to increase their control over the domain. Where specific product areas are excluded, control is lessened. Similarly, excluding specific marketing functions will weaken the degree of control that collaborating organisations are able jointly to exert on their external environment.

Form

The 'form' of collaboration refers to the constitutional characteristics of the collaboration. According to Terpstra and Simonin, the least developed form of collaboration is a non-equity arrangement. This involves members agreeing on methods of operation, joint promotion and so on, but the collaborating organisations do not share financial resources, funding their own contributions to the collaboration independently.

A more developed form of collaboration is the joint venture. This involves the collaborating organisations retaining financial independence, but may also involve the creation of an 'offspring' through the pooling or exchanging of resources. Meanwhile, the most evolved form of collaboration is said to occur when members acquire equity stakes in one another, leading to financial interdependency at the organisational level, rather than simply at the level of the collaboration.

Palmer (1998b), meanwhile, identifies another important feature of the form of collaboration: the governance style adopted. He depicts the governance style of collaborative agreements in the form of a continuum, with loose (less formal) governance styles at one end and tight (more formal) governance styles at the other. Loose governance styles are characterised by informal understandings, based largely on norms. Trust is implicit and its development serves as a risk-reduction mechanism that can obviate the need for more formal safeguards. Trust between the partners is vital as each can potentially give others access to its core competencies, especially when related to market resources (such as customer databases) or where collaboration involves the sharing of a brand name or brand image. Trust is also vital when operational resources (such as seconded staff) are involved.

As governance styles become tighter, greater reliance on a prescribed system of rules or some form of legal intervention is implied. Increasing formality implies increasing bureaucracy, which can include tightly written rules and procedures, such as sanctions when one party deviates from the rules. The downside of this increased formality is, however, reduced flexibility with respect to response to environmental change (WTO, 2002).

Mode

The 'mode' of collaboration refers to the intrinsic nature of relationships among the members involved. According to Palmer and Bejou (1995), there are two main dimensions to the mode of a given collaboration: the personal characteristics of individuals involved and the cultural characteristics of the organisation each is representing.

With regard to the first of these, Palmer and Bejou note that the dedication of senior managers to the collaboration has often been identified as a critical ongoing success factor for collaborations. In many cases, however, only junior members of staff are attached to the collaboration, and other partners may view this as denoting a lack of commitment on the part of that organisation. Whether junior or senior staff are attached to the collaboration can affect both its speed and direction, given that staff with different roles in the organisation and with different levels of responsibility are likely to have different individual interests, personal objectives and capabilities in respect of joint working. The convenor of the collaboration (if one is appointed) will play a crucial role in making the collaboration work and will need to apply a range of personal qualities in order to bring the key players together and facilitate their joint efforts. The role of the convenor is discussed in more detail in Chapter 7.

Differences in cultural values may also have an important impact on the speed and direction of collaboration, particularly in public–private sector collaborations where cultural values are likely to be most different. This can be particularly important in the tourism context where the public sector (transport, planning, policy) and private sector (tour operators, visitor attractions) must work together to produce the tourism product. Team-building among the participant representatives, with the aim of enabling parties to gain a shared vision and common values, can be critical to the success of such collaborations.

Each of these dimensions is likely to be strongly influenced by the number of organisations participating in a given collaboration. Much academic work on collaboration has tended to focus on bilateral ('dyadic') relationships, yet experts generally agree that there is a global trend towards greater number of partners becoming involved in a single collaboration. Moreover, many large organisations are now becoming involved in substantial portfolios of collaborative projects, which substantially increases the importance of organisational learning in collaboration theory. Organisations do not only learn from the experiences of former collaborations with the partners concerned in a given collaboration but they also learn from their experiences of other collaborations, with different sets of partners, that may be going on at the same time.

Motive

As we have seen in Chapter 5, the 'motive' for collaboration can include the desire to internalise the core competencies of other members, achieving economies in advertising and intelligence-gathering, joint development of new facilities, making a stronger case for the acquisition of resources, etc. The primary motive for collaboration is likely to differ from participant to participant and may change as the collaboration evolves.

There are many reasons why collaboration may arise in a given problem domain. For example, collaborative forms can develop as a result of a legal mandate, which may itself be the result of social pressure. In other instances, the motivation may be a perceived crisis. In many cases individual, personal motivations may be important; indeed, a 'champion' of collaboration may be critical to its success (Gray, 1985).

Environmental factors

Palmer and Bejou (1995) suggest that economic, social and political environmental factors affect all four of these key features of collaboration. To test this hypothesis, they conducted a survey of 54 tourism destination marketing 'alliances' in the UK and the US. Seventeen of these were Tourism Development Action Programmes (TDAPs) – an initiative of the English Tourist Board (ETB) designed to bring together stakeholders at the tourism destination level with the aim of promoting joint marketing and destination development. The other 37 alliances took the form of Visitor and Convention Bureaus (VCBs), which are usually initiated by local Chambers of Commerce in the US and tend to have very similar aims to their UK counterparts. So-called 'honey-pot' destinations were excluded from the sample as the major differences between the collaborations established to develop and market them were more likely to be product-related and less likely to be influenced by environmental factors.

Palmer and Bejou's sample was of local tourism destination marketing alliances, so in *coverage* terms their analysis focused mainly on differences in the functions covered by the alliances in their sample. Their results are summarised in Table 6.2. Palmer and Bejou suggest that the UK alliances were generally more mature, exhibiting a substantially wider functional coverage than their US counterparts. The authors suggest that the main reason for this wider functional coverage was that the UK alliances were formed with the explicit remit of strategic marketing planning, which inherently requires a wide coverage of marketing functions. The coverage of the US alliances, on the other hand, tended to be restricted mainly to promoting the destination. This more limited coverage was thought to reflect a greater mistrust of central planning and government intervention on the part of tourism organisations in the US, as well as greater belief in their own abilities to solve their own problems independently.

With regard to the *form* of collaboration, Palmer and Bejou argued that this was determined mainly by funding arrangements. The US alliances were largely funded by contributions from sales/occupancy taxes, with little in the way of grant assistance. The UK alliances, on the other hand, tended to rely much less heavily on taxation income and more on grants and loans from stakeholder organisations (which usually needed to be justified on a case-by-case basis). Meanwhile the US alliances did not tend to have tour operator equity interests, while in the UK this was common. In the UK tourism operators and local authorities contributed in three main ways: by purchasing equity in the alliance; by making loans to the alliance; and by making loans and grants for specific purposes.

Another difference in form was in the level of formality involved. Palmer and Bejou found a relative lack of formality in the US alliances. Whereas, in the US, 59% of respondents to the survey agreed that there

Table 6.2 Functional coverage of a sample of destination marketing alliances

	Percentage undertaking function	
	US sample *(n = 37)*	*UK sample* *(n = 17)*
Promotions of the area at exhibitions and in press, etc.	86.5	76.4
Hotel booking facility for incoming visitors	48.6	35.3
Routine collection of marketing research information	91.9	94.1
Regular dissemination of information to local tourism organisations	81.1	88.2
Operation of a visitor centre	86.5	29.4

Source: Palmer and Bejou, 1995

Note: the mislabelling of the column headings in the original has been corrected here were no written rules, with 73% agreeing that the arrangement was informal, in the UK these figures were smaller: 48% and 60% respectively. The greater formality evident in the UK alliances possibly reflected the more formal financial arrangements involved.

In respect of the mode of collaboration, the US sample tended to involve more partners than the UK sample: an average of 9.3 as opposed to 7.2. This was thought to be due in part to the greater perception that US alliances are publicly accountable, requiring wider representation of interest groups on the governing body. Meanwhile, the US representatives were less likely to have tourism industry experience than in the UK – 30% in the US, compared to 52% in the UK (Palmer & Bejou, 1995: 626) – with the US heads being more likely to be appointed for their political ability.

Finally, with regard to the *motives* for collaboration, Palmer and Bejou's study suggested that the primary motive among TDAPs in the UK was to draw in new forms of finance, particularly of funding from the ETB which required matching funds from public and/or private sources. Furthermore, the relevant legislation required that a local authority's expenditure should count towards their maximum spending budget unless it could be demonstrated that the venture was at 'arm's length' and not controlled by the authority. This created the need for a demonstrably independent alliance.

The motivation for collaboration in the US, meanwhile, was considered to be derived both from the private and public sectors. The former found that VCBs allowed them more scope to influence their shared domain than could be achieved through the existing channels established under the auspices of the Chambers of Commerce. With respect to the latter, meanwhile, local authorities found VCBs useful in enabling focus to be achieved in economic development while not adding to their expenditure. This was because the alliances were financed primarily through local taxation as opposed to direct expenditure on the part of the local authority.

The results of this study suggested that, despite being faced with a similar marketing problem, the two examples of tourism destination marketing alliance differed substantially in each of the four main features of collaboration established by Terpstra and Simonin. This was considered primarily to be due to the very different environments in which they were situated. Thus Palmer and Bejou concluded that it was not possible to identify any one 'ideal model' of tourism marketing collaboration. Indeed, the motives for collaboration will invariably by determined by the environmental context, while the best coverage, form and mode of a given instance of collaboration will depend on the environment in which it is taking place.

Selin's Typology of Sustainable Tourism Partnerships

Another instructive typology of collaboration in the tourism context is presented by Selin (1999), who identifies a number of dimensions upon which different sustainable tourism 'partnerships' in the US may be distinguished from one another. One particular dimension – geographical scale – is identified as having the potential to bring out helpful contrasts with each of the other dimensions. Thus, Selin presents a series of two-dimensional grids, with geographical scale taking the vertical axis in each case. The geographical scales chosen by Selin were community, state, regional and national. To illustrate the typology, a variety of US-based sustainable tourism 'partnerships' were then plotted conceptually on each of the two-dimensional grids.

Legal basis

According to Selin, the legal basis of a particular instance of tourism collaboration may vary from purely voluntary groups at one end of the spectrum to legally mandated or authorised collaborations at the other (see Figure 6.4). Voluntary collaboration is very often initiated by the community itself and tends to be grassroots in style. The examples used by Selin include watershed associations at the community level and

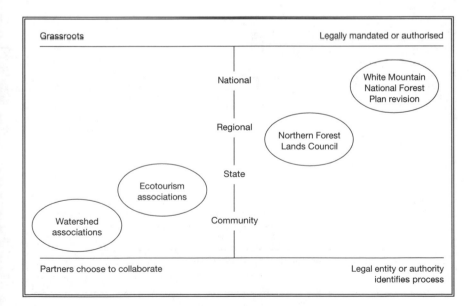

Figure 6.4 Geographic scale by legal basis

Source: Selin, 1999

ecotourism associations at various geographical levels (the Texas Natural Tourism Association being a good example of a voluntary, grassroots sustainable tourism collaboration at the state level). Legally mandated or authorised collaborative groups tend to be the result of public pressure for government at various levels to adopt a more 'participatory' style, more effectively involving various stakeholder groups in their major decision-making processes. Such collaboration tends to take the form of citizen advisory committees, task forces and working groups, which operate within an extended and opened-out planning and policy-making environment. Examples used by Selin are the Northern Forest Lands Council at the regional level and the recent revisions to the White Mountain National Forest Plan at the national level.

Locus of control

The second dimension employed by Selin is the locus of control of the collaboration (see Figure 6.5). This ranges from complete agency control at one end of the spectrum, through active consultation, seeking consensus, negotiating agreements, sharing authority and transferring responsi-

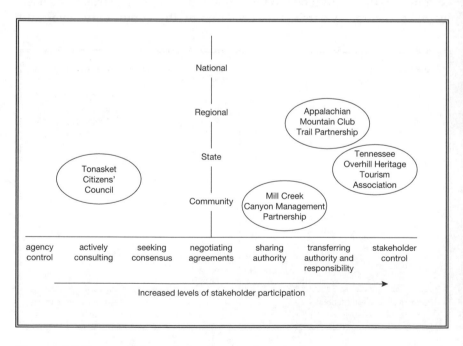

Figure 6.5 Geographic scale by locus of control

Source: Selin, 1999

bilities, to complete stakeholder control at the other. Examples employed by Selin include, at the agency control end of the spectrum, the Tonasket Citizens' Council. This involved a diverse group of stakeholders in rural Washington State providing input to the Forest Service in making decisions about the Okanogan National Forest. About 40 individuals were drawn in to sit on the council, assisting the Forest Service to balance the needs of recreation, tourism, timber production, wildlife and watershed conservation in its decision-making. At the other end of the spectrum, meanwhile, Selin's example is the Tennessee Overhill Heritage Tourism Association. Here stakeholder groups have taken primary control over all of the primary decision-making processes. Government and other agencies merely provide technical assistance and grant support to the group.

Organisational diversity and size

A further dimension identified by Selin is organisational diversity and size (see Figure 6.6). At one end of the spectrum, collaborating organisations are fewer in number and relatively homogeneous (in so far as participants are from one particular sector, e.g. commercial, non-profit

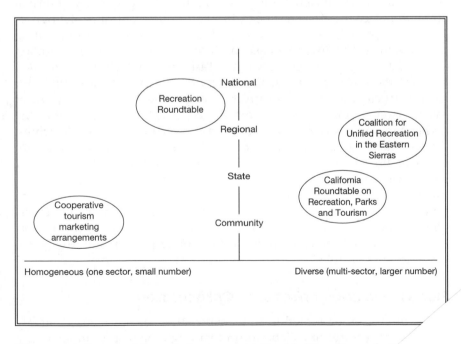

Figure 6.6 Geographic scale by organisational diversity and s~

Source: Selin, 1999

or public). Selin argues that a good example of this type of collaboration is co-operative marketing agreements. These can occur at anything from the community level (for example, where visitors to a visitor attraction are offered discounts at local restaurants), to the national level (for example, partnerships between car hire companies, hotels and airlines to provide frequent flier 'air miles' to their customers). At the other end of the spectrum, there tends to be a larger number of participating organisations, which come from a more diverse range of backgrounds. The example used by Selin to illustrate collaborations of this kind is the Coalition for Unified Recreation in the Eastern States, a broad-based coalition comprised of over 90 members representing some 50 federal, state and local government agencies, tourism businesses, user groups and environmental organisations.

Time frame

The final dimension identified by Selin is the time frame over which collaboration is envisaged (see Figure 6.7). At one end of the continuum are instances of collaboration that are convened with a short time frame in mind, often to address a particular crisis or take advantage of a passing opportunity. Such collaborations tend to establish a temporary, informal structure. Once the crisis has been brought under control or the opportunity has passed, the collaborating organisations return to operating autonomously. The example used by Selin of this kind of collaboration is the National Bighorn Sheep Center Task Force, which was convened to assist the town of Dubois, Wyoming, to design and raise funds for the construction of a visitor centre focusing on the bighorn sheep. After raising over $1 million to support the construction of the centre, the ownership and management were turned over to the town of Dubois. At the other end of the spectrum are instances of collaboration with a longer time frame. These tend to be more institutionalised in their legal form and structure, and tend to develop more formal decision-making processes. Selin's example of this kind of collaboration is the Southwestern Pennsylvania Heritage Preservation Commission, a federally mandated group set up in 1986 to disburse funds to support community-based heritage preservation projects and still (by 1999) operating in that role.

Stages of Inter-organisational Collaboration

The discussion presented in this chapter thus far has focused mainly on different features of collaboration that might be helpful in analysing it as a phenomenon. The frameworks developed here will be employed in Chapter 7, where the principal criteria for, and determinants of,

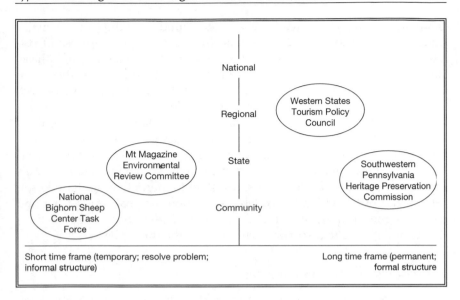

Figure 6.7 Geographic scale by time frame

Source: Selin, 1999

collaborative success will be explored. Indeed, many writers on the subject of collaboration have used such features in attempting to identify the principal success factors for collaboration in various contexts.

Other writers have, however, focused not on the features of the collaborative arrangement but on the various stages through which collaborations typically pass as they move from their conception to their ultimate demise. Indeed, several authors have proposed models of the collaboration life cycle. The stages are normally distinguished from one another by the nature of the tasks that are required of participants at that point in time. Proponents argue that identifying these key tasks and understanding how they might be performed more effectively will enable participants in the collaboration to make it more successful. Meanwhile, various internal and external environmental factors can interrupt, impede or even enhance the cycle, and these need to be identified and addressed for optimum performance of the collaboration. In this section we examine three such models. The first was developed by Gray (1985, 1989), based on the work of McCann and Chiles (1983).

Gray's three-stage model

Gray sets out a three-stage model through which collaborations typically develop. The first stage, termed the 'problem-setting' phase, involves identifying the key stakeholders in the problem domain and those stakeholders then reaching a mutual understanding of the major issues that need to be, and can be, addressed through a process of collaboration. In the following stage, known as the 'direction-setting' phase, stakeholders identify and share the values they hold in pursuing their individual goals and how they intend to approach the collaborative project. In this way, a sense of common purpose is developed among the stakeholders, giving life to their aspirations for the collaboration. In the third stage, which is the 'implementation' (or 'structuring') phase, the stakeholders institutionalise these shared meanings and collaborative processes, managing their interactions in an increasingly systematic manner. This enables the stakeholders to develop a system for perpetuating shared aspirations and order within the collaboration. Specific goals are set out and tasks assigned to particular members. Box 6.2 identifies the key actions that Gray argues are associated with each of the three phases.

Waddock's evolutionary model

Waddock (1989) also presents a three-stage model of the collaboration life cycle, based on the dynamics observed within five 'social partnerships', a review of existing case studies and the available literature on public–private sector collaboration. As such, Waddock (1989: 88) describes the model as 'synthetic'. The model is also described as 'evolutionary', in that the author is suggesting that there is a 'natural' development of collaborative arrangements starting from an initiation phase in which a partnership forum is set up. This then leads into an establishment phase in which the programmatic thrust is developed. The establishment stage then evolves into a final maturity stage in which the collaboration may, if successful, substantially broaden its agenda. Meanwhile Waddock identifies three main groups of tasks: issue-crystallisation, coalition-building, and purpose-formulation (and reformulation). While these activities tend to take place in roughly this sequence, none is identified exclusively with any one of the three stages identified by Waddock. Indeed, a more complex relationship is identified. This is illustrated in Figure 6.8.

Issue crystallisation

The activities constituting this process involve the participants shaping or forming the issue around which they intend to collaborate. This is to enable them to gain a shared understanding of the issue and begin to initiate joint action on addressing it.

Coalition-building

The second process involves integrating the key actors and balancing the power relationships among them. Working relationships are built

Box 6.2 Gray's developmental model of collaboration

Stages	Actions/Steps
Stage I: Problem-setting	• Define purpose and domain • Identify convenor • Convene stakeholders • Define problems/issues to resolve • Identify and legitimise stakeholders • Build commitment to collaborate by raising awareness of interdependence • Balance power differences • Address stakeholder concerns • Ensure adequate resources to allow collaborations to proceed with key stakeholders present
Stage II: Direction-setting	• Collect and share information • Appreciate shared values, enhance perceived interdependencies • Ensure power distribution among several stakeholders • Establish rules and agenda for direction-setting • Organise sub-groups if required • List alternatives • Discuss various options • Select appropriate solutions • Arrive at shared vision or plan/strategy through consensus
Stage III: Implementation	• Discuss means of implementing and monitoring solutions, shared vision, plan or strategy • Select suitable structure for institutionalising process • Assign goals and tasks • Monitor ongoing progress and ensure compliance to collaboration decisions

Source: Jamal and Getz, 1995, following Gray, 1985, 1989

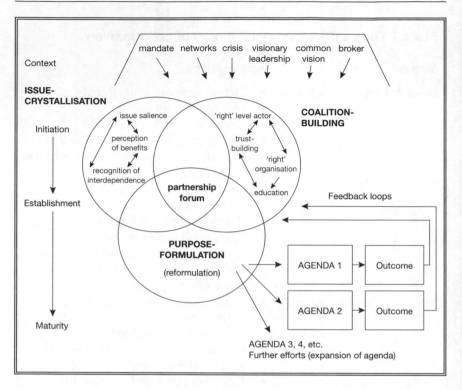

Figure 6.8 Evolutionary model of social partnership development
Source: Waddock, 1989

among the key players, enabling them to act effectively on the issues that have been identified and shaped in the issue-crystallisation process. Taken together, these two processes relate approximately to Gray's 'problem-setting' phase.

Purpose-formulation

   This process is roughly equivalent to Gray's 'direction-setting' stage and involves determining the scope or degree of domain overlap for participants, building consensus among participants on how to act in the problem domain and establishing jointly agreed goals for the collaboration. Participants' domains, which relate to the activities relevant to the collaboration, will typically overlap around areas of interdependence. Initially at least, the purpose of the collaboration may focus on some common problem or crisis that first brought the participants together. Waddock argues that, as outcomes become known, the purpose of the collaboration tends to be re-evaluated, often resulting in a broadening of focus.

Selin and Chavez's evolutionary model

Selin and Chavez's (1995) evolutionary model is essentially an extension of the developmental model set out by Gray, itself an extension of McCann and Chiles' (1983) original model. Selin and Chavez add an earlier and a later stage to Gray's model, giving the model five stages in all. They also add a set of feedback loops to the model (Figure 6.9).

The earliest stage of Selin and Chavez model is termed 'antecedents'. At this stage there are various forces operating on would-be participants – technological, political, social and economic – which draw organisations together to consider some problem (or set of problems) of common concern. These forces operate on their own, or in conjunction with one another, to catalyse collective action and create a 'problem domain' from the inter-organisational environment. The final stage of Selin and Chavez's evolutionary model, meanwhile, is termed 'outcomes'. These can be programmatic (the visible and tangible products of the collaboration), impacts or organisational benefits derived from the collaboration.

Selin and Chavez's model also extends that of Gray by introducing a set of feedback loops, as illustrated by the arrows passing back from the final stage of the model to each of the previous ones. Selin and Chavez argue, much as Waddock (1989) does, that there is a tendency for partnerships to undergo a cyclical re-evaluation of purpose, and that this often leads to 'a broadening of focus if the partnership is to flourish' (Selin & Chavez, 1995: 850). However, the authors also note that this re-evaluation can also lead to the demise of the collaboration if the problem remains unresolved, the partners lose interest in working together on it or the re-evaluative process causes the collaboration to develop a rift.

Caffyn's composite life-cycle model

The models presented above represent merely three examples of collaboration life-cycle models that might be applied in the tourism context. The logical thing to do would be to collect together such models and undertake a comparative analysis of their content, bringing out issues of common consensus and developing a composite model.

This, indeed, is the approach of Caffyn (2000), who examines 11 different life-cycle models that could be applied to tourism collaboration. These include the evolutionary model of tourism collaboration of Selin and Chavez (1995), as well as the 'Butler cycle' (Butler, 1980), which was first applied to analysing the dynamics of tourism destinations. Comparing and contrasting these, Caffyn arrives at the 'five summary phases' of the collaboration life cycle shown in Table 6.3, noting that most of the variation between the models is in the fifth and final stages.

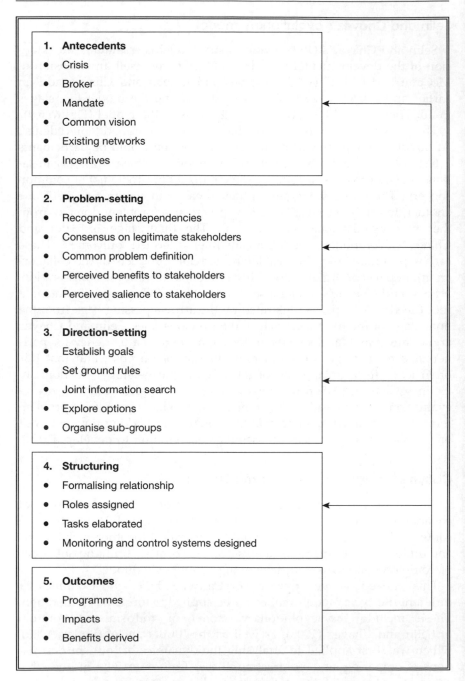

Figure 6.9 An evolutionary model of tourism partnerships

Source: Selin and Chavez, 1995

Table 6.3 Summary life-cycle phases and characteristics

Phase 1	Phase 2	Phase 3	Phase 4	Phase 5
Responding to external environment	Problem-definition	Development of identity	Full implementation-	Stagnation
Exploration of ideas	Coalition building	Formulation of procedures	Stability	Commitment questioned
Vision-formulation	Development of trust	Pursuit of mission	Monitoring	Uncertainty
Networking	Inventory	Explore options	Consolidation	Fewer options for innovation
Marshalling commitment	Assessment of needs	Form sub-groups	Co-ordination and administration	Loss of relevance
Creating a mandate	Choice of leader and staff	Personalised leadership	Decentralisation	Re-evaluation
Marshalling resources	Innovation	Build momentum	Tendering out and contracts	Purpose re-formulation
Developing a common purpose	Sense of mission	Expansion of activities		Adaption and Renewal
	Seeking legitimacy	High commitment		Domain expansion

Source: Caffyn, 2000

Based on this analysis, along with an in-depth case study of the North Pennines Tourism Partnership in England and comparative cases, Caffyn develops a composite tourism partnership life-cycle model (Figure 6.10).

The model comprises six phases in all. The most significant feature of this further developed model is that it includes an additional continuation (or 'after-life') phase at the end of the life cycle. Caffyn argues that, typically after nine years of operation, tourism collaborations tend to reach a point where their purpose is implicitly or explicitly re-evaluated. Some may continue much as before; some may be wound up; others may continue in a different form. Caffyn suggests eight 'after-life' options for the collaboration:

(1) The partnership could continue in more or less the same form, most likely because participants still see value in continuing with it.
(2) The collaboration may be absorbed into a bigger collaborative grouping, either with a broader focus or a wider geographical coverage.
(3) Various participants may take particular elements of the work of the collaboration and continue to progress them autonomously.
(4) The work of the collaborative group may be taken on by one of the participating organisations.
(5) The collaboration could continue in a more permanent form, for example as a limited company or a trust.
(6) The local community, business and/or voluntary organisations may wish to take over the management of the collaboration.
(7) The collaboration may spawn a series of smaller collaborative projects, which may be related at arm's length or completely independent from one another.
(8) The collaboration may finish completely, with no organisation taking up its role.

Conclusion

It should be clear from this chapter that drawing sharp distinctions between different kinds of collaboration is a very difficult task. While a number of writers have attempted to provide conceptually tight and practically useful definitions of different types of collaboration, each vying for ascendancy, as yet no clear winners have emerged. If anything, attempting to allocate specific terms to particular types of collaboration tends to increase confusion surrounding what counts as what, rather than dispel it. Even a brief examination of the many definitions that have been put forward (some of which are shown in the gallery of definitions forming the appendix to this chapter), reveals a picture that is far from clear.

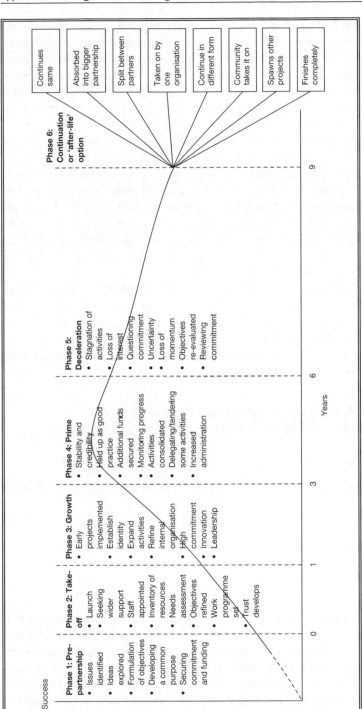

Figure 6.10 Composite life-cycle model

Source: Caffyn, 2000

Other writers have had more success in attempting to classify different forms of collaboration according to their major characteristics. Typologies based on more than one dimension, each based on a continuum of positions, have been popular and have met with some success in explaining what is important about collaboration. Arguably it is better to adopt a fairly broad definition of collaboration and to accept that there may exist a very wide range of collaborative relationships within it.

A number of life-cycle models of collaboration have also been developed, often in an attempt to identify the critical success factors for collaboration among organisations. Rather than to try to analyse collaboration according to its major attributes or features, life-cycle models attempt to identify the crucial tasks required at each stage of the evolution of a collaborative relationship. Improving the effectiveness with which these tasks are carried out will serve to make the collaboration function better, increasing the level of collaborative advantage that can be gained through the collaborative process.

But how is collaborative advantage acquired and maintained? Building on the various typological and life-cycle models developed in this chapter, the purpose of Chapter 7 is to review the critical success factors for inter-organisational collaboration. What makes collaboration successful and how can the performance of collaborative relationships between organisations be improved?

Appendix: A Gallery of Proposed Definitions of Collaboration and Allied Terms

Co-ordination

> Exchanging information for mutual benefit and altering activities for mutual benefit and to achieve a common purpose.
>
> Himmelman (1996: 27)

> The process whereby two or more organizations create and/or use existing decision rules that have been established to deal collectively with their shared task environment.
>
> Long (1997: 237)

> Coordination is characterized by more formal relationships [than co-operation] and understanding of compatible missions. Some planning and division of roles are required, and communication channels are established. Authority still rests with the individual organization, but there is some increased risk to all participants. Resources are available to participants and rewards are mutually acknowledged.
>
> Mattessich and Monsey, in Kvan (2000: 410–411)

Co-operation

Working together towards some common end.

Long (1997: 237)

Exchanging information for mutual benefit and altering activities and sharing resources for mutual benefit and to achieve a common purpose.

Himmelman (1996: 28)

Cooperation is characterized by informal relationships that exist without a commonly defined mission, structure or effort. Information is shared as needed and authority is retained by each organization so there is virtually no risk. Resources are separate, as are rewards.

Mattessich and Monsey, in Kvan (2000: 410)

Cooperative marketing groups are . . . groups of independent businesses that recognize the advantages of developing markets jointly rather than in isolation, but which may be unable to appropriate the benefits of cooperative activities directly.

Palmer (2002: 135)

The links that bring organisations together, thereby enhancing their ability to compete in the market place.

Lynch (2003: 818)

Where one or more firms work together to achieve interdependent goals. Typically, this is done on the basis of exchanging information, licensing arrangements, joint ventures and through trade associations.

Gilligan and Wilson (2003: 195)

Collaboration

When a group of autonomous stakeholders of a problem domain engage in an interactive process, using shared rules, norms, and structures, to act or decide on issues related to that domain.

Wood and Gray (1991: 146)

Exchanging information for mutual benefit and altering activities and sharing resources and enhancing capacity of another for mutual benefit and to achieve a common purpose.

Himmelman (1996: 28)

Collaboration for community-based tourism planning is a process of joint decision-making among autonomous, key stakeholders of an inter-organizational, community tourism domain to resolve planning problems of the domain and/or manage issues related to the planning and development of the domain.

Jamal and Getz (1995: 188)

Collaboration is taken to imply a very positive form of working in association with others for some form of mutual benefit ... the concern ... is ... with collaboration between organizations.

Huxham (1996: 7)

Collaboration [is] an intense form of mutual attachment, operating at the levels of interest, intent, affect and behaviour: actors are bound together by the mutually supportive pursuit of individual and collective benefit.

Cropper (1996: 82)

To work in association.

Long (1997: 237)

Collaboration is competition in a different form.

Hamel *et al.* (1999: 525)

Collaboration connotes a more durable and pervasive relationship [than co-operation or even co-ordination]. Collaborations being ... full commitment to a common mission. ... Authority is determined by the collaborative structure. Risk is much greater.

Mattessich and Monsey, in Kvan (2000: 411)

Wood and Gray define collaboration as a process where 'a group of autonomous stakeholders of a problem domain engage in an interactive process, using shared rules, norms and structures, to act or decide on issues related to that domain'. ... Normally collaborative interaction is considered a relatively formal process involving regular, face-to-face dialogue, these being features that distinguish it from other forms of participation.

de Araujo and Bramwell (2002: 1139)

Businesses are said to collaborate when, instead of (or perhaps as well as) competing, they choose to work together in pursuit of both parties' strategic objectives.

Evans *et al.* (2003: 391)

Partnership

Social partnerships involve an alliance among organisations to contend with a problem of social consequence that has an impact on but is not necessarily central to any of the partners' missions.

Waddock and Bannister (1991: 64)

An arrangement devoted to some common end among otherwise independent organizations.

Selin and Chavez (1995: 844)

A voluntary pooling of resources (labor, money, information, etc) between two or more parties to accomplish collaborative goals.

Selin and Chavez (1995: 845)

The collaborative efforts of autonomous stakeholders from organizations in two or more sectors with interests in tourism development who emerge in an interactive process using shared rules, norms and structures at an agreed organizational level and over a defined geographical area to act or decide on issues related to tourism development.

Long (1997: 239)

Partnerships are defined . . . as cooperative arrangements engaging companies, universities, and government agencies and laboratories in various combinations to pool resources in pursuit of a shared R&D objective.

Hagedoorn *et al.* (2000: 567)

Partnership is a dynamic relationship among diverse actors, based on mutually agreed objectives, pursued through a shared understanding of the most rational division of labor based on the respective comparative advantages of each partner. Partnership encompasses mutual influence, with a careful balance between synergy and respective autonomy, which incorporates mutual respect, equal participation in decision-making, mutual accountability, and transparency.

Brinkerhoff (2002: 216)

[A] long term commitment between two or more organisations for the purpose of achieving specific business objectives by maximizing the effectiveness of each of the participants.

National Economic Development Council,
in Naoum (2003: 73)

Strategic alliance

Co-marketing alliances are a form of *working partnership*. . . . They are contractual relationships undertaken by firms whose respective products are complements in the marketplace. They are intended to amplify and/or build user awareness of benefits derived from these complementarities.

Bucklin and Sengupta (1993: 32, original emphasis retained)

A strategic alliance, while encompassing joint ventures, goes beyond the more familiar joint ventures to include a myriad of non-equity arrangements.

Pekar and Allio (1994: 54)

Strategic alliances may be defined as organizational arrangements and operating policies through which separate organizations share administrative authority and form social links through more open-ended contractual arrangements as opposed to very specific, arm's length contracts. The concept of strategic alliances is connected to organizational structure, industry positioning, and competitiveness. Strategic alliances are concerned with the issue of how to obtain resources through partnership.

Witt and Moutinho (1995: 166)

Voluntary arrangements between firms involving exchange, sharing and codevelopment of products, technologies, or services.

Gulati (1998: 293)

A joint venture where ownership of an activity or operation is shared with a collaborator.

Piercy (1997: 252)

A business relationship established by two or more companies to co-operate out of a mutual need and to share in achieving a common objective.

Cateora and Ghauri (2000: 250)

A particular 'horizontal' form of inter-organisational relationship in which two or more organisations collaborate, without the formation of a separate independent organisation, in order to achieve one or more common strategic objectives.

Evans (2001: 229–230)

Strategic alliance is defined as an informal or formal arrangement between two or more companies with a common business objective.

Czinkota and Ronlainen, in
Gebrekidan and Awuah (2002: 679)

Strategic alliances are seen as a manifestation of interorganizational cooperative strategies that entail the pooling of skills and resources by the alliance partners in order to achieve one or more goals linked to the strategic objectives of the cooperating firms.

Czinkota and Ronlainen, in
Gebrekidan and Awuah (2002: 679)

Strategic alliances have the following characteristics: (i) the two or more firms that unite to pursue a set of agreed goals remain independent subsequent to the formation of the alliance; (ii) the partner firms share the benefits of the alliance and the control over performance of assigned tasks; (iii) the partner firms share the benefits of the alliance on a continuing basis in one or more key strategic areas (e.g. technology and products).

WTO (2002: 3)

Less-than-arm's-length agreements including: equity (joint ventures, minority equity positions, and equity swaps); and non-equity agreements (for joint R&D, joint product development, long-term sourcing agreements, joint marketing, reciprocal distribution, research consortia, barter switching agreements, and the less-than-arm's-length franchising and licensing agreements). The term does not include mergers and acquisitions, arm's-length sales contracts, and traditional arm's length distribution, franchising, and licensing agreements.

Dess *et al.*, in Gebrekidan and Awuah (2002: 679)

The formation of strategic alliances between two organizations combines competition and cooperation to create a collaborative strategy. ... Through strategic alliances, a firm can gain access to desired strategic capabilities by linking to a partner with complementary resources, or by pooling its internal resources with a partner possessing similar capabilities. ... Such alliances create synergies between resources that enhance or reshape competition within the market.

Chen and Chen (2003: 1)

Joint venture

New business entities that are owned by two or more firms that share resources and skills.

Pekar and Allio (1994: 54)

The joint venture is the creation of a jointly owned, but independent, organization by two or more separate parent firms through the partial pooling of assets.

Witt and Moutinho (1995: 166)

A collaborative arrangement between two or more companies. Joint ventures tend to be for limited time periods, usually for a project or similar. [They] can also take the form of multi-partner consortia.

Evans *et al.* (2003: 394)

Chapter 7

Collaborative Effectiveness and Inter-organisational Governance

Introduction

One thing that writers on the subject of collaboration seem to agree on is that collaboration is difficult (Huxham, 1996). Indeed, many empirical studies have reported spectacularly high failure rates of collaborative initiatives. According to Spyriadis (2002), empirical studies show that over half of all collaborative relationships are ultimately unsuccessful.

Gulati (1998) argues that one of the problems in interpreting the high failure rates that are often reported for inter-organisational collaboration is how best to measure collaborative performance. Donaldson and O'Toole (2002: 232) go so far as to suggest that, 'while all business performance is measured in a financial way in the long-term, there is little agreement on how to measure relationship performance in the long-term'. Meanwhile, 'relational performance is often excluded from models of relational development', with the broad assumption being made that 'relationships improve performance' (Donaldson & O'Toole, 2002: 233). Where studies have looked at the performance of inter-organisational collaboration, most have focused on the reasons for the termination of collaborative arrangements by the organisations involved. The problem with this approach is, first, that it may fail to distinguish between natural and untimely deaths. Indeed, some collaborative relationships are intended to be only temporary, while others may go on beyond their useful life due to inertia. Second, the approach implicitly assumes that a particular collaborative relationship is considered to be either a success or failure, making no allowance for the possibility of partial success and partial failure. Furthermore, it is quite possible that a particular instance of collaboration may be successful in certain respects but not in others; or that it is considered successful by some participants and not by others. This view is echoed by Spyriadis (2002), who points out that not all terminations can necessarily be viewed as failures; nor can all ongoing collaborations automatically be considered to be successful. Exit costs and barriers to withdrawal may keep 'failed' collaborations in existence beyond their 'natural' life span. Equally, it might be argued that termination is in fact a positive outcome of a 'completed' collaboration. Indeed, collaborations often terminate after meeting the participants' goals (Bleeke & Ernst, 1991).

Drivers of Collaborative Effectiveness

In spite of the problems identified above in interpreting what collaborative effectiveness might actually be, a number of writers have attempted to summarise the main determinants of collaborative effectiveness. Fyall (2003), for example, presents the following list:

- Involvement of key stakeholders.
- Good interpersonal relationships and development of trust between participants.
- Inclusive management style and organisational culture.
- Domain similarity and goal compatibility among participants.
- Duration and nature of previous relationships among participant organisations.
- Effective contractual conditions and exit barriers.
- An equity share agreement.
- Balance of management resources and power.
- Well-planned project, carefully chosen partners, balanced structure and high potential payoff relative to cost.
- Decisive leadership.
- Sound administrative support.
- Tight focus.
- Transparent implementation of policy.

In the context of social (i.e. public–private sector) partnerships, Waddock and Bannister (1991) derive the following list from an extensive literature review:

- Participants need to trust other participants.
- Representatives need to have adequate power to make decisions for their organisations.
- The appropriate participant organisations need to be included in the collaboration.
- Participants need to sense that there will be benefits to all the participants as a result of their collaboration.
- Participants need to recognise they are interdependent.
- Issues being dealt with need to be salient to participants.
- Participants need to feel that they add value to the partnership.
- Power needs to be balanced among the participant organisations.
- Collaborative objectives should be clear and well defined.

- Staff responsible for implementation must be competent.
- Feedback to participants has to be adequate.
- Leaders must articulate a strong vision about the purpose(s) of the collaboration.
- Strong leadership must exist within the collaboration.

Meanwhile, Spyriadis (2002) suggests the following possible themes for investigating the effectiveness of collaboration:

- Development of sufficient understanding of key policy-related issues in the alliance formation process.
- Emergence of network-level concepts.
- Success at every stage of the collaborative life cycle, especially partner selection (e.g. avoiding opportunists, finding partners who can fill specific roles in the alliance, ability to demonstrate commitment to the partnership, etc.).
- Complexity of collaboration.
- Clear aims expressed by each participant and detailed expectations of each.
- How the collaboration is managed – in particular, whether each participant has a positive attitude to managing and maintaining the collaboration.
- Number of participants.
- Integration of strategic, tactical, operational, interpersonal and cultural dimensions.
- Ability of the collaborative form to adapt to change.

Bramwell and Sharman (1999), meanwhile, present a framework for assessing the effectiveness of local collaborative tourism policy making (see Box 7.1). This divides the relevant drivers of effectiveness into three groups relating to the scope of collaboration the intensity of collaboration, and the degree to which consensus emerges among participants.

The alternative way of looking at the problem is to examine why collaborative arrangements are deemed to fail and/or the collaboration comes to an end. Indeed, much of the research into collaborative effectiveness that has been undertaken to date has focused on the reasons why collaborative relations terminate, rather than why they are considered to be successful (Gulati, 1998).

The UK's Museums and Galleries Commission (MCG, 1998) presents the following list of reasons for collaborative failure:

- Lack of clear objectives.
- Lack of staff time.
- Slow decision-making process.
- Changes in personnel.
- Lack of new ideas/new initiatives.

Box 7.1 Drivers of effectiveness in local collaborative tourism policy making

Scope of collaboration

- The extent to which the range of participating stakeholders is representative of all relevant stakeholders.
- The extent to which stakeholders see there are positive benefits to entice their participation.
- Whether the collaboration includes a facilitator and the stakeholders responsible for implementation.
- The extent to which individuals representing a stakeholder group are fully representative of that group.
- The number of stakeholders involved through the selected participation techniques.
- The extent to which there is initial agreement among participants about the intended general scope of the collaboration.

Intensity of collaboration

- The degree to which participants accept that collaboration is likely to produce qualitatively different outcomes and that they are likely to have to modify their own approach.
- When and how often the relevant stakeholders are involved.
- The extent to which stakeholder groups receive information and are consulted about the activities of the collaboration.
- Whether the use of participation techniques only disseminates information or also involves direct interaction among the stakeholders.
- The degree to which the dialogue among participants reflects openness, honesty, tolerant and respectful speaking and listening, confidence and trust.
- The extent to which the participants understand, respect and learn from each other's different forms of argument.
- The extent to which participants come to understand, respect and learn from each other's different interests, forms of knowledge, systems of meaning, values and attitudes.
- The extent to which the facilitator of the collaborative arrangements exerts control over decision-making.

Degree to which consensus emerges

- Whether participants who are working to build a consensus also accept that some participants will not agree or embrace enthusiastically all the resulting policies.

> - Extent to which there is consensus among the stakeholders about the issues, the policies, the purposes of policies and how the consequences of the policies are assessed and reviewed.
> - Extent to which consensus and 'ownership' emerge across the inequalities between stakeholders or reflect these inequalities.
> - Extent to which stakeholders accept that there are systemic constraints on what is feasible.
> - Whether the stakeholders appear willing to implement the resulting policies.
>
> *Source*: Bramwell and Sharman, 1999

- Lack of adequate negotiation.
- Responsibilities not sufficiently established at the outset.
- Lack of capital.
- Lack of communication and vacuum of objectives.

Spyriadis (2002), meanwhile, suggests the following key problems in collaboration:

- Uncertainty.
- Opportunism.
- Lack of alignment of partnership's objectives with those of the company.
- Company culture not supportive of collaboration.
- Dissatisfaction.
- Planning gaps.
- External relations.
- Conflicts of interests.
- Cultural differences.
- Reduced flexibility.

Lists of promoting and constraining factors such as those presented above tend to be based on theoretical analyses of collaboration, sometimes but not always substantiated by empirical studies of actual cases of collaboration. The purpose of this chapter is to review the body of theory and evidence on what makes collaboration successful and what causes it to fail. Why do some instances of collaboration evidently succeed while others fail? What are the important drivers of collaborative effectiveness and what factors impede it? How might inter-organisational governance be designed so as to maximise the chances of participating organisations meeting their individual and shared goals? A particular emphasis will be on the mechanics of inter-organisational governance, which is an issue that overarches many of the arguments to be presented.

Life-cycle Approach

The life-cycle approach to understanding the rationale for collaboration and the dynamics of the collaborative process has already been introduced in Chapter 6. Adopting a life-cycle approach can also be an effective way of structuring a theoretical analysis of collaborative effectiveness. By dividing the evolution of a collaboration arrangement into its component phases, it is possible to identify the 'pressure points' of the collaboration: the stages at which tasks critical to the success or failure of the collaborative arrangement are undertaken. In this way, important lessons for collaborative effectiveness may be drawn.

Gray's (1989) life-cycle model of collaboration is probably the most widely quoted of all such models. Indeed, several important studies have adopted it as a structure for analysing real-world collaboration. For example, Inskip (1993) reinterprets Gray's model to provide a list of key issues in the three main phases of collaboration. These are shown in Box 7.2.

Jamal and Getz (1995) also adopt Gray's life-cycle model of collaboration in their study of collaboration among stakeholders in the context of community-based planning at the tourism destination level. Box 7.3 identifies the key issues identified for facilitating the collaborative process at various stages of the collaboration life cycle.

The range of possible factors facilitating collaboration is evidently very wide. Fortunately, Jamal and Getz narrow down the focus considerably by arguing that two particular issues are critical in so far as they 'influence every stage of the collaboration process' (Jamal & Getz, 1995: 190). These relate, first, to the legitimacy of stakeholder process and, second, to the power relationships that develop as the collaboration proceeds. Both of these factors can inhibit the initiation and success of collaborative relationships. For example, the exclusion of key stakeholders at the beginning of the collaborative process may lead to problems in implementing decisions made by the collaboration, particularly if this restricts the collaboration's legitimacy as a valid decision-making body in the problem domain. Meanwhile, the issue of legitimacy of participating stakeholders is also considered to be critical (especially in the context of tourism) because of the complications introduced to the collaboration process by the often very large number of actual and potential participants, who may well have highly diverse and opposing interests. In such cases, difficulties experienced in collaboration may be directly related to differences in the value orientations of the various stakeholders.

Jamal and Getz go on to develop Gray's life-cycle model further by setting out a series of six propositions, each relating to a facilitator of

Box 7.2 Key issues in each successive phase of collaboration

Phase 1: Problem setting – goal: stakeholders agree and talk about the issues

Issue	*Question*	*Description*
Common definition of the problem	'What is the problem?'	Need agreement that a community issue causes problems important enough to collaborate. The problem must be common to several stakeholders.
Commitment to collaborate	'What's in it for me?'	Stakeholders feel that collaborating will solve their own problems. Need to be dissatisfied with current conditions. Shared values are key.
Identification of stakeholders	'Who should participate?'	An inclusive process that includes multiple stakeholders so the problems can be properly understood.
Legitimacy of stakeholders	'Who has the right and capacity to participate?'	Not only expertise but also power relationships are important.
Leader's characteristics	'Do I trust and respect the leader – the organization and the person?'	Collaborative leadership is key to success. Stakeholders need to perceive the leader as unbiased.
Identification of resources	'How can we fund the planning process?'	Funds from government or foundations may be needed for less well-off organisations.

Phase 2: Direction setting – goal: negotiating

Issue	*Question*	*Description*
Establishing ground rules	'What is acceptable and unacceptable behaviour?'	Gives stakeholders a sense of fair process and equity of power.
Agenda-setting	'What are the substantive issues we need to examine and decide?'	Stakeholders' different motivations for joining mean that establishing a common agenda may be difficult.
Organising subgroups	'Do we need to break into smaller groups to carry out our work?'	Large plenary committees need to be broken into smaller working groups.
Joint information search	'Do we really understand the other side of this negotiation?'	Parties have different sets of information and/or not enough information to make a judgement. Joint search can help find a common basis for agreement.
Exploring options	'What are all the possible options to solving our problems?'	Multiple interests mean that multiple options need to be considered before closure. Stakeholders' own interest are important.
Reaching agreement and closing the deal	'Are we all committed to going ahead on one option or a package of options?'	Stakeholders can agree on recommendations for a formal organisation or a joint voluntary course of action.

Continued on p. 196

Phase 3: Implementation – goal: systematic management of the inter-organisational relations

Issue	Question	Description
Dealing with constituencies	'How do we persuade our constituencies that this was the best deal we could get?'	Stakeholders need time to make sure that their constituents understand the trade-offs and support the agreement.
Building external support	'How do we ensure that organizations that will implement are onside?'	A concern that senior officials in government or business have not been briefed fully.
Structuring	'Do we need a formal organization to fulfil our agreement?'	Voluntary efforts can work. A formal organisation may be needed to co-ordinate long-term collaboration.
Monitoring the agreement and ensuring compliance	'How do we figure out assets, legal obligations and compliance with contracts?'	Time for lawyers and possible more legal/financial negotiations.

Source: Inskip, 1993, in Gray, 1996

one or more of the three stages of the collaboration process identified by Gray: problem-setting, direction-setting and implementation. Jamal and Getz emphasise that the propositions are based on the assumption that the domain is a turbulent one, where conflicts over planning and development exist, or where mechanisms for sharing ideas and developing directions are required. Turbulent domains are also characterised by a lack of well-defined inter-organisational processes (in other words, they are 'under-organised systems'). Jamal and Getz's six overarching propositions are as follows:

'1. Collaboration . . . will require recognition of a high degree of interdependence in planning and managing the domain.'

Stakeholder groups must believe that they need one another in order to address the problems they face, otherwise they will be tempted to embark on 'go-it-alone' initiatives, using their own resources and competencies. The risk with such strategies is, at best, that they will fail; at worst they may make the problem domain faced by the stakeholders even more complicated and turbulent. Stakeholders must therefore recognise that the problem domain in which they find themselves is fundamentally a shared one, and that collaboration is required in order to engage effectively with it.

Jamal and Getz go on to suggest that emphasising that community's shared resources and amenities are by definition limited may enhance stakeholders' perceptions of interdependence. Reminding stakeholders that tourism may have potential negative socio-cultural and/or environmental impacts that can affect the economic viability of the tourism industry may also help facilitate the collaborative process. Finally, it is worth reinforcing among stakeholders that tourism is inherently fragmented as an industry, and that the ability of any one sector to act alone is limited as a result.

'2. Collaboration will require recognition of individual and/or mutual benefits to be derived from the process.'

According to Jamal and Getz, the perception that there are to be substantial benefits associated with the collaborative action can be a more important precondition for collaborative success than recognition of the importance of the problem. A stakeholder organisation might well recognise the importance of an issue to the wider industry, but may not be inclined to collaborate in addressing it because it does not perceive there to be much benefit *to itself* in doing so. The organisation might consider other, non-collaborative ways of addressing the problem to be more appropriate. Alternatively, the organisation might feel that there are more important issues on its individual agenda that require

Box 7.3 Facilitating conditions and actions/steps for collaborative success

Stages	Facilitating conditions	Actions/steps
Stage I: Problem-setting	• Recognition of interdependence • Identification of a required number of stakeholders • Perceptions of legitimacy among stakeholders • Legitimate/skilled convener • Positive beliefs about outcomes • Shared access to power • Mandate (external or internal) • Adequate resources to convene and enable collaboration process	• Define purpose and domain • Identify convener • Convene stakeholders • Define problems/issues to resolve • Identify and legitimise stakeholders • Build commitment to collaborate by raising awareness of interdependence • Balance power differences • Address stakeholder concerns • Ensure adequate resources to allow collaborations to proceed with key stakeholders present
Stage II: Direction-setting	• Coincidence of values • Dispersion of power among stakeholders	• Collect and share information • Appreciate shared values, enhance perceived interdependencies • Ensure power distribution among several stakeholders • Establish rules and agenda for direction-setting • Organise sub-groups if required

Stages	Facilitating conditions	Actions/steps
		• List alternatives • Discuss various options • Select appropriate solutions • Arrive at shared vision or plan/strategy through consensus
Stage III: Implementation	• High degree of ongoing interdependence • External mandates • Redistribution of power • Influencing the contextual environment	• Discuss means of implementing and monitoring solutions, shared vision, plan or strategy • Select suitable structure for institutionalising process • Assign goals and tasks • Monitor ongoing progress and ensure compliance to collaboration decisions

Source: Based on Gray, 1985, 1989

priority attention and abandon interest in the problem that requires collaboration of some kind to solve effectively.

The mutual benefits of collaboration in the context of community-based tourism planning might include more effective and efficient tourism development, a greater degree of environmental and socio-cultural sustainability, or the avoidance of conflict in the tourism planning domain. Meanwhile, the individual benefits for community and environmental organisations might include the more effective represen-tation of some groups in the planning process or more resources for those groups to enable them to influence the planning domain. For the business organisations, the individual benefits of collaboration may lie in reduced uncertainty in the external environment, thereby improving their decision-making and potential for success. Public-sector organisa-tions might benefit individually from the more effective public-sector management of scarce resources, while for local residents the individual benefits might take the form of greater satisfaction with tourism's role in their community.

'3. Collaboration . . . will require a perception that decisions arrived at will be implemented.'

Jamal and Getz argue that successful collaboration requires both the legitimacy and power either to make or to strongly influence decisions. However, limitations of time or other resources, which will tend to be experienced in most instances of collaboration, may cause some would-be participants to be sceptical of the chances of the collaboration being successful. At later stages of the collaboration, participants may feel unwilling to share the power they currently possess over key resources in the problem domain, resulting in power struggles among participants. Such inter-organisational conflict may in turn lead to the underperfor-mance of the collaborative effort.

Collaborative success may well therefore depend on the partners addressing issues of legitimacy and power at an early stage. When the problem domain is very fragmented, as is often the case with tourism, receiving an external mandate by a national or regional authority might be necessary in order to establish the legitimacy of the collaboration and to neutralise power struggles as they emerge. Alternatively, these issues might be addressed from within the collaboration by appointing a convenor with the requisite legitimacy to motivate participation and ensure that power relations among the participating organisations remain well balanced. Whether or not a convenor is appointed, participants should have the perception that sufficient time, expertise and resources are available to ensure that the collaboration will last long enough to achieve its objectives.

'4. Collaboration . . . will depend on encompassing . . . key stakeholder groups.'

Many writers argue that successful collaboration requires that the relevant stakeholder groups are all properly identified and duly incorporated into the collaboration process. If a stakeholder group is poorly represented, or not represented in the collaboration process at all, their particular views will not be incorporated into the decision-making processes of the collaboration, nor will their interests be integrated into the objectives set for the collaborative effort. In such circumstances, collaborations should expect to meet with substantial external resistance, which will probably cause the collaboration to underperform. Different instances of collaboration will, of course, require different sets of stakeholders to be encompassed by the collaboration. Cost efficiency can be achieved by engaging stakeholder representatives who are skilled at representing the views of a broad constituency.

Jamal and Getz argue that, in the context of community-based tourism planning, residents are a crucial stakeholder group to incorporate. Meanwhile the nature of tourism as a public and social good implies that representatives from a range of levels of local, regional and national government organisations need to be integrated effectively into the collaboration.

'5. A convenor is required to initiate and facilitate . . . collaboration.'

The crucial role of the convenor has already been identified. Jamal and Getz, citing Gray (1989) argue that the convenor has a critical role to play, especially in the initial (problem-setting) stage, in identifying the key stakeholders and bringing them to the table. They go on to argue that the convenor should have sufficient legitimacy, expertise, resources and authority to perform this (and later) tasks, and might be drawn from such groups as the local Chamber of Commerce or the local tourism organisation. The role of the convenor in collaborative effectiveness is discussed further below.

'6. An effective . . . collaboration process . . . requires: formulation of a vision statement on desired tourism development and growth; joint formulation of tourism goals and objectives; self-regulation of the planning and development domain through the establishment of a collaborative (referent) organization to assist with ongoing adjustment of these strategies through monitoring and revisions.'

Finally, Jamal and Getz argue that, in order to ensure effective stakeholder participation at all stages and in all aspects of the collaboration, it is advisable to establish a 'referent organisation'. The major task of this organisation would be to monitor the participants' progress (or otherwise) towards the collaborative goals they have set out in their vision statement, and to assist the participants in making the necessary adjustments to their collaborative activities in order to remain on track in meeting them.

Thematic Approaches

While the collaboration life cycle is a popular conceptual framework within which to identify the major factors that are considered to promote or retard collaborative effectiveness, other work in the area has sought to identify particular themes that can be considered critical to the performance of the collaboration. These include, *inter alia*, partner selection, stakeholder involvement, external/internal uncertainty, governance mechanisms and the role of the convenor.

Partner selection

Kanter argues that North American companies that are considering joining together to collaborate have tended on the whole to be pre-occupied with the economics of the arrangement and therefore to miss out on the 'political, cultural, organizational and human aspects of the partnership' (Kanter, 1994: 97). Yet these aspects of the dynamics of collaboration can be critical, particularly at the formative stages of the collaboration when participants are selecting partners with whom they will need to collaborate effectively if the collaboration is to be successful.

Kanter suggests that the selection process will be more successful if companies look for three particular qualities in prospective partners:

- *Self-analysis.* Prospective partners should have thoroughly assessed the changing industry conditions and decided to seek to collaborate with like-minded organisations. It may also help if the executives have experience of finding good partners; collaboration with the first good-looking prospect is rarely successful.
- *Chemistry.* Partner representatives need to be able to get along well together. Kanter holds the human element to be just as important as the financial or strategic aspects.
- *Compatibility.* Collaboration will be more successful if partners are compatible on broad historical, philosophical and strategic grounds, sharing common experiences, values, principles and hopes for the future.

Based on this view, Kanter goes on to elaborate eight principles of successful partner selection, as shown in Box 7.4.

Bleeke and Ernst (1991) argue that collaboration involving participants of approximately equal strength is in principle more likely to succeed

---

Box 7.4 Eight I's that create successful we's

(1) *Individual excellence*: Both partners are individually strong and have something to offer to the partnership. Their motives for entering into partnership are therefore positive (to take advantages of these strengths) rather than negative (to mask weaknesses or escape difficulties).

(2) *Importance*: Joining the alliance must fit well with organisational objectives so that partners want it to work.

(3) *Interdependence*: The partners need each other – neither can succeed without the input of the other.

(4) *Investment*: Partners invest in each other, e.g. through equity swaps, which is a tangible sign of long-term commitment.

(5) *Information*: Communication is reasonably open and partners share the information needed to make the relationship work.

(6) *Integration*: Partners develop linkages and shared ways of working so that they can work together smoothly.

(7) *Institutionalisation*: The relationship is given a formal status, with clear responsibilities and decision processes.

(8) *Integrity*: The partners behave towards one another in an honourable way that justifies and enhances mutual trust.

Source: Kanter, 1994

---

than collaboration between the strong and the weak. The reason, they argue, is that the 'weak link' in the collaboration can easily detract from the competitiveness of the collaboration and cause friction between the participant organisations. Furthermore, it is likely that the weaker partner will find involvement in the collaboration too much of a distraction from improvements in other aspects of its business. In support of this assertion, Bleeke and Ernst refer to the results of a study of 49 cross-border alliances in which the success rate of collaborations involving two strong players was 67%, while the success rate of collaborations with unevenly matched players was only 33%.

Another observation made by Bleeke and Ernst (1991) is that most collaborative arrangements based principally on developing the competencies of a minor partner meet with failure or mixed results. They go on to argue that, for successful collaboration, all participants should bring complementary skills and capabilities. Skills transfer may result, but this should not be the primary purpose of the collaboration; rather it may be a useful spin-off.

Involvement of stakeholders

Many writers on the subject of collaboration suggest that involving *all* of the stakeholders in whatever problem domain is being acted in is critical to collaborative effectiveness (see, for example, Augustyn & Knowles, 2000). Wood and Gray (1991) argue, however, that it is not necessary for all of the stakeholders in the problem domain to be involved for successful collaboration to result. Drawing on a range of case study evidence, Wood and Gray argue that successful collaboration need in fact involve only a critical mass of key stakeholders, for example:

- Those that are most interested in working collaboratively.
- The most powerful and influential.
- The majority, so that social norms can be established and others can join later.
- The best organised, so that social pressure can be brought to bear on non-participants.

The presence or absence of stakeholders can, of course, have an impact on the interactions between participants, e.g. interfering with agreed outcomes by introducing new, damaging information or by calling the legitimacy of the collaboration into question. A study of a regional tourism partnership in Brazil by de Araujo and Bramwell (2002), for example, identified a critical limitation for the partnership as being a lack of serious involvement on the part of private-sector or non-government organisations. While this situation was felt to have some advantages, particularly in terms of the commonalities evident among members (including their generally positive attitude to tourism development), a major disadvantage was felt to be that the collaboration failed to incorporate the broad sweep of interests required in order for the project to establish a long-term, sustainable development perspective. Further, by not including community groups, resident associations and other interest groups, the chance to secure grassroots engagement in the project was foregone.

Uncertainty

Spyriadis (2002) argues that market uncertainty may enhance collaborative partnerships, while uncertainty within the alliance is likely to have a negative impact on the alliance. Box 7.5 summarises some of the major external and internal sources of uncertainty in the context of collaboration.

Box 7.5 Sources of uncertainty in collaboration

Internal uncertainties

- Goals – roles and expectations of the participants not specified.
- Partner abilities – partners may not have the required strengths.
- Latent conflict – conflict encountered in the course of the collaboration.
- Planning gaps – no detailed planning of significant tasks.
- Authority – clear procedures predetermined.
- Relationships – partners may not work well together.
- Performance – expected results may not be achieved.
- Benefits – inadequate revenues allocation or share of development.
- Commitments – unclear expected investments, duration, business volume or future rights.
- Opportunism – of one partner against the other.

External (market) uncertainties

- Economic environment – e.g. shifts in public policy, industry conditions, macro-economic variables.
- Market responses – e.g. unpredictable reactions of suppliers, customers, competitors.
- Partners' reactions – partners affected by various uncertainties.
- Liabilities – third parties involved.
- Government approvals – authorities may not grant needed rights.

Source: Adapted from Spyriadis (2002)

Governance mechanisms

Kanter (1994) argues that effective collaboration takes place when participants develop mechanisms (that is, structures, processes or skills) for bridging organisational and interpersonal gaps and achieving real value from the collaboration. The most productive relationships achieve integration at five levels, as shown in Box 7.6.

Augustyn and Knowles (2000), meanwhile, identify two factors critical to the performance of tourism collaboration in the city of York, England, both of which relate to the development of appropriate governance mechanisms. The first relates to the lack of a reward system for encouraging 'better-than-average' contributions on the part of participating organisations. The lack of such a system was considered to be a

---

Box 7.6 Levels of integration of collaborative mechanisms

- *Strategic integration*: involving continuous contact among leaders to discuss broad goals or changes within each company. Leaders should not strike the deal and then leave others to nurture it. The more contact top executives have with the collaboration the better.
- *Tactical integration*: bringing middle managers/professionals together to develop plans for specific projects or joint activities, to identify organisational changes that will link the partners together more effectively or to transfer knowledge.
- *Operational integration*: providing ways for people carrying out day-to-day work to have timely access to the information, resources or people they need to accomplish their tasks.
- *Interpersonal integration*: building the necessary foundation for creating future value by developing a more extensive and dense network of interpersonal ties.
- *Cultural integration* – requiring people involved in the relationship to have the communication skills and cultural awareness to bridge their differences.

Source: Kanter, 1994

---

constraining factor in the case of York. However, as Augustyn and Knowles note, criteria for determining what counts as a 'better-than-average' contribution to the collaboration are far from clear-cut, and would have to be determined by the participants in advance.

The second governance issues identified by Augustyn and Knowles in their analysis of tourism collaboration in York was that, from a practical perspective, continuous evaluation of performance is needed against the stated objectives of the collaboration. Such an analysis is critical in identifying areas for improvement within the collaboration and to facilitate future joint decision-making. If problems are identified in a timely manner they can be woven into the dynamic of the collaboration more effectively.

Some writers have argued that collaborations involving shared equity arrangements – i.e. joint ventures – are more likely to prove successful than those based on non-equity arrangements. Hanlon, drawing on the work of Flannagan and Marcus (1993), goes further to argue that joint ventures are more likely to be successful if one partner has a controlling share of the equity. Hanlon goes on to argue that holding 25% or more of the voting shares normally implies control in the context of airline alliances. Pekar and Allio (1994), meanwhile, note that business organisations are increasingly collaborating through non-equity arrangements, participants typically finding such governance forms to be more flexible. This flexibility can be critical in dynamic and fast-moving market environments where time is of the essence.

Bleeke and Ernst (1991), on the other hand, argue that what matters more is clear management control. Their study of 49 cross-border alliances, taken from a variety of locations and industries, suggested that alliances with an even split of financial ownership were just as likely to succeed as those where one party holds the majority interest. Counter to the commonly held view that fifty-fifty ownership will result in collaborative failure due to decision-making inertia, Bleeke and Ernst argue that when one partner has a majority stake it tends to dominate the decision-making process, often putting its own interest above those of other participants. This in turn can lead to both partners being worse off because they are not collaborating effectively with one another. The writers go on to argue that fifty-fifty ownership can be an advantage for at least two further reasons. First, it often implies that the collaboration is set up as an independent entity, with its own strong management. The second is that fifty-fifty ownership builds trust. This is because the success of each partner depends on the success of the collaboration as a whole, so that each partner has a stake in the success of all the others.

The role of the convenor

Many collaborative groups decide to appoint an external convenor. In other cases, a convenor will be appointed from within the membership of the collaboration. Writers have argued that the convenor can have an important influence on the effectiveness of the collaboration. This may in turn depend on their personal (or organisational) qualities, the resources at their disposal or the tactics they choose to adopt.

With regard to the personal qualities required of convenors of collaborative groups, Brandon (1993) suggests the following:

- Credibility as a person who is able to understand and empathise with particular participant views and concerns.
- Credibility as someone who is able to appreciate specialist considerations without necessarily being an expert in the area.
- Independence, or at least the ability to conduct meetings without being seen to side with a particular group or pursue a personal agenda.
- The ability to identify and weed out issues that are irrelevant or tangential to the main agenda.

- The ability to manage participants' expectations regarding the scope of the collaboration and the kinds of outputs that are likely to be generated.
- Authority to resist pressures to foreshorten or otherwise circumscribe the process of collaboration and exchange in order to achieve quick results.
- Recognition of the need to balance the requirements of bottom-up participation with top-down systems of management.
- Willingness to allow leadership to develop from within the group, so that the role of convenor might pass on when needed.

In determining whether it is better in terms of collaborative effectiveness to appoint an internal or an external convenor, Schuman (1996) suggests that the eight dimensions shown in Box 7.7 are important. Wood and Gray (1991), meanwhile, focus on the tactics employed by the convenor, which they argue are likely to vary according to the background of the convenor and to the nature of the mandate the convenor has been given.

With regard to the background of the individual or group called to perform the task of convenor, Wood and Gray note a considerable diversity in practice, ranging from prominent public individuals to

---

Box 7.7 Factors determining whether an internal or external convenor should be appointed

The use of a neutral convenor should be considered where:
- *Distrust or bias among the participants is apparent or suspect.* The convenor's job will be to facilitate the process and, as such, the convenor will play a critical role in decision-making. To give this power to any one participant may unbalance the collaboration and result in suboptimal outcomes being achieved.
- *One or more participants may feel intimidated by others and less willing to contribute.* Appointing a neutral convenor will provide participants with a neutral person before whom they feel less intimidated.
- *Rivalries between individuals and organisations are intense.* Participants will often be less willing to exhibit rivalry in the presence of a neutral outsider. The convenor's role in this situation will be to determine whether the rivalries that do emerge are useful to the collaboration or are likely to inhibit it.
- *The problem is poorly defined, or defined differently by different participants.* When people come together they are often more interested

in being understood than understanding others. The convenor's role will be to ensure that everyone's viewpoints are aired, listened to and built into the decision-making.

- *The problem domain is so broad that it becomes difficult for any person to think about it all at once.* In such circumstances, the convenor's job is to oversee the substantive process of the meetings, leaving the participants with the task of understanding the problem domain.
- *The participants find themselves in complex or novel situations, where experts are needed.* The convenor, as 'meta-decision maker', may be able to bring in expertise to the collaboration, particularly in situations that the participants have rarely, or never, encountered before.
- *A timely decision is required.* The convenor's role here is to act as 'collaborative parliamentarian', who chooses which procedural rules to apply and steers the collaborative group through their application, thereby speeding it up.
- *The cost of meeting is presently a barrier to collaboration.* Appointing an external convenor may help speed up and simplify 'meta-decisions', thereby reducing the costs of collaboration.

Source: Adapted from Schuman, 1996

environmental interest groups and from university research centres to business leaders. Wood and Gray go on to suggest that convenors drawn from some backgrounds are likely to adopt a highly formal style of convenorship, while those drawn from other backgrounds might be expected to adopt a less formal style. This, in turn, might have an important influence on the tactics the convenor could use to facilitate effective collaboration.

The tactics adopted by the convenor might also be expected to vary according to the type of intervention. Indeed, in some cases the convenor will have been invited to act in that capacity, in which case the convenor will adopt a 'responsive' role. In other cases the convenor may actively be seeking to bring about collaboration in the problem domain, in which case a proactive stance will be adopted.

Wood and Gray relate these two critical variables in the form of a matrix, which is shown in Table 7.1. The table identifies four main categories of tactic that the convenor of a collaborative group might adopt. These are:

- *Legitimation.* This involves the convenor acting as a source of legitimation for participants and the collaborative activities they

Table 7.1 Dominant modes and central attributes of convenors for
various types of interventions and influence

Type of intervention	Type of influence by convenor	
	Formal	*Informal*
Requested by stakeholders (convenor is responsive)	*Legitimation*: convenor needs to be seen as fair	*Facilitation*: convenor needs to be seen as trustworthy
Initiated by convenor (convenor is proactive)	*Mandate*: convenor needs to be seen as powerful	*Persuasion*: convenor needs to be seen as credible

Source: Wood and Gray, 1991

    propose. The convenor will need to be seen as being fair. Fairness
is required because the participants must be confident that the
convenor will not use the formal authority he or she has been given
in a one-sided or arbitrary manner.

- *Facilitation*. Here the convenor's role is to assist participants in
making decisions about collaborative actions. The convenor will
need to be viewed by participants as trustworthy. Trustworthiness
is required because the convenor has no formal authority to establish the collaboration, enforce rules or ensure outcomes and must
therefore rely on participants' trust to be effective.
- *Mandate*. Here the convenor will attempt to move the agenda
forward proactively, employing the mandate he or she has been
given by the collaborative group. The convenor will require a firm
mandate, since a mandated collaboration is only held together by
participants' fear of what they might lose out on if they are not
part of it.
- *Persuasion*. This involves the convenor proactively setting the
agenda and attempting to move it forward by convincing the participants of the benefits of collaboration. This will require credibility
on the part of the convenor, because the collaboration will be the
convenor's own idea, so he or she must come up with convincing and credible arguments for participation. The convenor must
also use his or her credibility, influence, knowledge of the interrelationships between participants and charisma to persuade
stakeholders to participate.

In many cases, of course, the convenor will be a group rather than an individual, so the above qualities will need to be exhibited at the group level. Wood and Gray go on to suggest that the convening group that actually tackles the problem domain is very often a *second-order collaborative alliance*. Often a smaller group, the *first-order collaborative alliance*, initiates the formation of this larger collaborative group. According to Wood and Gray this raises a number of interesting questions, for example are first- and second-order collaborative alliances governed by the same motivations? What leads the first-order alliance to seek to transform itself into the second-order collaborative alliance? Are the dynamics of first- and second-order alliances the same? Unfortunately there has to date been too little work on these crucial issues to provide really convincing answers to them.

Empirical Studies of Collaborative Effectiveness

As academic interest in the subject of collaboration has grown in recent years, and as business organisations are beginning to recognise the potential of collaborative working, so has the number of empirical studies of collaborative effectiveness also grown. Since it is not possible to present a comprehensive review of these studies given the space limitations of this book, a number of landmark studies will be covered in this section.

Governance style, partner interests and conflict

In their seminal study of collaboration in the context of co-marketing alliances, Bucklin and Sengupta (1993) used an ordinary least squares (OLS) regression model to test a number of hypotheses relating to the relative power of participants, their compatibility and the degree of conflict evident in the collaboration. Their model was based on responses to a survey of 98 co-marketing alliances. A mixture of parametric and non-parametric data was employed, the latter being measured on a number of attitudinal scales specially developed for the purpose. The findings of the model are briefly discussed here.

First, with regard to the balance of power between participants, the study found a strong negative relationship between power imbalances among the participants and the effectiveness of the relationship. Bucklin and Sengupta argue that this is because the presence of power imbalances in a relationship creates the potential for conflict. If, for example, the weaker party recognises its lack of power in the relationship, it is likely to take steps to limit its vulnerability. Such actions might take the form of involvement in competing alliances or a failure to commit its resources fully to the collaboration. If the stronger party recognises this potential, it too will limit its commitment to the collaboration. Bucklin and Sengupta's study also found a significant negative relationship between managerial imbalances and collaborative effectiveness. If one participant is not seen to be 'pulling its weight' by committing insufficient managerial resources to the collaboration, other participants will be less willing to put their full effort into the process. Similarly, participants that are not seen to allocate the expected managerial talent, in numbers or status, tend to be viewed with suspicion by other participants. This can create conflict in the collaboration, thereby detracting from its performance in meeting the goals set for it by the participants.

While conflict is a commonly observed feature of inter-organisational collaboration, it is not entirely clear whether it promotes or retards collaborative effectiveness. Many studies have found a negative relationship between conflict and effectiveness, suggesting that conflict within the collaboration can detract from its performance. Other writers have argued, however, that conflict resolution can result in positive outcomes, particularly if it results in organisational learning. Bucklin and Sengupta's study, however, found a strong negative relationship between conflict and collaborative effectiveness, suggesting that conflict rarely enhances collaborative effectiveness in practice. Bucklin and Sengupta go on to argue that making a distinction between functional and dysfunctional conflict may be helpful to participants in alliances, the key being to recognise the functional role of conflict and to learn to harness it towards meeting the objectives of the collaboration.

Bucklin and Sengupta's study also found a strong positive relationship between the project payoff, defined as the perceived strategic value of the project minus its development costs, and collaborative effectiveness. This finding supports Kanter's (1994) view, discussed earlier, that participants with clearly identified market opportunities and well-defined costs are more likely to collaborate with one another effectively.

With regard to partner compatibility, Bucklin and Sengupta used their empirical model to test two particular hypotheses. The first hypothesis – that greater organisational compatibility in terms of participants having similar problem domains and generally compatible goals will enhance the performance of the collaborative relationship – was strongly confirmed. This would tend to suggest that participants with similar management philosophies and joint interests are more likely to succeed in collaborating with one another. When such conditions are not met, conflict is likely to arise within the collaborative relationship that may retard its performance from the perspective of one, some or all of the participants.

The second hypothesis, that the longer and more stable the previous history of collaboration between the participants, the greater the effectiveness of the relationship, was also strongly confirmed. Bucklin and Sengupta suggest that a previous history of collaboration can contribute to collaborative effectiveness in two main ways. First, prior collaboration may enable participants to assess their compatibility more effectively, making them more likely to select partners with whom they share domain interests and similar ways of working. Second, Bucklin and Sengupta recognise that opportunistic behaviour is always likely to be a problem in inter-organisational collaboration. A level of mutual trust between the participants can, however, counterbalance this tendency, and this is more likely to develop if participants have collaborated together successfully in the past.

The central importance of trust and commitment in the collaborative relationship is confirmed in a recent study of 106 high-technology firms by Perry *et al.* (2002). Using an OLS model, the researchers found significant and positive relationships not only between trust and commitment but also between commitment (and termination penalties) and the perceived effectiveness of collaboration between the firms concerned. Thus trust is said to result in commitment, which in turn enhances the effectiveness of the collaboration.

Tourism co-marketing alliances

Bucklin and Sengupta's empirical work is, of course, on co-marketing alliances generally, so the question remains as to how far these findings are appropriate in the context of tourism marketing. Palmer (1998b) goes some way to answering this in his empirical study that looks specifically at tourism-related co-marketing alliances. Palmer's primary focus is on governance style. He adopts a loose–tight continuum. At one end of the continuum are instances of collaboration with loose (or 'informal') governance styles, while at the other are tight (or 'formal') ones. Palmer notes that business people tend to prefer looser governance styles, reverting to formality only when necessary. It is felt that excessive tightness can restrict creativity and innovation, which can be critical elements of the problem-solving activities of the collaboration. Loose inter-organisational governance styles are also said to be advantageous in that there is the potential for the collaborators to respond quickly to changes in their environment. Participants in the collaboration are thought to have more freedom to use their initiative without having to go through time-consuming decision-making systems. Against this, it is often said that excessive flexibility can lead to misunderstandings about mutual goals, resulting in problems about monitoring members' performance and exercising control over their behaviour. Furthermore, the informality of systems managed in a loose governance style may result in members failing to set their collaborative objectives properly or failing to structure their activities in the most appropriate ways for achieving such objectives.

Accordingly, Palmer developed two hypotheses to be tested. First, that 'local tourism marketing associations are more effective where they are associated with a "tight" governance style' (Palmer, 1998b: 188) and, second, that 'the effectiveness of local tourism marketing associations is greatest where there is a level of compatibility among members' (Palmer, 1998b: 190).

In order to test these hypotheses, Palmer employed a regression model based on data relating to 172 members of 13 local tourism associations in England in 1995. Independent variables were measured in the course of semi-structured interviews among a sample of officers of tourism destination marketing associations using a set of scales based on those employed by Bucklin and Sengupta (1993). Compatibility was operationalised in terms of respondents' perceptions of the extent to which they shared similar objectives and ways of doing business. Meanwhile the dependent variable, the effectiveness of the association, was considered more difficult to operationalise. In many cases, the objectives of the marketing associations were not specified in any great detail and directional goals were often more relevant than quantified goals. Even in the case of larger associations, it was noted that individual participants often have objectives that are different from those stated for the collaboration as a whole. A decision was taken, therefore, to adopt an 'inward-looking' definition based on the effectiveness of the collaboration as perceived by members. This was measured on a specially constructed scale and in a similar way to the independent variables.

A principal components analysis was conducted in order to identify suitable measures of governance style, member compatibility and collaborative effectiveness. These were then fed into a multiple least-squares regression model taking the following form:

$$\text{Effectiveness} = a + b_1(\text{governance style}) + b_2(\text{compatibility})$$

The results of the analysis were able to lend strong statistical support for the first hypothesis: that tightly governed associations were perceived by their members to be more successful than loosely governed ones. The most successful groups were found to be those with formal rules and conditions governing relationships between members and those that had an efficient and effective secretariat. The results also suggested that those associations that did not encourage discussion by members of the management of the association's objectives tended to perform more effectively. In essence, a style that 'is too loose could result in an association engaging in excessive discussion without achieving results which benefit members' (Palmer, 1998b: 196). This evidence points to the importance of achieving a tight governance style in the development of tourism marketing groups, especially at the destination level.

Meanwhile, the second hypothesis – that the effectiveness of local tourism marketing associations is likely to be greatest where there is a level of compatibility among members – was not supported by the data analysis. This finding contrasts with that of Bucklin and Sengupta, who found a strong positive relationship between the two variables. Palmer attempts to explain this finding with reference to the resource dependency theory of collaborative relationships (as discussed briefly in Chapter 5 of this book). More specifically, Palmer argues that, when participants possess similar competencies and resources, there is less scope for effective collaboration through the exchange of those competencies and resources. When there is a significant incompatibility between participants, a symbiotic relationship may emerge, sponsored by a mutually beneficial sharing of core competencies. The role of partner compatibility in determining collaborative effectiveness will be discussed in greater depth in the following section of this chapter.

These findings are generally supported by a follow-up study undertaken by Palmer (2002), which appears to use the same sample as was employed in his 1998 study. The study estimated a structural equations (LISREL) model in order to test the following hypotheses:

- A high level of commitment by members of a co-operative marketing association is positively associated with its perceived effectiveness.
- Co-operative marketing associations will be considered more effective by the members when members are drawn from diverse backgrounds.
- Formal methods of governing co-operative marketing associations are associated with high levels of perceived effectiveness.
- A high level of reciprocation of benefits and obligations between members leads to a high level of effectiveness for a co-operative marketing association.

Six indicators of the dependent variable and 15 indicators of the four independent variables (representing each of the hypotheses) were developed and operationalised using five-point attitudinal scales (as in Palmer, 1998b). The dependent variable was again operationalised in terms of participants' perceptions of the effectiveness of the collaboration.

The structural model gave strong support to the hypothesis that collaborative performance was positively associated with more formal governance styles, with the more effective associations having more formal rules governing relations between members, more efficient and effective secretariats and limits on the opportunities to discuss the management of resources. As such, the model supports Palmer's previous finding that stronger governance styles tended to be associated with tighter styles of inter-organisational governance.

While Palmer's previous study (Palmer, 1998b) found no significant relationship between the construct of participant compatibility and collaborative performance, the results of this model suggested a significant negative relationship between the two. In other words, dissimilarity among the participants' objectives is suggested by the model to promote collaborative effectiveness. Again, the suggestion here is that a diversity of competencies among participants is likely to result in symbiotic exchanges taking place, making it more likely that the participants perceive the collaboration to be successful.

The model also showed a significant positive relationship between participants' commitment to the association, which was operationalised in terms of clauses relating to exclusivity or withdrawal of membership, the frequency of attendance at meetings and whether the representative held a position in the association. The suggestion here is that commitment is associated with trust in the form of a virtuous circle, in which commitment deepens trust. Trust, in turn, will build more commitment, this resulting in greater levels of trust between participants. This confirms the view of Bucklin and Sengupta (as noted above) and is consistent with Morgan and Hunt's (1994) commitment–trust theory of relationship marketing.

The model could not, however, support Palmer's fourth hypothesis, which was that high levels of reciprocity and obligation between members tend to promote collaborative effectiveness. Palmer suggests that this may be the result of the complexity of the individual trade-off each participant experiences with regard to what their organisation puts into the collaboration and what they feel they are getting out of it in the way of benefits. Further refinements to the model would, according to Palmer, be needed in order to capture this complexity more fully.

Embeddedness in social networks

Kanter (1994: 97) argues that a fundamental feature of collaborative relationships is that they 'cannot be "controlled" by formal systems but require a dense web of interpersonal connections and internal infrastructures that enhance learning'. Meanwhile, Augustyn and Knowles (2000: 342) argue that the 'informational benefits of [such] social networks are critical for the ultimate success of the partnership'.

This leads on to the network approach adopted by Gulati (1998), who argues that relatively few studies to date have attempted to consider the impact of social networks on collaborative performance. A social network can be defined as 'a set of nodes (e.g. persons, organizations) linked by a set of social relationships (e.g. friendship, transfer of funds, overlapping membership) of a specified type' (Laumann *et al.*, in Gulati, 1998: 295). These networks might include 'supplier relationships, resource flows, trade association memberships, interlocking directorates, relationships among individual employees, and prior strategic alliances' (Gulati, 1998: 297). Hence collaboration, which entails the development of relationships between organisations, can be viewed as a sub-component of the organisation's social network. In other words, collaboration can be seen as one possible manifestation of the organisation's interlinked system of social relationships. It could be argued, therefore, that collaborations that are more deeply embedded in networks are more likely to be effective or last longer than others.

It is helpful to distinguish between relational embeddedness and structural embeddedness. The former focuses on the socialising relationships, or cohesive ties, that develop within networks. The more embedded in a network an organisation is, the stronger its cohesive ties within that network are likely to be. These cohesive ties condition how organisations participating in a network behave towards one another, engendering the free flow of information, reducing uncertainty and promoting trust among the organisations involved. Structural embeddedness, meanwhile, refers to the position that an organisation takes within a network. Writers have argued that organisations occupying similar positions in a network form a distinct status group, and that status can provide useful informational cues to actors regarding the likely behaviour of other actors in the network.

Embeddedness in social networks may therefore confer informational advantages to some or all of its participants. They may also enable participants to achieve control benefits, particularly when the organisation is situated between two others within the network. Such positioning may enable the intermediate organisation to create advantages for themselves by playing the other actors off against one another or by brokering tension between different players.

There is indeed some strong empirical evidence that alliances that are more embedded may perform better or last longer than those that are not. In one of the first such studies, Kogut (1989) found that alliances where members had previous ties were more likely to last longer. Levinthal and Fichman (1988) and Seabright *et al.* (1992) also found the duration of relationships to be affected not only by changes in task conditions that may alter resource interdependence but also by 'dyadic attachments' between firms. These are conditioned by the social structures in which firms are embedded and the continuity of boundary 'spanners' that result from a history of interaction between firms. More recently, a study by Gulati and Lawrence (cited in Gulati, 1998) of relationship embeddedness in the automotive industry found that, on average, sourcing arrangements based on more embedded relationships were associated with superior performance. Moreover, more embedded exchange relationships were seen to be particularly effective in situations of high uncertainty.

These findings are significant, in that they would seem to imply that embeddedness in networks, both extant and previous, may have an important influence on the effectiveness of collaboration. Given that large multinational organisations may well have a number of collaborations ongoing at the same time, this raises the issue of collaborative capability. Gulati (1998) suggests that some of these capabilities might be:

- Identifying valuable opportunities and good partners.
- Using appropriate governance mechanisms.
- Developing inter-organisational information-sharing systems.
- Making requisite relationship-specific investments.
- Initiating necessary changes in the collaborative relationship as it evolves while also managing participants' expectations.
- Managing conflict within the organisation arising from multiple collaboration membership.

However, the question of how these capabilities are developed and how they might influence the effectiveness of collaboration is still an open one. As Gulati (1988: 309) acknowledges:

> the performance of alliances remains one of the most interesting and also one of the most vexing questions. We now know that embedded ties differ in fundamental ways from other ties ... but we have less understanding of the extent to which alliances with embedded ties perform better or worse than other alliances and why.

Conclusion

The task of evaluating collaborative effectiveness is, unfortunately, hampered by definitional problems. First there is the problem of what is considered to be collaboration. Then there is the problem of determining the conditions under which collaboration might be considered to be effective. Many of the early studies of collaborative effectiveness focused simply on trying to ascertain the reasons for the termination of particular instances of collaboration, often on a rudimentary case-by-case basis. Researchers have, however, been making a determined effort to introduce empirical rigour to the study of collaborative effectiveness. Indeed, a number of valuable studies have been published in recent years.

The bad news for those looking for ready answers is, however, that these studies tend to suggest that there really is no simple formula for achieving effective collaboration. The factors that contribute to collaborative effectiveness are highly diverse and the relationships between them are very complex, as perhaps one might expect given that collaboration is essentially a social relationship. If the studies undertaken to date do tell us anything, it is that effective collaboration requires participants to adopt fundamentally new ways of thinking. This means abandoning competitive patterns of thought and behaviour and adopting instead a relationship perspective. When the organisation – or more precisely the individuals making decisions on behalf of the organisation – begin to recognise that they can do better by collaborating with other organisations in their problem domain rather than competing against them, the collaborative efforts in which they are participating will likely begin to flourish. By the same token, collaboration among those still deeply wed to the competition paradigm is more likely to meet with failure, or partial performance, than it is with unqualified success.

Part 4: Tourism Marketing Collaboration in Practice

Part 4 Introduction
Tourism Marketing Collaboration in Practice

The main objective of Part 4 of the book is to critically discuss the application of key theoretical perspectives outlined in the previous three parts of the book to specific instances of inter-organisational tourism marketing collaboration in three of the principal sectors of the tourism industry, namely transportation, accommodation and destinations. In order to provide some clarification and consistency for the remainder of the book, inter-organisational collaboration in the context of tourism marketing will be defined as:

> a process of joint decision-making among autonomous, key stakeholders of an inter-organisational, tourism marketing domain, using shared norms, rules or structures, to resolve marketing problems of the domain and/or to manage issues related to the development of the domain in marketing terms.

Consistent with the definitional framework provided by Jamal and Getz presented in Chapter 5, this definition is sufficiently broad and inclusive to encompass the vast array of issues pertinent to the initiation, dynamics and management of inter-organisational collaboration in the context of tourism marketing.

In order to examine the application and appropriateness of inter-organisational activity in pursuit of individual and collective goals in the context of tourism marketing a range of contemporary case material is to be included in the chapters that follow. For example, in Chapter 8, which examines the dynamics of inter-organisational collaboration among global airline alliances, Star Alliance represents the main focus of enquiry. Although the discussion is quite case-specific, a number of issues pertaining to the wider impact of global airline alliances on tourism are examined. Chapter 9 follows with an investigation into the application of collaborative marketing strategies among hotel consortia, with particular attention focused on the development of the Best Western organisation, the world's largest hotel 'chain'. Chapter 10 concludes Part 4 with a discussion of the collaborative marketing of the tourist destination in which, after a detailed introduction to the benefits and drawbacks of collaboration in the context of destinations, three case studies are introduced. The first case study focuses on two contrasting regional destinations in Queensland, Australia, and their divergent approaches to destination collaboration. The second case study looks at current attempts to develop tourism along the Mekong River in Southeast Asia and develop the Greater Mekong Subregion into a global destination. The third case study adopts a slightly different slant in that it represents a predominantly vertical approach to collaboration between destination marketing organisations (DMOs) and other components of the tourism product in attempts to engender repeat visitation among visitors. Through a case study based on the Stockholm Information Service in Sweden, evidence is presented to suggest that there exist considerable impediments to the implantation of relationship marketing strategies in the destination context.

Chapter 8
Global Airline Alliances

Globalisation and the Rationale for Airline Alliances

The last decade has seen a frenzy of alliance activity in the airline industry. According to data compiled by *Airline Business* magazine, the number of established alliances among airlines increased from 280 in 1994 to 502 in 1998 – an increase of nearly 80% (Hanlon, 1999). The data also suggested that more airlines were becoming involved in these alliances, the number of airlines involved in at least one inter-airline alliance rising by some 44%, from 136 in 1994 to 196 in 1998 (Hanlon, 1999). Most of these alliances comprised relatively uncomplicated arrangements, usually among only two airlines, and had a comparatively limited focus, typically just codesharing on specified routes. Codesharing first appeared in the US in the early 1960s, when American commuter airlines started using the same codes as the major carriers when connecting with them at their hubs. The practice has since grown apace. It involves 'two or more airlines agree[ing] to use the same designator code or flight number for connecting services in order to attract more business by extending their networks through partner carriers' (Malver, 1998: 19). Indeed, Morrish and Hamilton (2002) argue that, by 1985, almost all of the top 50 commuter airlines had entered into some form of codesharing agreement, the airlines involved accounting for some 75% of all commuter passengers at that time.

What characterises the development of airline alliances in recent years, however, is that a small number of truly 'global' alliances have emerged. Prominent among these are Star Alliance, Oneworld and SkyTeam. These alliances include almost all of the world's best-known international airlines, with big names such as British Airways, American Airlines, Lufthansa and Air France participating. Such alliances are on a scale never seen before. Morrish and Hamilton (2002) suggest that, by the end of the 1990s, the global alliances accounted for 63.6% of passenger traffic, 55.8% of passenger numbers and 58.4% of group revenues. At this time the main players had divided into four main alliances (see Table 8.1) and some commentators were predicting an extended period of relative stability. However, the collapse of the 'Qualiflyer' alliance in early 2002 as a result of the demise of its prime mover, Swissair, suggests that the situation is still in fact rather fluid. It must be acknowledged, therefore, that even the three remaining global alliances could be dissolved and perhaps reformed in different combinations over the coming years.

Table 8.1 Global airline alliances in 2001

		Passenger numbers (2001)	
		in 000's	*% share of alliance*
Star Alliance	Air Canada	23,100	9.5
	Air New Zealand	8174	3.3
	All Nippon Airways	6082	2.5
	Austrian Airlines	3609	1.5
	British Midland	6702	2.8
	Lauda Air	1801	0.7
	Lufthansa	39,694	16.3
	Mexicana Airlines	8699	3.6
	SAS Scandinavian Airlines	23,244	9.6
	Singapore Airlines	14,696	6.1
	Thai Airways International	18,721	7.7
	Tyrolean Airways	2335	1.0
	Varig Airlines	10,487	4.3
	United Airlines	75,457	31.1
		Total = 242,801 (13.2% world share)	100.0
Oneworld	Aer Lingus	6655	3.4
	American Airlines	78,178	40.4
	British Airways	40,004	20.6
	Cathay Pacific	11,269	5.8

		Passenger numbers (2001)	
		in 000's	% share of alliance
	Finnair	7540	3.9
	Iberia	24,928	12.9
	Lan Chile	4969	2.6
	Qantas	20,193	10.4
		Total = 193,736 (10.5% world share)	100.0
SkyTeam	Aeromexico	9475	4.7
	Air France	39,067	19.3
	Alitalia	24,926	12.3
	CAS Czech Airlines	2878	1.4
	Delta Airlines	104,943	51.7
	Korean Air	21,638	10.7
		Total = 202,927 (11% world share)	100.0

Sources: Morrish and Hamilton, 2002; www.atwonline.com, 2003
Notes:
(1) The 'Qualiflyer' alliance comprising DAT Belgian Airlines, Crossair, TAP Air Portugal, LOT Polish Airlines, Portugalia, Swiassair and Volare was disbanded in 2002 following the demise of its prime mover, Swissair.
(2) Some columns do not add to 100% due to rounding.

Another factor likely to affect the stability of global airline alliances in coming years is the turbulence major international airlines have been experiencing as a result of the recent wave of terrorist attacks, beginning in 2001 with the 9/11 atrocities in New York and Washington, DC, and continuing with further attacks in Kenya, Bali and Morocco. The significant fall in passenger volumes post-9/11 has left many international airlines with serious problems of overcapacity. This, in turn, has forced many airlines

to consider restructuring their businesses and to seek major cost reductions by closing down certain routes, decommissioning some of their aircraft, introducing painful across-the-board pay cuts, bringing in
controversial work-rule changes and, inevitably, shedding substantial
numbers of employees. By the end of 2002 three major international airlines in particular were experiencing serious financial problems: Air
Canada, United Airlines and American Airlines. United were the first to
feel the strain, shedding around 20,000 jobs in an effort to meet the US$2.56
billion annual cost savings required of them to remain financially solvent
(www.news.airwise.com, 2003). These efforts were, however, ultimately
fruitless, the airline being forced to file for bankruptcy protection in
December 2002. Air Canada was also forced into this position in March
2003, having accumulated some CAN$12 billion in debts and, with the out-
break of the second war in Iraq, being unable to stem its loss-making in a
'deteriorated revenue environment'. Even after filing for bankruptcy, Air
Canada was still reported to be making losses of around CAN$4 million
per day (www.news.airwise.com, 2003). American Airlines, meanwhile,
were only just able to prevent themselves from being forced into a similar
situation, even though the cost savings they required were much higher
than those of United – in the region of US$4 billion per year
(www.news.airwise.com, 2003). Ultimately, the combination of a round of
frantic pay deals with unions, major job losses and the renegotiation of
around 100 supplier and leasing contracts enabled American to succeed
where United and Air Canada had failed. Given the fate of the Qualiflyer
alliance when Swissair were forced out of business in 2002, whether
the respective global alliances – Oneworld in the case of American and
Star Alliance in the case of United and Air Canada – would have been able
to survive the demise of major players such as these is a moot point.
Arguably the trend towards non-equity alliances protects individual airlines from the negative consequences of a partner that has become bankrupt. On the other hand, it must be acknowledged that airline alliances are
only as strong as their weakest member, and that the failure of one partner to pull its own weight may seriously compromise the degree of collaborative advantage an alliance is able to achieve relative to competitor
alliances.

Airlines have often formed or joined alliances because their strategic
managers consider it unthinkable to stay outside such powerful business networks. Today's global airline alliances are so fully integrated
into the core businesses of airlines that membership confers a significant
market advantage on alliance participants. This is especially true in a
rapidly globalising world economy, which is undoubtedly more turbulent today than it has ever been. A major source of this turbulence is
growing macro-economic unpredictability as a result of greater international economic integration and the ever more complex interactions

that are taking place between the major macro-economic variables of these globalising economies. The air travel industry is considered to be especially vulnerable to such macro-economic variability, the demand for air travel tending to move in proportion to economic growth as measured by Gross Domestic Product (GDP) (Agustinata & de Klein, 2002). Forming or joining an alliance can be a good way of combating turbulence by reducing the airline's dependence on particular markets, regions or products. It also presents airlines with a means of securing access to new markets, helping them to extend their reach into areas in which their influence has been (and in many cases continues to be) limited by government regulation at the national level. Airlines also tend to see global alliances as a means of tackling the extreme turbulence of their market environment by enabling them to shift relatively effortlessly between weakening and emerging markets.

Global airline alliances are in many ways simply an extension of a process of consolidation that begun with the deregulation and liberalisation of air travel markets in the late 1970s and early 1980s. This led to a wave of new entry into the airline industry, with new airlines entering deregulated routes in an attempt to compete with incumbent airlines. In most regions a further wave of mergers and acquisitions then followed. However, the constraints of intergovernmental air service agreements and the restrictions usually placed on foreign ownership of national flag-carrying airlines implied that this consolidation took place primarily within national boundaries (Hanlon, 1999). Attempts to develop an extended international network by merger or acquisition of the airlines operating those routes were generally impeded by legislation and government intervention. Airlines were therefore forced to seek other solutions in order to exploit the opportunities and counter the threats of globalisation. Rod Eddington, Chief Executive of British Airways, reinforces this point when discussing the rationale behind airline alliances: 'Aero-politics prevent airlines consolidating in a conventional way. Governments appear to be in favour of consolidating so long as their airline is the consolidator. So alliances are a precursor to a sort of halfway house' (Nissé, 2003b: 5).

The response of the major international airlines was to convert their existing point-to-point route networks into hub-and-spoke networks. This entailed cutting many existing direct connections, leaving direct flights only between major city hubs. These hub airports would then be serviced by an array of spokes to other regional airports, usually serviced in partnership with domestic airlines. The result would be increased traffic densities on the spoke routes, enabling often substantial economies of density to be earned. Employing the hub-and-spoke system would also enable airlines to use larger aircraft, leading to further unit cost reductions. Economies of scope were potentially available as the aircraft served both direct and indirect markets at the same time. Finally, the use of hub-and-spoke networks enabled airlines to erect barriers to entry to their networks, which included not only the lower costs available to incumbent airlines but also the option to develop strategic entry barriers in the form of frequent-flier programmes (FFPs), computerised reservation systems (CRSs) and incentive commissions (Flanagan & Marcus, 1993; Pels, 2001). Consequently, competing airlines had little incentive (or, indeed, ability) to invade each other's hub-and-spoke networks.

According to Pels (2001: 5) airline alliances 'can be seen as a continuation of a process of concentration and consolidation in the aviation sector that was first characterized by the emergence of hub-and-spoke networks'. Airlines found that similar benefits could be achieved by joining up their hub-and-spoke networks through some form of alliance. Hence, Oum and Park (1997) suggest six major reasons for alliance formation in the global airline industry:

(1) Consumers tend to prefer airlines serving a large number of cities, so to attract more customers in a more competitive environment airlines need to be able to offer flights to a wide range of destinations worldwide. As alliance partners link up their networks they can provide a 'seamless' service, thereby expanding their network into new territories.
(2) Traffic feed between partners helps increase load factors and achieve economies of density. Partners may also be able to increase flight frequency without actually increasing the number of flights they themselves operate.
(3) Alliance members can reduce unit costs by taking advantage of economies of scale, increased traffic density and economies of scope.
(4) Frequency, schedule convenience and convenience of connections are seen by customers as major features of quality. By co-ordinating their activities, alliance partners can improve the quality of their services.
(5) An alliance can offer far more variety of itinerary and routing choices than a single carrier of a similar size.
(6) Members can take advantage of alliance-wide CRSs through the practice of codesharing. Flights sharing the same code are listed more than once on a CRS search. This has the effect of pushing competitor flights off the first booking screen, from which many travel agents prefer to book.

This is not to suggest, however, that today's global airlines alliances are entirely route-based in their orientation. Another distinguishing feature of today's global alliances is that their focus is much wider than it used to be, including not only agreements on the joint operation of routes but also collaboration on such wide-ranging issues as purchasing, aircraft maintenance, booking and sales, customer incentives, marketing and advertising and staff training. Hanlon (1999) also points out that, while airline alliances are predominantly horizontal and market-motivated, vertical and technology-based alliances are not unheard of. British Airways, for example, has extensive vertical linkages with companies in its supply chain, including hotel groups such as the Marriott, Hertz for car hire and Diners Club for charge cards. Meanwhile, a good example of a technology-based alliance in the airline industry is the KSS consortium wherein, through co-ordinated purchasing decisions, member airlines are able to specialise in different aspects of aircraft maintenance: one in airframes, another in landing gear, another in engines and so on.

Despite the many widely accepted benefits of alliances there are, however, several potential drawbacks with the practice. Perhaps the most evident to the customer arises when, having originally booked with their preferred carrier, they learn that they will be flying with an alliance partner instead. This can have considerable 'knock-on' effects. Most notably, airlines participating in alliances need to address issues of service expectation and service quality, and brand perceptions and brand imbalance. Adverse alliance perceptions may also have a negative impact on individual brands that may have taken considerable time, care and cost to establish. Customer relationships are also at the mercy of alliance partners where common standards across the alliance are expected. Thus, while airlines can improve their finances and yields by closely co-ordinating and integrating their operations through the realignment of their resources via alliances, attention needs to remain on the needs and wants of customers if alliances are to be successful in the medium to long term.

Malver (1998) provides a further example of the importance of airline–customer relationships with regard to business-to-business markets. In the late 1990s a number of the world's largest buyers of corporate travel, namely American Express, Hogg Robinson Business Travel International and Carlson-Wagonlit, accused Star Alliance of failing to be price competitive. Although no evidence was found to support such assertions, it raised the attention of the European Union and Star Alliance was warned that strict conditions would be imposed on its operations if they were found to be anti-competitive.

Another important concern is the segregation of the world's airlines into 'strategic blocks'. This can make it difficult for airlines wishing to collaborate with other airlines 'outside' their alliance to do so. This 'strategic inflexibility' is also likely to occur on occasions when alliances will sometimes take precedent over individual airlines with regard to the demands made on people and resources. At the same time, global airline alliances, simply by their size and reach, bring with them risks relating to trust, commitment and the ability to manage considerable cross-cultural issues.

There also exists the fear that eventually alliances will eliminate fair competition between the member airlines unless the 'open-skies' environment is guaranteed. The ambiguous impact of airlines on competition is a real concern. While alliances can increase service quality and efficiency, this is often at the cost of competition in some markets. The overall net result for consumers is therefore uncertain (OECD, 2000). Also, by accepting fairly standard oligopolistic assumptions and interactions, one can conclude that an alliance will increase the partners' traffic and profits on alliance routes between continental hubs. However, these gains come at the expense of non-allied airlines. There is thus 'an incentive for non-allied airlines to enter alliances, and alliances are likely to beget more alliances' (Park and Zhang, 1998, in Morley, 2003: 39). Already duopolistic situations are in existence on certain routes, thus highlighting the need to get connected. Malver (1998: 21) takes up this point by concluding that:

> the greater the number of airlines there are in the same alliance, the greater the possibility that it will result in oligarchy when the member airlines join all their operations. Passengers will then end up flying with the one and only mega monocarrier which controls the markets and sets the routes and fares.

A number of studies have been conducted on the benefits and drawbacks of airline alliances, the most notable being those by Morrison (1996), Oum *et al.* (1996, 2000), Park and Cho (1997), Park and Zhang (1998) and Schweiterman (1995). However, recent theoretical and empirical investigations by Morley (2003: 49) provide a very useful summary of the principal benefits and drawbacks of global airline alliances as shown in Box 8.2.

Functional Coverage of Airline Alliances

Airline alliances are clearly not simply about the co-ordination of routes and route networks. In an effort to determine the features of airline alliances that lead to successful outcomes, Rhoades and Lush (1997) developed a typology based on two major characteristics: the degree to which resources are committed to the alliance; and the complexity of the particular arrangement (see Table 8.2). This, they argue, is superior to Bleeke and Ernst's typology (see Chapter 6), which is based on the *outcomes* of collaboration and hence only really useful in classifying alliances once they have concluded.

Codesharing

This practice involves airlines selling the seats of other carriers as though they were their own. Codesharing is most often used to join up

---

Box 8.2 Benefits and drawbacks of global airline alliances

- No single airline is able to offer a truly global service and network on its own in the current regulatory environment, so alliances offer the only way to do this and to build a global brand.
- Alliances avoid violating international regulatory instructions which limit, and sometimes prohibit, the purchase of equity in other airlines by having partners around the world with local knowledge, political connections, cultural affinity and experience.
- Airline alliances appear to offer airlines the potential to cut costs.
- Hence, alliances offer the potential for fare reductions.
- Generally, fares do fall as a consequence of alliances, but perhaps not by the full extent of the realised cost savings.
- Alliances can improve airline economics through integration of networks and feeding passengers to partners.
- Alliances between formerly competing airlines on a route can reduce competition to the disadvantage of travellers.
- Reduced competition can result in fewer flight services and higher fares.
- Alliances will bring customer-service benefits, such as integrated schedules, reduced waiting times at hubs between connecting flights, easier information sourcing and booking and easier connections.
- Alliances provide a means for airlines to offer (virtually) many more services than they otherwise could.
- Alliances provide a means for non-market leaders jointly to increase their competitive position against a market leader on a route, and thus to increase competition to the benefit of the non-leader airlines and travellers.

Sources: Based on Morley, 2003; OECD, 2000

---

connecting flights, which are sold and displayed as if they were operated by the same airline. Air travellers have always shown a strong preference for booking connecting flights with the same airline, and codesharing enables airlines to meet this demand without having to commit to operating each and every possible route. In effect, a bilateral flight network is established. Codesharing also makes the combined flight more likely to be purchased on CRSs (Evans, 2001), since the sharing of a single code makes the flights concerned more likely to appear on the

Table 8.2 Rhoades and Lush's typology of airline alliances

		Complexity of arrangement		
		Low	Moderate	High
Commitment of resources	High	(III) Computerised reservation systems	(VI) Management contracts	(IX) Equity governance
	Moderate	(II) Blocked-space agreements, revenue sharing, 'wet lease' and franchising	(V) Joint service	(VIII) Joint marketing
	Low	(I) Codesharing	(IV) Insurance and part pooling	(VII) Baggage handling, ground maintenance and facilities sharing

Source: Rhoades and Lush, 1997

first screen of a search for suitable flights. Many travel agents prefer to book flights for their customers from this first screen and it is reported that it is from the first screen that 70% to 90% of all flights are booked (Rhoades & Lush, 1997). Involving low levels of interaction and resource commitment, codesharing is a very popular alliance activity. Indeed, the World Tourism Organization (WTO, 2002) suggests that codesharing alone accounts for something like 70% of all airline alliances.

Blocked-space agreements, revenue sharing, 'wet lease' and franchising

These are essentially codesharing agreements, but they typically involve a greater commitment of resources on the part of one or more alliance member, and hence imply a greater burden of risk than simple codesharing. A 'wet lease' involves one airline leasing the aircraft and staff of another, then selling and operating the flight as though it were its own. The arrangements are normally more accommodating for the hiring airlines than a straightforward commercial deal (French, 1997). Franchising involves one airline renting the brand name and image of another, which it then applies to its own operations, selling them as though they belonged to the airline from which the brand image is being rented. Slightly more complicated are blocked-space agreements, which involve one airline agreeing to allocate a number of seats on one or more of its flights to another airline for a pre-agreed cost – a kind of partial wet lease (Rhoades & Lush, 1997). The responsibility for selling those seats to passengers then falls on the 'leasing' airline, which benefits by gaining access to additional flight codes on the major CRSs. The airline supplying the seats, meanwhile, benefits from having higher load factors on their flights, with the leased seats being paid for whether or not they are occupied. Revenue sharing or 'revenue pooling' involves two or more airlines that are operating a particular route agreeing to share the revenues generated by that route, often on the basis of the capacity contributed by each carrier. In some cases only a proportion of the revenue is 'pooled', up to a maximum percentage of seats sold. These forms of collaboration have generally become less popular in recent years as airlines have begun to collaborate on the basis of complementary networks of routes rather than competition on a given route.

Computerised reservation systems (CRSs)

Given the greater use of information technology in the booking of flights, a number of CRSs have been developed which give airlines much greater power to monitor and manage their sales. Airlines use this power to operate yield-management systems and frequent-flier programmes.

Examples of CRSs in the European context include Amadeus (comprising Air France, Lufthansa, Iberia and Sabena) and Galileo (comprising British Airways, KLM, Swissair, Austrian, Aer Lingus, Air Portugal and Olympic). These different systems have varying coverage of the main national markets, so that membership of one of them brings favoured access to the markets it covers. CRSs also generate huge volumes of marketing data that become available exclusively to members of that particular system. The sharing of CRSs does not normally involve significant interaction among the participants once the system has been established and the staff suitably trained. The resource commitment associated with CRSs tends, however, to be substantial and this is a major reason why the development and operation of CRSs tends to be collaborative.

Insurance and part pooling

Some airlines have found it expedient to spread out the cost of insurance by purchasing it jointly and to pool spare aircraft parts so as to increase their availability. The latter is particularly useful among airlines that have similar route networks, share facilities and own relatively small fleets of aircraft. Insurance and part pooling implies a limited commitment of resources, partly because the airlines involved would have to purchase the parts and insurance anyway, and partly because of the cost savings that may be gained by joint purchasing. At the same time, a moderate amount of co-ordination is required in order to ensure that parts are interchangeable and stocks are properly maintained, making this form of collaboration rather more complex than those previously discussed.

Joint service

Usually offered within a codesharing agreement, joint-service agreements enable airlines with complementary route structures to blend their flights, enabling them jointly to provide a 'seamless' service to as many destinations as possible. As alliance partners link up their networks in this way, they are able to offer services to a wider range of destinations, to gain access to attractive airports and to service 'thin' routes where passenger numbers would normally be too low to enable the airline to offer its own service. An example of the latter is the joint service agreement between Qantas and Air Vanuatu, which enabled the former to add this route to its network despite the relatively low load factors (Oum & Park, 1997). The co-ordination required for joint-servicing agreements implies moderate levels of both resource commitment and the complexity of the arrangements.

Management contracts

Management contracts involve the alliance participants agreeing to allow management experts, drawn from within the group of participating airlines, to manage a specified subset of the airlines' operations. The aim is typically to ensure consistency of decision-making, with the top-level management of the various participating airlines taking a hands-off approach. This implies a moderate level of complexity and a high level of resource commitment (in the form of expert personnel who are loaned to the management contract by one or more of the participating airlines).

Baggage handling, ground maintenance and facilities sharing

These arrangements all imply low levels of resource commitment but relatively high levels of complexity. Baggage handling agreements involve two or more airlines working together to ensure that their systems function smoothly, and may be particularly beneficial to an airline that has large number of passengers transferring from one flight to another at non-hub airports. Ground maintenance agreements imply airlines agreeing to service each other's aircraft, which again can save significant time and trouble at non-hub airports. Facilities sharing, meanwhile, can help airlines gain access to the gate and hangar space they need, these being increasingly congested at many major airports around the world.

Joint marketing

Airlines alliances often involve joint-marketing activities for two reasons. First, marketing and promotion can form a major element of the cost base of major world airlines, which compete in an increasingly competitive global market. Joint marketing can enable economies of scale to be earned in this important business function. Collaboration in marketing also recognises that some airlines have superior local knowledge and experience to others in respect of certain products and markets (French, 1997). Second, significant marketing benefits can be reaped by emphasising the global reach and connectivity of the combined networks of alliance members. For example, many of the world's major airlines now operate reciprocal FFPs. These are loyalty-reward schemes based on travellers earning points (or 'air miles') according to the type of ticket bought, which they can accumulate and later spend on further flights offered by the same airline, discounts, upgrades, concessions on care hire and so forth. Airlines are increasingly finding it beneficial to collaborate by linking their FFPs, allowing customers to spend their points on flights offered by partner airlines as well as their own. Hence, for example, British Midland, Air Canada, SAS and United have linked their FFPs for some time. Joint marketing implies a moderate level of resource commitment due to the resources that need to be made available to such marketing campaigns. At the same time, such arrangements are likely to be highly complex due to the significant co-ordination required to prepare them and the high levels of trust required among participants to collaborate successfully in this vital area of their business (Rhoades & Lush, 1997).

Equity governance

Equity sharing or swapping represents a form of airline alliance that involves high levels of both resource commitment and organisational complexity. Not only is a substantial financial commitment often involved, but such arrangements also typically involve top-level management participating in the board governance of partner airlines. Equity-governance arrangements appear to be becoming less popular among airlines in recent times (Oum & Park, 1997). However, Hanlon (1999) points out that this need not imply that the significance of equity governance is waning if – as indeed seems to be the case – such arrangements are involving increasingly heavier stakes.

Alliance Structures

In addition to the above, Morley (2003) provides an alternative typology of airline alliance structures. This originates from a study conducted by Gemini Consulting (Howarth & Kirsebom, 1999). Morely stresses that, although alliances range from 'loose' to 'formal' structures, they are generally 'loose' in that:

- It is not necessary for success or profitability that major assets are managed jointly – readily established linkages such as terminal facilities and booking systems are sufficient.
- The assets, resources and services provided by an airline to the alliance are not readily separated from the providing airline itself, but are an essential part of it.
- Splitting off the major assets provided by an airline to the alliance into a separate organisation would be very risky, as the other members of the alliance could readily appropriate them.

Morely concludes that there are three levels relevant to global airline alliances, each depending on the overall commitment given to the alliance by member airlines: co-ordination; sharing of strategy and operations;

and unification. The first, co-ordination, focuses on the expansion of the network and the marketing gains to be made, with some co-ordination of capacity, collaboration and sharing of information. The majority of airline alliances can be bracketed under this heading, including the Oneworld alliance which can be viewed in its entirety in Figure 8.1. This having been said, while Oneworld is predominantly a very large 'co-ordination' alliance, there are evidently some much closer alignments involving equity stakes taking place. For example, British Airways currently holds a 9% share in Spain's Iberia and a 19.491% share of Australia's Qantas. Under normal conditions, cost savings of 'co-ordination' alliances occur through co-ordination of external purchases with only small gains to be achieved from operational and utilisation efficiencies (see Table 8.3). One of the negative implications of looser alliance forms is that the individual member airlines are more prone to competitive behaviour and so remain a competitive threat to other airlines in the alliance. Much depends on trust and goodwill and a sense of 'collaborative spirit'. Thus, in 'co-ordinated' alliances, the balance of power (and control), the ability of partners to negotiate with each other and the ability of member airlines to counter the strength of key players are all highly significant. This latter point applies particularly to Oneworld, where British Airways and American Airlines between them account for almost 83% of all routes, 70% of all daily departures and approximately 72% of all passengers (see Figure 8.1).

The second level of alliance is that of 'sharing of strategy and operations'. This alliance type involves a much tighter integration of scheduling and marketing and is best evidenced by Star Alliance (see following case study). The third, and most extreme form of alliance is that of 'unification', where the alliance is achieved through the acquisition of major equity stakes and has as its *raison d'être* the common control of a unified organisation. This quite rare form of alliance is best demonstrated by the recent announcement that Air France and KLM of the Netherlands are to merge (economist.com, 2003). Although technically a merger, for regulatory reasons Air France-KLM (as the new company is to be known) is more like a 'unified' alliance. Indeed, full mergers have thus far tended to founder because of fears on the part of the airlines involved of losing certain entitlements to fly particular routes and some of their prized airport landing slots if their national flag-carrier status is ceded. This new 'merger' has managed to work around such legislation through the adoption of a highly complicated organisational structure in which KLM's Dutch identity will be protected. In essence, KLM has become an 'independent' subsidiary of the Air France-KLM holding company. Numerous airlines have spent months and even years trying to conclude similar deals, but this represents the first really 'big' deal which, overnight, is set to create Europe's biggest airline. However, it is a very

	oneworld	Aer Lingus	American Airlines	BRITISH AIRWAYS	CATHAY PACIFIC	FINNAIR	IBERIA	LANCHILE	QANTAS
Destinations	563	32	243	223	42	51	101	47	75
Countries/Territories	136	13	49	94	25	27	40	19	16
Daily departures	8,509	148	4,519	1,385	140	253	984	237	843
Passengers (m)	227.5	7	125	39.6	11.2	6.2	25.2	5.2	20.2
Employees	254,421	5,635	105,500	49,988**	14,500	9,425	26,200	10,173	33,000
Fleet (operated)	1,974	33	1,098	320	78	60	146	50	189
Operating revenue (m)	–	€958	US$17,229	£8,340*	HK$33,090	€1,640	€4,690	US$1,428	A$11,319
Operating expenses (m)	–	€894.2	US$20,629	£8,450*	HK$28,340	€1,580	€4,441	US$1,378	A$10,691
Operating profit (m)	–	€63.8	–US$3,300	–£110*	HK$4,750	€60.0	€249	US$50	A$631
Frequent flyer programme	Yes	TAB (Travel Award Bonus)	AADVANTAGE	Executive Club	Asia Miles	Finnair Plus	Iberia Plus	LanPass	Qantas Frequent Flyer
Airport lounges	Yes	Gold Circle Club	Admirals Club and Flagship Lounges	Executive Club, Concorde, First, and Club World/Club Europe	Cathay Pacific First and Business	Golden Gate, Silver Wings, Long haul lounge, Domestic lounge, Finnair Lounge (ARN)	Salas VIP	Salon VIP	Qantas Club, First and Business
Number of lounges	More than 380	10	50	222	50	55	75	17	52
Chief Executive	Peter Buecking	Willie Walsh	Gerard Arpey	Rod Eddington	David Turnbull	Keijo Suila	Xabier de Irala	Enrique Cueto Plaza	Geoff Dixon
Headquarters	Vancouver, Canada	Dublin, Ireland	Fort Worth, Texas, USA	London, UK	Hong Kong	Helsinki-Vantaa, Finland	Madrid, Spain	Santiago, Chile	Sydney, New South Wales, Australia
Year of formation	1999	1936	Traces its origins back to 1926	Traces its origins back to 1919	1946	1923	1927	1929	1920
Ownership	100% owned by its member airlines	95% owned by the Irish Government. 5% owned by employees	Wholly owned subsidiary of AMR Corporation, which is a publicly traded company on the New York Stock Exchange	Publicly quoted company, with shares traded on the London and New York Stock Exchanges	Public company listed on the Hong Kong and London Stock Exchanges. Major shareholders are Swire Pacific Ltd (45.1%) and CITIC Pacific Ltd (25.4%)	Publicly quoted on Helsinki Stock Exchange and in SEAQ system on the London Stock Exchange. Finnish Government is majority shareholder with 59%	9% owned by British Airways, 1% by American Airlines, 30% by institutions, 60% floated on Madrid Stock Exchange	Publicly traded company, with 5.4% traded on the New York Stock Exchange, and 11.4% traded on the Santiago Stock Exchange in Chile. Majority shareholders hold the remaining 83.2% of the Company	Public company listed on the Australian Stock Exchange. British Airways is a major shareholder with 19.491%
Website address	www.oneworld.com	www.aerlingus.com	www.aa.com and www.amrcorp.com	www.british airways.com	www.cathay pacific.com	www.finnair.com	www.iberia.com	www.lanchile.com	www.qantas.com.au
Related carriers	–	–	American Eagle, AmericanConnection, TWA LLC	BA CitiExpress, British Mediterranean, Comair, GB Airways, Loganair, Maersk Air Ltd, Regional Air, Sun-Air	–	–	Air Nostrum	LanExpress, LanPeru	QantasLink: Airconnex, Airlink, Eastern Australia Airlines, Southern Australia Airlines, Sunstate Airlines

Table 8.3 Composition of estimated cost savings from contrasting airline alliance structures (percentages of cost base)

Alliance type	*Finance and utilisation saving*	*Airline operation saving*	*External saving*	*Total saving*
Co-ordination	0.1	0.8	1.0	1.9
Sharing	0.7	2.3	2.6	5.6
Unification	2.6	5.2	3.6	11.4

Source: Adapted from Howarth and Kirsebom, 1999, as featured in Morley, 2003

bold initiative, and not without risk in so far as the belief still remains that mergers of large international airlines are very difficult to achieve successfully. The previous failed merger attempts between BA and KLM, and BA and American Airlines, are testament to the veracity of problem. This said, British Airways is currently in talks to create a 'unified' alliance with Swiss, the airline created out of the demise of Swissair two years ago (Nissé, 2003a). Not only would Swiss join the Oneworld alliance but it is also its intention to apply to the European Commission for 'antitrust immunity' for an alliance to share routes, landing rights and facilities. BA already has such a deal with Qantas and has applied to the Commission for a similar deal with Iberia. Significantly, the deal is likely to rest on Swiss agreeing to substantial cuts in staffing and the number of long-haul aircraft it operates. However, with the airline running up a considerable deficit, this medicine may be the only remedy.

Commentators argue that the current merger between Air France and KLM is likely to be beset with considerable challenges, not least due to the major differences that exist in respect of corporate and national cultures. However, in order to accommodate both airlines' wishes, the

Figure 8.1 Oneworld alliance statistics

Source: www.oneworldalliance.com/pressroom/section_data/facts/ F000cd01.doc (accessed 23 May 2003)

Notes: All figures are for main airline and related carriers covered by the *Oneworld* agreement. All financial figures are for the most recent fiscal year. Operating figures are the latest published.
* Figures do not include BA non-owned franchise airlines. Include exceptional items.
** Excludes BA CitiExpress.

two airlines are to retain their own brands. With combined revenues of €19 billion, the two airlines are planning cost savings of a mere €600 million. In view of the structure of the deal, it is perhaps understandable that the cost savings will be limited. For example, the group will retain both Paris' Charles de Gaulle airport and Amsterdam's Schiphol as hubs, along with all their associated costs. In addition, despite the fact that both airlines have considerably large staff numbers, no redundancies are planned of a compulsory nature. Partly driven by the heavy union presence in both airlines, this fact alone will make it very difficult indeed for Air France-KLM to achieve the necessary cost savings that served as the catalyst for the negotiations that led to their merger in the first instance. The fact that both airlines use different types of aircraft serves as a further impediment to the joint company achieving substantial cost savings.

Early predictions are that the anticipated outcomes of the Air France-KLM initiative are over-optimistic, despite the fact that the opportunity to save costs was clearly one of the key drivers. One particular challenge will be the difficulties in separating assets and appropriating resources equitably. There is, however, likely to be one clear beneficiary in the deal – the SkyTeam alliance – for it has clearly strengthened its market standing against the other two major airline alliances: Oneworld and Star Alliance. Significantly, Delta Airlines of the US is a key member of SkyTeam. With KLM's long-established partnership with Northwest Airlines, which in turn has a separate marketing alliance with Delta and Continental (again of the US), there is a strong chance that all four airlines will end up in SkyTeam and therefore serve as a significant competitive threat to both Oneworld and Star Alliance. This is particularly significant due to the fact that antitrust regulators have discouraged full mergers because of the dominance of each airline at its regional hub in the US.

One further distinction between alliance types is again provided by Morley (2003): namely the extent to which the alliance is 'complementary' or 'parallel' in nature with regard to their networks and services. For example, a 'complementary' alliance is where carriers have separate, non-overlapping route networks and connections and feed traffic to each other. A parallel alliance, on the other hand, involves airlines that were competitors on important routes prior to the alliance. In this case, competition can often be reduced as a consequence, with cartel-like behaviour taking place, usually to the detriment of the consumer. Both complementary and parallel aspects are evident in all three of the big three global airline alliances, albeit to varying degrees.

In conclusion, although there remains talk of a so-called 'open-skies' deal, in which airlines' nationalities would become less important, negotiations remain at a very early stage and are likely to go on for years rather than months. In the interim, developments of the Air France-KLM nature are likely to continue as is the strengthening of existing alliance groupings.

Case Study: Star Alliance – The Collaborative Strategy Process

In order to shed light on the collaborative strategy process for international airline alliances, Figure 8.2 is put forward as a possible analytical framework. This framework, first proposed by Evans (2001), will serve as a lens through which Star Alliance will be examined in depth.

Introduction

Launched in May 1997 as the first truly global airline alliance, Star Alliance today comprises Air Canada, Air New Zealand, All Nippon Airways (ANA), Asiana Airlines of Korea, Austrian Airlines Group, British Midlands International (bmi), Lauda Air, LOT Polish Airlines, Lufthansa, Mexicana, SAS Scandinavian Airlines System (SAS), Singapore Airlines, Spanair, Thai Airways International, Tyrolean Airways, United Airlines and Varig. Star Alliance is widely considered to be the most advanced alliance of its type, and has a vast array of products and services within its domain, as evidenced in Box 8.2.

Table 8.4 demonstrates that, across most criteria, Star Alliance is the clear market leader: although it must be emphasised that these statistics exclude the current 'merger' between Air France and KLM, and the knock-on effects for SkyTeam, due to the recent nature of these events. Recent awards include 'Best Airline Alliance' in 2002 by *Business Traveler Magazine* and the 'World's Leading Airline Alliance' at the Ninth Annual World Travel Awards, 2002.

Strategic context

With regard to Star Alliance's sense of corporate purpose, its mission and vision statements leave for little ambiguity. Its mission is clear in that it exists to contribute to the long-term profitability of its members beyond their individuality. The key role of the alliance is to facilitate co-operation and integration of member airlines while allowing them to make economies and retain their individual identities wherever possible. Although the focus of the alliance will doubtless change

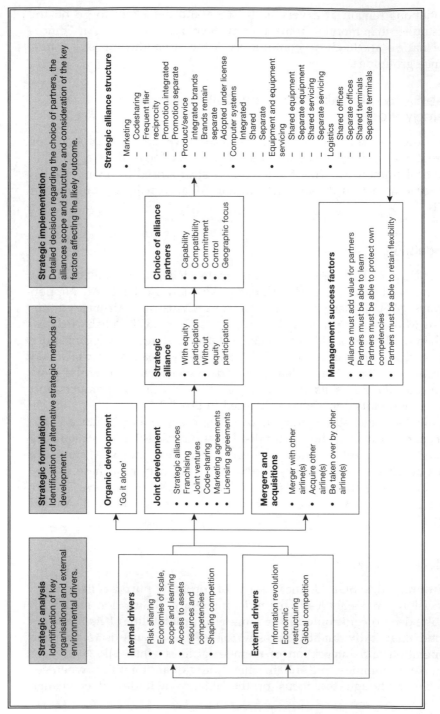

Figure 8.2 The collaborative strategy process for international airlines

Source: After Evans, 2001

Box 8.2 Star Alliance: Key benefits, 2002

- Twelve principal airlines serving over 729 destinations in 124 countries.
- Co-ordinated timetables for smooth transfer between partner airlines.
- Extensive codesharing.
- With certain exceptions, the ability to earn and redeem bonus points in the Star Alliance members' respective loyalty programmes.
- Special airport services for passengers with 'Star Priority' (confirmation from waiting lists, baggage check-in, etc.).
- Access to some 500 lounges worldwide.
- All of the alliance's timetables and routes are available in all major electronic reservation systems.
- Star Alliance 'Round the World' fares and Star Alliance 'Airpasses' for travel in Europe, Asia/Pacific, North America, Mexico and Brazil.
- StarAlliance.com, a website with information and links to member airlines' reservation services.
- Star Alliance Convention Plus, a product programme designed for conference organisers and participants.
- Joint ticket offices in selected major cities.
- Joint service functions at selected airports (ticket office, check-in, lounges, etc.).
- 'Star Connection Teams' to assist passengers in making connections at selected airports.
- Improvements in checking through baggage to final destinations.
- Joint development of ICT infrastructure and new alliance-wide products and services.
- A joint training programme in functional and cultural areas for employees of member airlines who work with customers.
- Close co-operation in the areas of safety and the environment.

Source: SAS, 2002

---

over time, its vision is bold in that it states that Star Alliance is to be the leading global airline alliance for the frequent international traveller. At the current moment in time this vision holds true, with the alliance spanning 729 destinations in 124 countries with over 2000 aircraft. Star Alliance is a true market leader with global market presence.

Table 8.4 Key figures for Star Alliance 2001/2002

	Passengers/ year (million)	Destinations	Countries	Aircraft	Daily departures	RPK (billion)	Annual operating revenue (US$ billion)	Employees
Air Canada	23.1	160	26	328	1583	67.0	6.9	40,000
Air New Zealand	7.8	46	15	88	477	22.4	3.4	9500
All Nippon Airways	43.0	54	9	139	610	51.6	9.4	13,000
Austrian Airlines Group	7.2	125	67	94	397	14.2	2.0	7700
British Midlands International	6.7	23	10	53	273	4.3	1.2	4,800
Lufthansa	43.9	327	89	280	1640	90.9	16.7	32,000
Mexicana	8.3	53	10	59	348	13.1	1.4	6500
Scandinavian Airlines	22.1	86	33	199	810	23.6	3.8	7556

Singapore Airlines	14.8	64	37	92	204	69.1	4.6	14,000
Thai Airways International	18.6	77	35	81	271	45.2	2.9	26,000
United Airlines	75.0	117	26	559	3695	187.6	16.1	84,000
Varig	10.5	136	19	85	385	26.0	2.6	16,900
Star Alliance	**281.0**	**729**	**124**	**2057**	**10,700**	**615.0**	**71.0**	**261,956**
Oneworld	187.0	568	135	1504	8600	426.20	42.2	273,495
SkyTeam	207.0	507	112	1324	7600	352.8	36.6	186,051
KLM/Northwest Airlines	70.0	306	64	916	3000	175.6	15.9	78,973

Source: SAS, 2002

Note: RPK refers to Revenue Passenger Kilometres, this being the number of paying passengers multiplied by the distance they are flown in kilometres.

Strategic analysis

Both external and internal pressures are such that all international airlines are experiencing hard economic times after a run of two or three years of terrorist atrocities, economic gloom, union pressure and the short- and long-term financial costs of a major shortfall in pension products leaving many airlines with a significant hole in their finances. Under such circumstances it is more important than ever that alliances such as Star Alliance focus on bringing bottom-line benefits to member airlines beyond their individual capabilities. The fact that alliances offer considerable opportunity to increase revenue and measures to derive cost efficiencies goes a long way to sustain their popularity as strategic vehicles for effectively managing turbulence in the marketplace. Identified as an 'inevitable result of the regulatory framework within which the international airline industry operates [where] regulatory and legal restrictions often prevent the full ownership of airlines by foreign companies' (Evans, 2001: 239), alliances are clearly the only viable market entry mechanism for the foreseeable future. According to Jaan Albrecht, Chief Executive of Star Alliance, if individual members had:

> continued to operate as separate airlines, the loss of feeder traffic would have forced them to scale back their networks in a much more drastic way. Global airline alliances offer a depth of market penetration that has allowed the participating airlines to reduce frequencies and destinations to a much lesser degree than otherwise would have been necessary. (staralliance.com, 2003)

Evans, meanwhile, offers a contrasting viewpoint, which is that alliances represent 'unstable and transitory forms of organisation, a "second-best" solution that is disturbingly likely to break up under commercial pressure' (Evans, 2001: 239). No evidence exists to date in the external environment to suggest that this is likely to happen, although the current difficulties being faced by United Airlines, the largest individual airline within Star Alliance, does provide some cause for concern. In the autumn of 2002, United Airlines was forced to seek 'Chapter 11' bankruptcy protection in the US. To date, largely due to the fact that United continues to provide services much as before, no damage has been done to the alliance. However, the situation could deteriorate rapidly if United were to fail to recover and exit the alliance (aviationnow.com, 2003). Although Star Alliance is rumoured to be preparing a rescue package for United Airlines, aid in the form of loans is in reality more likely to come from Lufthansa and Air Canada, who, fearful for the future of an alliance without United, may be willing to bail the airline out. This having been said, a recent agreement between Lufthansa and United has gone a long way towards alleviating the problem. This involves the two airlines transforming their transatlantic alliance into a joint venture-like operation that is expected to contribute US$90 million annually to the carrier's revenues. Individually, United Airlines has a number of recovery strategy initiatives it is hoping to implement to reverse its fortunes. According to Glenn Tilton, Chief Executive of United Airlines, it is hoped that United will:

- Maintain its current hub system (Chicago, Denver, Washington Dulles, San Francisco and Los Angeles).
- Strengthen the Star Alliance with its foreign alliance partners. United clearly acknowledges that the alliance is bringing passengers into its domestic airline system. If anything, more connections are needed rather than fewer.
- Reduce operating costs which are acknowledged as being among the highest in the industry.
- Make all flights profitable. Currently 30% are unprofitable, most of these related to flights to and from non-hub airports.
- Create a new entity that will provide low-cost services that successfully compete with other low-cost carriers such as Jet Blue and Southwest in the US.
- Withdraw full-service flights from non-hub routes (staralliance.com, 2003).

As well as United Airlines, Varig of Brazil is also experiencing considerable financial difficulty at the time of writing. Although less substantial than the problems United is facing, the difficulty is such that it is calling upon the sense of collective 'team spirit' that has been such a strong feature of Star Alliance since its conception over six years ago. In that time, Star Alliance has gone to incredible lengths to protect its members. As well as providing support to Air Canada to prevent a takeover attempt, it is currently offering to do the same for Thai Airways International in order to keep the struggling airline in the alliance.

On a different note, there are also worries about the position of Air New Zealand. Now that Qantas, a member of the Oneworld alliance, owns a share of Air New Zealand, there is a real chance that Air New Zealand will 'switch' alliances. Although this is unlikely to happen for a while due to the very integrated nature of Star Alliance, it is not expected that both Qantas and Air New Zealand will remain in competing alliances in the longer term. This represents a perfect example of how individual competitive activity can impact significantly on alliance membership and ultimately on alliance success.

In spite of these internal worries, there is little doubt that all members of Star Alliance continue to benefit greatly from alliance membership. For example, membership in Star Alliance is highly advantageous for SAS, particularly with regard to higher revenues gained from partners' passengers feeding into the network. Since the launch of Star Alliance, additional passengers and revenues have risen by 60% for SAS. In 2002, this 'interline revenue' accounted for 10% of the group's total passenger revenues in 2002. In the same period, passenger traffic added from SAS to the other Star Alliance members grew by nearly 60% (SAS, 2002).

Strategy formulation

There can be little doubt that, in the world of international airlines, most airlines, whether willingly or as a matter of last resort, accept that alliances are the only choice. Of course it can be argued that the benefits of alliances can probably be achieved more completely and efficiently through mergers and acquisitions. However, unless the regulatory and legal restrictions are lifted to make such strategies possible, alliances will remain the 'next best alternative' for the foreseeable future.

This having been said, alliances in general can grow and are growing organically. There is also evidence to suggest that alliances will collaborate with other alliances or alliance partners when circumstances are deemed suitable and the rewards sufficiently attractive. One particular competitive threat to all airline alliances is the emergence in recent years of very robust and dynamic 'no-frills' entrants into the domestic and international airline markets. While the large, predominantly former national-flag carriers have been busy collaborating, the likes of Easyjet and Ryanair in the UK have taken the initiative and recast the ground rules of competition in a number of markets and on particular key routes. The response from alliances has been further differentiation and an expansion of the products and services on offer. Some individual airlines, however, have taken the competitive battle head-on with the launch of their own 'no-frills' carriers: bmibaby being the very successful response from bmi with more than 700,000 passengers carried in the first nine months of operation. In 2002, bmi reported a record growth in passenger numbers and an improved operating performance in what they described as an exceptionally tough trading environment for the airline industry (bmi, 2003). Much of this success is attributed to the new segmentation strategy which saw the launch of the 'no-frills' subsidiary. This initiative alone improved the major indicators of economic efficiency for the group, with a 30% improvement in passengers carried per employee and a 20% reduction in overhead costs per available seat kilometre.

One of the principal decisions for those wishing to pursue alliance strategies is whether to adopt 'with-equity' or 'without-equity' models. Star Alliance is an equity alliance in that the company is fully owned by its members. This is true also of the competing Oneworld and SkyTeam alliances. The extent to which such 'with-equity' models survive in the longer term is open to debate however. The loyalty and commitment of alliance partners is crucial for success, the outcome of the Air New Zealand–Qantas–Oneworld scenario perhaps setting a precedent for the rest of the industry to follow. The other option available is the model adopted by Air France and KLM. However, the somewhat muted response from other airlines, and the distinctly cool response from the stock market, suggests that currently a nervous 'knee-jerk' response may not be desirable.

As mentioned earlier in the chapter, Star Alliance is widely regarded to be the most advanced airline alliance with regard to its sharing of strategy and operations. The question now is how to take the project forward. According to Jaan Albrecht, Chief Executive of Star Alliance, the alliance has 'achieved a level of maturity that allows it to concentrate on the deeper integration of the member airlines, including the realisation of cost savings' (TAI, 2003b: 53). However, the possibility of future new partners has not been written off, assuming they have a culture, management style and geographical coverage that are compatible with Star Alliance. One potential future partner is Emirates, the Dubai-based Middle Eastern airline. Although the airline is making noises to the effect that it does not wish to join an alliance, preferring instead to rely on bilateral agreements, it is clear that Emirates represents a key target for Star Alliance, as it does for Oneworld and SkyTeam. The huge amount of tourism-related investment in and around Dubai in recent years has contributed to Emirates being one of the few airlines continuing to grow rapidly post-9/11. Its geographic location is also of interest in that it represents a convenient 'stop-over' destination in the Middle East for airlines wishing to connect with carriers to Southeast Asia, the Far East and Australasia.

Strategy implementation

Organisational structure and maturity are viewed as the principal competitive advantages for Star Alliance in comparison to its competitors, in that 'one carrier – one vote' brings the openness, transparency and level playing field deemed necessary to cultivate a culture of effective collaboration. More importantly, the conditions are right for the development of trust. The alliance has an Alliance Management Board (AMB), a body which oversees all alliance activities on behalf of the 16 member airlines, which is currently chaired by Graham Atkinson, Senior Vice-President, Worldwide Sales and Alliances, United Airlines. Although one senior member from each of the carriers makes up AMB, bmi does in fact have two seats due to the unique way in which the company is structured (the chairman actually owns the company and remains actively involved in its running). There exists a local Star Alliance

Steering Council in each country, while Star Alliance Services GmbH, formed in 2002, and which again is jointly owned by the alliance partners, serves as the organisational vehicle for product development, marketing and administration. It is based in Frankfurt.

Marketing, products and services

One of Star Alliance's particular qualities is its ability to remain innovative in the face of considerable competition and economic pressures. It has, in fact, been responsible for establishing many firsts among global airline alliances. For example, May 2002 saw the launch of Star Alliance Conventions Plus – a highly flexible, tailor-made, conference travel solution. Responding to a burgeoning demand in the market, Star Alliance was the first airline alliance to offer a product exclusively targeting conference travel. Two years before, Star Alliance introduced its first global television advertising campaign aimed at enhancing the brand image among business travellers. Launched globally in pan-regional efforts in Europe, the Asia-Pacific and Latin America, the media strategy focused on channels that reached international business travellers while *en route* and included integrated TV campaigns, direct mail and Internet campaigns. Before that, in October 1999, Star achieved another alliance first by developing a global Internet tool which enabled travellers to book seats on any alliance member's flight through a personal computer or laptop. One further example relates to the launch of a CRS alliance display in July 1999 that enables intermediaries to check schedules and availability of Star Alliance flights in a single display that shows only member airline direct flights and connections for a chosen itinerary. This innovative display allows the Star Alliance network to build brand awareness and enhance the level of customer service worldwide.

The development of the Star Alliance brand is central to the development of the alliance, with the consistent promotion of the brand through a variety of channels being one of the alliance's most important attributes. In accordance with its mission and vision, the Star Alliance brand reads as 'Star Alliance, The Airline Network for Earth'. One of the principal channels for the development of the brand are the aircraft themselves. In March 2003, Asiana Airlines became the first airline to showcase the new livery, with the Star Alliance name painted in bold letters across a white fuselage and the familiar alliance logo fully covering the vertical stabiliser. The aircraft will thus serve as a flying billboard on Asiana's extensive route network. Eventually, the new livery is to be adopted by all alliance partners with at least one aircraft donning the new livery to begin with, and a rolling programme being co-ordinated thereafter in line with scheduled maintenance or repair, or delivery of new aircraft. This has important implications for branding as the operating carrier will be identified by its own logo located on the forward part of the aircraft fuselage below the Star Alliance name (TAI, 2003a). The rationale behind such a move is that it will go a long way towards enhancing the visibility and awareness of the brand and serve as a catalyst for further brand development opportunities.

There is little doubt, however, that development of the Star Alliance brand remains at an early stage. Although there appears agreement as to how the new livery should be used, the extent to which each individual airline is aware of how the combined brand names (for example Star Alliance and Lufthansa) increase the 'combined' value, or potentially damage one of the partners, is unclear (Schreiber, 2002). In short, the question is, to what extent does becoming part of the wider alliance's brand 'ecosystem' have value? Brand values, as identified in Chapter 3, can be either tangible or intangible. The tangible benefits of alliance membership appear very clear. What perhaps is less certain after six years of operation is the extent to which the more intangible elements of the brand, such as alliance culture, service delivery and service quality, have yet to permeate all elements of the domain brand.

One of the main causes of conflict among alliances seems to have been avoided in the case of Star Alliance in that problems often arise when most organisations wish to be lead or strategic brands. Hill and Lederer (2001) suggest that discussion needs to take place in operating the alliance so that partners are clear which brand in the alliance is the lead brand, which is the strategic brand and which are supporting brands. In essence, this is the same as the problem of deregulation versus consolidation, in that most airlines are in favour of consolidation so long as their airline is one of the consolidators. To assist alliance partners, Schreiber (2002) proposes the Brand Get–Give Analysis where:

Brand Value of Partnership = (Get divided by Give)
× Knowledge + Intangibles

This approach suggests that the value of collaboration to a company's brand is based upon what one can get from the potential relationship and what one must give up to get these things of value. Schreiber goes on to argue that 'win-win' situations are not always the most suitable approach and that understanding domain 'value' collaboration is the key. With the focus of most airline alliances on cost and efficiency gains, it is perhaps understandable that branding is often considered as an afterthought. This is demonstrated by Star Alliance in that, while it is very well advanced as an airline alliance, serious branding developments are only now beginning to take shape – six years after the alliance was launched.

One of the principal marketing benefits of Star Alliance is the reciprocal relationship in existence between all partners' FFPs, where points can be redeemed by each airline in the alliance. The Star Alliance network makes this process easier and quicker, in that not only can the customer earn and redeem points and air miles across the whole network, but every flight taken counts towards higher status in the individual partners' FFPs. Although each programme provides unique and valuable benefits, when travellers reach status levels in the individual airlines' FFPs, they are eligible for the equivalent Star Alliance status level. With Star Alliance Gold or Star Alliance Silver status, travellers then receive additional worldwide travel benefits. Prior to August 2002, award tickets could only combine two Star Alliance members at the most. The current transparent and 'fully integrated' nature of the alliance-wide programme offers travellers considerable benefits, particularly with regard to convenience and flexibility. By eliminating the need to use two or more award tickets to reach certain destinations, Star Alliance Awards have in some cases also reduced the total number of air miles required for award travel to those destinations. An 'Around-the-World' award is also now available within most Star Alliance Awards charts. The approach adopted by Star Alliance towards FFPs is typical of its approach to all aspects of the alliance, in that it encourages each partner airline to maintain its own FFP while giving customers the chance to take full advantage of the entire Star Alliance network, thus adding flexibility (staralliance.com, 2003).

Computer systems and equipment

One area where Star Alliance really does demonstrate its 'sharing' culture is with regard to its computer systems and equipment. For example, to improve the FFP award ticket-booking process, as introduced above, Star Alliance developed an alliance-wide computer function that enables its member airlines to book available seats in 'real time' on all other Star Alliance airlines. The function, called Redemption Availability and Sell (RAS), creates an alliance-wide ability to deliver faster award bookings and more flexibility in the choice of available flights.

A further example applies to procurement and the use of collective buying power. This is best demonstrated by the signing of an agreement in April 2003 with Novell Inc. This arrangement represents a new strategic sourcing relationship, where benefits of joint procurement for all alliance partners and sophisticated information and identity management solutions are on offer. While the need to source independently of other airlines in the alliance makes economic sense on most occasions, the collective relationship with Novell Inc. is likely to generate substantial cost savings for the individual airlines within Star Alliance. This is a clear example of how the dynamics of Porter's Five Forces model have changed as a consequence of collaboration. Whereas before the global airline alliances came into being the balance of power probably existed with the suppliers to the international airline industry, the formation of these mega-alliances has tipped the balance of power in favour of the airlines through the collective buying power of alliances.

In addition to alliance-wide sourcing, Star Alliance intends to deploy a Novell Nsure secure identity management solution to enhance and improve information flow and security across its information techno-logy backbone known as StarNet. Originally launched in September 2000, StarNet links all member carriers and allows information exchange. Interestingly, Lufthansa is a prime contractor, although an open tender-ing process did occur. In essence, StarNet represents a common ICT infrastructure that links together all the separate computer networks of the Star Alliance member carriers. The network provides real-time access to information and enables improved customer servicing across the entire alliance. The Novell Nsure secure identity management solution provides Star Alliance with the power to provide secure ICT integration across the alliance, while allowing each of the member airlines to continue leveraging the technologies and investments they already have in place. The Novell solution is intended to provide Star Alliance with a cost-effective solution that will allow controlled access to network information across multiple platforms without compromising security. Collectively, it is believed that the financial savings alone of centralised systems could amount to millions of US dollars (staralliance.com, 2003).

More recently, Star Alliance signed an agreement with Rockwell Collins, a global leader in aviation electronics. This further development is aimed at standardising and simplifying the member airlines' fleets in order to reduce capital requirement and maintenance costs (staral-liance.com, 2003). Again, it demonstrates the commitment of Star Alliance to maximising the benefits of alliance membership for its partner airlines. This search for benefit maximisation and cost reductions is also evidenced by the move by Star Alliance to scrutinise all aspects of operations. For example, where outside contractors are currently involved, perhaps in ground handling, contracts are to be reviewed and where feasible replaced by a Star Alliance member organisation undertaking the contract on behalf of all Star Alliance members. Cost savings are clearly a major rationale, as is the desire to seek continuity of service, preferably within the alliance itself. Further cost-saving measures currently under explo-ration include establishing locations where access can be made available to facilities owned by member airlines at airports. Where possible, the actual number of facilities will be reduced in order to offer a superior alliance-wide product. These developments alone are testament to the sense of energy and drive behind the expansion and further improve-ment of the operational aspects of Star Alliance.

Management success factors

Understandably, it is a strategic imperative that the alliance must add value for partners. Similarly, partner airlines must be able to learn continuously from each other, be able to protect and potentially exploit their own competencies – as in the case of Lufthansa and its pivotal role in StarNet – and, when necessary, be able to retain individual 'strategic flexibility'. This latter point is particularly relevant to the development of Star Alliance in that within the wider alliance a number of partners have particularly close working relationships with each other – almost alliances within the alliance. For example, Lufthansa is clearly Scandinavian Airlines' most important and valuable partner in that it delivers approximately 60% of all Scandinavian's interline revenue (SAS, 2002). Moreover, SAS reciprocates with Lufthansa by roughly the same percentage. In addition, the airlines represent one another in their home markets, with co-ordinated marketing and sales activity. Passenger service at airports, aircraft maintenance, technical services and a certain level of co-ordination in aircraft fleet development and joint purchases are other areas of co-operation which benefit both the individual airlines and Star Alliance more generally.

Scandinavian Airlines also participates in the European Cooperation Agreement (ECA) with Lufthansa and bmi. The aim of the ECA is to create a competitive intra-European traffic system through the integration of the three airlines' route networks within the European Economic Area (EEA) to and from London Heathrow and Manchester airports in the UK (SAS, 2002). Approved by the European Commission for a period of eight years until the end of 2007, the ECA is struggling to create a profitable return, principally due to the numerous negative external pressures impacting on travel post-9/11. Although not as yet highly profitable, the existence of the ECA demonstrates the ability of partner airlines to work collectively with other airlines within the wider alliance.

The ability to retain some degree of strategic flexibility outside the wider alliance is something that nearly all partner airlines benefit from within Star Alliance. For example, Scandinavian Airlines operate a network of co-operative agreements outside the principal alliance with a number of often much smaller national and regional players. At the current point in time, SAS co-operates with the likes of airBaltic in Latvia, Skyways in Sweden and Cimber Air in Denmark; the purpose being to extend their overall network to routes where they would not normally make a profitable return. Other partners include Maersk Air, Estonian Air, Icelandair and Air Greenland (SAS, 2002). Similarly, Singapore Airlines has an equity partnership with Virgin Atlantic. This is achieved through mutual airline growth, such as complementary route networks, high service standards, excellent brands, a more extensive FFP presence, the availability of more passenger lounges and airport facilities for passengers to utilise and growth for trade and tourism in the region (singaporeair.com, 2003).

One very interesting development relates to the recent development of Opodo – a pan-European 'independent' company owned by nine of Europe's leading airlines. What is in effect an online travel service designed to counter the competitive threat from traditional tourism intermediaries, Opodo represents a cross-alliance development in that representatives of all three main global airline alliances are involved in the initiative. For example, Air France (SkyTeam), British Airways (Oneworld) and Lufthansa (Star Alliance) each hold a 22.8% interest in the company, with Alitalia (SkyTeam), Iberia (Oneworld) and KLM each holding a 9.14% interest, and Aer Lingus and Finnair (Oneworld) and Austrian (Star Alliance) owning the rest. Opodo has been launched with the deliberate aim of becoming the European leader of online travel purchases and regaining influence of the traditional and e-travel agents, with the German, British, French and Italian markets the primary targets. Although the concept is proving very popular, the cross-connections between airlines from the three key global airline alliances adds an interesting dynamic to the development of inter-organisational collaboration among international airlines. This is particularly so when one considers aspects of trust, commitment, information provision and accessibility, and the unification of systems and IT networks to facilitate the project's development. This having been said, this demonstration of 'horizontal' inter-organisational collaboration enables the airlines to compete with some very strong Internet players and enables the airlines to obtain external economies of scale in production, and power in purchasing or distribution in an environment which is intensely competitive.

Conclusion

There is little doubt that there remain considerable challenges on the competitive horizon both for Star Alliance specifically and for airline alliances more generally. Nor is there any great doubt that, for the foreseeable future at least, strategic alliances are likely to 'continue to be a dominant feature of business strategy within the international airline industry' (Evans, 2001: 241). Indeed, this viewpoint is shared by Morley (2003: 48), who states that 'airline alliances have proved to be a major feature of international airlines' responses to the need to change their ways of operating in an industry which is still heavily governed by regulatory constraints'. Morley continues by stating that alliances are clearly likely to continue in the short term, although the threat of unexpected and innovative responses remains a distinct possibility. One threat on the horizon is that greater scrutiny is likely to be a permanent feature of alliances in that international regulators will continue to explore the complex web of internal activity that is global airline alliances.

Although existing global alliances are not necessarily in a stable or final form, new alliances are unlikely in that most of the principal airlines are already firmly established in such structures. This is not to say, however, that opportunities for switching are unlikely to occur. This is particularly pertinent in respect of the situation facing Air New Zealand of Star Alliance and its growing relationship with Qantas, a key member of the competing Oneworld alliance. If 'switching' does begin to establish itself as a strategy, there is a strong prospect that it will serve as a catalyst for an alliance 'arms race'. This view is adopted by Hamel (1991), who considers competing airline alliances to be in a 'race to learn in which the winner will eventually establish dominance in the partnership thereby leading to instability' (cited in Evans, 2001: 36). If this were to occur, it is clear that collaboration in the context of international airlines is really just competition in a different form. The extreme outcome of such a scenario is that one large 'mega'-alliance will reign supreme in the global market for air travel, doubtless accompanied by a monopoly-induced increase in prices to travellers. The alternative, and perhaps more realistic outcome, in the medium term at least, is that lower fares will result from further integration and cost efficiencies gained by alliances and the greater competition that will arise from increasing competition between the various alliances and between alliances and other airlines, in particular the low-cost carriers. Irrespective of which scenario comes to fruition, the most likely marketing outcome is that the alliances themselves will become the 'umbrella brands' with the individual airlines becoming 'sub-brands' of the wider collaborative domain.

The recent Air France-KLM initiative is clearly one that requires considerable scrutiny over the coming months and years. Indeed, if greater liberalisation of the regulatory structure is to occur, then other international airlines, especially the likes of Lufthansa and British Airways, may be encouraged to adopt a similar strategic response. If this should happen, codesharing could become but a distant memory, with airlines moving towards strategies of merger and acquisition. According to Morley (2003: 48) 'airlines are likely to be encouraged in this direction, when allowed, by the potential economies of scale and scope, and by a belief that they will be able to learn from and overcome the difficulties experienced in cross-national mergers in other industries'.

One final comment relates to the distinction between complementary and parallel alliances. Whereas complementary alliances are not widely believed to impact negatively on competition and clearly improve the airlines' economies, the same viewpoint is not generally held for parallel alliances. With parallel alliances, there is sufficient evidence available to discourage them in that they can have a severe impact on competition, with fewer flights, reduced service levels and less traffic a very real possibility. It is these alliances that will serve as the greatest threat to market harmony and will clearly raise alarm bells for anti-competitive agencies. They are thus to be discouraged if the integrity of airline alliances as an effective 'customer-friendly' inter-organisational form is to continue.

Chapter 9
Hotel Consortia

Introduction

Like the wider tourism industry in which it is situated, the hotel industry is complex, fragmented and highly competitive, and over recent decades has witnessed tremendous growth. Through a combination of acquisitions, mergers and various forms of collaboration, a great deal of consolidation and concentration has taken place across the industry, to the extent that the 10 largest chains of hotels now account for well over 3 million rooms. On the other hand, this represents less than one-fifth of the total world supply, with only 26% of all hotel rooms being marketed under the brand names of the top 50 global companies (WTO, 2002). The vast majority of the hotel industry therefore remains under independent ownership, although the scale and reach of independents varies enormously (Roper, 1995).

It is widely acknowledged among independent hotel operators that working in isolation from one another is becoming ever less tenable as a strategy. For example, independents of all kinds are now more than ever before finding their own competitive strategies being influenced by those of large corporate chains, especially in terms of the proliferation of market opportunities provided by global distribution systems and the seemingly infinite capabilities of the Internet. In particular, independent hotels are increasingly coming under threat as a result of the 'marketing muscle, the technology to attract customers and the operational efficiencies to generate profit' of the major chains (Weinstein, 2001: 5).

Arguably, in this mature and highly competitive marketplace, the key to prosperity for independent hotels – many of which are very small in comparison to the ever more global markets in which they are operating – is growth and greater visibility. These two strategies will afford independents greater market penetration and increased geographic market coverage, and will afford them greater opportunities for destination marketing and the benefits to be derived from economies of scale

260

(Dev & Klein, 1993). Recognising this, independents continue to pursue new ways of increasing their market shares. They are cognisant that, with the globalisation of the industry and worldwide advances in technology, staying visible and increasing profitability necessitates the use of sophisticated marketing support expertise and global technology, as well as access to wider national and even international markets. All this must be achieved in a way that maximises market opportunities while ensuring the most effective representation in the marketplace at minimum transaction costs (Morrison & Harrison, 1998).

For independent hotels, three principal options exist to counter the growth among hotel chains and the accompanying threat to their market segment: affiliation with a major hotel chain; exploiting specific niche markets; and membership of a consortium. The benefits of the first option, affiliation with a major hotel chain, can be considerable. In particular, the independent hotel is able to draw from the chain's brand image and reputation, as well as to benefit from their increased marketing power, managerial expertise and range of financing opportunities. However, lack of overall control and strategic inflexibility, a long-term contract and payment of royalties may represent substantial drawbacks to affiliation with one of the major hotel chains. There has also been a proliferation of powerful marketing and promotional alliances on a global scale.

Rather than using capital to build and open new hotels, hotel chains are forging alliances with other hotel chains. For example, in the mid-1990s, Copthorne/Scandic and SAS/Radisson formed powerful marketing alliances that sought to capitalise on the geographic strength and size of the companies involved (Sall, 1995). With these sales and marketing agreements, each chain's position was strengthened without the need for investment in new hotels. The second option is to enter and exploit niche markets. Indeed, in spite of the growth of the large hotel chains, there remains space in the marketplace for niche operators. This has recently been evidenced in the UK by the growth of 'boutique hotels' such as Malmaison. The third option is to join one of the growing number of consortia that currently exist in the marketplace. Generally viewed as collaborative arrangements between hotels designed to improve their competencies, advance their market and improve their competitive position, while at the same time retaining independence of ownership, consortia usually vary in terms of the degree of commitment, control, cooperation and organisational formality. It is on this form of collaboration, the hotel consortium, that this chapter concentrates.

Defining the hotel consortium

Over the past two decades, hotel consortia have grown both in number and in influence to become a highly significant sector of the wider hotel industry. Indeed, joining together into consortia is widely regarded to be an important lifeline for the survival of small and independent hotels (Morrison, 1994). In the UK alone there are in excess of 30 hotel consortia, comprising around 1600 hotels and 54,000 bedrooms. The growth in numbers has been accompanied by the evolution of the sector from simple locational marketing or representation groups, to complex, multi-layered organisations that manage a combination of corporate functions. Over 20 years ago, Littlejohn (1982) referred to hotel consortia as organisations of hotels that together unite resources in order to establish joint purchasing and trading arrangements and to offer marketing services. Littlejohn went on to suggest that these aims and objectives are usually achieved through the setting up of centralised offices, and that the consortium's activities are often financed through a levy or subscription on the member hotel units. More recently, Evans (1990: 8.1) provided a more general definition, where a consortium was identified as 'a group of firms coming together for a common benefit'. In a similar vein, Gilbert and Zok (1992) referred to a hotel consortium as an organisation of hotels that combine resources to establish corporate management services such as marketing and promotional activities, purchasing, personnel and training. Morrison and Harrison (1998: 351), meanwhile, defined a hotel consortium as 'a grouping of predominantly single, independently owned hotels that share corporate costs, such as marketing, while retaining independence of ownership and operation'. More recently, Knowles (1999) clarified four generic definitional aspects of hotel consortia, those being:

(1) A group of hotels that combine resources to establish joint purchasing and trading arrangements and operate marketing through a common central reservation office (CRO) that is usually financed by a levy on the hotel member units.
(2) A number of independently owned units that affiliate in order to benefit from the access to greater resources that would not be possible on their own.
(3) An organisation of hotels that pool their resources in an effort to establish corporate management services, such as purchasing, personnel, training, marketing and public relations.
(4) A collection of hotels with similar standards and voluntary membership, paying a fee for marketing and sales service, run exclusively for the benefit of the consortium.

Types of hotel consortium

In attempting to distinguish between different types of hotel consortium, Slattery *et al.* (1985) identified five distinct categories, namely:

- *The marketing consortium.* This was the original type of consortium to be formed with the intent of providing access to marketing expertise to the small, independent hotel. Membership in this consortium allowed members to compete with the hotel chains for the accommodation customer. Such consortia took one of two strategic positions: either location marketing, which promoted hotels from within a specific region with the support of a local or regional tourist board; or niche marketing, in which the members involved were from within a specified market segment, whether national or international. For example, Small Luxury Hotels of the World (SLH) (see Box 9.1) has developed a niche target market for the affluent and discerning guest.
- *Marketing and purchasing consortia.* These evolved from the marketing consortia that were committed to increasing membership numbers. With larger numbers they were able to negotiate reduced prices for bulk purchases, thus generating cost savings for members. The prospect of such savings and reduction in purchasing costs were deemed to be a considerable attraction for prospective members. Slattery *et al.* (1985) and Dundjerovic (1999) suggest that both Best Western Hotels (see Box 9.1 and later case study) and Consort Hotels (see Box 9.1; now part of Best Western Great Britain) are representative of this type of consortium.
- *Referral consortia.* In this type of consortium, hotels demonstrate a collaborative relationship with airlines whereby the hotels receive bookings through the airlines' reservation systems. This collaborative form provides exposure for hotels in international travel markets, which have often proved difficult for hotels to penetrate on their own.
- *Personnel and training consortia.* Rather than be driven by revenue generation or cost reduction, personnel and training consortia are driven by individual hotels pooling their resources with regard to personnel, training and skills development.
- *Reservation systems.* These consortia provide a reservation system network for hotels throughout the range of the market. They provide a wide choice of size, location and prices for the potential hotel customer. They also provide comprehensive marketing services for its members. The largest of these reservation systems is REZsolutions, with its coverage of around 25,000 hotels, 80 brands and 3 million rooms (Dundjerovic, 1999).

Box 9.1 Examples of hotel consortia

Small Luxury Hotels of the World (SLH)

SLH brings together more than 290 of the world's finest-quality hotels and offers the ease of booking and familiarity of an international hotel chain, while at the same time retaining and promoting the unique character, individuality and independence of each of its member properties. Created in 1991 as the result of a merger between Prestige Hotels Europe and Small Luxury Hotels & Resorts of North America, the two groups combine over 30 years experience of international hotel marketing. SLH was formed to represent the collective interests of the most luxurious, independent, exclusive hotels and resorts around the world. The consortium's activities are designed to provide similar economies of scale to those achieved by the big international hotel chains, while maintaining the individuality and independence of each of its member properties. In 1995, SLH merged with the Asian and Pacific properties of Select Hotels and Resorts International, creating a global membership and adding marketing services and reservations coverage in these regions. By 1997, the consortium's membership exceeded 230 hotels in over 30 countries; by the latter half of 2002 this had increased to more than 290 hotels in over 50 countries.

Best Western

Best Western represents the world's largest hotel chain with over 4,000 hotels in 80 countries, is a not-for-profit organisation owned by its members, with a highly recognised brand name that allows its members to retain their individuality yet still achieve the benefits of a hotel chain for minimal cost. Members are provided with a wide range of services that include domestic and international reservation systems, worldwide marketing, sales and advertising, brand identity, design facilities, quality assurance, customer service and various education and training services. All these services are offered in an effort to increase the profitability of the individual member hotels. Members are not subjected to long-term contracts as these can be renewed annually.

Consort Hotels

Consort Hotels is a consortium that offers a variety of benefits to members, including access to new business and new markets, access to a central reservation system, referral between hotels through a nationwide network of similar properties and access to an overseas sales office, all of which helps the independent hotel to market itself internationally. In addition, professional advice, training and recruitment services and group purchasing benefits are available. Membership also provides a voice in government, as well as 'club membership' and the camaraderie that it facilitates (Evans, 2001).

Pride Hotels of Britain
Pride Hotels of Britain is a collection of the finest privately owned hotels in Britain with 36 properties, in addition to a small cruise ship, *Hebridean Princess*, and a luxurious touring train, *The Royal Scotsman*. Pride Hotels of Britain was initially set up to address the marketing needs of its hotel members. One particular feature of the Pride consortium is its dedicated recruitment initiative which helps individuals to find employment across its full range of hotels.

Benefits and Drawbacks of Consortium Membership

Benefits

The benefits of consortium membership are many and varied. For example, once they are able to afford the membership fee or subscription, independent hotels can benefit from collective marketing, attendance at trade shows and travel exhibitions, event sponsorship, marketing communications and media familiarisation tours. Murray (1997) suggests that joining a consortium makes all these benefits available at a cost that is affordable to any property determined to be one of the leaders in its area. Figure 9.1 identifies a number of benefits of consortium membership that will be advantageous to independent hotels, especially those that are small in size.

Scale economies are clearly one of the principal magnets for consortium membership. In fact, Dundjerovic (1999) claims that the main reason for the existence of any type of consortium is to provide independents with some of the benefits of a chain hotel, notably scale economies. Achieving scale economies can lead to increased room yield and reduced costs, while enabling the hotel to maintain its independence of ownership and operation (Slattery, 1992). Knowles (1999) adds that the possibility of attracting extra business, particularly from markets previously inaccessible to the independent, unaffiliated hotel, is another major benefit of consortium membership. Hotel consortia usually specialise in the provision of corporate marketing services for the individual hotel member, and by joining a consortium independents gain the advantages of more established chains while still retaining their independence. Benefits of consortium membership can also be categorised as tangible and intangible. Tangible benefits include:

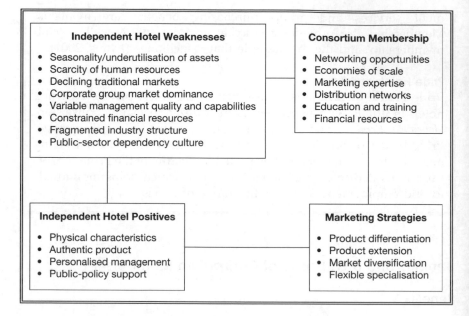

Figure 9.1 Justification for consortium membership

Source: Adapted from Morrison, 1994

(1) Financial benefits:
- Increased income through greater visitor numbers.
- Reduced administrative costs.
- Joint development of projects at lower cost.
- Reduced investment exposure and risk.
- Marketing cost economies of scale in the form of branding, product/service testing, advertising and promotion.
- Effective use of resources in technology development.

(2) Operational benefits:
- Creation of new and improved performance.
- Strengthening of operations through innovative and enhanced processes, thus adding to the technical skills base.
- Managerial control over a horizontally integrated value chain.
- Innovation benefits derived from the pooling of skills, information and expertise.
- Generation or use of core and secondary technology.
- Bargaining leverage of suppliers and intermediaries.

(3) Marketing benefits:
- Geographic strengthening and widening of market access.

- Shaping competition by providing new and joint market opportunities.
- Enhanced growth through overcoming market entry barriers.
- Maintenance of the ability to meet specific local market demands, market research and development.
- Shared and enhanced brand image.
- Theme-based marketing, improving prospects for market penetration.
- Strengthened product line.

All of the advantages above are gained through the consortium's provision of access to:

- Networking opportunities.
- Economies of scale.
- Technology and distribution networks.
- Educational and training support.
- A computerised reservation system (CRS).
- Purchase discounts through a central purchasing facility.
- Referral business from the consortium's hotels in other countries.
- Public-relations activities and media exposure.
- Professional marketing advice.

As well as:

- Participation in numerous marketing projects including key international trade markets and shows.
- Mention in the consortium's guide and traveller's handbook.

Increasingly, consortium membership results in an association with similar hotels and access to an extensive and lucrative marketing tool, namely a global distribution system (GDS), which provides a direct link to the overseas trade. No single, independent hotel is permitted access to a GDS, which would normally only be open to chains or consortia (Clark, 2001). In the current global marketplace, the success of the consortium rests on its ability to provide its members access to technology relatively inexpensively. For example, Unirez, a hotel consortium, is successful because of its ability to provide a high-tech application service provider (ASP) solution. ASP allows hotels to access reservations and other systems through the use of the Internet while the service provider houses and manages the technology. Utell, one of the world's largest hotel consortia, offers access to all channels on an international basis. They believe that access around the world and around the clock, as well as access to a GDS, the Internet and voice-recognition reservation systems, are the most important things they can provide for their members. In addition to tangible benefits, there are also benefits of an intangible nature. Such benefits pertain to the gains achieved through the diffusion of management expertise and generic skills to the members of the consortium. These benefits are achieved through the pooling of skills, information and expertise of members with similar characteristics.

With the above benefits on offer, it is clear that many independent hotels view consortium membership as a means of gaining authority in the marketplace through greater marketing muscle and lower purchasing costs (Ivory, 1993). Furthermore, members of consortia are expected to benefit from the development of discussion forums, strategic planning, effective domestic and international marketing strategies, as well as market research that is now undertaken by the consortium as a whole rather than by the individual hotels. This 'collective entrepreneurship', as it is described by Morrison (1994), can lead to increased profits for the independent hotel as well as to the broader promotion of the destination as a whole (Briggs, 1994; Murray, 1997), while preserving the individuality and independence of each member hotel (Knowles, 1999).

Drawbacks

There are, however, certain costs associated to consortium membership. Morrison (1994), for example, identifies the following:

(1) *Financial costs*. These are the costs associated with supporting the co-ordination, administration and marketing activity of the consortium.
(2) *Operational costs*. These may include the reduction in innovation and entrepreneurship of the individual hotel. Vulnerability due to mutual dependency and uncertainty may also be a problem, as might the conflict that may arise from the division of authority and decision-making power. There is always the potential for imbalances between benefits and commitment to arise, for the imposition of a standardised product and trading format and for inter-member conflicts.
(3) *Marketing costs*. These may include a loss of flexibility and quick response to the needs of the market, the erosion of individual competitive position through the creation of a weakened bargaining position and suppression of individual identity in order to enhance the brand image of the consortium.

In trying to determine if consortia are indeed beneficial to the survival of the small and independent hotel, a number of opinions exist. Morrison and Harrison (1998), for example, question the extent to which the promise of benefits is actually translated into real benefits for consortium members. In a similar vein, Dundjerovic (1999) points out that the longevity and success of consortia in attracting new members indicate that operators of small and independent hotels believe them to be of value to their survival at regional, national and international levels.

However Dundjerovic further states that consortia only provide the scale economies of hotel chains and that they can never duplicate such chains in respect of their often superior specialisation, external financing and career development.

Consortium Trends

Growth and evolution of consortia

Since the mid-1990s, hotel consortia have clearly been getting bigger and they have arguably been getting better too (Shundich, 1996). Considerable improvements in reservations technology and management support saw the generation of additional membership benefits through the more effective tracking of guest histories and hence improved database marketing. Although there was no actual increase in the number of hotels in consortia during the mid-1990s, a considerable increase in the number of reservations was evident, most notably in electronic form. By 1997, however, the trend had turned to globalisation and consolidation. Dela Cruz (1998) argues that size of consortia had become a crucial success factor and, as had been the case with corporate hotel chains, this led to a burst of mergers and acquisitions. Such activity was most prevalent among consortia based on shared reservation systems. For example, in the mid to late 1990s, two major reservation providers, Utell and Anasazi, merged to form REZsolutions. Dela Cruz (1998: 76) states that, according to the vice-president of marketing for REZsolutions, there was 'a need for a one-stop-shop environment which provides integrated solutions, whether that's global distribution systems, technology solutions, the ability to process data, capture data or mine that information'.

By the end of the 1990s, reservation-provider consortia had been continually improving their technological abilities and widening their global distribution systems, thus providing independent hotels with a degree of 'visibility' comparable to corporate chain hotels. There had also been as much consolidation among consortia as among the corporate hotel chains, the development of the Internet leading to much of the growth and added sophistication of the services provided by consortia. More recently, Miller (2000) states that, during the period of economic boom, global hotel chains were able to invest heavily in information technology. As a result, the independent hotel consortium has had to change in order to compete successfully in the 'techno-driven' hotel industry. With the increase in technology the reservation/referral systems were both changing and evolving into full-service companies, or else increasing their presence through mergers, alliances, joint ventures or partnerships.

One such full-service company is Indecorp, created by Preferred Hotels and Resorts, which is a consortium of independent hotels, resorts and brands. With Indecorp, independent brands can join together to increase revenue through cost savings and economies of scale, and secure financing and the capital needed for technology acquisition. The goal of Indecorp is 'to protect the independent market and support its brands on the world market place' (Miller, 2000: 64). It aims to do this by providing strategic management, reservations, purchasing, customer relationship management and e-commerce technologies that the independent would be unable to achieve on its own, while still allowing the independents to protect and preserve their independence (Chipkin, 2001). All in all, Indecorp aims to be an umbrella corporation in which multiple brands, i.e. hotel consortia, will be sharing technologies and loyalty programmes, while retaining their most important individual characteristics.

Another consortium that is evolving is The Leading Hotels of the World. It has grown from a not-for-profit reservation service organisation into a full-service, luxury marketing company, with four joint-venture companies that provide group sales, advertising, marketing and public relations, financial services and quality assurance services and hotel inspections (Miller, 2000). The Leading Hotels of the World has also formed a number of alliances with luxury service companies such as Crystal Cruises and Avis; product manufactures like Louis Vuitton, Hennessy and Christian Dior; and up-market travel agencies such as Virtuoso. Perhaps more significantly, it has also formed a strategic alliance with another luxury-oriented consortium, Relais et Chateau. This alliance, which represents 800 of the world's finest hotels and restaurants, has been described as a 'business-to-business solution' and not a merger or acquisition (Miller, 2000). The members' incentive to form this 'solution' was based on their geographic proximity, similar customer base and shared commitment to quality. By combining their competitive advantages, both The Leading Hotels of the World and Relais et Chateau have been able to enhance the reputation of their brands and consolidate their worldwide leadership in the luxury end of the market. For the future, they plan to establish joint marketing programmes and to develop state-of-the-art technological developments that will include interlinks between their two websites, the opening of an Internet portal and the sharing of databases. The alliance will also be highlighted in each other's directories, so that guests are encouraged to combine their stays between the two companies.

Nowadays it is difficult to distinguish between the main types of consortium as many are changing their form and offering considerably more services to their members than ever before. This added complexity has a number of sources. First, a single hotel can belong to several different types of consortium simultaneously. Second, consortia are no longer available only to independent hotels but also now to chain hotels.

Third, the business formats of different consortia have not only become very complex but they also vary considerably from one consortium to another (Knowles, 1999). Formerly the activities of the consortium depended upon the type of consortium. Now all consortia undertake activities to increase revenue or to mirror those of the hotel chains. These activities might include:

- Promotion, with the establishment of brand names and brand imaging.
- The establishment of distribution channels, such as CRSs and GDSs.
- Product and price standardisation.

The major hotel consortia are now competing vigorously with each other for members as, more recently, growth has remained static, with some consortia actually losing members. One of the main barriers to consortium membership is the high cost of membership, with fees ranging from US$600 to US$12,000 per year. Another challenge to the survival of consortia is the depletion of the pool of potential new members, as the increasing presence of the large chain hotels erodes the number of independents available. Arguably the greatest threat, however, is the development of Internet technology. Nowadays it is both easy and inexpensive for any hotel to go online, and this has given even the smallest independent hotel access to the most distant consumer and vice versa (Clark, 2001). Indeed, Clark argues that consortia have responded to these challenges not only by consolidating but also by making full use of the Internet, particularly by adopting reciprocal strategies in the form of websites featuring one another's properties.

Consortium marketing strategies

The provision of marketing benefits constitutes the main attraction for membership of a hotel consortium. Small and independent hotels cannot individually afford the marketing strategies and projects required to compete successfully with the major chain hotels. Such chain hotels have substantial marketing and financial resources and, as a result, considerable marketing capabilities. These comprise national and even international coverage, access to inter-property and central reservation systems and connection to a global distribution system. This, coupled with an organised and motivated sales force, a high degree of flexibility and adaptability to changing market conditions and the strength of well known brands, provides the chain hotels with the tools to compete successfully against the independents (Imrie & Fyall, 2001). Imrie and Fyall suggest also that branding is to be one of the key marketing management practices for the future. More often than not, small and independent hotels cannot achieve a successful brand image or provide an effective branded product on their own. Hence, some affiliation or marketing alliance with other hotels is advantageous. For many hotels, the customer advantages of branding are unattainable if the 'loose management control that consortia have over their members prevents the delivery of consistent brand standards – both in the consistency of the provision of high quality technical attributes and in the consistency of delivery of functional attributes' (Imrie & Fyall, 2000: 48).

Marketing strategies adopted by hotel consortia do, however, differ from one to another in significant ways. For example, some consortia, such as Small Luxury Hotels of the World, involve members actively in the running of the organisation. In this instance, the consortium expects its members to take a full part in marketing decisions. However, in contrast, other consortia, such as Flag, predominant in the Asia-Pacific region and including brands such as Comfort Inn, Quality Inn, Clarion and Flag, prefer their members to concentrate on the daily running of their own establishments (Ivory, 1993). Satchell (1995), meanwhile, reports that Pride Hotels of Britain (see Box 9.1 on p. 264), which has both international and diagonal 'non-hotel' affiliations, established a marketing committee to raise its profile as well as to develop policies to identify new business opportunities and increase customer demand. They also had a marketing agent in the US that distributed brochures to promote Pride Hotels of Britain to US travel agents. This consortium also established links with a group of independent innkeepers in the US where reciprocal marketing activities were launched. In contrast again, the marketing strategy of the Distinctly Different consortium of bed-and-breakfast establishments, now known as Arcadian Hotels, was based mainly on public relations. Brochures with press releases were mailed to a specially compiled press list. This helped to produce a steady flow of enquiries as well as media visits to member properties. The distribution of brochures to countries such as the US and France provided international coverage (Batchelor, 1997).

A further example is provided by Morrison and Harrison (1998) in their study of marketing techniques used by Consort Hotels. At the time of the study, the consortium included 180 independently owned and operated hotels in the UK, whose facilities were promoted jointly both at home and abroad. With the increase in the use of electronic distribution systems, the consortium was able to address the challenges of collaboration in a number of ways. First, by the pooling of resources, the small independent hotels were able to access the technology and marketing expertise offered by the consortium. In their rebranding of both business and leisure markets, member hotels were selected for targeted promotions according to their suitability, rather than each hotel trying to access all markets. This helped to enhance the effectiveness of the hotels' marketing strategy, to strengthen individual competitive position and to increase the consortium's bargaining power over its competitors. Second, membership of Consort Hotels gave small independent hotels access to an electronic distribution system and, therefore, access to the global marketplace. This access was gained without the high, fixed costs of individual technological installations. All members of the consortium shared installation costs along with the operating and technological transaction costs associated with obtaining business. Third, collective membership in the consortium generated a critical mass of hotels, which yielded the potential to achieve the consolidated power of a brand image, which is a necessity in the mature and saturated global market. The independent hotel, therefore, had a more visible, prominent position in the 'electronic shopping mall' that the hotel market has become. This visibility facilitates consumer accessibility and consistency of available information.

In 1998, Scotland Hotels of Distinction was the largest marketing consortium of independently owned country and town house hotels in Scotland. Some of the strategic objectives of Scotland Hotels of Distinction for 1998–2000 were to build the consortium brand within member hotels and improve member networking and internal monitoring systems while generating overseas business through the central reservation office (Morrison & Harrison, 1998). In an effort to achieve these objectives, the marketing strategy of the Scotland Hotels of Distinction involved the following components:

- *Explicit differentiation*. This involved the building and establishing of the brand in an effort to enhance the profile of the consortium as well as to define and promote the benefits of the individual hotels and the tourism destination as a whole.
- *Market mining*. In order to profit from the core of the committed tourists in and to Scotland, the consortium selected the off-peak, domestic business tourist as its main target market.
- *Innovative product extensions*. These included the promotion of added-value romantic breaks from the autumn to the spring in the UK through making use of press advertisements, direct mail and reader promotions.
- *Market diversification*. This was designed to generate business in the shoulder and off-periods, through a campaign of sustained marketing communications in specialist magazines and via a post-card-mailer programme.

Consortium effectiveness and member expectations

A recent study by Carimbocas (2003) provides some valuable insights into evaluating the current experiences of consortia members and their expectations for the future. Using a questionnaire survey conducted in the summer of 2003, Carimbocas questioned the effectiveness of the hotel consortium as a method of survival for small and independent hotels in the UK. In particular, the study explored the extent to which hotel consortium membership continues to meet and overcome the challenges of today's competitive and increasingly global marketplace. By interviewing consortium management personnel and surveying consortium members, both sides of the consortium equation were explored. Interviewees were all representatives of well-known consortia with high-profile international images and included Small Luxury Hotels of the World, MacDonald Hotels, Pride Hotels of Britain and Jarvis Hotels. Of those surveyed, virtually all were members of the above consortia, although the survey did target a wider cross section. A number of key findings arose from the study.

Motivation for consortium affiliation

For small and independent hotels, the potential for growth and increased profitability remains the clear motivation behind consortium membership. One respondent argued that:

> if you are not part of a brand, be it a chain or marketing association, then you will be at risk because it is well known that branded hotels outperform non-branded hotels. This is because large hotel chains have the management expertise, benefit from economies of scale and are able to implement international marketing campaigns that keep them in the forefront of the market.

A further respondent added to the above statement be expressing his belief that:

> independent hotels will never be able individually to match the momentum of the corporate hotels in the current marketplace and only through joining with others can they hope to survive.

All interview respondents were in agreement that small and independent hotels need to be more visible in the new global marketplace and have greater access to a larger market if they are to survive. Perhaps unsurprisingly, access to wider markets, international representation, increased visibility and improved sales and productivity proved to be the most frequent responses when asked about the rationale behind consortium membership. With the widespread availability of the Internet, access to global distribution systems was not deemed as significant as has perhaps been the case in the past. Likewise, although the academic literature suggests that hotels would experience reduced costs as well as benefit from discussion forums, strategic planning and support in recruitment and the training of personnel, little evidence was unearthed by Carimbocas to support these assertions. This was also true of members searching simply for reduced marketing costs. For example, one respondent replied that members of the Small Luxury Hotels of the World consortium are:

> wealthy and operate at the upper end of the market and could stand alone, but they choose to belong to the consortium because they want to be leaders in the provision of luxury accommodation, synonymous with their brand.

For a number of other respondents, however, the imposition of a standardised product and the loss of marketing autonomy and decision-making flexibility were causes for concern.

Consortium structure and governance

The relationship between the consortium and its members is important to the effectiveness and stability of the organisation, and ultimately to its eventual success. As discussed in Chapter 7 in the context of collaboration more generally, the degree of formality in the governance of consortia varies from one consortium to another. The smaller consortia, which are usually member-controlled, exhibit the loosest bonds between members, with very little formality. In contrast, larger consortia frequently are limited companies, and often have more formal governance structures and styles of management. These differences in formality affect the organisation's objectives and effectiveness, as well as the members' influence on the consortium and vice versa (Knowles, 1999). For many independent hotels, consortium membership is frequently regarded as a transitional step rather than a strategy for long-term growth. In fact, 60% of consortia last no more than four years and fewer than one in five last up to 10 years. In general, these alliances fall apart because of a lack of well-defined strategic goals at the outset (WTO, 2002).

In accord with the findings of Palmer (2002), Carimbocas also came to the conclusion that consortium effectiveness and stability can best be achieved through more formal organisation structures, wherein all parties know and accept the rules and regulations that govern the operation. Without structures and rules, collaborative 'inaction' is more common in hotel consortia. However, all interviewees in the Carimbocas study belonged to consortia that were party to formal governance structures. For example, Small Luxury Hotels of the World has a board of directors and an appointed chairman. The organisation operates on a voting system where the members have an input as to how the organisation is to be operated through meetings held throughout the year. There are strict quality standards to be adhered to, with regular inspections throughout the year to enforce and maintain them. A similar practice holds true for Pride Hotels of Britain, whose members also work on the board and decide on the direction of the business. Pride Hotels of Britain operates essentially as a club, so if a hotel wishes to join it has to gain the votes of existing members. Again, this serves as a mechanism to ensure quality standards are maintained.

Consortium choice and withdrawal

Choosing one consortium over another is often a question of greatest exposure and market visibility. Although more prominent among international rather than local, regional or national consortia, this was an issue raised across the board among respondents to the Carimbocas study. As with the previous finding, consortia were also chosen on the strength of their brand, which was considered to be synonymous with higher standards and improved image. Again, lower costs were deemed to be less important than the coverage, visibility and market reach of the consortium.

Multiple membership of competing consortia is an interesting option that is often overlooked when discussing consortium membership. However, multiple membership is relatively common, in that members are again looking to maximise their market coverage and reach. Multiple membership is most common where individual hotels are members of local, regional and maybe international consortia and where they are perhaps targeting different market groups at different times of the year.

Withdrawal and the short-term nature of many consortium affiliations are commonplace and an accepted dynamic of the business of marketing consortia among hotels. In the Carimbocas study, for example, withdrawal, although not widespread, had taken place among a number of the respondents. The cost of membership was not, however, the most significant issue. The principal reason for withdrawal was either that expected benefits were not being received or that the member considered there to have been a drop in the overall standard of service being given by the consortium. One further issue that may be more prevalent as a catalyst for withdrawal in the future is the exclusive nature of some membership contracts for consortia. For example, the inability to become members of any other consortia is likely to serve as a barrier to remaining, irrespective of the benefits of membership of that consortium.

Growth and perceived future of consortia

In the early part of this chapter it was stated that the entire hotel industry is continuing to grow through powerful marketing and more prominent collaboration. Consortia in particular are deemed to be following in the footsteps of the hotel chains, who themselves are forming alliances with other hotel chains in order to strengthen their market position without the need to build more hotels. Size of consortia is thus becoming important as the entire hotel industry becomes more and more concentrated and consolidated in its character. The perception of many of the respondents to the Carimbocas study is that with so many mergers and acquisitions in the industry it is difficult to envisage independent hotels remaining unaffiliated in the future. On the other hand, one respondent commented that:

> there has always been consolidation within the hotel industry and it is increasing. Standardisation is also on the increase but each hotel or group will fall into its own niche for there will still be the need for individual hotels with their own individual style.

However, with the increasing trend towards globalisation and consolidation, the study concludes that consortia will increasingly be forced to evolve, merge and consolidate. Globalisation has undoubtedly led to increased competition, and with the advent of new entrants on the domestic market and with the improved technology now readily available, all hotels and hotel groups have to innovate and evolve in order to continue to create value. The study further concludes that this evolution is vital to the very survival of consortia and independents. One respondent claimed that:

> consortia have to change to meet the demands of the market, not just for [their] own sake and that of [their] members but for the sake of those independents that remain unaffiliated. If we can't seem to offer what they need, then the independents won't stand a chance against the chains. And, if we can't achieve these goals on our own, then we either get out of the business or get a partner.

Interestingly, since the completion of the study, two major hotel consortia have in fact formed a major strategic alliance, and in so doing have capitalised on their market position, strengthened the awareness of the brand and consolidated their global leadership in the luxury end of the market.

Case Study: Best Western – The World's Largest Hotel Chain®

Originally founded in 1946 as an informal 'referral system' between hotels, today Best Western represents the single largest hotel 'chain' in the world. With more than 4000 independently owned and operated hotels throughout the world, Best Western represents one of the best examples of collaborative marketing throughout the entire tourism industry. Of particular note is that it offers member hoteliers the advantage of retaining their independence while providing the benefits of a full-service, international hotel affiliation with global benefits (Best

Western, 2002). Not only is the consortium over 50 years old, but it has grown, matured and expanded at a rate not seen elsewhere in the industry. For example, by the end of the 1970s, Best Western was accommodating 15 million guests and generating US$1 billion in room sales. By the early 1980s, it was widely regarded as the world's largest chain of independently owned hotels. In sheer scale, Best Western is unique in that, while global airline alliances are clearly expanding at an extremely rapid pace, they remain immature organisational structures by comparison.

Best Western represents a model that is often held up as 'best practice' in the industry and one that serves as a benchmark for others. With a 99% retention rate in recent years among its member hotels, the 'collaborative' business model clearly retains its appeal, welcoming 158 new hotels in the US, and 143 international hotels in 2002 alone. With regard to its financial performance, revenues from fees and dues were approximately 2% higher in 2002 than in 2001, principally due to increasing membership numbers. Furthermore, revenue from affiliation fees increased by 21%, while that from international reservation fees increased by 8%, primarily due to increased reservation fees and increased volume through the central reservation system, and the payment of prior-year losses by affiliate organisations (Best Western, 2002). Revenue from self-funding programmes also increased in 2002, this time by 6%. After the considerable difficulties experienced post-9/11, 2002 proved to be a very encouraging year for Best Western.

Using the 'coverage-form-mode-motive' typology advocated by Terpstra and Simonin (1993), as introduced in Chapter 6, the remainder of this case study will examine the Best Western consortium of hotels in more depth, the aim being to investigate the dynamics of this successful instance of collaborative marketing.

Coverage

With regard to its market coverage, geographical scope and provision of marketing functions, Best Western is very much the global market leader. The consortium has a very deliberate sense of corporate purpose. Its mission statement is to 'serve the collective interests of members and guests. By focusing on satisfaction and brand loyalty, we will ensure that Best Western is more valuable than any other brand in our industry' (www.bestwestern.com, 2003). Best Western's principal reason for existence, therefore, is to increase the profitability of its members, primarily middle to upper-middle-class hotels. The Automobile Association of America rates 63% of Best Western hotels in the US and Canada as two- or three-diamond, while nearly 80% of all hotels in Europe receive three- or four-star rating, locating the chain at the upper-middle end of the market with prices set accordingly. Although prices clearly vary according to season, the average daily rate is approximately US$72 in the US.

Although started in California, Best Western's head office is located in Phoenix, Arizona, with reservation and operation centres in Phoenix and Glendale, and multilingual, consolidated reservation offices in Dublin, Sydney and Milan. It also has over 20 sales offices around the world with territories as far afield as New Caledonia, Macedonia and Yemen recently joining the consortium. Its newest international sales office is in Beijing, in the People's Republic of China, where Best Western is hoping to benefit from the significant growth in demand for tourism and hospitality. The international arm of the business alone provides reservation and brand-identity services for more than 1500 members in 79 countries outside the US and Canada. With over 1500 corporate employees worldwide, Best Western is clearly global in its coverage of the market and delivery of its member services. Its wide range of member services include:

- Domestic and international reservation systems.
- Representation and listings in all major global distribution systems, including Amadeus, Sabre, Galileo and Worldspan.
- Worldwide marketing, sales and advertising (which includes the distribution of millions of travel guides and atlases around the world).
- Brand identity.
- Gold Crown Club International, Best Western's fully international frequent-traveller programme currently endorsed by more than three million members worldwide.
- Website presence (which includes a profile of each property, corporate information and online reservations).
- Facility design.
- Quality assurance.
- Customer service.
- Education and training services.

Best Western was in fact one of the very first hotel brands to provide booking capability on the Internet – as long ago as 1995. Today, more than 35% of the company's total reservations bookings are made through its website, on which nearly all of the brand's hotels feature. This site recorded 182 million hits in 2000 alone. Developments into m-commerce are also now taking place with new applications for wireless users being prepared for the market. Education and training is one aspect of their portfolio that is taken particularly seriously in that it warrants its own website. This very popular site contains over 1500 pages of content, 700 best-practice recommendations and a marketing plan template for individual hoteliers. Other services are made available to members but on a separate fee basis. These include, for example:

- Central purchasing.
- Special marketing opportunities.
- Telecommunications network programmes.

In addition to the above, Best Western has recently launched BestRequests®, a uniform worldwide package that brings together 16 of the most frequently requested guest amenities and services. This new brand proposition includes a continental or hot breakfast, free local phone calls (up to 30 minutes) and long-distance access, data-port connections in all guest rooms, irons, ironing boards and coffee/tea makers in all rooms and so on. The brand is also now committed to designating 50% of all rooms as non-smoking. It is believed that this brand commitment to customers will go along way to confirming the brand values of 'value' and 'convenience' in the minds of the customers.

In addition to the individual brand benefits, inter-organisational collaboration extends outside the hotel sector in that Best Western shares 'partnership' with numerous players in the international tourism industry. One of their newest partners is Thai Airways International, bringing to 10 the number of airlines represented in the hotel brand's Gold Crown Club International frequent traveller programme. This represents yet more evidence of the emerging trend towards diagonal forms of collaboration, and of the further opportunities for market 'connectivity' and benefits to be derived from co-branding.

Form

Best Western is quite categorically a not-for-profit membership organisation for independently owned and operated hotels. It is not a publicly traded company and is membership-driven, inasmuch as each member has a voice in the operation of the company. It is an equity form of collaboration in that it is funded by fees and dues paid by the member hotels, although other services are made available to members on a separate fee basis whereby the fees are assessed specifically for the service in question. Although it is clearly accountable to its members, Best Western operates a relatively 'tight' form of governance in that it is managed by an executive board just like any normal publicly listed company. With over 1500 employees worldwide, it has managed to retain its 'individual' style by avoiding unnecessary bureaucracy wherever possible. With regard to its income streams, Best Western has one of the lowest fee structures of any major chain in the industry while at the same time offering members complete flexibility. This is exercised by the short-term nature of most contracts whereby members can renew their membership on an annual basis. Members are free to leave the organisation at any time or even transfer membership for a minimal fee if the property is in good standing. This said, with a 99% retention rate in recent years among its member hotels, the freedom to leave clearly serves as an exit strategy that is seldom adopted by its members. It is perhaps this freedom to leave which serves as a major draw to Best Western in the first instance, and as a major driver for the organisation itself to meet the needs and wants of its members. In this instance, the collaborative business model appears to work to the benefit of its members.

Mode

With regard to the intrinsic nature of the relationships among its member hotels, it would probably be fair to say that, although Best Western provides the necessary frameworks and environment to encourage further networking and collaboration, the majority of members are rather individualistic in their outlook and approach to business. Best Western serves very effectively individual members' markets and marketing needs. Outside this quite specific remit, member hotels remain effectively in competition with hotels both outside and inside the consortium. It is very common for a number of hotels of a similar quality and from the same town or city to be members of Best Western. Therefore, although most members benefit from the collaborative strength of the Best Western brand they frequently remain in direct competition with other hotels also benefiting from membership of the consortium, This clearly has some impact with regard to business relations between member hotels within the organisation.

In order to enhance the 'family' nature of the brand, however, Best Western recently implemented its very first 'Best Western for a Better World' global community relations week. Designed to develop a sense of community spirit and encourage hoteliers to 'give something back' to local communities, this represents an interesting development designed to permeate the organisation in the years to come.

Motive

Quite clearly, the considerable marketing benefits on offer to independently owned and operated hotels are significant and represent the principal motivation for hoteliers joining the organisation. Although there are certain fee implications, in that the fees may be prohibitive for many smaller hotels and represent a hole in the budget of larger hotels which would have spent the membership fee on individual, competitive marketing strategies, the benefits are such that Best Western retains all but 1% of its member hotels on an annual basis. In view of the competition in the marketplace and the increase in number of consortia, be they national or international in scope, this is a considerable achievement. The fact that members are free to leave whenever they wish and can be members of any number of other consortia offers individual members considerable flexibility and freedom. Perhaps this freedom represents Best Western's greatest strength in that it facilitates a culture of meeting the needs and wants of its members on a continual basis. For Best Western and its 4000 plus members, collaboration is clearly a concept that works and delivers real benefits.

Conclusion

Today, mergers and acquisitions represent the most common method of expansion in the hotel industry, and this is no less the case in the consortium sector. Most major hotel chains have expanded by consolidation, either with the creation of international strategic alliances or through mergers and acquisitions with already established chains or consortia. Sharing resources, risks and costs is a fast, efficient and inexpensive way of expanding one's influence. Back in 1995 Morrison stated that the further growth of consortia lies in the process of consolidation. With consolidation, the strength of hotel consortia now has the added potential to raise the performance of the individual members. These consolidations provide consortia with: improved economies of scale in the form of buying power; market coverage and operational benefits; economies of replication in the form of recurrent and fixed capital costs; and economies of scope with regard to specialisation and global coverage.

Industry analysts predict that there will be yet further consolidation of hotel consortia (www.world-tourism.org, 2003). According to industry professionals and analysts, however, smaller hotel groups and consortia should not feel overly threatened by the increased consolidation within the hotel industry. Martin Gerty of Howarth UK, for example, notes that, while consolidation leads to smaller numbers of larger players, there will always be scope for the smaller groupings that have niche markets (Anon., 1997). Other professionals agree that the processes of globalisation and consolidation will not squeeze groups out of business, arguing that there is in fact room in the marketplace for everybody (Anon., 1997).

Peter Cass of Preferred Hotels and Resorts asserts that the access to global distribution systems no longer provides competitive advantage for consortia with the widespread availability of the Internet. He insists that the traditional reservation affiliations have given way to the need for strategic positioning and that consortia must change their focus and structure in order to succeed in the new marketplace. He states that the main hope for the future success of consortia is 'to provide all the support and marketing of chains and franchise systems without actually licensing the brand' (quoted in Dela Cruz, 2000: 76).

There is little doubt that the way hotels are owned, marketed and managed has undergone significant change in recent times. Recent economic slowdown and the increasing threat of global terrorism serve as significant external threats and, according to Weinstein (2000), hold the entire industry hostage, forcing it to respond according to new realities. As with larger chains, hotel consortia are also affected by these global changes, as well as by the impact of hotel group mergers and other competitor activity. The large chains will continue to threaten consortia, especially the smaller players, but there is little doubt that they can survive as long as they remain adaptable. Independent consortia are moving rapidly and creatively in building their core competencies by representing fine hotels and developing and maintaining high quality standards for their constituent properties. Small consortia are also continuing to grow, albeit at a slower rate than the large chains. One emerging strategy for consortia wishing to remain competitive is to form yet further marketing partnerships and alliances, often in related business areas such as in travel, car hire, retailing and online businesses (Chipkin, 2001). In conclusion, it seems ironic that the fate of many independent hotels is to become part of yet further consortia in order for them to retain their 'independence' in the future. In this instance, the pivotal question is whether strategies of collaboration are merely reinforcing the drive towards consolidation in the accommodation sector, and perhaps even in the wider tourism industry.

Chapter 10
Destination Collaboration

Introduction

The tourist destination lies at the very heart of the travel and tourism system, representing as it does an amalgam of products that collectively provide a tourism experience to consumers. Referred to by Kotler *et al.* (1993) as 'tourism-place' products, destinations comprise the attractions, amenities and activities, ancillary services and points of access that collectively represent the 'focus of facilities and services designed to meet the needs of the tourist' (Cooper *et al.*, 1998: 102).

It might be argued that the very nature of the tourist destination product requires the application of the relational approach to marketing, as advocated by Helfert *et al.* (2002) and discussed in Chapter 2 of this book. Indeed, the multiplicity of components that make up the destination product, the complexity of the relationships that exist between them and the intensification of this complexity due to the large tendency for a large number of different stakeholders to be involved are such that the tourist destination is widely acknowledged to be one of the most difficult entities to manage and market (Sautter & Leisen, 1999). The complexity of the tourist destination as a product to be marketed is further increased when the consumer dimension is taken into consideration. For example, individual customers of the destination product will frequently differ in their perceptions, expectations and desired satisfactions of the 'tourism-place'. Few, if any, are likely to regard the destination as a neatly encapsulated bundle of suppliers, as might be the case from the supply perspective (Buhalis, 2000). The task of managing the tourist destination is therefore never going to be an easy one. The destination is likely not only to have multiple stakeholders, multiple components and multiple suppliers, but also to convey multiple meanings to multiple markets and market segments.

While the tourism destination is clearly a difficult product to market effectively, tourism destination marketers are also likely to continue to face considerable challenges in the future. The work of Bennett (1999), for example, identifies a range of possible future pressures for destination marketers, including the need to take account of the needs, wants and expectations of more mature and knowledgeable customers, and the corresponding need for more up-to-date and reliable information upon which to base such decision-making. Bennett also recognises the significant pressures caused by the continued presence and influence of intermediaries with respect to destinations, along with a corresponding imbalance of channel power for destinations in the tourism system. With regard to technological and transportation pressures, advances in effective destination management systems have taken place which now afford them necessity status, while the continuing growth of discount airlines and the plethora of new destinations continue to ensure fierce competition among destinations for tourist spend. In spite of these considerable pressures, however, Bennett considers the traditional 'dividing line' between the public and private sectors to be the principal catalyst for change; a dividing line that Bennett considers to have been holding back the potential of destination marketing for far too long.

More recently, King (2002) acknowledges the existence of a number of similar pressures. However, he also raises the spectre of traditional distribution channels being increasingly bypassed in the future by more direct contact between the consumer and the supplier. He also suggests that a shortening of booking lead times is likely, as is a gradual demise in the demand for mass tourism products leading to a greater pressure for the destination to deliver satisfactions and meet expectations of an increasingly independent tourist. King is very critical of many existing destination marketing organisations (DMOs), particularly insofar as they remain focused on 'what the destination has to offer' and continue to use 'mass marketing techniques more suited to the passive customer' (King, 2002: 106). He advances this theme by suggesting that the customer is now very much an active partner in the marketing process. For destinations to be a success, marketers will therefore need to engage the customer as never before, as well as be able to provide them with the types of information and experience they are increasingly able to demand. It is now 'the customer who can decide how and when they access their travel and tourism information and how and through what process they access and purchase their travel and tourism arrangements' (King, 2002: 106).

In the same study, King advances a number of so-called 'new realities' for destination marketers. These include the need for:

- Even greater emphasis on a strong brand image, with clearly identified and projected brand values that resonate with key target segments.
- More direct engagement with the customer to identify their holiday motivations, anticipate their needs and fulfil their aspirations.

- The establishment of ongoing, direct, two-way and networking consumer-communication channels, and for key customer relationship strategies to take place with the eventual development of mass customisation marketing and delivery capabilities.
- Greater emphasis to be given to the creation and promotion of holiday experiences that link key brand values and assets with the holiday aspirations and needs of key customers.
- A move away from a relatively passive promotional role to include greater intervention, facilitation and direction in the conversion process.

Related to the first of these 'new realities' identified by King, it can be argued that one of the biggest hurdles for destination marketers is their limited ability to build destination-wide brands. The lack of product control and the tight budgets they tend to experience, as well as the potential for political interference, all inhibit the ease with which brands can be developed. This in turn helps to explain why there is such a paucity of brand innovation in the destination sector as compared to other sectors within the tourism industry. This viewpoint is shared by Scott *et al.* (2000: 202) who argue that:

> the difficulties of co-ordination and control have the potential to undermine a strategic approach to marketing based on destination branding because campaigns can be undertaken by a variety of tourist businesses with no consultation or co-ordination on the prevailing message or the destination values being promoted.

Hopper (2002), meanwhile, identifies many of the above issues as contributing to why London has achieved so little sustained impact in terms of brand positioning.

Rather than explore the dynamics of some of these forces, the issue here is the extent to which many of them are in fact leading destinations to seek new, innovative ways of collaborating in order to meet both individual and collective destination goals. In this respect, Buhalis (2000: 99) suggests that 'failure to ensure and maintain a balance effectively jeopardises relationships between stakeholders and threatens the achievement of the strategic objectives and the long-term competitiveness and prosperity of destinations'. For destination marketing to be effective and succeed, it is clear that destinations need to bring all of the individual partners together to collaborate rather than compete, and to pool resources towards developing an integrated marketing mix and delivery system (Buhalis & Cooper, 1998).

King (2002) refers to this move towards greater collaboration as the 'network economy', in that DMOs will probably enter into strategic relationships with industry partners who can together provide a seamless experience for the customer. This is because it will be the 'relevance of the experience they offer the customer, rather than the destination they promote, which will be the key ingredient for success in the future' (King, 2002: 108). This viewpoint is shared by Bennett (1999), who calls for much more collaboration between all those involved in the destination product in order to take destinations forward. Collaboration is not considered as a luxury in this instance, but as a necessity for destinations to survive in the face of considerable competition and environmental challenges. In particular, traditional political boundaries need to be broken down, with a preference for autonomous DMOs that are out of the direct control of the public sector. According to Buhalis (2000: 99), 'destination management and marketing should act as tools and facilitators to achieve a complex range of strategic objectives, which will ultimately need to satisfy the needs and wants of stakeholders'. However, while they may be accountable for the delivery of destination marketing plans, DMOs are effectively only 'co-ordinators' in that they are unable to control all of the marketing activities in the destination or the mixes of individual players operating within the destination's boundaries. Unilateral marketing is common among individual businesses. Multilateral behaviour is, however, more prevalent in the context of DMOs. In essence, both competitive and collaborative behaviour needs to be recognised and managed in a co-ordinated and complementary manner. Ultimately, failure to develop collaborative approaches to marketing within the destination will hinder destination development, especially when the destination is getting larger.

The preceding two chapters have already demonstrated the movement away from adversarial models of marketing towards a growing recognition of the potential to be achieved by working in collaboration with others, be it among international airlines (Chapter 8) or hotels (Chapter 9). The vital question to be answered in this chapter, therefore, is to what extent can destinations themselves also benefit from collaboration?

Benefits and Drawbacks of Destination Collaboration

According to Palmer and Bejou (1995: 617), 'a *free market* solution to tourism destination marketing in which there is no collaboration among stakeholders gives rise to a number of potential problems for them'. There are three main reasons for this:

(1) Stakeholders are able to create less promotional impact on potential visitors by working independently than by joining together to put in place a promotional campaign in which resources are pooled.
(2) Market mechanisms typically fail to support and share the benefits of the collective promotion of an area. If some of the businesses in

an area paid for a promotional campaign, there would be no effective means of preventing those who did not pay for it from receiving a share of the benefits.

(3) In the marketing planning process, stakeholders can achieve their objectives more effectively by recognising their interdependencies. Strategic planning by the private sector can, however, be made more difficult in the absence of input from the public sector.

A number of destinations are beginning to acknowledge the inadequacies of the free market, competitive approach, and to accept the need for collaboration between the main stakeholders in the destination domain. For example, Jayawardena (2000) argues that the future success of the Caribbean as a destination lies ultimately in greater co-operation, teamwork and communication, and in a united effort by all the principal stakeholders. Likewise, in the context of London as a tourist destination, Hopper (2002) suggests that collaboration among key agencies within the destination is essential to enable agreement on the key messages to be transmitted to customers and to ensure a degree of consistency in decision making. To counter the dramatic drop in tourist numbers to London in the aftermath of the outbreak of foot and mouth disease in 2001, the London Tourist Board launched a highly successful 'Summer in the City' marketing campaign in partnership with short-break tour operator, Superbreak. Similarly, in response to the events of 9/11, the London Tourism Action Group was initiated, this being a collaborative action-response destination-marketing strategy led by the London Development Agency and including a wide range of London organisations and tourism industry bodies – even the Office of the Mayor.

Demands for collaborative action to help counter problems in the development and marketing of destinations are by no means a new phenomenon. For example, over a decade ago Bell (1992) argued that collaboration among Bali's tourism industry was essential in overcoming the island's perceived migration 'down market'. At the same time, Holder (1992) indicated that co-operation among the public and private sectors in tourism in the Caribbean was not merely desirable but a necessity in view of the particular characteristics of the tourism industry. With distinct problems evident between the public and private sectors in terms of lack of trust, mutual suspicion and disrespect, and a failure on the part of either party to understand the other's role, Holder suggested that unilateral visions of development were myopic insofar as the 'interests of the public and private sectors so closely converge' (Holder, 1992: 157–158). Public–private sector collaboration should in theory be an attractive proposition, as there is usually a congruence of objectives between the two sectors.

Studies such as those by Ayala (1997), Barkin and Pailles (1999), Long (2000), Minca and Getz (1995), Roberts and Simpson (2000) and Timothy (1998) examine destination collaboration at the local level (intra-destination collaboration) with a focus on destination development. Meanwhile, work by Sonmez and Apostolopoulos (2000) reflects upon the role intra-destination collaboration can play in resolving conflict between communities on the island of Cyprus. Another study by Standeven (1998) argues for the cohesive force of collaborative marketing as a vehicle to drive the development of sport tourism in view of the responsibilities for sport and tourism being both dispersed and fragmented.

Other studies, such as those by Darrow (1995) in the Caribbean and Henderson (2001) in the Greater Mekong Subregion, explore the means by which destinations can work in partnership with other destinations in improving the inter-regional, inter-state and inter-destination product. The question of inter-destination collaboration has been mooted much in the past but progress to date on achieving it has been somewhat patchy. For example, back in the late 1980s Teye (1988) outlined the need for greater regional co-operation among destinations in Africa, with joint promotion and marketing being just one of many avenues for potential collaboration. Building on the back of long-haul travel trends and the migration to multi-destination trips, inter-destination marketing collaboration was considered by Teye to be crucial to long-term success. Indeed, it was tourism marketing that provided 'the primary reason for whatever regional co-operation exists in developing countries' (Teye, 1988: 222). This view was driven by the observably narrow base for tourism existing in some countries, such as Zambia, and the availability of complementary tourism products in neighbouring countries and those bordering the Indian Ocean, such as Kenya, Tanzania, Mauritius and the Seychelles. In the mid-1990s, Wahab (1996) identified the constraints on the growth of tourism in Egypt only to conclude that international collaboration with other Middle Eastern countries was the way forward.

A number of advantages do, therefore, exist with respect to collaboration within and among destinations. These include:

- Reduction in risk through strength in numbers and interconnectedness within and across destinations.
- Efficient and effective exchange of resources for perceived mutual benefit.
- The generation of increased visitor flows and positive economic impacts.
- The potential for collaborative initiatives to counter the threat of channel intermediary powers.
- In peripheral locations, collaboration serving as a significant vehicle to broaden the destination domain.

- The ability to counter greater standardisation in the industry through the use of innovative collaborative marketing campaigns.
- The potential to develop destination-wide reservation systems and two-way dialogue with customers through technological collaboration, whereby the emerging technologies can facilitate relationship-building and customer relationship-management programmes.
- Further collaboration on the Internet, so affording DMOs the ability to reach large numbers of consumers, to transmit information and offer products at a relatively low cost, to provide complete and more reliable information, to make client reservations quickly and efficiently and to reduce the costs associated with producing and distributing printed materials.

In addition, Hill and Shaw (1995: 26) argue that 'co-operative marketing may be particularly advantageous when a country's tourism product is underdeveloped or when existing products are in an advanced stage in the product life cycle and it is desirable to attract new markets and/or formulate new products'. Similarly, Prideaux (2000) argues that collaboration in a promotional sense often starts at the destination level at the 'national' stage of the resort-development spectrum. This involves joint campaigns, with state, local government and local business campaigns taking place alongside campaigns between hotels and major attractions.

Destination collaboration is, however, far from widespread. Indeed, there remain a number of constraints and drawbacks to collaboration both within and between destinations. These include:

- General mistrust and suspicion among collaborating partners due to governance or structures that are inappropriate for moving the shared project forward.
- Inability of various sectors within the destination to work together due to excuses of a political, economic or even interpersonal nature.
- Instances where particular stakeholders fail to recognise the real value of collaboration and remain closed to the benefits of working together.
- The frequent disinterest in collaboration from 'honey-pot' attractions, where the need to work more closely together is discounted due to their own individual success in the marketplace.
- Competition between municipal authorities that administer separate geographical regions within a recognised destination resulting in inertia.

The problems involved in instigating effective destination collaboration are well illustrated in the model proposed by Prideaux and Cooper

(2002), as shown in Figure 10.1. Out of three destination marketing scenarios, Model B is identified as their 'preferred' option since it represents the middle ground in so far as equilibrium is established between destination-wide marketing and marketing efforts conducted by individual businesses.

For destination-marketing collaboration to succeed, the DMO needs to act as a strong 'unifying force' that is able to discourage the conception of splinter groups, which at a later stage can frustrate or otherwise oppose destination-wide strategies. If a strong counter-body does emerge, this may well generate significant confusion in the marketplace and engender dysfunctional behaviour within the destination.

Opportunities for Destination Collaboration

Collaboration is, nevertheless, likely to represent the sine qua non for successful destination marketing in the future. Tourism destinations are clearly complex domains which almost always involve a wide range of stakeholders, the constraints and aspirations of whom are typically highly divergent. As such, inter-organisational collaboration, often in the form of public–private sector partnerships, is a popular strategy for tourism destinations. Some of the areas on which such collaborative relationships often focus within and between destinations include the following.

Information gathering

Given the complexity of the destination domain, sufficient high-quality information tends to be at a premium for collaborative partnerships at the tourism destination level. The partnership organisation will typically need to collect, assimilate and analyse a range of data pertaining to the various stakeholder groups bound together in the collaboration. This may include, for example, data on their economic status, the distribution and control of tourism resources, and stakeholder opinions on, and aspirations for, the development of tourism. Visitor surveys are particularly important and the task of undertaking these often falls to the collaboration. Destination-level collaborative partnerships may also wish to monitor national trends and conduct market research (Ritchie & Brent Ritchie, 2002). A good example of this strategy in action is in the city of York, England, where successive public–private sector collaborations have devoted considerable time and effort to gathering, making use of and disseminating information, including the updating of an economic impact model (Augustyn & Knowles, 2000).

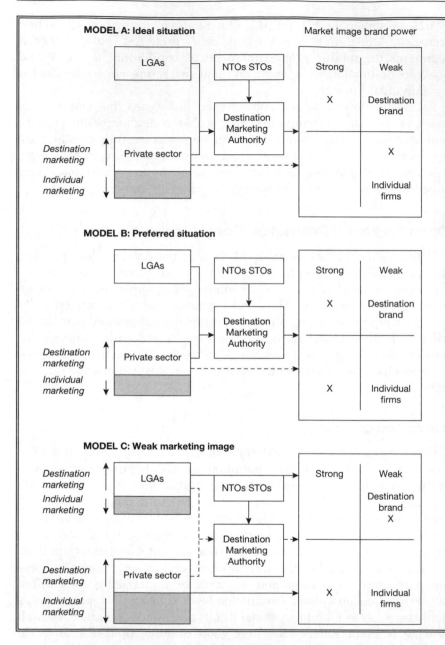

Figure 10.1 Destination marketing scenarios

Source: Adapted from Prideaux and Cooper, 2002

Note: In the above figure, STOs refer to state tourism organisations, while NTOs refer to national tourism organisations.

Product development

Given the complex and interrelated nature of the destination product, co-ordination often represents a barrier to the innovation of new destination-level tourism products, as well as to the development of existing ones. Destination partnerships often have an important role to play in enabling the co-ordination of the many stakeholder groups that will typically need to be involved in such activities. For example, Caffyn (2000) identifies several such activities undertaken by the North Pennines Tourism Partnership (England), including the development of walking itineraries, assisting the development of a network of camping barns, improvements to existing visitor attractions and the development of new visitor attractions. The partnership also initiated the erection of boundary signs for the North Pennines Area of Outstanding Natural Beauty, helped set up the North Pennines Farm Holiday Group and funded a number of arts and crafts initiatives in the area.

Another example relates to two former metropolitan areas of Yorkshire, England, those being Kirklees and Calderdale. These districts were formed when a former metropolitan county was abolished, and are centred on Huddersfield and Halifax respectively. In the mid-1980s the districts worked together in what was at the time considered an unusually close way, pooling efforts and resources to market themselves as a single entity (Bowden, 1991). This helped to reconfigure the public's perception of the area from a rather stereotypical image based on the districts' industrial past (Bowden, 1991) to one that reflected the area's considerable variety of countryside features and attractions. Joint promotion and rebranding to 'Pennine Yorkshire' enabled the districts to combine resources, people and budgets, and this contributed immensely in bringing tourists to a hitherto little-known corner of England.

Product marketing and promotion

Another task that often falls to tourism partnerships by virtue of the fragmented and complex nature of the tourism destination domain is product-marketing. By collaborating, participating organisations can achieve a number of important marketing advantages, including the ability to have a stronger presence at major international trade fairs and travel shows. Palmer and Bejou (1995), for example, found that more than three-quarters of their sample of tourism partnerships in the UK and the US undertook such activities. Many collaborative groups also compile and publish tourism directories for the destination, which can also be distributed to the travel trade as a promotional exercise. In case of York, England, collaborative marketing activities have also included the promotion of the city to rail travellers, coach parties and school groups (Augustyn & Knowles, 2000).

Visitor management

The focus of collaboration at the tourism destination often falls on visitor management, with the design, construction and operation of a central visitor information centre being a fairly common goal. Selin and Chavez (1995), for example, analyse the various stages of collaboration involved in the Eagle Valley Partnership, Colorado, where the idea of a visitor information centre emerged as a major focus of collaboration. After three years of collaborative work, the visitor information centre opened in 1991, comprising a centre–museum complex, rest rooms, a picnic area, a boating access ramp and a caboose (cabin) donated to the project. Collaborative efforts can also focus on the activities taking place within the visitor information centre, including the development of electronic reservation systems, web-based visitor information systems and so on.

Training and employment initiatives

While individual tourism businesses may wish to keep their training in house for fear of losing hard-fought competitive advantage to their competitors, generic training schemes can often be effectively promoted and delivered on a collaborative basis. Such training might include pre-season training for seasonal and new employees in customer care (such as the Welcome Host scheme), which has been the case in York (Augustyn & Knowles, 2000).

Networking and encouraging stakeholder support

If collaboration is to meet its objectives effectively, those involved must work to ensure that the major stakeholders remain committed to the collaborative method of working. This means that the collaborative efforts must be seen to benefit stakeholders, especially insofar as collaborative advantage is actually being achieved. It is imperative, therefore, that the collaborative partnership does not neglect activities that maintain stakeholder support and promote the strategy of partnership. In the case of the North Pennines Tourism Partnership, for example, regular newsletter postings and local exhibitions were undertaken to ensure a good flow of communication about the work and achievements of the partnership (Caffyn, 2000). The partnership also took the lead in collaborating with the North Pennines Tourism Association in setting up the North Pennines Festival.

Destination Collaboration in Action

The chapter will now introduce three short case studies in order to illustrate the dynamics of destination collaboration in practice. The first case study focuses on Queensland, Australia's principal tourism state, and contrasts attempts by two regional destinations, the Gold Coast and the Sunshine Coast, to develop and market themselves in a collaborative manner. The second case study explores some of the issues resulting from attempts to collaborate between nations in the establishment of a broader, cross-national destination domain. With its focus on the Greater Mekong Subregion (GMS), collaboration between China, Myanmar, Laos, Thailand, Cambodia and Vietnam highlights some interesting collaboration dynamics. The third case study takes a slightly different slant and looks at how destinations are exploring the benefits to be attained from the adoption of relationship-marketing strategies to engender repeat visitation and loyalty among consumers. With an example taken from the Stockholm Information Service, Sweden, this case study identifies the need for both collaboration within the destination, predominantly of a vertical nature, and collaboration with the final consumer as two vital ingredients for the successful implementation of relationship marketing at the destination level.

Intra-destination collaboration

A study conducted by Scott *et al.* (2000) reports on a series of destination 'nodes' that were identified by Tourism Queensland, the DMO for the State of Queensland, Australia. These were Tropical North Queensland, Brisbane, the Gold Coast, the Sunshine Coast and the Whitsundays. Each destination 'node' was identified as having distinct destination attributes and target markets, alongside a sufficiently developed tourist industry to warrant a portfolio approach to their management as a destination. This case study, which originates from work conducted by Prideaux and Cooper (2002), reports on two of these nodes, namely the Gold Coast and the Sunshine Coast. The study explores some of the aspects of the relationship between destination marketing and the actual growth of the two destinations. The principal focus of the case study is on the relationship between destination-marketing organisations, destination stakeholders and the local government authorities at both 'node' destinations.

The rationale for selection of these two destination 'nodes' was quite straightforward: they had similar institutional arrangements; both were located in a coastal area and had access to an international airport; and both were actively promoted by common state tourism organisations (STOs) and the national tourism organisation (NTO). Furthermore, the same domestic and international airlines serviced both destinations, both offered coastal and rainforest experiences and both were equidistant from Brisbane. Meanwhile, the outcome of previous collaboration was that, whereas the Gold Coast had become more successful in attracting the international market, the Sunshine Coast demonstrated a stronger domestic bias. Interestingly, the Gold Coast demonstrates the potential benefits for destinations that adopt a single marketing organisation, while the Sunshine Coast demonstrates a situation where multiple marketing organisations operate in a large destination.

Gold Coast

The Gold Coast is without question the principal mass tourism development in Queensland, benefiting from excellent transportation links with Brisbane, the state capital. The Gold Coast is administered by a single local government authority (LGA), known as the Gold Coast City Council (GCCC). Tourism was recognised early on in the destination's life cycle as an important contributor to the economy and, largely because of this, a much more professional approach was adopted from the 1960s onwards. In the late 1960s, the GCCC joined the Australian NTO, the Australian Tourist Commission (ATC), in an overseas mission to Japan. Later missions to Singapore and New Zealand demonstrated the destination's proactive approach to developing international markets, using a variety of formal and informal marketing strategies.

The present-day organisation of tourism in the Gold Coast is under the auspices of the Gold Coast Tourism Bureau (GCTB), which actively leads a large number of destination marketing initiatives. For example, the GCTB:

- Organises joining promotions sponsored by the public sector.
- Offers advice to prospective investors.
- Assists in the preparation of submissions to attract meetings, incentives, conventions and exhibitions (MICE) tourism.
- Monitors tourism trends.
- Prepares background information for LGAs.
- Acts as host to visiting journalists, trade buyers and tour operators.
- Distributes marketing material directly to the public as well as through a variety of channel intermediaries.

In addition to the above, the Gold Coast International Tourism Committee (GCITC), an association of 18 major destination operators, actively promotes the destination to the travel trade. However the GCTB and the GCITC market a single destination brand, 'Brand Gold Coast', which promotes a unified image to the world. Public-sector support has been consistent, with the participation of the state tourism authority, Tourism Queensland, and the ATC being instrumental to the growth in the number of international visitors to the destination. Quite clearly, there has always been a significant 'collective' spirit evident on the Gold Coast with respect to tourism, with the accommodation, attractions and tour operations sectors heavily supportive of the actions of the DMO. In short, the Gold Coast has been able to engender an environment and a set of formal and informal intra-destination relationships conducive to collaboration.

Sunshine Coast

The Sunshine Coast lies to the north of Brisbane, slightly closer in proximity than the Gold Coast. Unlike the Gold Coast, the 'nodal' area is managed by three independent LGAs: Noosa Shire Council, Maroochy Shire Council and Caloundra City Council. The three authorities have quite divergent interests and views with respect to tourism. For example, Noosa Shire Council exhibits a strong environmental and ecological protection focus. Maroochy Shire Council (which legislates for the largest and most rapidly developing community in the region), on the other hand, has actively encouraged development in the past. Caloundra City Council, meanwhile, is perhaps the keenest of the three authorities on further development at present. It is therefore not so surprising that tourism has been developed unilaterally in the past, this despite a major coastal highway linking the three shires and excellent transportation links to Brisbane. Despite an airport development at Maroochydore, which is particularly beneficial for inter-state tourism, close proximity to the international airport at Brisbane has delivered only limited benefits with regard to attracting inter-state and international visitors.

There has always been considerable competition between the three shires at the 'local' level, and indeed some tension. After a variety of previous organisational forms, Tourism Sunshine Coast (TSC) surfaced in the late 1980s with funding from Tourism Queensland, the individual LGAs and members of the TSC. However, although TSC is the recognised regional tourism authority, destination collaboration has been almost impossible to achieve, with the long history of rivalry between the LGAs and non-government interest groups impeding progress. Referring back to Figure 10.1 (p. 292), Model C is the destination marketing scenario which best describes the historical, and current, situation in the Sunshine Coast. In this instance, self-interest and opportunistic behaviour is apparent, with the overall marketing impact being diluted through diverse marketing activity and a longstanding failure to develop fully the collaborative 'destination domain'. Not only has this led to confusion in the minds of both customer and consumer, but it has also resulted in the dilution of promotional funds, has encouraged individual businesses to pursue unilateral marketing strategies and has led to the emergence of short-term selling strategies. The lack of unity at the 'nodal' destination has also led to investor uncertainty and the unnecessary competition for tourism expenditure.

In its defence, the Sunshine Coast has received fewer funds than its competitor south of Brisbane, and now requires inter-state visitors to use the 'hub' at Brisbane International Airport due to the collapse of Ansett Australia and the withdrawal of direct flights from Melbourne and Sydney. Although this is clearly an impediment to growth, the long-standing lack of collaboration has clearly hindered the development of tourism across the 'domain destination'.

Conclusions

In their original study, Prideaux and Cooper (2002: 49) concluded that:

> where there is strong co-operation between the private sector and LGAs at representative DMO level and where all key stakeholders in the tourism industry have supported a single brand strategy, the destination can anticipate considerable growth, as demonstrated by the Gold Coast.

Conversely, they concluded that:

> where there is a lack of unity or where there are multiple marketing bodies with multiple brands representing the same primary desti-nation there is considerable danger that primary market research will not be undertaken and that marketing strategy will degener-ate into unco-ordinated selling campaigns. (Prideaux & Cooper, 2002: 49)

This certainly seems to have been the case with the marketing of the Sunshine Coast, in that disunity, along with a confused and inconsis-tent external image, have contributed a great deal to creating an uncertain environment for tourism-related investors – an outcome highlighted in work by Ryan (2002). Furthermore it is significant that many tourists do not now restrict themselves to a single destination. Returning to the orig-inal comment made by Buhalis (2000) that the destination is often perceived quite differently by different groups of tourists, collaborative branding is, in part, a response to tourist behaviour at the destination as perceived by themselves.

Prideaux and Cooper (2002) conclude that the key elements to successful destination marketing include:

- Close co-operation, not competition, by LGAs if there is a number of LGAs administering the destination.
- A progressive employment of marketing strategies and tools over time according to geographically defined markets.
- Adoption of a single brand for the destination.
- Adoption of a marketing structure that closely adheres to Model B in Figure 10.1 (p. 292).

Although the situation in the Sunshine Coast appears to have persisted over a long period of time, Heath and Wall (1992) suggest that problems related to collaboration between local authorities and destination-marketing organisations can be overcome, or at least reduced, by establishing greater consensus between stakeholders on the domain 'sense of purpose' as part of a more participative management approach. Greater collaboration is, therefore, viewed as a precondition for effective brand building, which, in turn, becomes a catalyst for further growth.

Inter-destination collaboration

This second study, which focuses on the Greater Mekong Subregion, develops the theme of destination collaboration further by looking at an example of inter-destination collaboration or collaboration between one or more countries in pursuit of a common goal – typically increased tourist visitation and expenditure. The origin of such collaboration is built on the premise that collaboration will be advantageous to a country when the outcome of the initiative exceeds that which the country acting alone would produce using similar resources (Hill & Shaw, 1995). In essence, inter-destination collaboration is where one or more countries collaborate to establish a common identity and promote themselves as a single tourist destination.

Greater Mekong Subregion

The Greater Mekong Subregion (GMS) in Southeast Asia is centred on the region through which the Mekong River flows (Figure 10.2). From the Himalayas to its delta in Vietnam, the Mekong flows through Yunnan Province in China, Myanmar, Laos, northeast Thailand, most of Cambodia and, eventually, Vietnam. The area clearly has an abundance of natural, cultural and historical resources that provide considerable potential for tourism development. Tourism is deemed by the individual governments to be a vehicle for achieving economic growth and a higher standard of living for its citizens. However, with a range of political and security issues besetting the region throughout the past three decades, the GMS represents a considerable destination-building challenge.

The Asian Development Bank (ADB) provided the initial impetus for subregional collaboration. In the early 1990s, the ADB recognised the region as a single entity 'with scope for integrated and cooperative development, incorporating tourism' (Henderson, 2001: 151). The fact that the six countries shared political boundaries, natural resources and history provided the catalyst for the ADB. The belief was that the region provided an excellent opportunity to benefit from collaborative advantage through inter-destination tourism collaboration. The challenge was, however, significant, in that, despite sharing much in common in respect of their

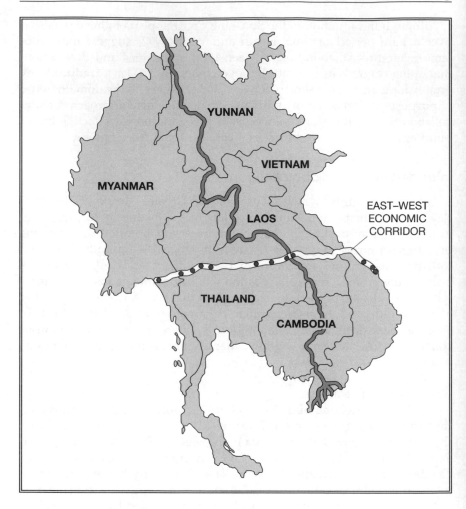

Figure 10.2 The Greater Mekong Subregion and the East–West
Economic Corridor

Source: www.visit-mekong.com, 2003

tourism products and overall levels of product maturity, the countries
are in fact very different. For example, while Thailand is one of the most
mature tourist destinations in the region, Laos and Myanmar are
probably two of the poorest countries in the world, with very limited
basic infrastructure and services. The ADB recognised the marketing
power of the Mekong River and believed that, with effective marketing
between the six countries, the river could in fact become a very powerful
touristic icon.

Despite best efforts, much goodwill and all good intentions, progress was deemed to be slow in the early stages, with a succession of collaborative forms not managing to advance the project rapidly. In 1997, progress was hastened with the establishment of the Agency for Coordinating Mekong Tourism Activities (AMTA), located at the headquarters of the Tourism Authority of Thailand (TAT) in Bangkok. Today, AMTA is the permanent secretariat to the Tourism Working Group (TWG), which was originally formed in 1994. Its principal objectives are to:

- Co-ordinate Mekong tourism activities and especially marketing.
- Co-ordinate tourism skills development.
- Help strengthen relationships among participating NTOs.

Designed to accelerate the momentum of subregional inter-destination collaboration, progress has been made in respect of:

- Joint tourism marketing and promotion.
- Travel facilitation.
- Training in basic tourism skills.
- Mekong River tourism infrastructure planning and development.

In respect of the last of these points, efforts are being made to bring the region's airlines and tour operators into closer contact with each other so as to form a reliable and integrated airline network. There is also the East–West Economic Corridor (EWEC), which also provides a valuable land link between four of the six nations. The EWEC, which is about 1,600 km long, is the only land link which connects the Indian Ocean with the Pacific. As can be seen in Figure 10.2, the EWEC provides a ready framework for co-operation. Potentially, the cultural heritage and varied natural geography of the EWEC make it a further subregional tourist destination in itself.

For the GMS, the principal international tourist markets identified for growth are the US, Japan, Taiwan, Australia, France, Germany and the UK. A wide range of marketing communications media has been produced to target these core markets, including publications, guides, brochures and maps. To strengthen marketing efforts further, a Marketing Task Force was established in 2000. More recently, a dedicated website has been established (www.visit-mekong.com), which for the first time brings the full range of tourism products and destinations in the GMS direct to the consumer.

Such an ambitious inter-destination initiative is always likely to encounter problems. For example, the negative implications of such an initiative may include:

- Conflict occurring with demands for greater regional and local autonomy.

- Insufficient government support and funding.
- Political disturbances in one country and the negative impact of the country image tarnishing other nations and impacting adversely on their tourism.
- Inconsistencies in national policies and systems.
- Political and commercial sensitivities.

Although there still remains a lack of empirical data about collaborative forms in which countries share assets in pursuit of a common goal, Henderson (2001) proposed 10 key criteria upon which the effectiveness of the GMS could be benchmarked. The first five criteria originate from a study conducted by Hill and Shaw (1995) in Australia:

- Close proximity to one another compared to their proximity to the origin market.
- *En route* air service connections.
- Similar standards in tourism products.
- Compatible tourist attractions.
- Many multinational tourism enterprises.

To these, Henderson (2001) adds five further criteria:

- Appropriate political and economic systems and stability.
- Compatible stages of tourism development.
- Ease of movement.
- Presence of an effective and unifying image.
- Favourable travel industry attitude towards the implementation of public sector initiatives.

Each of the above criteria is now to be examined with regard to the status of inter-destination tourism within the GMS:

- *Proximity*: the six countries of the GMS clearly share a close geographic proximity to one another relative to the distance from their predominantly long-haul markets.
- *En route air service connections*: with Bangkok dominating as the 'hub' airport, an extensive timetable now exists that connects all the key destinations within the GMS.
- *Similar standards in tourism products*: although significant measures are being put in place to reach this target, Thailand is clearly more advanced than the other five countries at present in respect of tourism infrastructure and quality of the tourist offer. It is hoped that, over time, this target will be achieved.
- *Compatible tourist attractions*: there exists a considerable diversity of attractions in the GMS, although there is clearly also some potential for duplication and overlap. On the other hand, each country has its own distinct character as a tourist destination, which

is a reflection of their differing geography, history, economics and social and political contexts. Major attractions in the GMS include indigenous hill tribes in northern Thailand and Vietnam and minority tribes in Yunnan Province. There are also the Angkor Wat temple in Cambodia and the former Laotian capital of Luang Prabang, both designated UNESCO World Heritage Sites. In addition, the GMS offers numerous other heritage sites, particularly of an armed conflict and ex-colonial genre.

- *Multinational tourism enterprises*: these exist in abundance in Thailand but to a lesser extent in the other five countries. This reflects Thailand's relative maturity as a tourist destination.
- *Political and economic systems and stability*: a number of pan-regional organisations have offered support to the development of tourism in the GMS, such as the Association of Southeast Asian Nations (ASEAN) and the Pacific Area Tourism Association (PATA). Recently, SARS has clearly served as a major impediment to growth and regional stability. However, other more long-standing issues, such as military dictatorship in Myanmar, Communist control in Laos, Yunnan and Vietnam, and the military power and political influence of the Thai armed forces, have all, on various occasions, impacted on the speed of economic growth. Investment levels and infrastructural developments have been affected, while the deep-rooted legacy of suspicion and hostility in certain areas is a historical inheritance that is difficult to ignore. More recently, there has also been a move towards more opportunistic bilateral developments between countries, which ultimately may undermine multilateral collaborative initiatives. The power of Thailand in the alliance is also an issue, as Thailand is clearly the economic driver behind many of the tourism initiatives.
- *Compatible stages of tourism development*: this is clearly an issue in that Thailand outperforms all the other destinations put together. With less historical baggage of internal strife and war, Thailand has experienced a much more stable climate for development than any of its neighbours, especially Cambodia, Vietnam and Myanmar. However, inclusion of Thailand in the GMS brings with it substantial experience of tourism development and economic influence which can only benefit the other five countries.
- *Ease of movement*: this is an essential prerequisite for tourism development. In addition to integrated airline systems and land communications, such as the EWEC, the smooth operation of immigration and issuing of visas is vital, as are cordial cross-border regulations integral to the development of tourism within the GMS. At present, visa policies are restrictive, especially for overland crossings and multiple entry. The facilitation of intra-GMS travel is clearly vital for the development of tourism within the GMS.

- *Image*: the need to forge a common identity and establish a consistent and coherent brand image for the GMS has begun to be addressed with the recent launch of the GMS website. As Henderson (2001: 157) states, 'multiple destinations participating in a strategic alliance require a unifying theme or meaningful image to which tourists, the tourism industry, and investors can respond'. Considerable progress needs to be made here, but the launch of its own website represents a definite step in this direction.
- *Travel industry support*: although the travel industry has expressed much commercial interest in the GMS product, there remains unease and concern over issues pertaining to security and the liberalisation of visas and cross-border controls.

Conclusions

The fact that many of the above criteria are very difficult to measure serves as an impediment to determining the overall degree of success achieved by the GMS collaborative initiative. Likewise, the fact that the entire GMS project is ongoing makes it difficult to make conclusions as to its effectiveness. The project has a dynamic to it which is evolving on a daily basis. This having been said, it would appear that, for the collaborative tourism entity (the GMS) to succeed fully, a far closer partnership is required among the individual NTOs and other associated agencies. There is also the requirement for greater private-sector involvement, as is there a need for many more 'packages' or 'heritage trails' to be developed that facilitate the selling of the GMS as a single product.

As things stand, it is clear that not all of the 10 criteria are being met. However, the GMS remains an ambitious attempt to ignite tourism development in five regions, which, apart perhaps from Thailand, are desperate for economic development and an upgrade in living standards for their host communities. If harnessed further in the future, there still remains hope that the GMS can serve as the catalyst for future development, regional harmony and economic prosperity in the region.

Destination relationship marketing

This final case study, originating from work by Fyall and Callod (2003) and Fyall *et al.* (2003), adopts a slightly different slant in that it represents a predominantly vertical approach to collaboration between DMOs and other components of the tourism product in an attempt to engender repeat visitation among visitors.

Although the relevance of loyalty is acknowledged in the wider marketing literature (Sheth & Parvatiyar, 2000), the phenomenon has received limited attention in the tourism destination literature (Oppermann, 2000).

This may be attributed to the volume and frequency requirements within short time frames for relationship marketing to succeed and the very different purchasing patterns typically found in leisure travel markets. However, work by Riley *et al.* (2001) suggests that the loyalty status of a destination visitor may be translated into one where the visitor values the destination, prefers it to other potential places to visit and ultimately feels devoted to it. Thereafter, the visitor may feel that switching costs would be incurred in changing to another destination. Defined as such, it is clear that destination loyalty is more suited to attitudinal or composite, rather than behavioural, measures of decision making, as indeed was posited by Jacoby and Chestnut (1978). Irrespective of whether a particular case supports destination loyalty as a function of attitudinal or composite loyalty measurements, it is pertinent to evaluate how a tourist's propensity to discontinue or to continue to visit the destination is formed, since this is the basis for any loyalty-building strategy.

Determinants of repeat visitation by tourists to destinations include the friendliness of the destination's residents (Ross, 1993), cultural amenities, natural attractions and activities (Court & Lupton, 1997) and past experience and destination familiarity (Oppermann, 1999). However, the above conclusions are drawn from single studies on single destinations, so their relevance may not be universal. This is particularly so with regard to the link between satisfactory experience and repeat visitation, whereby Bowen and Shoemaker (1998) stress that many tourists report high levels of satisfaction yet fail to return. Bowen and Shoemaker do, however, accept that loyal tourists do tend to make more frequent purchases, demonstrate increased willingness to broaden the base of their purchasing behaviour over time, engage in 'partnership actions' such as influencing others through word-of-mouth advertising, show decreased price sensitivity and are less sensitive to offers from competitive destinations. Furthermore, Reid and Reid (1993) argue that loyal tourists tend to visit more frequently, tend to be a stable source of income and can be more profitably served than new buyers. On the other hand, Oppermann (1997) suggests that repeat tourists to a destination visit considerably fewer attractions, despite on average staying longer, and notes that the expenditure of repeat tourists tends to be slightly lower. Work by Pyo *et al.* (1998), meanwhile, suggests that repeat tourists tend to seek relaxation rather than activities, and that repeat tourists are more likely to be visiting friends and relatives. However, it is the frequent inability of tourism destination marketers to determine whether or not their tourists are on a repeat visit, how often they have visited in the past and with what regularity that can seriously impair the design and implementation of successful relationship marketing (Oppermann, 1998). Despite this, there is evidence to suggest that tourism destination marketers still consider the perceived benefits of relationship marketing worth pursuing.

It is in many ways immaterial whether one views relationship marketing as a tactical 'currency' promotional activity, as a strategic tool whereby a supplier seeks to 'tie in' customers or as a fundamental business philosophy (Palmer & Mayer, 1996). Indeed, all three pose significant challenges for the marketing of tourism destinations. More important, perhaps, is the need to select those customers necessary to achieve maximum profitability/value for both parties (Newell, 1997), to ensure high quality standards through a constant dialogue with customers as well as a constant wish to improve (Ballantyne, 1994), to extend marketing to the entire organisation (Payne *et al.*, 1996), to deliver a value to the customer that motivates him or her to stay in the relationship (Fournier *et al.*, 1998) and to develop long-term relationships wherein supplier and customer can work as 'partners' (Grönroos, 1994). The tourism destination that wishes to engage in relationship marketing needs to heed the above principles if tourist loyalty and repeat visitation are to be achieved.

The Stockholm Information Service, Sweden

For effective relationship marketing to succeed, the aforementioned core elements of the activity need to be examined in the light of the available resources and competencies of the organisation, as well as the forces and circumstances that surround it. These elements serve as a framework for examining the potential of relationship marketing within the Stockholm Information Service (SIS), which is the DMO responsible for the co-ordination of the marketing of the city of Stockholm as a tourist destination.

Selection of the right customers: Based on the value each visitor can provide the destination over time, minus the costs of serving the same visitor, destinations need to effectively select their 'right' visitor base. Criteria may include:

(1) *Frequency and volume of purchase*: this may prove problematical for destinations, as it is attitudinal more than behavioural loyalty that is the focus for the SIS.
(2) *Total spending patterns*: although market surveys may provide the SIS with an indication of how much different visitor groups spend at the destination, the organisation has no direct way of controlling a specific visitor's pattern of expenditure, unless initiatives of co-operation to share and jointly compile data among all actors are taken.
(3) *Proportion of purchase*: the SIS has very limited knowledge of frequency of visits and consequently partial knowledge of the

proportion of visits Stockholm represents for visitors. Just as for frequency and volume, these measures are, however, of less import-ance to the SIS due to its focus on attitudinal loyalty.

(4) *Probability of purchase*: probability of purchase is the tool used by the SIS in its analysis of customer 'attitudinal' attractiveness in the European market. Couples/families with medium-to-high incomes and a desire for independent travel have been chosen on the belief that this group has a higher-than-average propensity to consume the product and develop a positive attitude towards it. As a result, the SIS sees value in investing more in this group and has created the Stockholm Project – a partnership between th SIS, Scandic Hotels and SAS Airlines – to serve them.

Total quality: Relationship marketing establishes the need for strong overall quality and constant quality improvement within the organisa-tion (Ballantyne, 1994). In the case of a tourism destination, the visitors' quality perceptions are thought to reflect the total trip experience, and all factors of the destination have an impact on experienced outcome and on the quality image of the destination (Murphy *et al.*, 2000). This highlights the importance for a tourism destination management organ-isation to:

(1) *Ensure overall quality of the destination product*: as the tourism desti-nation is an amalgam of independent actors, ensuring the quality of the product and its marketing is a significant challenge. It is recog-nised by the SIS that successful collaboration, essential if Stockholm is to become a competitive tourism destination.

(2) *Achieve excellence of quality*: current strategies conducted by the SIS to address this issue include the implementation of extensive visitor surveys, the setting up of a quality management committee, the launch of quality standards, existence of systems to monitor service performance and handle customer complaints and initiatives to enhance employee satisfaction.

Marketing extended to the whole organisation: In its attempt to achieve this goal, the SIS has recognised the importance of staff as a vital link in the quality of the destination, and has identified the need for specific staff guidance. However, due to limited financial and human resources, the SIS can only play a minor role in the development of a suitable marketing culture among its staff members. In reality, the SIS relies instead on the organisational cultures of its suppliers and its ability to form effective partnerships with key actors.

Added customer value: An organisation pursuing a relationship-marketing strategy creates more value for its customers by improving its perform-ance and/or by reducing customers' non-monetary costs through strategies of customisation. This may be in the form of direct-marketing material, service delivery or experiential aspects of consumption. It has been argued that such an organisation develops tighter ties with its customers than one which seeks to reduce monetary costs (Grönroos, 1994). A tourism destination may, however, encounter specific problems in the customer process. For example, specific problems for the SIS include the co-ordination and collection of information and the ability actually to deliver added value. The value perception visitors receive from a tourism destination is dependent on the performance of each indepen-dent actor, despite the fact that the destination is consumed as a single product. Efforts of all actors must therefore be co-ordinated to deliver value to visitors.

Long-term co-operation: The time perspective in relationship marketing has moved beyond the single transaction to focus on long-term part-nership-building with the customer (Grönroos, 1994). This long-term co-operation covers all forms of contact between the organisation and the customer, and, as such, has far-reaching implications. It is mostly a matter of how close the organisation can become to its customer, and, as a result, the long-term perspective is dependent just as much on customer attitudes as it is on the strategies of the organisation. With its current strategic emphasis on increasing awareness and repeat visita-tion, for the SIS to adopt a longer-term orientation the problem of infrequent purchase by visitors, the issue of increased buyer confidence, and both visitors' and the SIS's value of a relationship all need to be addressed.

Conclusions

The highly competitive global market for tourists serves as a catalyst for tourism destinations to seek more innovative 'relationship' marketing strategies so as to engender a degree of loyalty and stimulate lucrative repeat business within their visitor base. This case study demonstrates that, in the case of Stockholm, although its destination life-cycle posi-tion suggests that loyalty building ought to be a strategic imperative, the particularities of the tourism destination product complicate the building of relationships with the end consumer: the visitor. In turn, these complications appear to diminish the suitability and value of relationship marketing for tourism destinations.

In a context of many destinations competing in price-driven, low-margin markets, the costs and benefits to be derived from relationship marketing require significant research before tourism destinations are able to accept the concept as a new paradigm or potential solution to maintain/expand their share of the market for visitors. In view of the inherent imbalance of power, resources and experience between tourism-destination 'actors', generating cohesion, mutual trust and respect within the tourism system stands as a significant challenge for those marketing tourism destinations in the future.

Conclusion

In concluding this chapter, it is probably fair to say that the three case studies adopt a predominantly positive approach to the adoption of collaborative marketing. The one element that they have in common, however, is the lack of a robust mechanism to test fully the extent to which it is in fact the collaborative aspects of their marketing strategies that have delivered the major benefits. Accurate measurement, monitoring and control is a perennial problem for all marketers, irrespective of one's sector, in that so many variables can impact upon the success, or otherwise, of marketing campaigns. However, this is a particular problem for those involved in collaborative marketing.

In view of the above, it is instructive to conclude with an examination of a recent study by Dwyer (2003), which goes some way towards challenging the so-called 'standard view' of the benefits of collaborative destination marketing by suggesting that the much-communicated benefits may in fact not be economically valid after all. Dwyer, indeed, suggests that there are in fact 'very few areas of tourism research that have more immediate implications for practitioners than the area of cooperative destination marketing' (2003: 103). Much of the argument proposed by Dwyer is based on the premise that there remains an insufficient understanding of the internal dynamics of collaboration and that many of the so-called economic benefits have not yet fully been tested empirically. According to Dwyer (2003: 96), the view that 'transactions and administrative costs aside, a destination will always reap positive economic impacts from cooperative marketing if it experiences greater injected tourism expenditure as a result of participation in this form of activity' is a dangerous assumption to make and one upon which investors are advised to proceed with caution.

There are in fact two principal reasons for destinations to collaborate in the context of destination marketing. The first is where two or more destination players perceive mutual benefits or gains to be derived from collaboration. The second is where a resource dependency perspective is evident, wherein collaboration is expected to improve overall control over scarce resources in the environment. For inter-destination examples of collaboration, Wing (1994) propagates the view that clear benefits accrue from increased visitation, quoting Sri Lanka, Nepal and the Maldives as examples of good practice. Dwyer counters this, however, by suggesting that:

> [the] implication of this view is that where cooperative destination marketing increases overall visitation to a region, individual destinations will gain if they experience increased visitor expenditure regardless of any change in their individual shares of the collective market. (Dwyer, 2003: 97–98)

Whether collaboration is intra-destination, as in the case of the Gold and Sunshine Coasts example, or inter-destination, as in the GMS example, Dwyer argues that this assumption is in fact dependent on the particular mix of industries in collaborating destinations, suggesting that losses may occur if the mix is imbalanced.

This viewpoint, if corroborated, clearly has important implications for stakeholders involved in destination collaboration and the overall effectiveness of collaboration outcomes. In his study of destination collaboration across Australia, Dwyer (2003: 99) concluded that:

> in general, the Australian states to gain most from additional tourism are those having a higher share of their Gross State Product (GSP) accounted for by the air transport and aircraft industries, and by local industries dependent on sales to tourists, and a lower share of their GSP accounted for by industries in the traditional export sectors of agriculture and mining.

If true, this may have important consequences for further destination collaboration. Destinations considering collaboration to be a vehicle to achieve individual and collective outputs, be it at the subregional, regional, state or national level, will need to consider fully:

- Their rationale for collaboration.
- Their expected benefits, particularly economic benefits.
- The opportunity cost of 'going it alone'.
- The extent to which greater visitation levels are likely to serve as a catalyst for even further economic development.
- The destination 'industry mix'.

This latter point relates directly to Dwyer's findings in that those destinations that are most dependent on export earnings in primary and secondary industrial sectors are most likely to suffer adverse economic effects from tourism growth. Although there is clearly some merit in this viewpoint, arguably these comments can equally be applied to tourism growth in general. In all cases, and whatever the industry-mix context, prescriptions for destination collaboration should only ever be made once the destination has a full understanding of the needs of stakeholders and the constraints of their environments (Palmer & Bejou, 1995). And, rather than relying on across-the-board increases, collaborating partners should perhaps strive to increase their 'domain' share of visitors. A consequence of this, however, is the potential for opportunistic behaviour and the creation of imbalance within the collaborative form, leading possibly to mutual mistrust, suspicion and ultimately to inertia for fear of the others 'losing out' and, ultimately, the return to more adversarial forms of competitive marketing.

Part 5: From Competition to Collaboration in the Tourism Industry

Part 5 Introduction

From Competition to Collaboration in the Tourism Industry

The fundamental philosophy of marketing is that the key to the organisation achieving its goals is for it first to determine the needs and wants of various target markets and then to deliver the desired satisfactions more efficiently and effectively than its competitors. Despite many advances in marketing theory and practice over the years, this basic philosophy has remained the accepted orthodoxy. However, in the face of major changes in the business environment, particularly the accelerating trend towards globalisation in recent times, serious questions now have to be asked of the traditional 'adversarial' orientation of marketing. In particular, how appropriate is this marketing orientation in meeting the demands of the increasingly dynamic, complex and turbulent marketplace?

In this book we argue that the forces of change are now such that this established marketing paradigm is becoming increasingly untenable in the global marketplace. Instead, the adoption of more 'relational' collaborative approaches to marketing is necessary. Marketing conducted by an organisation without reference to the relationships it either already has, or perhaps might have, with other key stakeholders in the problem domain will increasingly find itself unable to meet its objectives. Likewise, if the collaborative dimension is overlooked or ignored, marketing strategies of the future are likely to lack relevance and therefore be ineffective.

An important proposition underpinning this view is that the marketing domain is essentially one in which collaboration is increasingly not just advantageous but obligatory. To accommodate this collaborative approach to marketing it will be necessary for organisations to change their philosophies, modes of operation, management practices and strategic decision-making. Organisations need to learn how to develop and maintain partnerships with a range of stakeholders, as well as to find new collaborative ways to secure market advantage and deliver superior added value.

The central premise of this book is that the unilateral, adversarial, competitive orientation of marketing that has dominated marketing theory for so long is in fact facing a powerful challenge in the form of collaborative, multi-party, relational marketing. Christopher *et al.* (2002: 129) refer to this as 'network marketing', arguing that:

> The realisation that individual businesses no longer compete as stand-alone entities, but as collaborative networks, has been perhaps one of the most significant breakthroughs in management thinking in recent years. We are now entering the era of 'network competition' where the prizes will go to those organisations that can best structure, co-ordinate and manage relationships with their partners in a network committed to creating customer and consumer value through collaboration.

This argument is considered to be particularly valid in respect of the marketing of tourism. As set out in Chapter 2, tourism is a highly complex and multi-sectoral industry, where no single organisation provides or has control over the entire product. Successful delivery of the wider tourism product is dependent on close working relationships, inter-dependencies and interactions with numerous other stakeholders and is therefore particularly relevant to the collaborative marketing paradigm.

Collaboration between organisations is certainly not a new phenomenon. What is new, however, is its emergence as a decision-making paradigm, arising from bodies of knowledge relating to relationship marketing, network marketing, stakeholder theory and inter-organisational collaboration. This paradigm has the potential to transform marketing thinking and practice, particularly in the tourism industry. In attempting to understand the full implications of this paradigm, Parts 1 and 2 of this book have explored the 'traditional' market paradigm, based on the pursuit of competitive advantage, while Part 3 has examined theories of inter-organisational exchange. Three sector-based case studies, presented in Part 4 of the book, have then attempted to apply some of the important insights of inter-organisational exchange theory to the practice of tourism marketing.

Chapter 11, which follows, attempts to draw together a synthesis of the above, utilising the structure of the strategic tourism marketing planning process. The focus is on how the tourism organisation might achieve collaborative advantage through the application of a collaborative marketing approach. The material is structured as responses to a series of questions, presented below, that arise out of the foregoing chapters of the book. These are intended not only to represent a focus for our conclusions on the subject of collaborative marketing but also to serve as catalysts for future research in this area. The questions all have one theme in common: to what extent can existing models, theories, concepts and principles of 'adversarial' competitive marketing advance the adoption and effective practice of 'relational' collaborative marketing in tourism? In effect, the philosophical underpinning of the notion of market orientation, the marketing strategy process and the implementation of marketing programmes themselves require scrutiny and revalidation from a 'relational' collaborative perspective. The aim is not to dismiss the frameworks and models that have served the marketing discipline so well, for so long, but to explore their suitability for the underpinning of strategic marketing planning for collaborating firms and organisations in the tourism industry.

Situation Analysis

- To what degree, and with what consequences (either positive or negative), are individual competitive and joint collaborative visions compatible with one another, consistent with stakeholder expectations and in accord with employees' or participants' understanding of the overriding strategic direction of the organisation?
- What mechanisms are in place to co-ordinate the activity between competing and collaborating organisations, thereby ensuring successful delivery of the corporate vision and mission?
- How compatible are the individual organisation's goals and objectives with those of the collaborative domain, and how compatible are the goals and objectives of the collaboration with the participating organisation's goals and objectives?
- With regard to PEST analysis, how do macro-environmental factors impact upon parallel competitive and collaborative marketing practice and to what extent is PEST analysis equally valid to both competitive and collaborative market environments?
- Do some environmental factors carry more weight than others when determining strategy in collaborative environments?
- In the destination life cycle, are the four life-cycle stages of equal importance to competitive and collaborative marketing? Are the duration of each stage and the marketing responses deemed appropriate in situations of competitive marketing equally valid in the context of collaborative marketing?
- Are situations of parallel competitive and collaborative marketing by organisations reflected in the life-cycle model?
- Is the Five Forces model suitable for situations of collaborative marketing, are amendments required to the model to represent the collaboration context more accurately, and how may relationships vary between suppliers, buyers and competitors in contrasting competitive and collaborative environments?

- To what extent is an amended version of strategic group analysis necessary to accommodate more accurately the relational networks that exist in the collaboration domain? Is the model of equal value to both competitive and collaborative situations? To what extent can the strategies of competing and collaborating organisations be successfully analysed using the same model?
- Are the various components of the marketing audit of equal value to both competitive and collaborative environments?
- How are issues pertaining to confidentiality, trust and proprietary skills accommodated in the marketing audit, and are there likely to be significant information gaps in the context of collaboration?
- How readily are collaborating organisations prepared to contribute equitable amounts and quality of information to marketing information systems?
- Are there likely to be significant information gaps in the collaboration context? Is a marketing information system a realistic proposition in a collaborative domain?
- What are the system and organisational dynamics of developing such a tool for information and research in the context of collaboration?
- What are the necessary linkages and sources of 'added value' for collaborative marketing activities and organisations? What are the likely sources of friction of analysing such organisational competencies and attributes in a collaborative setting? Moreover, how is 'value added' to be measured in the context of collaborative marketing?
- Which organisational resources are funded, allocated and used for competitive and collaborative marketing activity? To what degree are resources allocated equitably between competitive and collaborative marketing? How is resource use monitored in each situation?
- How appropriate is the Brand Pyramid in situations of collaborative co-branding and what are the customer perceptions of co-branding with regard to the thematic, stylistic and core attributes and values of the brand? How do competitive and collaborative brands actually compete with or complement one another in the marketplace?
- How valuable is the Branding Iceberg in situations of co-branding and to what extent do the competitive and collaborative brands 'above' and 'below' the line compete with or complement one another?
- What evidence is there of conflict and friction in the 'below-the-line' management of co-brands and how compatible are organisational attributes and competencies in situations of co-branding?

- How appropriate are the BCG and GE matrices in the context of collaborative marketing? What are the likely resource implications for alternative forms of collaborative marketing and how suitable are the existing criteria as bases for analysis?
- How suitable is the destination market matrix to multiple destination collaborative marketing strategies? Are the four life-cycle stages equally valid to multiple destination collaboration situations? What are the most appropriate variables for analysis along each axis?
- Are the fundamentals of a competitive SWOT analysis equally valid to competitive and collaborative marketing situations? To what extent are customers able to distinguish sufficiently the critical success factors of a collaborative marketing initiative to make the consumer-oriented SWOT a worthwhile model to enhance effective 'collaborative' strategic marketing planning?

Strategic Tourism Marketing Planning

- Can the generic strategy option of the collaborative domain sit comfortably alongside the generic strategies of the participant organisations? How do organisations conducting parallel competing and collaborating marketing strategies reconcile their generic strategies?
- How might an organisation's selected generic strategy contribute to its choice of collaborating partner?
- How does an organisation's market position impact on its choice of partner(s) in collaborative marketing situations and on the effectiveness of its relationship with other collaborating partners?
- How does an organisation's market position impact on the structure, governance and outcome of a collaborative form?
- How might offensive and defensive strategies vary in competitive and collaborative situations? Are offensive and defensive strategies more suited to one situation than another and is it possible to implement offensive and defensive strategies at the same time in parallel competitive and collaborative environments?
- How may the implementation of push and pull approaches to strategy vary in competitive and collaborative market conditions?
- To what extent is strategic overlap likely to occur in contrasting competitive and collaborative situations?
- How compatible are the marketing objectives determined for the individual organisation and those of collaborating partners, and how likely are the marketing objectives of the collaborative form to satisfy the marketing objectives of the individual organisation?
- Who determines the marketing objectives of the collaborative marketing form and what resource implications may there be for

individual partners in meeting the requirements of the collaborative marketing objectives?

- How are organisations able to reconcile their segmentation, targeting and positioning decisions in parallel competitive and collaborative market situations?
- What are the resource implications for individual collaboration partners in meeting the requirements of the collaborative decision on segmentation, targeting and positioning?
- What are the basic characteristics of the collaborative form and how do its shared rules, norms and structures contribute to the successful achievement of collaborative marketing outcomes?
- What are the underlying motives for tourism marketing collaboration?
- How does the fragmented nature of the tourism industry contribute to the need for tourism marketing collaboration?
- How do the characteristics of each individual sector within the tourism industry contribute to the need for inter-organisational collaboration in order to achieve tourism marketing outcomes?
- How does the turbulence in the wider tourism environment contribute to the need for tourism marketing collaboration?
- How does the turbulence evident in each individual sector within the tourism industry contribute to the need for inter-organisational collaboration to achieve tourism marketing outcomes?
- What is the overriding domain orientation of the inter-organisational form?
- What is the theoretical basis upon which inter-organisational collaboration is built and what implications are there for the shared rules, norms and structures of the inter-organisational form?
- How do the theoretical foundations of the inter-organisational collaborative form impact on the successful achievement of tourism marketing outcomes from the problem domain?

Strategic Tourism Marketing Implementation and Control

- What degree of autonomy is deemed appropriate and necessary for the successful achievement of collaborative marketing outcomes?
- What are the life-cycle characteristics of the inter-organisational collaborative form? How might the different stages, both individually and collectively, contribute to the achievement of desired outcomes?
- How is interactivity nurtured in the collaborative form?

- What actions or decisions result from inter-organisational collaboration and how do they compare with the predetermined marketing objectives of the collaborative form?
- What are the key features of the inter-organisational collaborative form and how are they likely to impact on the achievement of desired outcomes?
- To what extent do the joint outcomes of tourism marketing collaboration surpass the sum of individual tourism marketing outcomes that could be achieved in the absence of collaboration?
- What are the desired qualities of partners with whom to collaborate?
- What is the ideal partner mix for successful achievement of the collaborative marketing domain?
- In what situations is the individual or co-brand used and how do organisations manage the convergence or divergence of brand values in the context of collaboration?
- What level of representation and coverage are warranted by individual and collaborative messages, brands and associated values?
- How do competing and collaborating organisations reconcile pricing decisions, customer-perceived value and brand consistency in addition to achieving differential advantage in the marketplace when operating in unilateral or multilateral environments?
- To what extent are collaborative forms influential in seasonal pricing strategies, where payments are made throughout the channels of distribution and in situations where multiple objectives exist, various stakeholder demands need to be met and the collaborating partners demonstrate significantly different patterns of ownership?
- In pursuit of higher yield through the effective delivery of yield-management systems, what efforts are being made to integrate existing yield-management systems across the collaborative domain?
- How do the communication objectives vary in parallel competing and collaborating environments? Who ultimately determines and pays for the wider collaborative marketing communications strategy?
- What structures can be put in place to minimise duplication of communication and how can all the collaborating partners' interests be accommodated while at the same time maximising the benefit of the collaborative message?
- What issues are apparent as a result of collaboration in respect of organisations' use of intermediaries?
- How may channel structures, power and overall channel influence vary in accordance with inter-organisational collaboration?
- How do competing and collaborating organisations reconcile decisions relating to the extended marketing mix with regard to service delivery and the service encounter?

- What are the principal drivers of collaborative effectiveness and what factors impede it in the context of tourism marketing?
- What is the most effective form of inter-organisational governance to maximise the chances of participating organisations meeting their individual and shared marketing goals?
- What measures are available to minimise internal uncertainty and opportunistic behaviour within the inter-organisational form?
- What role do the selection and actions of the convenor play in the overall success? What are the most suitable criteria for the convenor of an inter-organisational tourism marketing collaboration?
- What are the opportunity costs of inter-organisational collaboration?
- What structures and processes are in existence to accommodate the evaluation, monitoring and control of collaborative marketing initiatives?
- To what extent are issues of trust and commitment a prerequisite for effective evaluation, monitoring and control?
- To what extent are issues of evaluation, monitoring and control taken into consideration when determining the governance of inter-organisational forms?
- What are some of the operational and managerial implications of collaborative evaluation, monitoring and control?
- Are existing evaluation, monitoring and control policies, practices and procedures adequate for collaborative marketing initiatives?

Chapter 11
Conclusions

The Collaborative Strategic Tourism Marketing Planning Process

Figure 11.1 presents a conceptual framework of the 'collaborative' strategic tourism marketing planning process. The aim is to present a synthesis of the bodies of knowledge of strategic marketing and inter-organisational collaboration. The schematic diagram has its origins in the collaborative strategy process for international airlines developed by Evans (see Figure 8.2, p. 244). Figure 11.1 differs from Evans' schematic in two main ways. First, while Evans' framework related specifically to airline alliances, the intention of our schematic diagram is to apply it to collaboration in tourism more generally. Second, while the purpose of Evans' framework of analysis was to incorporate in one single schematic the two previously unrelated bodies of knowledge, corporate strategy and inter-organisational collaboration, the intention of Figure 11.1 is to relate tourism marketing and inter-organisational theory.

Figure 11.1 illustrates the three key stages of the strategic marketing planning process: the situational analysis; strategic marketing planning; and strategic marketing implementation and control. However, within the second and third stages of the process, strategic marketing theory is synthesised with theoretical components of inter-organisational collaboration to provide a 'route map' for the making of collaborative marketing strategies. Although there is no significant change in the elements in the first stage as compared with 'traditional' marketing theory, a number of questions arise which require addressing if organisations are to achieve collaborative advantage through the adoption of collaborative marketing strategies in the stages that follow. In the second stage, however, the consideration of collaboration strategies begins to exert an influence. Organisations need to decide if their marketing objectives are to be best met through organic, 'go-it-alone' strategies; through other joint strategies such as franchising or joint ventures; through merger or acquisition strategies; or through the adoption of collaborative marketing strategies.

323

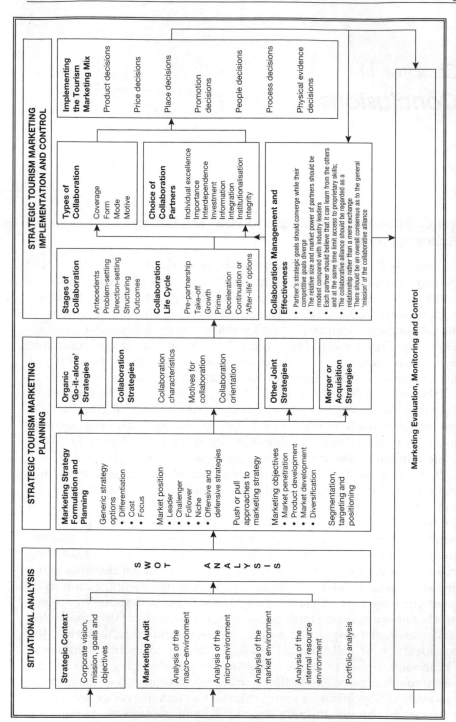

Figure 11.1 The collaborative strategic tourism marketing planning process

At this stage, the characteristics of collaboration need to be well understood, and the motivations for collaboration should be clarified. This stage also offers an opportunity for organisations to undertake some critical self-analysis of their orientation towards collaboration before entering into such arrangements. Once these issues have been gone through, the question is then one of implementation. Organisations need to appreciate and come to terms with the different stages of collaboration, as well as the kinds of decisions they can expect to encounter as the collaboration goes through the various stages of its life cycle. The most suitable type of collaborative form then needs to be chosen, with close attention being paid to its coverage, form, mode and motive. Organisations then need to identify the combination of partners most suitable for the achievement of collaborative advantage prior to the actual implementation of the marketing mix. With regard to the evaluation, monitoring and control aspects of the strategic marketing planning process, although this will clearly take place after implementation of the mix, specific evaluation of the management and effectiveness of the inter-organisational collaborative form will also need to take place. This will feed into the generic evaluation, monitoring and control systems, and serve as a catalyst for the review of the suitability of the collaborative form adopted and the suitability of the chosen partners in effectively meeting the objectives of the collaboration.

Figure 11.1 perhaps conveys the impression that, at the beginning of the process, the organisation is not involved in any kind of collaboration. This may be the case, although, as the adoption of collaborative marketing strategies continues in the increasingly global market place, tourism organisations are more and more likely to be beginning the strategic marketing planning process, conducting both competitive and collaborative marketing strategies at the same time. In other words, when beginning to redraft their strategic marketing plan, some organisations will have previous experience of collaboration while others will be considering the adoption of collaborative marketing strategies for the first time. This issue will feature in discussions throughout this chapter, but it is appropriate at this juncture to stress that the conceptual framework provided in Figure 11.1 does not show this dynamic and hence does not identify this as a potential source of conflict. This is because the framework is intended solely as a vehicle to address the collaboration components of the strategic marketing planning process.

Situational Analysis

The underlying purpose of the situational analysis is to identify the key external opportunities and threats facing the organisation, as well as to ascertain the strengths and weaknesses internal to the organisation.

Set within the context of the wider organisational 'sense of purpose', as demonstrated through its vision, mission, goals and objectives – its strategic context – situational analysis provides the necessary foundation for decision-making evident in the second and third stages of the collaborative strategic tourism marketing planning process.

Strategic context

From the outset it needs to be stressed that marketing decisions, be they strategic or operational, need to be made in a manner that is consistent with the overriding vision, mission, goals and objectives of the organisation. All organisations, irrespective of their pattern of ownership, exhibit a 'sense of purpose'. Most demonstrate a unilateral, competitive sense of existence, which identifies the nature of their business and general strategic direction. For example, United Airlines, part of Star Alliance, aims to be recognised worldwide as 'the airline of choice'. This is significant, in that, despite the fact that the airline acknowledges the considerable benefits of Star Alliance membership, its corporate 'sense of purpose' remains ultimately adversarial in orientation. The tendency for organisations to retain individual sense of purpose was demonstrated in Chapter 8. When United Airlines filed for bankruptcy protection in December 2002, the attempts by Lufthansa and Air Canada to 'rescue' United were not by means of their existing collaborative arrangements but through more traditional merger and acquisition strategies.

Chapter 8 proposed that no international airline is truly able to compete globally and reach out to global markets without being a member of a 'strategic alliance'. Likewise, Chapter 9 suggested that very few independent hotels or hotel groups are able to market themselves effectively without being members of a 'consortium'. Chapter 10, meanwhile, highlighted that single tourism destinations able to afford the marketing necessary to compete in distant markets and thereby bypass 'partnerships' are few and far between. However, airlines, hotels and tourism destinations all have their own individual organisational visions, missions, goals and objectives, which establish their direction and sense of purpose for the future. The question for each of them is to what extent their individual competitive and joint collaborative ambitions are compatible with one another, consistent with stakeholder expectations and in accord with employees' understanding of the overriding strategic direction of the organisation.

To date, it would appear that very few organisations, if any, have included reference to any previous experience of, or aspirations for, collaboration in their vision and mission statements. If, however, the trend towards collaborative marketing strategies continues, it might be expected that collaborative values, ambitions and expectations will achieve greater prominence in the future vision, mission, goals and objectives of individual organisations. As collaboration becomes more established as a vehicle for achieving the organisation's marketing objectives, and the success or otherwise of collaboration has a greater impact on the organisation's 'financial' bottom line, the involvement of collaborating organisations and the changing expectations of stakeholders will have to be integrated into the equation.

There is, of course, an increasing number of organisations that do in fact set out specifically to collaborate. The example of Best Western in Chapter 9 is testament to this. Its mission is stated as: 'to serve the collective interests of members and guests ... by focusing on satisfaction and brand loyalty [thereby to] ensure that Best Western is more valuable than any other brand in our industry'. With its origins going back over 50 years, Best Western has set the precedent for a number of 'me-too' competitors. This demonstrates the positive impact of collaboration in the hotel sector. In the case of Best Western, collaboration is central to its corporate sense of purpose and permeates the entire organisation.

The same is true of Star Alliance, which through its one-member-one vote inter-organisational form offers a clear sense of corporate purpose. The mission of Star Alliance is clearly collaborative in that it exists to contribute to the long-term profitability of its members beyond their individual capabilities. The key role of the alliance is to facilitate co-operation and integration of member airlines, while still allowing them to make economies of scale and scope, as well as to retain their individual identities wherever possible. Although the focus of the alliance will undoubtedly change over time, its vision is constant in that it states that Star Alliance is to be the leading global airline alliance for the frequent international traveller. At the moment this vision holds true, with the alliance spanning 729 destinations in 124 countries with over 2000 aircraft. Interestingly, however, this sense of purpose still demonstrates something of a competitive or 'adversarial' orientation in that the alliance is seeking to become the world's leading global airline alliance, presumably by out-competing its two key rivals, Oneworld and SkyTeam. Quite clearly, all three alliances are in competition in their quest to become the foremost global airline network, each putting into practice the shared concepts, competencies and connections in their 'value-creating networks'.

The issue of implementation is fundamental to organisational mission statements, in that it is the mission that explains how the vision is to be reached. More often than not, organisational values and standards of behaviour are included in such statements. For those contemplating collaboration, such items are worthy of scrutiny when seeking suitable collaborative partners. It is also advisable for organisations to reflect on their rationale for collaboration, as well as to investigate the rationale for collaboration among potential partners. The prospect of collaboration, even if it not actually acted upon, will more than likely have an increasing impact on the determination of organisational 'sense of purpose' in the future. For example, organisations may wish to include reference to ideals, culture and structures that are collaboration-friendly and are of a tone and content compatible to seeking partners at a later stage of the strategic tourism marketing planning process.

The above applies also to the compatibility of the individual organisation's goals and objectives with those of the collaborative domain, as well as to the compatibility of the goals and objectives of the collaboration with those of the participating organisations. In establishing organisational goals and objectives at the corporate level, financial criteria presently tend to predominate. However, the more established inter-organisational collaboration activity becomes, the more 'corporate' goals and objectives will have to reflect this. At the same time, 'value networks' will have to be made explicit in their financial returns – something that to date has perhaps not been especially evident in practice. In the setting of goals and objectives at the corporate level, it is important to recognise the point made by Kanter that effective collaboration is best in situations where strategic goals converge and where competitive goals diverge. Global airline alliances are a good example of this principle, in that, although individual airlines may share ambitions in the global marketplace, each retains its own competitive goals that are set within geographic boundaries and are often route-specific. In this way strategic 'collision' or 'duplication' can be avoided. By linking into a global network, would-be competitors are able to extend market reach at reduced cost and effort.

Marketing audit

At the wider 'corporate' level, an understanding of the external and internal environments is necessary before generic strategy options and corresponding marketing programmes can be selected. Chapter 3 introduced a range of existing 'standardised' models that have become marketing strategy 'icons' over recent decades. Without exception, they all came about in response to single-firm situations and were developed in economic times that were quite different from those of today. In the following section, the various components of the marketing audit will be analysed in turn in order to evaluate their continued suitability, either for an organisation considering the adoption of collaborative marketing strategies for the first time or for one with previous experience.

Analysis of the macro-environment

In providing an overview of external events, forces and circumstances in the external macro-environment, PEST analysis has proved to be an enduring and powerful framework. Indeed, a wide range of political, economic, socio-cultural and technological developments were highlighted in Chapter 1 as the key drivers of collaboration, and in this sense PEST analysis is clearly valid to both competitive and collaborative market environments. Of course, the PEST framework offers no simple solutions, but it does provide a useful synthesis of macro-environmental factors that decision makers can use as a platform from which to act.

Of special interest, however, is how decision makers reconcile particular factors when developing strategy inside and outside the collaborative domain. For example, restrictions in international shareholdings have been instrumental as a catalyst for the creation of global airline alliances, However, within the collaborative domain, the persistence of such restrictions can become a cause of friction and possible inertia. This is due to the inability of certain organisations to 'walk the talk' with respect to deregulation, which can generate frustration and a lack of trust among partner airlines. In this way, a macro-environmental factor which contributed significantly to the emergence of global airline alliances could actually become the major catalyst to their demise. Indeed, if airlines existed in a truly free-market situation, it is more than likely that collaboration would not exist in its current form: 'adversarial' acquisition and merger activity would be more than likely to predominate.

Some factors will of course always carry more weight than others in determining strategy in collaborative environments. PEST factors will always exist – the issue is how an organisation should react to them as part of a collaborative entity. With regard to events such as 9/11 and SARS, theory would suggest that there is strength in numbers. However, taking the case of airlines, clearly it is mainly individual routes and carriers that suffer. Indeed, all the major US airlines have individually experienced considerable trading difficulties post-9/11, and have received only very limited assistance from federal government. To date, the ability and will of partner airlines to help them out have been somewhat limited. And, as was stated in Chapter 8 in the case of United Airlines, it is difficult to envisage Star Alliance without United as its largest single partner. However, as things stand, there appears to be very little more that Star Alliance can do. The threat of takeover of Thai Airways International and the response of Star Alliance as a collaborative form is eagerly awaited.

By adopting the concept of the global airline alliance, international airlines have clearly responded in a suitable collaborative manner to the globalising macro-forces they encounter in their external environment. What is so ironic, however, is that the adoption of such inter-organisational forms has itself reinforced the trend towards even greater concentration and consolidation in the industry. Finally, with regard to international airlines, one factor that is likely to pose a threat in the future is the very real menace of even greater scrutiny from the authorities. Regular examination is likely to be a permanent feature of global airline alliances, in that international regulators will continue to explore the complex web of internal activity within the inter-organisational domain.

Further to the use of PEST analysis, the destination life cycle and its predecessor the product life cycle pose a number of problems for organisations already collaborating. This is simply because the focus of analysis is always on a single destination or a single product. For destinations, although life cycle analysis might be a very useful framework for understanding the dynamics of destination development and the marketing responses required at various stages of development, it clearly makes the starting assumption that the organisation is making its strategy under basically adversarial, competitive conditions. Although, in the context of collaboration, the stages of development are likely to be much the same, the 'collaboration curve' is more than likely to be a different shape, reflecting instead conditions in the wider collaborative destination domain. At the same time, the individual destination curve is likely to be impacted upon, either positively or negatively, by the success or otherwise of collaborative efforts. The comments by Dwyer in Chapter 10 are highly pertinent in this respect; the assumption that all destinations will benefit from inter-destination collaboration may not in fact hold true in all situations.

A conspicuous feature of the case study of destination collaboration in the Greater Mekong Subregion, as set out in Chapter 10, is that the partner destinations are clearly at very different stages of their destination life cycle. Whereas Thailand, as the region's most mature destination, is likely to be considering latter-stage issues, such as possible repositioning, the opportunity for market development or even new product development, this is clearly not going to be the case for Laos, which finds itself at the very earliest stages of destination development. The model, as it stands, therefore does not accommodate the complexities of inter-organisational collaboration. In this respect, the collaboration life cycle proposed by Caffyn, and featured in Chapter 6, is perhaps a more suitable framework, even if its utility is mainly at the implementation stage of the strategic tourism marketing planning process.

The international airlines comprising the major global airline alliances, as featured in Chapter 8, are also clearly at rather different stages of development, although the majority are probably in what would be described as the mature phase. In contrast, global airline alliances themselves are still immature as inter-organisational forms and remain very much in their infancy. For the likes of Star Alliance, Oneworld and SkyTeam, the learning curve has been very steep indeed, with all collaborating airlines having to learn 'on the job' and develop strategy in an emergent fashion rather than through the prescriptive process dominant in the academic literature.

Analysis of the micro-environment

For a number of years, Porter's Five Forces model has stood its ground as a very simple but effective framework for facilitating understanding of the single organisation's micro-environment. The five forces are, of course: competitors, new entrants, buyers, suppliers and the existence and impact of substitutes. The five forces are all clearly relevant to the collaborative context. Commencing with competitors, competitive rivalry is normally greatest when rivals are of a similar size in that they all strive for a dominant market position. Thus, although competitive rivalry among international airlines is strong, it is nothing perhaps when compared to the future competitive situation facing the three main global airline alliances.

Regarding buyers, a typical outcome of collaboration, be it among airlines, hotels or destinations, is that the power of buyers of the collaborative product is reduced. This will doubtless be hastened further if the airline alliances, hotel consortia and destination partnerships develop further their own intermediary activity, thereby weakening the power base of the major travel intermediaries. The example of Opodo, as discussed in Chapter 8, is a good example in that it represents a collaborative vehicle by which nine airlines have joined forces to counter the competitive threat of traditional travel intermediaries.

Similar to the outcome for buyers, the bargaining power of suppliers is also likely to decrease as a result of continuing collaboration. Although the purchase of specialised inputs will always be necessary, the procurement of many inputs can be reduced in price through collaborative action. The example of the recent supply agreement between Star Alliance and Novell Inc., as discussed in Chapter 8, is a good one in that it represents a strategic procurement relationship in which there will be benefits of joint purchasing available for all alliance partners, particularly in the form of sophisticated information and identity management solutions. This illustrates very clearly how the dynamics of Porter's Five Forces model have changed as a consequence of collaboration. Whereas before the global airline alliances came into being the balance of power probably existed with the suppliers to the international airline industry, the formation of these mega-alliances has tipped the balance of power in favour of the airlines through the collective buying power of their alliances.

The threat of new entrants poses some interesting questions despite the fact that the majority of the major international airlines are already represented in existing alliances. Although a large number of airlines have yet to get 'connected' in the new world order of global airline alliances, this is not so for the major industry players. There is, however, clearly room for new alliances – although it is unlikely that they are to be a serious competitive threat to the existing 'Big Three' – as is there room for alternative 'niche' operators which reject collaboration in favour of the traditional adversarial approach to competition: the 'no-frills' air-lines being a good case in point here. Although dismissed initially by the traditional international airlines, the strategic flexibility of the 'no-frills' carriers clearly has accelerated their growth in recent years. And, although there have existed opportunities for collaboration, acquisition strategies seem to have been the order of the day to date, vis-à-vis the acquisition of Go by Easyjet and the acquisition of Buzz by Ryanair.

Finally, Porter's original model introduces the threat of substitutes as a driving force in determining organisational strategy. This is very much the case in the context of the tourism industry. At the destination level in particular, the enduring fear is that people, tourists, actually stop trav-elling and undertake other activities in their free time. It is in the interests of all destinations, and in fact everybody involved in travel and tourism, that people continue to travel. Hence, the greater the collaboration within the tourism system as a whole, the greater the efficiencies and the higher the levels of product satisfaction that will prevail. The Greater Mekong Subregion represents a good example of this dynamic taking place, in spite of some quite formidable obstacles.

Although still highly relevant, the Five Forces model could offer more value to tourism marketers if it were more inclusive of some of the existing trends in the macro-environment. As regards alternative models that reflect better current market conditions and forces of change, that advocated by Thurlby, which is outlined in Chapter 3, is ideally placed to complement Porter's original model. With six forces, namely regula-tion, new entrants, customer expectation, improved digital information, synergistic alliances and organisation re-invention, Thurlby's model is arguably much more relevant to instances of collaboration.

In addition to Thurlby's six forces, it would probably also be benefi-cial to incorporate further forces of a collaborative genre, such as partner pressure, control and power in inter-organisational forms, cultural influ-ence, degree of strategic flexibility and financial pressures. Rather than show how they might impact on collaboration effectiveness, the issue here is what impact such pressures might have on the strategic direc-tion of the inter-organisational form and on the individual 'partner' organisations. These are questions at the very core of collaboration activity, inasmuch as what may be beneficial to the inter-organisational form might in some way or ways be detrimental to the organisation as an individual.

It can be argued that the issue is really one of balance, in that all forms of inter-organisational collaboration carry benefits and costs to participants, with compromise being virtually the only guaranteed outcome. One model that goes some way towards addressing these issues is the Four Links model, as advocated by Lynch and presented in Chapter 3 of this book. Identification of the nature, depth and impact of an organisation's relationship with government links and networks, complementors, informal co-operative links and networks and formal co-operative linkages is essential to providing a true and accurate account of the possible impact of the organisation's collaborative environment on its ability to determine unilateral and multilateral strategy. The important conclusion here is that both Thurlby's revision of the Five Forces model and Lynch's Four Links model warrant greater prominence in the collaborative strategic tourism marketing planning process.

This conclusion also applies to strategic group analysis, albeit perhaps to a lesser extent. While Chapter 3 notes Drummond and Ensor's proposition that the notion of an industry is too broad to facilitate a useful understanding of an organisation's real competitive position, the analysis of strategic groups can serve as a very useful model for inter-organisational competitive situations. For example, Figure 3.2 (p. 66) highlighted strategic groups in the airline industry, and the same kind of analysis could easily be applied to strategic alliances. On the other hand, with only three primary global airline alliances in existence, application of such analysis may not be especially beneficial in that each alliance is in reality competing on the same territorial base: global market coverage.

Analysis of the market environment

The collection, analysis, dissemination and sharing of information represents one of the biggest hurdles to the effective implementation of collaborative marketing. This is because it goes to the heart of issues relating to confidentiality, trust and proprietary skills. The example of the SIS, presented in Chapter 10, and its attempts to develop relationship marketing strategies at the destination level provide a very good example of the difficulties of developing effective marketing information systems within the collaborative domain. Unless trust is established within the collaborative domain, information gaps will always exist and in turn will hinder the development of the domain entity. Although only a possibility at the present time, the potential switching of Air New Zealand from Star Alliance to the competing Oneworld alliance demonstrates the ease with which sensitive market and partner information can be 'shared' with competitors.

Hence, while the various components of the marketing audit are of value both to competitive and to collaborative environments, the ability and willingness of partners to gather the information involved is open to question. This said, the greater the integration of loyalty marketing programmes, such as airline frequent-flier programmes and hotel frequent-guest programmes, the more collaborative in orientation will marketing information systems become. Greater consolidation and concentration of key competencies, such as the provision of accurate, up-to-date and relevant information through integrated ICT systems, not only brings with it financial economies but also offers considerable benefits to the partner organisations with respect to integrated booking systems, yield-management provision and customer-tracking systems.

Analysis of the internal resource environment

In analysing the organisation's internal environment, one of the most useful models for analysis developed in recent decades has been Porter's Value Chain. As identified by Doyle (see Chapter 3 of this book), organisational competitiveness is no longer dependent on the effectiveness of its internal and cross-functional networks. Instead, organisational competitiveness today is increasingly dependent on the organisation's external networks and collaborative relationships. This point was also made by Ashkenas *et al.* (see Chapter 1 of this book), who argue that the value chain has come to represent the single most significant concept by which organisations and enterprises are linked together. Indeed, in many cases the individual organisation's value chain is merely part of a myriad of value chains that interlink to form an extensive system for delivering solutions to customers. Therefore, it is the effectiveness with which marketers manage the entire supply chain and network of collaborating partners that will determine the future competitiveness of the organisation. Originally a single firm concept, the value chain today represents more of a value web, value constellation or value network, with it being virtually impossible for organisations to manage the entire value chain in competitive isolation. The issue among collaborating partners then becomes one of what competencies and resources are chosen to contribute to the value web.

The hierarchy of resources model is also highly relevant at this juncture as it represents an alternative vehicle to identify the internal resources of the organisation. When contemplating collaboration, organisations need to consider the degree to which peripheral, base, core or breakthrough resources are to be included in the collaborative domain. All organisations will wish to retain some degree of independence with regard to their proprietary skills. However, in the future, forces in the external environment are likely to be such that more and more resources previously considered to be of proprietary value are likely to be shared among partners in search of collaborative advantage. The concepts of the value chain and hierarchy of resources clearly resonate strongly with many issues pertaining to inter-organisational collaboration.

One internal resource fundamental to organisations is the value attached to its brand. Both the Brand Pyramid and Branding Iceberg, introduced in Chapter 3, are useful models for identifying the variables that constitute a brand and the relationships between such variables. Branding is central to the organisation's 'corporate sense of purpose' and thus the extent to which brands work in collaboration with others, be it in a formal or informal sense, is highly significant: there are clearly going to be impacts by association. Although other internal resources may be deemed more important in the early stages of inter-organisational collaboration, brands represent the most visible aspect to the customer and, therefore, need to be handled with considerable care.

Star Alliance is an excellent example of the emerging value of collaborative 'co-brands' and the effectiveness of 'co-branding' as a strategic weapon. In this instance, co-branding is being used as a strategy to increase the scope and influence of both individual partners' brands and the brand representing the collaborative domain. It also serves as an ideal innovative mechanism and opportunity for the individual and collective brands to become more distinctive in the marketplace. In essence, co-branding represents a form of collaboration between two or more brands with significant customer recognition, in which all the participants' brand names are retained. Commentators argue that the recent merger between Air France and KLM is likely to face major challenges, not least due to the considerable differences that exist with regard to corporate and national cultures. However, in order to accommodate both airlines' wishes, as well as to overcome regulatory restrictions, the two airlines are to retain their own brands, at least for the meantime.

The Branding Iceberg and Brand Pyramid both serve as useful models to help identify the key assets and competencies of brands, while they also serve as excellent vehicles to identify the real action points of collaboration and value chain linkages, which could be service delivery, research and development, low-cost operations or cost-effective market access. For the future, collaborating partners need to question the value of retaining their brand independence and have suitable systems in place to monitor and measure customer reaction and behaviour. Indeed, success in an organisation's branding strategy will ultimately be determined by what customers think they are buying into.

Portfolio analysis

Rather than manage a portfolio of products, collaboration typically involves the management of a portfolio of relationships. This has implications for resources in that caution needs to be applied to the management of resources across the individual organisation's full portfolio of relationships. Quite clearly, existing portfolio models, most notably the BCG and GE matrices, refer to single organisational contexts.

Moreover, it is clear that such models are focused on product-market scenarios and the consequent demand on resources. In the context of inter-organisational collaboration, the first stage in managing a portfolio of relationships is usually to identify the nature of those relationships. For example, are relationships ad hoc or ongoing, strategic or operational alliances?

Although the BCG and GE matrices have served the strategic marketing literature well, there are good reasons to believe that product-market matrices are insufficient to deal with the more complex dynamics of inter-organisational collaboration. For example, although with the BCG matrix individual organisations are able to base their decisions on market growth rate and their share of the market relative to competitors, in the context of collaboration the organisation's closest competitor may in fact be situated within the same collaborative marketing domain.

If the existing BCG model was to be applied to global airline alliances, it would suggest that all three key alliances are seeking to be the 'star' product: high growth market; high relative market share; and cash neutral. In reality, although one can question the actual rate of market growth, all three are relatively close in respect of their market shares. No one alliance has a substantial lead in the market as yet, even though alliance strategies have so far relied heavily on signing up additional partners suitable for guaranteeing ever more global market access. However, despite the weakness of its empirical base, and its ignorance of the concept of sustainable competitive advantage, it can be argued that, in a large number of situations, the generic characteristics and resource outcomes of the BGC model still make it a useful addition to the collaboration strategic marketing toolbox. What is required are more imaginative and creative axes which will work more effectively in the context of collaboration, enabling organisations to identify particular resource requirements and commitments and the impacts these may have on other aspects of their business. Different investments will be required at different stages of inter-organisational collaborative relationships.

Despite the weaknesses and limited use of the BCG in inter-organisational collaboration and the determinants of strategy, the slightly more flexible GE matrix is likely to offer a more robust and worthwhile outcome for those wishing to manage a portfolio of relationships. The key is clearly in the determination of the axes (industry/market attractiveness and collaborative strengths) and the identification of suitable variables and weightings. For example, the criteria identified to maximise collaborative effectiveness in Chapter 7 could quite easily be applied using the GE matrix framework to a particular inter-organisational setting. Possible variables could be the nature and scope of networks, existing partnership activities, duration of existing relationships, strength of value chain systems, flexibility of organisational culture in which collaboration is expected to take place, collaborative orientation and mindset of the chief executive, partner reach, geographic coverage and/or the nature of exit barriers.

For inter-organisational collaboration among destinations, the value of the destination market matrix also requires further scrutiny. The destination market matrix is clearly market-driven rather than product-driven. The problem for a domain destination like the Greater Mekong Subregion, however, is the ability to gather together, record and interpret sufficient qualities of data to complete such a model in the first instance.

Although a product issue rather than a market issue, one of the outstanding features of the various destination examples in Chapter 10 is that each individual destination within the collaborative domain is at a different stage of its own life cycle. Thailand, for example, is at a mature stage of development, while Laos is very much at the less-developed end of the spectrum. The model may serve the collaborative domain well but the implementation of resources will relate back to the individual destination's vision, mission and goals, the objectives of the organisation and the overall significance of tourism in the wider economy. Of particular note, however, is the fact that the target markets chosen for the Greater Mekong Subregion are all relatively mature in their own life cycles, and as a result tend to share similar patterns of market behaviour. In this regard, the model is wholly applicable to collaboration.

SWOT analysis

Simple, immediate and readily accessible, SWOT analysis is also a highly flexible and sound analytical framework. Able to provide a summary 'position statement' of the internal strengths and weaknesses and external opportunities and threats relevant to either an organisation or a collaborative domain, SWOT clearly has value in both unilateral and multilateral settings. The essentially subjective nature of the technique means that it has to be carried out in an extremely focused manner, but, provided it is applied with utmost care, SWOT analysis can provide a ready platform for the determination of strategy. One major weakness perhaps is the extent to which customers are able to distinguish sufficiently the critical success factors of a collaborative marketing initiative in order to make the model worthwhile in respect of inter-organisational collaboration. For example, in the context of global airline alliances, many of the questions pertaining to service expectation and quality, service delivery and the nature of the service experience may be lost in an inter-organisational maze. For example, determining what partner airline does what, when and where, and to what standard, would prove difficult for a passenger faced with some of the more complex codesharing arrangements that exist. In such circumstances, the key question of who is ultimately responsible when something goes wrong is a rather difficult one to answer.

In closing discussion of the situational analysis stage of the collaborative strategic tourism marketing planning process, it is clear that, despite the majority of concepts, models and frameworks initially being developed for analysis of external and internal single organisation situations, the majority are to some degree applicable in the context of inter-organisational collaboration. What is required are imaginative approaches to their usage, the identification of more applicable axes and variables and the inclusion of complementary inter-organisational collaboration concepts, models and frameworks. The organisation's surroundings increasingly need to be viewed as a network of inter-organisational relationships, rather than as an anonymous, unilaterally, competitive market.

Strategic Tourism Marketing Planning

Marketing strategy formulation and planning

Once the necessary foundations for decision making have been established through completion of the situation analysis, the second stage of the collaborative strategic tourism marketing planning process begins: strategic marketing planning. It is at this stage of the process that the decision to collaborate, or not as the case may be, takes place. The second stage incorporates all aspects of marketing strategy formulation and planning and commences with consideration of the generic strategy options facing the organisation.

Generic strategy options

The question of generic strategy direction is one that has proved difficult for virtually every international airline, in that the vast majority have deliberately selected the safe 'middle ground'. This is despite the fact that the 'stuck-in-the-middle' option is dismissed so readily in the strategy literature. Perhaps to a lesser degree the same is also true of global airline alliances, in that they all have similar breadth and market reach, and they are all trying to differentiate themselves from one another. In times of market turbulence, the strategic 'middle ground' may be a safe choice for a while, providing a 'time out' and the opportunity to 'hedge one's bets'. In the case of international airlines, this explanation can in part be attributed to the constraining nature of regulation.

Perhaps a more difficult situation is where an airline like British Airways, which for the past 20 years or so has continually presented itself as one of the premium, full-service airlines with a particular focus on business travel, signs up to a strategic alliance which includes partners that may be perceived as incompatible with its individual strategic direction. Through the selective choice of partner airlines and the integration of value networks, it is expected that collaborative advantage will prevail. This appears to be the case to date; but the salient question is, at what cost? British Airways reported a downturn in pre-tax profits for the third quarter of 2003 to £110 million, a fall of some 53%. This followed a drop in revenues and yields and a £40 million one-off cost associated with union disputes and strikes in the summer of 2003. Although this can be, and has been, blamed on a number of factors, there is always likely to be some concern that the strategic inflexibility of collaboration may contribute to these problems. At the moment, global airline alliances are perhaps still too young to provide a definitive answer to this question.

The competitive threat from 'no-frills' airlines continues to grow, however, and this fact alone confirms the veracity of the need to focus on one particular generic strategy option. It is also true that the 'no-frills' airlines have been very radical and innovative in the marketplace, this being entirely outside the domain of collaboration.

For organisations with no collaboration experience, the choice of generic strategy is a decision which comes with no strings attached. For organisations already conducting parallel competing and collaborating marketing strategies, such as British Airways, the ability to reconcile their sometimes conflicting generic strategies can prove problematical. On the other hand, recent discounting and heavy price-related promotional campaigns by British Airways have been focused quite specifically on particular routes and particular competitors in an attempt to limit the damage spreading to its wider business interests. Significant, however, is the fact that British Airways is conducting defensive marketing strategies in response to the very real threat from the 'no-frills' airlines, which in the UK are currently exerting significant influence on the ground rules of competition. Then again, it is notable that British Midland International has been able to maintain its position within the Star Alliance in addition to developing a successful 'no-frills' carrier: bmibaby. Evidence provided in Chapter 8 suggests that, to date, this 'dual' strategy has worked well, and indeed continues to go from strength to strength.

For independent hotels and hotel groups, most of the collaborations in existence appear to adopt a differentiation or focus strategic approach, with very few, if any, adhering to the cost principles of Porter discussed in Chapter 4. This also appears to be the case among destinations, in that most seek to adopt the differentiation route. Within the Greater Mekong Subregion this holds true despite the fact that the six individual countries making up the domain region have significantly different cost bases.

Market position

Existing and desired future market positions are important in that they both help set the benchmark for strategic decision making. In the case of the Greater Mekong Subregion collaboration, for example, it is hard to envisage Laos, Vietnam or Cambodia becoming the regional market leader for many years to come in terms of their tourist numbers and/or expenditure. If these destinations are content to remain market followers or market nichers, then one could argue that there remains little reason for inter-organisational collaboration. If, on the other hand, they demonstrate more ambition in the marketplace, then the power of collaboration can provide a vehicle for this. The various market positions of competitors clearly have implications for later partner choice if collaboration is the chosen strategic path, and will impact on the third stage of the collaborative strategic tourism marketing planning process, where the type of collaboration, governance structure, collaboration membership and outcomes of collaboration are to be determined.

For existing inter-organisational forms, such as Star Alliance, which explicitly states its aim to be the world's principal global airline alliance, not only does market position impact on its own strategic direction but it is clearly likely to impact on the future strategic direction, of the partners' individual strategies as they converge over time and a domain sense of collaborative purpose is established.

With regard to the use of appropriate offensive and defensive marketing strategies, if the organisation is outside collaboration then it has the freedom to chose. However, once it becomes a member of an alliance, consortium or partnership, then certain limitations begin to surface with regard to the individual organisation's strategic decision-making. For example, in the case of international airlines, any decision to cut routes, downgrade in-flight services or alter timetables on an individual basis will clearly have ramifications for other alliance members in the short-to-medium term.

To date, the considerable cost and potential for retaliatory action from the adoption of frontal attack strategies means that they have been limited to competitive rather than collaborative situations. For example, frontal attack strategies are frequently used in the 'no-frills' sector to good effect, and are clearly to the benefit of the discount traveller. Although costly to implement, the adoption of such strategies has been instrumental in growing market share and developing the overall size of the discount market. More common among global airline alliances are flank attacks, where selected market segments, for example specific routes, are targeted. The adoption of such strategies often represents the beginning of a partner search, in that an attempt is made to fill gaps in the global network. This can also be the case for the adoption of encirclement strategies, where each of the three major airline alliances seeks to 'crowd out' others from the marketplace and, in turn, further the consolidation and concentration of the industry. The example of Opodo, as discussed in Chapter 8, illustrates the effective implementation of a bypass attack, in that the partner airlines have collectively moved into a new area of business through the development of new technologies and channels of distribution in order to counter the competitive threat of existing travel intermediaries. Finally, guerrilla attacks tend to be confined to the 'no-frills' sector, although in the UK alliance players such as British Midland International and British Airways have conducted aggressive price-discounting promotions on a regular basis to serve as a competitive challenge to the 'no-frills' carriers. The adoption of such competitive action demonstrates the use of one strategy for the domestic market and another for the wider global network. To date, as a result of their scale and structure, global airline alliances have been unable to accommodate guerrilla tactics at short notice in response to competitive pressures.

Push or pull approaches to marketing strategy

Closely related to the above discussion, as well as to the earlier discussion relating to the analysis of the micro-environment, the decision to adopt push or pull marketing strategies will usually depend on a number of factors, not least the decision-making processes of consumers, the nature of the channels of distribution and the power of individual organisations or inter-organisational forms in those channels. The example of Best Western demonstrates how independent hotels and hotel groups can 'at a stroke' enhance their visibility in the marketplace and deliver more effective push strategies. At the same time, the vast majority of independent hotels, while maybe using the Best Western brand to good effect, will continue to undertake traditional push campaigns, especially at the local level. The adoption of both pull and push approaches to marketing strategy should in most cases be complementary, and this applies in collaborative as well as competitive settings.

Marketing objectives

As discussed in Chapter 4, the Ansoff matrix remains that framework that is most frequently referred to with regard to the setting of marketing objectives. Such analysis enables the potential areas in which core competencies and generic strategies may be deployed to be mapped out. For organisations not currently involved in inter-organisational collaboration, this perhaps represents one of the key moments in deciding when and how, in accordance with the organisation's wider 'corporate' objectives, their marketing objectives are to be met. This could be through organic 'go-it-alone' strategies, merger or acquisition strategies, collaboration or other joint strategic options. For those already involved in one or more collaborative arrangement, this represents an occasion to review previous marketing strategies in light of the individual organisation's new 'corporate' objectives. The freedom to make decisions is clearly related to any existing collaborative involvement and the size, strength, power and influence of the individual organisation within the alliance, consortium or partnership.

Segmentation, targeting and positioning

The final, and perhaps most important decision prior to deciding whether or not collaboration strategies are necessary, involves determining the bases of segmentation, target markets and market positioning. Prior to engaging in inter-organisational collaboration, all organisations, be they airlines, hotels or destinations have the freedom to choose whatever strategies they deem appropriate. As discussed above, however, once collaboration has been adopted as a modus operandi, organisations will have to reconcile their segmentation, targeting and positioning decisions within parallel competitive and collaborative market situations. Clearly this will have resource implications and will impact on all aspects of implementing the marketing mix in the third stage of the collaborative strategic tourism marketing planning process. This particularly applies to aspects of customer expectations and branding. The decision by Star Alliance to reciprocate fully their partner airlines' frequent-flier programmes and to standardise awards is testament to the gradual convergence and safe middle-ground, 'stuck-in-the-middle' strategy of many international airlines, as well as to the general convergence of buying behaviour among international leisure customers and business travellers.

Once collaboration has been adopted as a strategic vehicle, new bases of segmentation can be adopted that break away from existing stereotypical criteria. For example, new bases of segmentation, such as the success of relationships, network categories, loyalty and commitment among partners, could further enhance the inter-organisational collaborative marketing domain. In the case of the Greater Mekong Subregion collaboration, the potential problems of multiple motivations and the complexity of managing different groups of visitors with different expectations has been avoided through the agreement among partner countries that similar markets will be targeted to each individual country for the domain product. In turn, the positioning statement will incorporate those attributes that are to establish a collaborative advantage for the inter-organisational domain.

Collaboration strategies

It is at this juncture that the decision needs to be made among individual organisations as to how they wish to proceed in the achievement of their marketing objectives. In the case of international airlines, the external environmental forces are such that alliances are deemed to be the only mechanism for the foreseeable future. This was highlighted in Chapter 8 by Jaan Albrecht, Chief Executive of Star Alliance, in that, if individual members of Star Alliance had continued to operate as separate airlines, the loss of feeder traffic would have forced them to scale back their networks in a much more drastic way in view of the very turbulent market environment post-9/11. Membership of a global airline alliance clearly offers individual airlines a depth of market penetration that has allowed the participating airlines to reduce frequencies and destinations to a much lesser degree than otherwise would have been necessary. Although perhaps a 'second-best' option, the extent to which they have truly been put under commercial pressure is open to debate. This having been said, the 'safety-in-numbers' analogy has clearly benefited the likes of Varig of Brazil and Thai Airways International with their respective problems. Likewise, since the launch of Star Alliance, additional passengers and revenues have risen by 60% for SAS Scandinavian Airlines. In 2002, this 'interline revenue' accounted for 10% of the group's total passenger revenues. In the same period, passenger traffic added from Scandinavian Airlines to the other Star Alliance members grew by nearly 60%.

One can question the extent to which stakeholders understand and have input into the overriding strategic direction of the organisation. At present, it is questionable whether they really have a say, or indeed whether it is ultimately down to them as to whether or not the collaboration meets its objectives. This issue highlights one of the fundamental challenges of collaboration. Collaboration may serve well at a corporate level but operationally such arrangements are often difficult, time-consuming and resource-intensive to implement. For employees, there is always the fear that collaboration is merely a precursor to future merger, or even acquisition. At the same time, global airline alliances, simply by their size and reach, bring with them risks relating to trust, commitment and the ability to manage considerable cross-cultural issues and, therefore, represent a considerable management challenge.

Collaboration characteristics

Prior to committing the organisation to inter-organisational collaboration, it is advisable to become familiar with the basic characteristics of the collaborative form and how shared rules, norms and structures can contribute to the successful achievement of collaborative marketing outcomes. Clearly collaboration, be it among international airlines, independent hotels and hotel groups or tourist destinations, represents both challenges and opportunities. However, clear appreciation of these challenges and opportunities is perhaps not aided by the lack of a single, tightly defined concept. Consistent with the adoption of the definition presented at the beginning of Part 4 of this book, organisations electing to adopt collaboration as a vehicle to achieve their marketing objectives need to recognise that: stakeholders are independent; solutions emerge by dealing constructively with differences; joint ownership of decisions is required; stakeholders need to assume collective responsibility for the ongoing direction of the domain; and, finally, collaboration is an emergent process, where collaborative initiatives can be understood as emergent organisational arrangements through which organisations collectively cope with the growing complexity of their environments.

Ultimately, organisations wishing to collaborate with others are seeking to achieve collaborative advantage. The example of StarNet, a common ICT infrastructure that links together all the separate computer networks of Star Alliance members and that provides real-time access to information, enabling improved customer servicing across the entire alliance, is testament to the benefits that can be achieved through collaboration.

Motives for collaboration

Understandably, organisations vary in their motives for adopting interorganisational collaborative marketing strategies, the literature being replete with examples of why organisations come together to form collaborative arrangements. Chapter 5 introduced a number of frameworks, that by Beverland and Brotherton proving particularly useful where eight key motivations were postulated:

- Market entry and market position-related motives.
- Product-related motives.
- Product/market-related motives.
- Market structure modification-related motives.
- Market entry timing-related motives.
- Resource use efficiency-related motives.
- Resource extension and risk reduction-related motives.
- Skills enhancement-related motives.

For the Greater Mekong Subregion, the Asian Development Bank recognised that the region could be seen as a single entity, with scope for integrated and co-operative development. Tourism was viewed as being a part of this, and collaboration was seen as the only means of achieving the vision. As discussed in Chapter 10, a variety of collaborative formats were tried prior to a more formal approach being adopted with the launch of the Agency for Coordinating Mekong Tourism Activities in 1997. Despite considerable difficulties, including insufficient government support and funding, as well as inconsistencies in national policies and systems, the motivation to develop a domain destination spanning six countries has benefited from a collaborative approach. One argument adopted by this book is that the fragmented nature of the tourism industry serves as a catalyst in itself for collaboration to be the development vehicle in tourism. This is especially so at the destination level.

Described as 'collective entrepreneurship' by Morrison and Harrison, and discussed in Chapter 9, inter-organisational collaboration can lead to increased profits for the independent hotel as well as to the broader promotion of the destination as a whole, while preserving the individuality and independence of each member hotel. In this instance, Best Western represents a highly suitable vehicle for the independent sector to counter the competitive threat from an increasingly consolidated and concentrated hotel accommodation sector. Again in Chapter 9, the example of Scotland Hotels of Distinction is useful in that it demonstrates the strength of collaboration in the accommodation sector; in this instance helping to achieve explicit differentiation, innovative product extensions and market diversification for the consortium. Although to date consortium membership provide only the scale economies of hotel chains, as the concept matures and develops the future may see a time when hotel consortia are able put up a serious challenge to the major hotel chains in respect of specialisation, external financing and career development.

One very useful tool is the matrix put forward by Chaston and presented in Chapter 5. This matrix serves as a valuable addition to the collaborative strategic marketing planning process and complements the Ansoff matrix in assisting organisations to clarify their strategic options and choices in their potential adoption of inter-organisational collaboration.

Collaboration orientation

It has already been argued that collaboration is fundamental to the collective development of the wider tourism industry, and that organisations should reject the independent strategies that have traditionally been formulated at the individual level and focus their efforts on working in the inter-organisational domain. This may be so, but what is to be the overriding domain orientation of the inter-organisational form and what is the theoretical basis upon which inter-organisational collaboration is to be built? Out of the three approaches discussed in Chapter 5, the two most common theoretical approaches are resource dependency theory and the theory of relational exchange. Whereas the theory of resource dependency is based on power and control, in that interdependencies exist among organisations because individual stakeholders in the domain own or have control over vital resources, the theory of relational exchange is based on more altruistic foundations, whereby trust, commitment and mutual dependency are prerequisites for success. Thus, whereas resource dependency theory views the collaboration process as one of organisations attempting to achieve competitive advantage by accessing resources that lie out of their individual control, for relational exchange theory collaboration is the result of organisations recognising the interdependence of problems in their domain and the benefits of developing reciprocal relationships aimed at solving them.

In each of the examples introduced in Part 4 of the book, there are aspects of both of these theoretical orientations in the resulting forms of collaboration. International airlines, although demonstrating considerable relational exchange behaviour once in the alliance structure, are driven by the need to access global markets and the fear of being excluded from the emerging 'network' nature of the industry. In particular, collaboration enables international airlines to extend their reach into areas in which their influence has been limited by government regulation at the national level. Airlines also tend to see global alliances as a means of tackling the extreme turbulence of their market environment by enabling them to shift relatively effortlessly between weakening and emerging markets. Independent hotels and hotel groups, meanwhile, although clearly benefiting from the relational dynamics of the likes of Best Western, predominantly enter consortia in order to achieve cost-effective, 'technology-driven' access to distant markets. Furthermore, without access to Thailand's considerable tourism infrastructure and resources, the relational orientation inherent within the Greater Mekong Subregion would actually deliver very little. In a way, whether or not organisations understand and acknowledge the rationale behind collaboration may not be important. However, the authors would argue that, by understanding the forces that drive collaboration and the underlying motivations for adopting inter-organisational collaboration strategies, the resulting implementation and control of collaborative marketing strategies are more likely to deliver successful outcomes.

Strategic Tourism Marketing Implementation and Control

Stages of collaboration and the collaboration life cycle

When deciding upon collaboration as a vehicle to achieve marketing objectives, the numerous studies discussed throughout the book, but particularly those considered in Chapter 6, suggest that there exist a number of quite distinct stages in the 'life cycle' of collaboration. Although there remain numerous opportunities for further research in this area, it can be argued that, whether one looks at the example of Star Alliance in Chapter 8, Best Western in Chapter 9 or the Greater Mekong Subregion in Chapter 10, each inter-organisational form has evolved over a period of time in an emergent manner. Most studies relate back to the pioneering work conducted by Gray, as introduced in Chapter 6, which advocated a three-stage model of collaboration: problem-setting, direction-setting and structuring. This model was extended by Selin and Chavez, who concluded that five key stages exist: antecedents, problem-setting, direction-setting, structuring and outcomes. This model was developed further by Caffyn with the development of the collaboration life cycle, again introduced in Chapter 6.

While the relatively long-established Greater Mekong Subregion project remains in relative infancy, after only six years of operation Star Alliance has, according to its chief executive, reached a level of maturity that enables it to concentrate on the deeper integration of the member airlines, including the realisation of cost savings, rather than on the search for further partners. Clearly comparisons can be made with the concept of the destination life cycle and product life cycle. For example, in Chapter 10, following the work of Hill and Shaw, it is argued that co-operative marketing may be particularly advantageous when a country's tourism product is underdeveloped, or when existing products are in an advanced stage in the product life cycle and it is desirable to attract new markets and/or formulate new products. Similarly, Prideaux argues that collaboration in a promotional sense often starts at the destination level at the 'national' stage of the resort development spectrum. This typically involves joint campaigns between states, local government and local businesses taking place alongside campaigns between hotels and major attractions.

One very useful aspect of Caffyn's life-cycle model is the existence of eight post-collaboration 'after-life' options. This is significant in that recognition is given to the fact that, once the marketing objectives have been met, the inter-organisational 'sense of purpose' moves on. For example, the collaboration life cycle suggests that the inter-organisational form can be:

- Continued.
- Absorbed into a bigger 'competitive or complementary' grouping.
- Dissolved in that individual partners learn from collaboration and take the ideas forward individually.
- Taken over by one partner who takes control/leads the collaboration.
- Continued in a more permanent form.

- Taken over by a stakeholder who assumes control over the collaboration.
- Divided up into a number of spin-offs.
- Simply discontinued.

The historical development of Best Western is testament to the strength and enduring qualities of its inter-organisational credentials, while the numerous changes that have taken place with the development of the Greater Mekong Subregion attest that, although the inter-organisational structures have not always been sufficiently robust to take the initiative forward, the belief in and commitment to the inter-organisational domain has been maintained throughout. As for the three major global airline alliances, they remain in a mature phase of development with no sign of 'closure' in the short-to-medium term.

Types of collaboration

Throughout this book it has become clear that drawing sharp distinctions between different types of inter-organisational collaboration is very difficult and, indeed, not especially helpful. In reality, one has to accept that there exist a variety of different forms that are effective in different situations, with each form passing through a similar life cycle, albeit at different speeds and with different outcomes. The development of a suitable typology of inter-organisational forms is thus very difficult. That having been said, Rhoades and Lush provide a useful typology of airline alliances, as outlined in Chapter 8, based on the degree to which resources are committed to the alliance and the complexity of the particular management. Meanwhile Morley, in the same chapter, offers an alternative typology based on alliance structures. Thus, whereas Oneworld is described as a 'co-ordinated' alliance – where the balance of power (and control), the ability of partners to negotiate with each other and the ability of member airlines to counter the strength of key players is highly significant – Star Alliance is described as a 'sharing' alliance in that far tighter integration of scheduling and marketing activities is evident. Most significant at the moment is the 'unified' nature of the Air France-KLM development where, in reality, KLM is to become an 'independent' subsidiary of Air France-KLM, a holding company. This very original development represents an advancement of existing alliance structures, with this new inter-organisational form accommodating considerable external environmental pressures.

In the case of hotel consortia, although a variety of configurations were highlighted in Chapter 9 – a mixture of location or niche marketing consortia, marketing and purchasing consortia, referral consortia, personnel and training consortia and collaborative reservation systems – the groupings are in fact very similar insofar as they continue to develop, differentiate and offer ever more services over time. Of all the typologies outlined in Chapter 6, most notably those advocated by Dev and Klein, Huxham and Selin, that provided by Terpstra and Simonin – coverage, form, mode and motive – serves as a particularly useful framework to explain the inter-organisational dynamics of collaborative forms. This was put to good effect in Chapter 9, where a detailed critique of the Best Western hotel consortium was set out. Best Western's coverage is global in that it offers a full-service marketing product across the world, in addition to extending its benefits outside its traditional hotel sector in respect of sharing 'partnership' with numerous non-hotel players in the international tourism industry. This represents yet more evidence of the emerging trend towards diagonal forms of collaboration, and further opportunities for market 'connectivity' and benefits to be derived from co-branding. As a collaborative form, Best Western is a not-for-profit consortium, which clearly exists to serve its members. It has adopted an equity format funded by fees and dues paid by member hotels, yet it also demonstrates tight governance in the form of an executive board. Best Western affords members considerable flexibility in that it offers rolling one-year contracts wherein membership can, if desired, be discontinued or transferred for a small fee. In terms of mode, Best Western represents a facilitating network, albeit individual in outlook with considerable marketing benefits serving as the catalytic motive for membership. This having been said, numerous other criteria, including direction, duration, commitment, organisational type, hierarchical complexity, formality of governance, equity arrangements, risk, the number of partners and the legal nature of the collaboration, are all equally relevant in different situations.

Although the different sectors appear to demonstrate particular preference to their 'own' form of collaboration, the important conclusion to draw is that each strives to maximise the benefits of collaboration fully and to deliver sufficient collaborative advantage to make inter-organisational collaboration worthwhile. It is for this reason that the synthetic definition of collaborative marketing introduced in Part 4 of the book remains, in the opinion of the authors, that which is most appropriate for the future study of the phenomenon. This sees collaborative marketing being described as a process of joint decision-making among autonomous, key stakeholders of an inter-organisational, tourism marketing domain, to resolve marketing problems of the domain and/or manage issues related to the marketing and development of the domain.

Choice of collaboration partners

Irrespective of the coverage, form, mode and motive of collaboration, one of the key issues in implementing effectively any alliance, consortium or partnership is ensuring that the most appropriate partners are recruited in order to maximise collaborative advantage. Clearly those responsible for initiating collaboration need to establish the desired qualities of partners with whom to collaborate and identify the preferred partner-mix for successful achievement of the collaborative marketing domain. In providing a guideline for partner selection, Kanter's Eight I's, as presented in Chapter 7, represent a very useful 'generic' framework upon which to base partner selection decisions. Also presented in Chapter 7, Wood and Gray offer an alternative, complementary set of guidelines which propose that truly effective inter-organisational forms need to include those stakeholders most interested in working collaboratively; the most powerful and influential stakeholders; the majority of stakeholders, so that social norms can be established and others can join later; and the best-organised stakeholders, so that social pressure can be brought to bear on non-participants. These latter points are of particular relevance to global airline alliances in that, over a relatively short period of time – just six years – Star Alliance has been able to nurture a very strong domain culture, an increasingly integrated domain-wide brand and significant representation from its members.

Implementing the tourism marketing mix

The true test of an inter-organisational form is clearly the extent to which it delivers collaborative advantage and meets the objectives set for it. Despite considerable debate in the field of services marketing as to the application and worthiness of the Seven Ps framework, arguably it remains a useful structure upon which to organise discussion on the implementation of the tourism marketing mix.

Perhaps the most important product-related decisions for collaborating partners are the extent to which the individual or collaborative 'co-brand' is used and how partners manage the convergence or divergence of brand values in the context of collaboration. Schreiber's Brand Get–Give analysis, which was introduced in Chapter 8, provides a useful vehicle for understanding the 'domain' value of collaboration and serves as a complementary tool to the more established Brand Pyramid and Branding Iceberg models outlined in Chapter 3. The benefits of collaborative branding are well demonstrated by the example of the Small Luxury Hotels of the World consortium in that, despite the cost of membership, and the strength of their individual hotel brands, members choose to belong to a consortium which offers them the potential to be true leaders in the provision of luxury accommodation, an orientation which they see as being synonymous with their own brands. For the majority of independent hotels and hotel groups, 'brand' membership is becoming more and more important in that, with the greater concentration and consolidation evident in the industry, independents are never going to be able to match the momentum of the corporate hotel chains in the marketplace, and only through collaboration and the benefits of collaboration co-branding can they hope to survive.

In many ways, branding represents the most visible component of the integration of stakeholder effort. In the example of global airline alliances, however, what is not yet clear is the extent to which customers are actually buying into the collaborative or individual brand. Out of the three major global airline alliances, Star Alliance – 'The Airline Network for Earth' – has perhaps been the most active in developing a collaborative co-branding strategy. However, although there appears general agreement as to how the new livery should be used, the extent to which each individual airline is aware of how the collaborative and individual brand names (for example Star Alliance and Lufthansa) increase the combined value, or potentially damage individual partners, is unclear. For the future, the question has to be to what extent does becoming part of the wider alliance's brand 'ecosystem' bring real value. Brand values, as identified in Chapter 3, can be either tangible or intangible. The tangible benefits of alliance membership appear very clear. What perhaps is less certain after six years of operation is the extent to which the more intangible elements of the brand, such as alliance culture, service delivery and service quality, will permeate all elements of the domain brand.

Interestingly, despite advances in product development and domain-brand consistency, considerable variation still remains in the prices set by partners in inter-organisational collaborations. Clearly there is always going to be pressure to set prices in competitive situations so as to counter short- to medium-term competition, while, when setting prices within the inter-organisational context, the nature of the relationships, interactions and interdependencies among partners will clearly impact on decision making. This applies across the board, in that international airlines, independent hotels and hotel groups and destinations all exhibit quite different cost bases, infrastructural requirements and supplies of labour and are, therefore, subject to quite different macro- and micro-environmental pressures. However, the pressure to converge towards an alliance median is likely to grow as the collaboration develops, if only to reflect better the corporate position and sense of purpose of the inter-organisational domain.

Seasonality is one factor that impacts significantly on pricing across all sectors of the tourism industry, as does the ownership and commitment to the cause among collaboration partners. As with many aspects of managing collaboration, the setting of prices is all about managing differences, variety and cross-cultural dynamics. From a positioning perspective, however, the customer is likely to expect a certain degree of consistency and standardisation across the domain brand. There is, nevertheless, likely to emerge a fear among customers of the extent to which partners share pricing information and act collaboratively on pricing decisions. Collusion among partners in the setting of prices is a genuine fear, in that many inter-organisational forms are contributing to the 'perceived' and 'real' further concentration and consolidation of their particular sector within the tourism industry. To date, the relevant regulatory authorities have found it difficult to arrive at any collusion on this matter. It is clear, however, that this will remain an issue of concern for the future.

One significant benefit still to be derived from inter-organisational collaboration is the ability to pursue higher yield through the effective delivery of 'domain' yield-management systems. Such a development clearly hinges on the sharing of domain-wide information, something only made possible once trust and commitment have been cemented across the entire inter-organisational arrangement. The likely benefits are considerable, in that relationship marketing and customer-relationship management strategies then become a viable option for alliances, consortia and partnerships. Although there remain a number of hurdles at the destination level, as evidenced by the Stockholm Information Service in Chapter 10, the integration of frequent-flier programmes by Star Alliance is evidence of significant integration of support systems at the domain level, as is the example of Opodo discussed in Chapter 8. This clearly represents an area where there remains considerable scope for expansion in the future, and one area that is likely to lead to the further consolidation of inter-organisational collaboration across the tourism industry as a whole.

Channel intermediaries play such a significant role in the tourism system that it comes as no surprise that airlines, hotels and destinations consider the attraction of domain-wide systems, increasing power and control within the distribution chain and the opportunity to counter the threat from both traditional and emerging e-intermediaries as significant drivers towards the adoption of collaborative marketing strategies. Earlier discussions on the analysis of the micro-environment outlined the changing power base that successful collaboration can deliver, and certainly in the case of hotel consortia greater prominence within the distribution chain and access to a much larger, and very often more international, marketplace serve as key antecedents for collaboration. Potentially the key element of the marketing mix impacted on by collaboration, the balance of power can very quickly shift among suppliers of the tourism product and tour operators and travel agents, with the cost and control element between both sides shifting in favour of those organisations adopting the collaborative marketing route.

One of the more recent elements to be considered in the context of inter-organisational collaboration is the issue of promotion. The emphasis of collaboration to date quite clearly has been on enhanced market access, global reach and service-support systems and processes, and on domain development. However, the benefits to be gained by promotional domain strategies can be considerable. For members of Best Western, the world-wide promotion of independent hotels offers considerable advantages, as does the collective development of imagery promoting the Greater Mekong Subregion. This is also true of the international 'multilateral' promotion of Queensland's Gold Coast in comparison to the 'unilateral' efforts to promote the Sunshine Coast, as discussed in Chapter 10. As with decisions pertaining to the use and communication of the domain brand, inter-organisational promotional decisions to date are very much of a 'suck-it-and-see' nature, with little historical precedent to underpin decision-making.

As for decisions pertaining to implementation of the extended marketing mix, the cross-cultural dynamics of global airline alliances in particular contribute to the 'people' element, and its impact on product delivery, the service encounter and experiential aspects of delivering the brand that are difficult to put into place. Partner airlines in all three of the major global airline alliances maintain to some extent their tradi-tional 'adversarial' flag-carrier mentality, which serves as an impediment to more integrated adoption of the domain culture, evidenced most recently in the innovative union between Air France and KLM, where the decision has been taken not to attempt to merge corporate cultures. Strong individual corporate cultures, significant union power, national pride and perhaps a little fear on the part of management to make the cuts necessary to make the 'union' between the two organisations more in tune with the expectations of the stock markets, demonstrate the considerable barriers to closer inter-organisational collaboration among international airlines. In this context, alliances are clearly a 'second-best' form of organisational structure to accommodate the dynamic forces in the external macro-environment.

The initiation and development of value-chain networks and enhanced connectivity in the interdependent system that is tourism resonate strongly with the process component of the extended marketing mix. The referral system that was the origin of Best Western, the early codesharing arrangements that were the origins of airline alliances, and the web developments behind the marketing of the Greater Mekong Subregion all demonstrate the importance of process within the collabor-ative tourism marketing mix. Evidenced within the Branding Iceberg in Chapter 3, it is more often than not the service support systems and processes that underpin successful outcomes derived from inter-organisational collaboration.

The final aspect of the extended marketing mix, that of physical evidence, is so closely intertwined with the development of domain brands and related items such as livery, uniforms and domain logos that this most tangible of elements really should perhaps be considered at the very outset of inter-organisational collaboration, rather than representing, more often than not, an 'afterthought' in the minds of those initiating such strategies. The Air France and KLM development is testament to the 'national' issues at stake in many situations of this kind, the question for the future being the extent to which such decisions are driven by the customer rather than the supply-side orientations of airlines, hotels and destinations.

Collaboration management and effectiveness

The one consistent question asked by every participant of inter-organisational collaboration is quite simply: what makes collaboration successful and how can the performance of inter-organisational collaborative relationships between organisations be improved? Chapter 7 explored these issues in depth, albeit without coming to a firm conclusion. The comments of Huxham presented in Chapter 7 are significant in that little argument exists among writers to counter the claim that collaboration is difficult. The comments made by Donaldson and O'Toole, also presented in Chapter 7, are also worth mentioning in that much of the difficulty attributed to collaboration is how one actually measures effectiveness and success. Donaldson and O'Toole suggested that, while the majority of business performance is measured in a financial way in the long term, very little agreement, if any, has been reached as to how relationship performance should be measured in the long term. They concluded that relational performance is in fact frequently excluded from models of relational development due to an underlying assumption that relationships simply must improve performance. Similar comments were made by Dwyer in Chapter 10, when in the context of inter-destination collaboration he argued that there remains an insufficient understanding of the internal dynamics of collaboration and that many of the so-called economic benefits have yet fully to be tested empirically.

As with all aspects of marketing, collaborative marketing strategies are subject to numerous variables that can impact on performance and outcomes. Interestingly, far more attention in the academic literature has to date been given to the reasons for termination and 'failure', rather than to collaboration performance per se. Reasons for failure, or not meeting objectives, are of course numerous. Factors such as not identifying clear objectives at the outset, uncertainty and self-serving behaviour within the collaboration, inertia, lack of time, personnel and resources, and a conflict of culture can all play their part. It is undoubtedly true that empirical studies by Bucklin and Sengupta on the collaboration in the context of co-marketing alliances, and Palmer with specific reference to tourism-related co-marketing alliances, both of which are discussed in Chapter 7, have started to clarify the debate. On the other hand, work by Kanter counters this desire to 'measure' collaboration by arguing that a fundamental feature of collaborative relationships is that they simply cannot be controlled by formal systems. Instead, a dense web of inter-personal connections and internal infrastructures that enhance learning are the key to success. These contrasting viewpoints highlight very different prescriptive and emergent approaches to understanding and implementing inter-organisational collaboration.

Chapter 7 nevertheless identifies a plethora of lists that claim to identify the necessary prerequisites of collaborative success. Work by Bramwell and Sharman identified three strands of success: the scope of collaboration the intensity of collaboration, and the degree to which consensus emerges. While their analysis was applied to local collaborative tourism policy making, it clearly carries currency across other tourism sectors. Likewise, the study by Jamal and Getz identified six overarching propositions for collaborative success based upon the legitimacy of the stakeholder process and the power relationships that develop as the collaboration proceeds. Originally identified in Chapter 7, the six propositions are:

(1) Collaboration will require recognition of a high degree of interdependence in planning and managing the domain.
(2) Collaboration will require recognition of individual and/or mutual benefits to be derived from the process.
(3) Collaboration will require a perception that decisions arrived at will be implemented.
(4) Collaboration will depend on encompassing key stakeholder groups.
(5) A convenor is required to initiate and facilitate collaboration.
(6) An effective collaborative process requires: formulation of a vision statement on desired tourism development and growth; joint formulation of tourism goals and objectives; and self-regulation of the planning and development domain through the establishment of a collaborative (referent) organisation to assist with ongoing adjustment of these strategies through monitoring and revisions.

In a similar vein, Kanter's study across industrial sectors concluded that, to maximise the benefits of collaboration:

(1) Partners' strategic goals should converge while their competitive goals diverge.
(2) The relative size and market power of partners should be modest compared with industry leaders.
(3) Each partner should believe that it can learn from the others and at the same time limit access to proprietary skills.

(4) The collaborative alliance should be regarded as a relationship rather than a mere exchange.
(5) There should be an overall consensus as to the general 'mission' of the collaborative alliance.

The extent to which the prescriptions contained in the above lists are borne out in the case studies featured in this book are clearly open to interpretation. In the case of the Gold Coast versus the Sunshine Coast example in Chapter 10, the difference in the outcomes between the single marketing organisation of the Gold Coast and the multiple marketing organisations of the Sunshine Coast is very significant. Although the Sunshine Coast example would appear to adhere to the majority of Kanter's five criteria for success, the evident lack of consensus as to the general 'mission' of the domain destination has clearly hindered progress. The historical self-interest and opportunistic behaviour of the three 'partner' authorities is apparent, with the overall marketing impact being diluted through diverse marketing activity and a long-standing failure to develop fully the collaborative destination domain. Not only has this led to confusion in the mind of both customer and consumer, but it has also resulted in the dilution of promotional funds, encouraged individual businesses to pursue unilateral marketing strategies and led to the emergence of short-term selling strategies. The lack of unity at the 'nodal' destination has also led to investor uncertainty and unnecessary competition for tourism expenditure.

Those destination collaboration criteria identified for the Greater Mekong Subregion in Chapter 10 are testament to the fact that it is very difficult indeed for a totally 'generic' set of criteria to carry value across the various sectors of the tourism industry. Even in this case, however, the fact that many of the identified criteria are so difficult to measure serves as an impediment to determining the overall degree of success achieved by the collaborative initiative. Likewise, the fact that the Greater Mekong Subregion collaboration is ongoing makes it difficult to conclude as to its effectiveness. Nonetheless, it does appear that, for the collaborative tourism entity to succeed fully, a far closer partnership is required among the individual NTOs and other associated agencies. There is also the requirement for greater private-sector involvement, as is there a need for many more 'packages' or 'heritage trails' to be developed that facilitate the selling of the Greater Mekong Subregion as a single product.

In the case of international airlines and their membership of global airline alliances, the five criteria advocated by Kanter serve as a useful benchmark for measuring effectiveness. However, given the fate of the Qualiflyer alliance, when Swissair were forced out of business in 2002, it is highly questionable as to the extent to which Star Alliance, Oneworld and SkyTeam are sufficiently robust as inter-organisational forms to survive the demise of one of their major partners. The trend towards non-equity alliances has so far tended to protect individual airlines from the negative consequences of a partner that has become bankrupt. However, airline alliances are only as strong as their weakest member, and the failure of one partner to pull its own weight may seriously compromise the degree of collaborative advantage an alliance is able to achieve relative to competitor alliances. Indeed, the recent collapse of the Qualiflyer alliance suggests that alliances are by no means permanent landmarks. Even the three remaining global alliances may be dissolved and perhaps reformed in different combinations over the coming years.

For independent hotels and hotel groups within the Best Western consortium, the short-term 'rolling' nature of contracts and the freedom to transfer offer a degree of flexibility that, to date, is not available to individual destinations and airlines to the same degree. The ever closer integration of international airlines within their inter-organisational forms has perhaps created a situation where turning back is no longer an option. For independent hotels and hotel groups, however, the relationship between the consortium and its members is important to the effectiveness and stability of the organisation and ultimately to its eventual success. As discussed in Chapter 7 in the context of collaboration more generally, the degree of formality in the governance of consortia varies from one to another. The smaller consortia, which are usually member-controlled, exhibit the loosest bonds between members, with very little formality. In contrast, larger consortia frequently take the form of limited companies, and often have more formal governance structures and styles of management. These differences in formality affect the organisation's objectives and effectiveness as well as the members' influence on the consortium and vice versa. For many independent hotels and hotel groups, consortium membership is frequently regarded as a transitional step rather than a strategy for long-term growth. And while Best Western records a retention rate of 99%, evidence in Chapter 9 suggests that 60% of consortia last no more than four years and fewer than one in five last up to 10 years.

In concluding this aspect of the collaborative strategic tourism marketing planning process, it can be suggested that, until a definition of what truly constitutes collaboration is universally agreed upon, the problem of determining the conditions under which collaboration might be considered to be effective will continue. The fact that no consistent 'prescriptive' solution exists may not be such a problem, however, for much of the success of collaboration lies in the mindset of the partners. The abandonment of competitive patterns of thought and behaviour and adoption of 'relational' collaborative orientation, as advocated by Helfert *et al.* and discussed in detail in Chapter 2, will contribute strongly to more effective collaborative performance in that more and more organisations will 'walk the talk'. As concluded at the end of Chapter 7, collaboration among those still deeply wedded to the competition paradigm is more likely to meet with failure, or partial performance, than it is with success.

Marketing evaluation, monitoring and control

Conducted in parallel with the monitoring of the effectiveness of inter-organisational forms in meeting the goals and objectives of the collaborative strategic tourism marketing plan, the generic evaluation, monitoring and control of the strategic marketing plan in the context of collaboration requires additional metrics to those advocated in Chapter 4. A good example in this area of activity is SAS Scandinavian Airlines, which has fully integrated its alliance activity into its monitoring systems in that it is able to monitor 'interline' revenue with its alliance partners, most notably Lufthansa, and to evaluate its inter-organisational performance through sophisticated systems. Meanwhile, the monitoring of domain yield and sales by alliance partners is facilitated by StarNet, Star Alliance's common ICT infrastructure that links together all the separate computer networks of the Star Alliance member airlines. However, although the problem of monitoring has arguably been one of the downfalls of collaboration, the technologically driven airlines have a considerable advantage over destinations, for example, in that the lack of sufficiently robust information bases in the destination domain frequently hinders progress, whether this is intended to be achieved by the adoption of either collaborative or competitive marketing strategies.

With the adoption of collaborative marketing strategies, to some degree organisations are entering into 'boundaryless' multilateral co-operative environments, where issues of responsibility and accountability are often difficult due to unclear reporting structures, different reporting time scales and measurement inconsistencies. The challenge for the future is to adopt monitoring, evaluation and control systems that enable individual and collaborating organisations to respond quickly if problems arise in the course of the strategic marketing planning process. If inter-organisational forms become cumbersome and unable to act in a flexible manner to serious problems of a short-term nature, the development of trust and commitment – two prerequisites for effective evaluation, monitoring and control – will be severely tested. The challenge is to grow and become solid in purpose, but to have governance structures that can respond to external events and competitive activity speedily.

Concluding Comments

In the study conducted by Helfert *et al.*, as discussed in Chapter 2, it was argued that an organisation's 'surroundings' should be seen as a network of inter-organisational relationships, rather than as an anonymous market. The study also concluded that market orientation on a relationship level can be interpreted in terms of the resources the organisation employs and the activities it undertakes further to the process of relational exchange. The question to be addressed here is the extent to which this does in fact represent a new 'collaborative' marketing paradigm.

Without question, from early beginnings in the late 1980s and early 1990s, strategic marketing began to draw from the inter-organisational relationship literature with the overriding argument being that emphasis would shift away from 'customer focus' to 'mutual dependence' through networks based on skills and resources that partners could bring to the relationship. This debate has continued to grow in the new millennium with Christopher *et al.* (2002: 121) outlining the movement away from transaction economics and resource-based views of the firm, towards a business model that is based on:

> [the] idea of the firm as an element in a network that competes through the way it leverages the resources and capabilities of its individual members. Each member of the network specialises in that aspect of the value-creation process where it has the greatest differential advantage. This model of business activity sees the network, not the individual firm, as the value delivery system.

The above clearly represents a movement away from the 'single-firm' transactional business model, in that the emerging 'collaborative' marketing paradigm implies that sustainable advantage lies in managing the complex web of relationships that link highly focused providers of specific elements of the final offer in a cost-effective, value-adding network. According to Christopher *et al.* (2002: 124), 'the key to success in this new competitive framework is, arguably, the way in which the network of alliances and suppliers are welded together in partnership to achieve mutually beneficial goals'. They go on to suggest that, to be truly agile, collaborating networks need to exhibit a number of distinguishing characteristics:

- They need to be market sensitive.
- They need to share the same information.
- They need to ensure that the exchange of information is facilitated by process alignment, i.e. that the core business processes of network partners connect easily.

Competition is clearly no longer between individual organisations, but between their supply chains or networks. In this case, the future lies with the ability of individual organisations to partner with others in an effective manner in delivering the desired outcomes demanded by the market in a complex, dynamic and turbulent macro- and micro-environment.

Although one can quite easily interpret the above paradigmatic shift as being both a philosophy of conducting business and a 'relational' management process, this is perhaps missing the point. The debate has moved on inasmuch as the question of whether to collaborate has now been superseded by that of who are the most suitable partners with whom to collaborate and in what form should such collaboration take place. For example, rather than simply asking whether or not to pursue collaboration as a strategy, the following three questions have now assumed greater prominence:

- Which relationships offer the greatest value potential?
- What level of benefits should be provided to relationships?
- How should these benefits/resources be delivered?

Consistent with the work of Morgan and Hunt, introduced in Chapter 2 of this book:

- A firm will trust its relationship partner when both partners share similar values, when communication in their relationship is healthy, and when their relationship history is not characterised by one partner maliciously taking advantage of the other.
- Relationship commitment arises not only from trust and its antecedents, but also from the direct effects of shared values and the belief that partners would be difficult to replace.
- More than half the differences in levels of co-operation from one relationship to the next can be explained by relationship commitment, trust and their antecedents.

The future lies with value, value exchange, and value enhancement driven and delivered by value networks. Through network knowledge, value can be created and shared by interactions that emerge from within networks of relationships. Collaboration, therefore, is as important, if not more so, than competition in the new world order. In the words of Christopher *et al.* (2002: 229) 'it is networks that compete, not firms'. They go on to suggest that 'it is not merely a shift in language but a shift in ideas about how value is created and an acknowledgement of new organisational forms'.

This book has endeavoured to integrate the literatures of tourism marketing and inter-organisational collaboration in an attempt to provide a synthesis of what the authors believe to be the necessary catalyst to further the level of analysis and critical debate on what are presently the most significant matters relating to collaborative marketing in the tourism industry. It is hoped that the contents of this book will facilitate the future analysis of collaboration opportunities, help formulate collaboration strategy and, most importantly, implement collaboration effectively.

To close, hopefully this book has raised more questions than it has attempted to answer. The emerging adoption of inter-organisational collaborative marketing strategies has demonstrated the dynamics, energy and permeating influence of the phenomenon across the entire tourism industry. Clearly questions and challenges remain, such as the need for greater accountability for collaborative forms, greater evidence to support collaboration decision-making and detailed cost-benefit analysis, the impacts of multiple network membership, the most effective governance and management styles, and perhaps the greatest research vacuum to date: collaboration as viewed through the eyes of the customer. After all, what the customer buys into ultimately determines the success, both now and in the future, of any marketing strategy – be it implemented through traditional 'adversarial' competitive strategies or those that adhere to the philosophy advocated in this book: the emerging 'relational' collaborative marketing strategy.

References

Paper-based Sources

Aaker, D. (1992) *Strategic Market Management*. Chichester: John Wiley & Sons.

Abell, D.F. and Hammond, J.S. (1979) *Strategic Marketing Planning: Problems and Analytical Approaches*. Englewood Cliffs, NJ: Prentice Hall.

Agustinata, B. and de Klein, W. (2002) The dynamics of airline alliances. *Journal of Air Transport Management* 8 (4), 201–211.

Anon. (1997) Do hotel marketing consortia work? *Hotel and Catering Business* (October), 28–32.

Ansoff, I. (1987) *Corporate Strategy*. London: Penguin.

Appiah-Adu, K., Fyall, A. and Singh, S. (2000) Marketing culture and customer retention in the tourism industry. *Service Industries Journal* 20 (2), 95–113.

Ashkenas, R., Ulrich, D., Jick, T. and Kerr, S. (1995) *The Boundaryless Organisation*. San Francisco, CA: Jossey-Bass.

Augustyn, M.M. and Knowles, T. (2000) Performance of tourism partnerships: A focus on York. *Tourism Management* 21 (4), 341–351.

Ayala, H. (1997) Resort ecotourism: A catalyst for national and regional partnerships. *Cornell Hotel and Restaurant Administration Quarterly* 38 (4), 34–45.

Badaracco, J.L. (1991) *The Knowledge-Link: How Firms Compete Through Strategic Alliances*. Boston, MA: Harvard Business School Press.

Baker, M.J. (2001) *Marketing: Critical Perspectives on Business and Management Parts I to V*. London: Routledge.

Ballantyne, D. (1994) Marketing at the crossroads. *Asia–Australia Marketing Journal* 2 (1), 20–26.

Balmer, J.M.T. (2001) The three virtues and seven deadly sins of corporate brand management. *Journal of General Management* 27 (1), 1–17.

Barkin, D. and Pailles, C. (1999) NGO and community collaboration for ecotourism: A strategy for sustainable regional development in Mexico. *Tourism Recreation Research* 24 (2), 69–74.

Batchelor, R. (1997) A distinctly different case study. *Insights* (July), C1–C7.

Bateson, J. (1977) Do we need service marketing? In *Marketing Consumer Services: New Insights*. Report No. 77–115, Boston, MA: Marketing Science Institute.

Bell, C.A. (1992) Bali: How to maintain a fragile resort. *Cornell Hotel and Restaurant Administration Quarterly* 33 (5), 28–31.

Bennett, O. (1999) Destination marketing into the next century. *Journal of Vacation Marketing* 6 (1), 48–54.

Berry, L. (1980) Services marketing is different. *Business* 30 (3), 24–29.

362

Berthon, P., Hulbert, J.M. and Pitt, L.F. (1997) Brands, brand managers, and the management of brands: Where to next? Report No. 97–122, Boston, MA: Marketing Science Institute.

Best Western (2002) *Annual Report*. Phoenix, AZ: Best Western.

Beverland, M. and Brotherton, P. (2001) The uncertain search for opportunities: Determinants of strategic partnerships. *Qualitative Market Research: An International Journal* 4 (2), 88–99.

Blackett, T. and Boad, B. (1999) *Co-branding: The Science of Alliance*. Basingstoke: Macmillan Business Press.

Bleeke, J. and Ernst, D. (1991) The way to win in cross border alliances. *Harvard Business Review* (November–December), 127–135.

Bleeke, J. and Ernst, D. (1995) Is your strategic alliance really a sale? *Harvard Business Review* (January–February), 97–103.

bmi (2003) *Press Release*, 17 April 2003.

Bowden, S. (1991) Pulling together in the Pennines: A tale of two districts. *Tourism Enterprise* 76, 10.

Bowen, J. and Shoemaker, S. (1998) Loyalty: A strategic commitment. *Cornell Hotel and Restaurant Administration Quarterly* 39 (February), 12–25.

Briggs, S. (1994) Powerful partnerships: Setting up and running a marketing consortium. *Insights* 6 (3), A69–A72.

Booms, B.H. and Bitner, M.J. (1981) Marketing strategies and organization structures for service firms. In J. Donnelly and W.R. George (eds) *Marketing of Services* (pp. 47–51). Chicago, IL: American Marketing Association.

Boone, J.M. (1998) Hotel–restaurant co-branding: A preliminary study. *The Cornell Hotel and Restaurant Administration Quarterly* 38 (5), 34–43.

Bradley, S., Hausman, J. and Nolan, R. (1993) *Globalisation, Technology and Competition: The Fusion of Computers and Telecommunications in the 1990s*. Boston, MA: Harvard Business School Press.

Bramwell, B. and Lane, B. (2000) *Tourism Collaboration and Partnerships: Politics, Practice and Sustainability*. Clevedon: Channel View.

Bramwell, B. and Sharman, A. (1999) Collaborating in local tourism policymaking. *Annals of Tourism Research* 26 (2), 392–415.

Brandon, K. (1993) Basic steps toward encouraging local participation in nature tourism projects. In K. Lindberg and D.E. Hawkins (eds) *Ecotourism: A Guide for Local Planners* (pp. 134–151). North Bennington, VT: The Ecotourism Society.

Brassington, F. and Pettit, S. (1997) *Principles of Marketing*. London: Financial Times Pitman Publishing.

Brinkerhoff, J.M. (2002) Assessing and improving partnership relationships and outcomes: A proposed framework. *Evaluation and Program Planning* 25 (3), 215–231.

Bucklin, L.P. and Sengupta, S. (1993) Organizing successful co-marketing alliances. *Journal of Marketing* 57 (2), 32–46.

Buhalis, D. (2000) Marketing the competitive destination of the future. *Tourism Management* 21 (1), 97–116.

Buhalis, D. (2001) The tourism phenomenon: The new tourist and consumer. In S. Wahab and C. Cooper (eds) *Tourism in the Age of Globalisation* (pp. 69–96). London: Routledge.

Buhalis, D. and Cooper, C. (1998) Competition or co-operation: The needs of small and medium sized tourism enterprises at a destination level. In E. Laws, B. Faulkner and G. Moscardo (eds) *Embracing and Managing Change in Tourism* (pp. 324–346). London: Routledge.

Butler, R.W. (1980) The concept of a tourist area cycle of evolution: Implications for management of resources. *Canadian Geographer* 24 (18), 5–12.

Butler, R.W. (1999) Sustainable tourism: A state-of-the-art review. *Tourism Geographies* 1 (1), 7–25.

Buttle, F. (1986) *Hotel and Food Service Marketing*. London: Holt, Rinehart and Winston.

Caffyn, A. (2000) Is there a tourism partnership life cycle? In B. Bramwell and B. Lane (eds) *Tourism Collaboration and Partnerships: Politics, Practice and Sustainability* (pp. 200–229). Clevedon: Channel View.

Calantone, R.J. and Mazanec, J.A. (1991) Marketing management and tourism. *Annals of Tourism Research* 18 (1), 101–119.

Carimbocas, C. (2003) Hotel consortia: Ten years later. Unpublished Masters thesis, Bournemouth University, UK.

Cateora, P.F. and Ghauri, P.N. (2000) *International Marketing* (European edn). London: McGraw-Hill.

Chaston, I. (1999) *New Marketing Strategies*. London: Sage.

Chen, H. and Chen T.-J. (2003) Governance structures in strategic alliances: Transaction cost versus resource-based perspective. *Journal of World Business* 38 (1), 1–14.

Child, J. and Faulkner, D. (1998) *Strategies of Co-operation: Managing Alliances, Networks and Joint Ventures*. Oxford: Oxford University Press.

Chipkin, H. (2001) Is independents' day at hand? *Lodging* 26 (11), 44–48.

Christopher, M., Payne, A. and Ballantyne, D. (2002) *Relationship Marketing: Creating Stakeholder Value*. Oxford: Butterworth-Heinemann.

Clark, S. (2001) Multiple choices. *Caterer and Hotelkeeper*, 15 February, 31–32.

Cooper, C., Fletcher, J., Gilbert, D., Shepherd, R. and Wanhill, S. (1998) *Tourism Principles and Practice* (2nd edn). Harlow: Pearson Education Limited.

Cox, K.K. and McGinnis, V.J. (1982) *Strategic Marketing Decisions: A Reader*. Englewood Cliffs, NJ: Prentice Hall.

Court, B. and Lupton, R. (1997) Customer portfolio development: Modelling destination adopters, inactives and rejectors. *Journal of Travel Research*, 30 (2), 35–43.

Cravens, D.W. and Piercy, N.F. (1994) Relationship marketing and collaborative networks in service organizations. *International Journal of Service Industry Management* 5 (5), 39–53.

Cravens, D.W. and Woodruff, R.B. (1986) *Marketing*. Reading, MA: Addison-Wesley.

Cropper, S. (1996) Collaborative working and the issue of sustainability. In C. Huxham (ed.) *Creating Collaborative Advantage* (pp. 80–100). London: Sage.

Crotts, J.C., Buhalis, D. and March, R. (eds) (2000) *Global Alliances in Tourism and Hospitality Management*. New York: The Haworth Hospitality Press.

Crotts, J.C. and Wilson, D. (1995) An integrated model of buyer–seller relationships in the international travel trade. *Progress in Tourism and Hospitality Research* 1 (2), 125–140.

Dale, C. (2000) The UK tour-operating industry: A competitive analysis. *Journal of Vacation Marketing* 6 (4), 357–367.

Darrow, K. (1995) A partnership model for nature tourism in the eastern Caribbean islands. *Journal of Travel Research* 33 (3), 48–51.

Davidson, H. (1997) *Even More Offensive Marketing*. London: Penguin.

de Araujo, L.M. and Bramwell, B. (2002) Partnership and regional tourism in Brazil. *Annals of Tourism Research* 29 (4), 1138–1164.

Dela Cruz, T. (1998) Consortia 25. *Hotels* 32 (7), 49–76.

Dela Cruz, T. (2000) Consortia 25. *Hotels* 34 (7), 76–78.

Dev, C.S. and Klein, S. (1993) Strategic alliances in the hotel industry. *The Cornell Hotel and Restaurant Administration Quarterly* 34 (1), 42–45.

de Wit, B. and Meyer, R. (1998) *Strategy: Process, Content, Context: an International Perspective.* London: International Thomson Business Press.

Domke-Damonte, D.J. (2000) The effect of cross-industry cooperation on performance in the airline industry. In J.C. Crotts, D. Buhalis and R. March (eds) *Global Alliances in Tourism and Hospitality Management* (pp. 141–160). New York: The Haworth Hospitality Press.

Donaldson, B. and O'Toole, T. (2002) *Strategic Market Relationships: From Strategy to Implementation.* Chichester: John Wiley & Sons.

Douma, S. and Schreuder, H. (1991) *Economic Approaches to Organizations.* Hemel Hempstead: Prentice Hall.

Doyle, P. (2000) *Value-Based Marketing: Marketing Strategies for Corporate Growth and Shareholder Value.* Chichester: John Wiley & Sons.

Drucker, P. (1973) *Management Tasks, Responsibilities, Practices.* New York: Harper Row.

Drummond, G. and Ensor, G. (1999) *Strategic Marketing: Planning and Control.* Oxford: Butterworth-Heinemann.

Dundjerovic, A. (1999) Consortia: How far can they go towards helping independent hotels compete with chains? *Tourism and Hospitality Research* 1 (4), 370–374.

Dwyer, L. (2003) Cooperative destination marketing: Revisiting the assumed economic impacts. *Pacific Tourism Review* 6 (2), 95–105.

Edgell, D.L., Kurtis, M.R. and Agarwal, A. (1999) Strategic marketing planning for the tourism industry. *Journal of Travel & Tourism Marketing* 8 (3), 111–120.

Elmuti, D. and Kathawala, Y. (2001) An overview of strategic alliances. *Management Decision* 39 (3), 205–218.

Emery, F. and Trist, E. (1965) The causal texture of organizational environments. *Human Relations* 18 (1), 21–35.

Evans, M. (1990) The hotel consortium: There's safety in numbers. *Insights* (May), A8.1–A8.5.

Evans, N. (2001) Collaborative strategy: An analysis of the changing world of airline alliances. *Tourism Management* 22 (3), 229–243.

Evans, N., Campbell, D. and Stonehouse, G. (2003) *Strategic Management for Travel and Tourism.* Oxford: Butterworth-Heinemann.

Evans, M.R., Fox, J.B. and Johnson, R.B. (1995) Identifying competitive strategies for successful tourism destination development. *Journal of Hospitality and Leisure Marketing* 3 (1), 37–45.

Faulkner, B. (1998) Developing strategic approaches to tourism destination marketing: The Australian experience. In W.F. Theobald (ed.) *Global Tourism* (2nd edn) (pp. 297–316). Oxford: Butterworth-Heinemann.

Fayos-Sola, E. (1996) Tourism policy: A midsummer night's dream? *Tourism Management*, 17 (6), 405–412.

Flanagan, A. and Marcus, M. (1993) Airline alliances: Secrets of a successful liaison. *Avmark Aviation Economist* 10 (1), 20–23.

Fournier, S., Dobscha, S. and Mick, D. (1998) Preventing the premature death of relationship marketing. *Harvard Business Review* 76 (January–February), 43–50.

Frechtling, D.C. (1987) Five issues in tourism marketing in the 1990s. *Tourism Management* 8 (2), 177–178.

French, T. (1997) Global trends in airline alliances. *Travel & Tourism Analyst* 4, 81–101.

Fyall, A. (2003) Marketing visitor attractions: A collaborative approach. In A. Fyall, B. Garrod and A. Leask (eds) *Managing Visitor Attractions: New Directions* (pp. 236–252). Oxford: Butterworth-Heinemann.

Fyall, A. and Callod, C. (2003) Destination relationship marketing. Paper presented at 13th International Research Conference of CAUTHE, Coffs Harbour, Australia, February.

Fyall, A., Callod, C. and Edwards, B. (2003) Relationship marketing: The challenge for destinations. *Annals of Tourism Research* 30 (3), 644–659.

Fyall, A., Garrod, B. and Leask, A. (2001) Scottish visitor attractions: A collaborative future? *International Journal of Tourism Research* 3 (3), 211–228.

Fyall, A. and Leask, A. (2002) Managing visitor attractions: A collaborative approach. *Insights* (January 2002), A93–A97.

Fyall, A., Oakley, B. and Weiss, A. (2000) Theoretical perspectives applied to inter-organisational collaboration on Britain's inland waterways. *International Journal of Hospitality & Tourism Administration* 1 (1), 89–112.

Fyall, A. and Spyriadis, A. (2003) Collaborating for growth: The international hotel industry. *Journal of Hospitality and Tourism Management* 10 (2): 108–123.

Garrod, B. and Fyall, A. (1998) Beyond the rhetoric of sustainable tourism? *Tourism Management* 19 (3), 199–212.

Gartner, W. (1996) *Tourism Development*. New York: Van Nostrand Reinhold.

Gebrekidan, D.A. and Awuah, G.B. (2002) Interorganizational cooperation: A new view of strategic alliances – the case of Swedish firms in the international market. *Industrial Marketing Management* 31 (8), 679–693.

Gilbert, D. (1989) Tourism marketing: Its emergence and establishment. In C. Cooper (ed.) *Progress in Tourism, Recreation and Hospitality Management* (Vol. 1) (pp. 77–90). Belhaven: London.

Gilbert, D. and Zok, S. (1992) Marketing implications of consolidation in the hotel industry. *Journal of Hospitality and Leisure Marketing* 1 (1), 51–69.

Gilligan, C. and Wilson, R.M.S. (2003) *Strategic Marketing Planning*. Oxford: Butterworth-Heinemann.

Go, F.M. and Appelman, J. (2001) Achieving global competitiveness in SMEs by building trust in interfirm alliances. In S. Wahab and C. Cooper (eds) *Tourism in the Age of Globalisation* (pp. 183–197). London: Routledge.

Godfrey, K. and Clarke, J. (2000) *The Tourism Development Handbook*. London: Cassell.

Goeldner, C.R., Ritchie, J.R.B. and McIntosh, R.W. (2000) *Tourism: Principles, Practices, Philosophies*. Chichester: John Wiley & Sons.

Gray, B. (1985) Conditions facilitating interorganizational collaboration. *Human Relations* 38 (10), 911–936.

Gray, B. (1989) *Collaborating: Finding Common Ground for Multiparty Problems*. San Francisco, CA: Jossey-Bass.

Gray, B. (1996) Cross-sectoral partners: Collaborative alliances among businesses, government and communities. In C. Huxham (ed.) *Creating Collaborative Advantage* (pp. 57–79). London: Sage.

Gray, B. and Hooley, G. (2002) Market orientation and service firm performance: A research agenda. *European Journal of Marketing* 36 (9/10), 980–988.

Grönroos, C. (1989) Defining marketing: A market-orientated approach. *European Journal of Marketing* 23 (1), 52–60.

Grönroos, C. (1994) From marketing mix to relationship marketing: Towards a paradigm shift in marketing. *Management Decision* 32 (2), 4–20.

Grossman, R. (1997) Co-branding in advertising: Developing effective associations. *The Journal of Product & Brand Management* 6 (3), 191–201.

Gulati, R. (1998) Alliances and networks. *Strategic Management Journal* 19 (4), 293–317.

Hagedoorn, J. (1993) Understanding the rationale of strategic technology partnering: Interorganizational modes of cooperation and sectoral differences. *Strategic Management Journal* 14 (5), 371–385.

Hagedoorn, J., Link, A.N. and Vonortas, N.S. (2000) Research partnerships. *Research Policy* 29 (4/5), 567–586.

Hall, C.M. (1999) Rethinking collaboration and partnership: A public policy perspective. *Journal of Sustainable Tourism* 7 (3/4), 274–289.

Hamel, G. (1991) Competition for competence and inter-partner learning within international strategic alliances. *Strategic Management Journal* 12 (5), 83–104.

Hamel, G., Doz, Y. and Prahalad, C. (1999) Collaborate with your competitors and win. In B. de Wit and R. Meyer (eds) *Strategy: Process, Content, Context* (2nd edn) (pp. 525–532). London: Thomson Learning.

Hanlon, P. (1999) *Global Airlines: Competition in a Transnational Industry* (2nd edn). Oxford: Butterworth-Heinemann.

Haywood, K.M. (1990) Revising and implementing the marketing concept as it applies to tourism. *Tourism Management* 11 (3), 195–205.

Haywood, K.M. (1992) Identifying and responding to the challenges posed by urban tourism. *Tourism Recreation Research* 17 (2), 9–23.

Heath, E. and Wall, G. (1992) *Marketing Tourism Destinations: A Strategic Planning Approach*. Chichester: John Wiley & Sons.

Helfert, G., Ritter, T. and Walter, A. (2002) Redefining market orientation from a relational perspective: Theoretical considerations and empirical results. *European Journal of Marketing* 36 (9/10), 1119–1139.

Henderson, J. (2001) Strategic alliances and destination marketing in the Greater Mekong Subregion. *Pacific Tourism Review* 4 (4), 149–159.

Hill, S. and Lederer, C. (2001) *The Infinite Asset: Managing Brands to Build New Value*. Boston, MA: Harvard Business School Press.

Hill, T. and Shaw, R.N. (1995) Co-marketing tourism internationally: Bases for strategic alliances. *Journal of Travel Research* 34 (1), 25–32.

Himmelman, A.T. (1996) On the theory and practice of transformational collaboration: From social service to social justice. In C. Huxham (ed.) *Creating Collaborative Advantage* (pp. 19–43). London: Sage.

Hoffman, K.D. and Bateson, J.E.G. (1997) *Essentials of Services Marketing*. Fort Worth, TX: The Dryden Press.

Holder, J. (1992) The need for public and private sector cooperation in tourism. *Tourism Management* 13 (2), 157–162.

Holloway, J.C. and Plant, R.V. (1988) *Marketing for Tourism*. London: Pitman.

Hopper, P. (2002) Marketing London in a difficult climate. *Journal of Vacation Marketing* 9 (1), 81–88.

Houston, F.S. (1986) The marketing concept: What it is and what it is not. *Journal of Marketing* 50 (2), 81–87.

Howarth, G. and Kirsebom, T. (1999) *The Future of Airline Alliances: Current Thinking, Strategic Direction and Implications*. Sutton: Gemini Consulting and Reed Business Information Systems.

Hrebiniak, L. and Joyce, W. (1984) *Implementing Strategy*. New York: Macmillan.

Huber, G.P. (1984) The nature and design of post-industrial organizations. *Administration Science Quarterly* 30 (8), 928–951.

Hulbert, J.M. and Pitt, L. (1996) Exit left centre stage? The future of functional marketing. *European Journal of Marketing* 14 (1), 47–60.

Hunt, S.B. (1970) The nature and scope of marketing. *Journal of Marketing* 40 (2), 17–28.

Huxham, C. (1993) Pursuing collaborative advantage. *Journal of the Operational Research Society* 44 (6), 599–611.

Huxham, C. (1996) Collaboration and competitive advantage. In C. Huxham (ed.) *Creating Collaborative Advantage* (pp. 1–18). London: Sage.

Imrie, R. and Fyall, A. (2000) Customer retention and loyalty in the independent mid-market sector: A United Kingdom perspective. *Journal of Hospitality and Leisure Marketing* 7 (3), 39–53.

Imrie, R. and Fyall, A. (2001) Independent mid-market UK hotels: Marketing strategies for an increasingly competitive environment. *Journal of Vacation Marketing* 7 (1), 36–74.

Inskip, R. (1993) A study of facilitating interorganizational collaboration. Paper prepared for the CAIS/ASCI Conference, Antigonish, Nova Scotia, Canada.

Ivory, M. (1993) Consorting together. *Voice* 2 (4), 18–20.

Jackson, B.B. (1985) Build customer relationships that last. *Harvard Business Review* (November–December), 120–128.

Jacoby, J. and Chestnut, R. (1978) *Brand Loyalty Measurement and Management*. New York: John Wiley & Sons.

Jamal, T.B. and Getz, D. (1995) Collaboration theory and community tourism planning. *Annals of Tourism Research* 22 (1), 186–204.

Jarillo, J.C. (1988) On strategic networks. *Strategic Management Journal* 9 (1), 31–41.

Jayawardena, C. (2000) An analysis of tourism in the Caribbean. *Worldwide Hospitality and Tourism Trends* 1 (2), 122–136.

Jobber, D. (1998) *Principles and Practice of Marketing* (2nd edn). Maidenhead: McGraw Hill.

Jobber, D. (2001) *Principles and Practice of Marketing* (3rd edn). Maidenhead: McGraw Hill.

Johnson, G. and Scholes, K. (1997) *Exploring Corporate Strategy* (4th edn). London: Prentice Hall.

Kanter, R.M. (1994) Collaborative advantage: The art of alliances. *Harvard Business Review* (July–August), 96–108.

Kanter, R.M. (1995) Thinking locally in the global economy. *Harvard Business Review* (September–October), 151–160.

Kapferer, J.N. (1997) *Strategic Brand Management*. London: Kogan Page.

King, J. (2002) Destination marketing organisations: Connecting the experience rather than promoting the place. *Journal of Vacation Marketing* 8 (2), 105–108.

Kitchen, P.J. (1993) Marketing communications renaissance. *International Journal of Advertising* 12 (4), 367–386.

Knowles, T. (1999) *Corporate Strategy for Hospitality*. Harlow: Addison-Wesley-Longman.

Kogut, B. (1989) The stability of joint ventures: Reciprocity and competitive rivalry. *Journal of Industrial Economics* 38 (2), 183–198.

Kohli, A.K. and Jaworski, B.J. (1990) Marketing orientation: The construct, research propositions and managerial implications. *Journal of Marketing* 54 (2), 1–18.

Kotler, P. (1983) *Principles of Marketing* (2nd edn). Englewood Cliffs, NJ: Prentice Hall.

Kotler, P (2001) *A Framework for Marketing Management*. Englewood Cliffs, NJ: Prentice Hall.

Kotler, P., Armstrong, G., Saunders, J. and Wong, V. (1999a) *Principles of Marketing* (2nd European edn): Englewood Cliffs, NJ: Prentice Hall.

Kotler, P., Bowen, J. and Makens, J. (1999b) *Marketing for Hospitality and Tourism* (2nd edn). Englewood Cliffs, NJ: Prentice Hall.

Kotler, P., Bowen, J. and Makens, J. (2003) *Marketing for Hospitality and Tourism* (3rd edn). Englewood Cliffs, NJ: Prentice Hall.

Kotler, P., Haider, D. and Rein, I. (1993) *Marketing Places*. New York: Free Press.

Kotler, P. and Levy, S.J. (1969) Broadening the concept of marketing. *Journal of Marketing* 33 (1), 10–15.

Krippendorf, J. (1987) *The Holidaymakers: Understanding the Impact of Leisure and Travel*. Oxford: Butterworth-Heinemann.

Kvan, T. (2000) Collaborative design: What is it? *Automation in Construction* 9 (4), 409–415.

Leask, A., Fyall, A. and Garrod, B. (2002) Heritage visitor attractions: Managing revenue in the new millennium. *International Journal of Heritage Studies* 8 (3), 247–265.

Levinthal, D.A. and Fichman, M. (1988) Dynamics of interorganizational attachments: Auditor–client relationships. *Administrative Science Quarterly* 33 (3), 345–369.

Levitt, T. (1960) Marketing myopia. *Harvard Business Review* (July–August), 3–13.

Levitt, T. (1983) The globalization of markets. *Harvard Business Review* (May–June), 92–102.

Littlejohn, D. (1982) The role of hotel consortia in Great Britain. Service Industries Review 2 (1), 79–91.

Long, P. (1996) Inter-organisational collaboration in the development of tourism and the arts 1996: The Year of visual arts. In M. Robinson, N. Evans and P. Callaghan (eds) *Culture as the Tourist Product* (pp. 255–278). Sunderland: Business Education Publishers.

Long, P. (1997) Researching tourism partnership organizations: From practice to theory to methodology. In P. Murphy (ed.) *Quality Management in Urban Tourism* (pp. 235–252). Chichester: John Wiley & Sons.

Long, P. (2000) Tourism development regimes in the inner city fringe: The case of Discover Islington, London. In B. Bramwell and B. Lane (eds) *Tourism Collaboration and Partnerships: Politics, Practice and Sustainability* (pp. 183–199). Clevedon: Channel View.

Lumsdon, L. (1997) *Tourism Marketing*. London: International Thomson Business Press.

Lynch, R. (2003) *Corporate Strategy* (3rd edn). Harlow: Pearson Education Limited.

Macneil, I. (1980) *The New Social Contract: An Enquiry into Modern Contractual Relations*. New Haven, CT: Yale University Press.

Magun, S. (1996) *The Development of Strategic Alliances in Canadian Industries: A Micro Analysis*. Working Paper No. 13, Industry Canada.

Malver, H. (1998) *Service in the Airlines: Customer or Competition Oriented?* Stockholm: Stockholm University.

March, R. (1994) Tourism marketing myopia. *Tourism Management* 15 (6), 411–415.

McCann, J.E. and Chiles, C.L. (1983) Design guidelines for social problem-solving interventions. *Journal of Applied Behavioral Science* 19 (2), 177–189.

McDonald, M. and Christopher, M. (2003) *Marketing: A Complete Guide*. Basingstoke: Palgrave Macmillan.

McDonald, M. and Payne, A. (1996) *Marketing Planning for Services*. Oxford: Butterworth-Heinemann.

McDonald, M. and Wilson, H. (2002) *The New Marketing: Transforming the Corporate Future*. Oxford: Butterworth-Heinemann.

McIntosh, R.W., Goeldner, C.R. and Ritchie, J.R.B. (1995) *Tourism: Principles, Practices, Philosophies* (7th edn). Chichester: John Wiley & Sons.

McKercher, B. (1995) The destination-market matrix: A tourism market portfolio analysis model. *Journal of Travel and Tourism Marketing* 4 (2), 23–40.

MGC (1998) *Collaboration Between Museums: A Report for the Museums & Galleries Commission*. London: Museums & Galleries Commission.

Middleton, V.T.C. (1988) *Marketing in Travel and Tourism*. Oxford: Butterworth-Heinemann.

Middleton, V.T.C. (1998) *Sustainable Tourism: A Marketing Perspective*. Oxford: Butterworth-Heinemann.

Middleton, V.T.C. (2001) *Marketing in Travel and Tourism* (3rd edn). Oxford: Butterworth-Heinemann.

Miller, C. (2000) Consortia react and reinvent to compete. *Hotels* 34 (11), 63–68.

Minca, C. and Getz, D. (1995) Public and private sector cooperation in destination planning: A comparison of Banff and Niagara Falls. *Tourist Review* 50 (4), 49–59.

Morgan, M. (1996) *Marketing for Leisure and Tourism*. London: Prentice Hall.

Morgan, R.M. and Hunt, S.D. (1994) The commitment–trust theory of relationship marketing. *Journal of Marketing* 58 (3), 20–38.

Morley, C. (2003) Impacts of international airline alliances on tourism. *Tourism Economics*, 9 (1), 31–51.

Morrish, S.C. and Hamilton, R.T. (2002) Airline alliances: Who benefits? *Journal of Air Transport Management* 8 (6), 401–407.

Morrison, A.J. (1994) Marketing strategic alliances: The small hotel firm. *International Journal of Contemporary Hospitality Management* 6 (3), 25–30.

Morrison, A.J.. and Harrison, A. (1998) From corner shop to electronic shopping mall? *Progress in Tourism and Hospitality Research* 4 (4), 349–356.

Morrison, S.A. (1996) Airline mergers: A longer view. *Journal of Transport Economics and Policy* 30, 237–250.

Mullins, L.J. (2002) *Management and Organisational Behaviour* (6th edn). Harlow: Financial Times Prentice Hall.

Murphy, P. (1997) *Quality Management in Urban Tourism*. Chichester: Wiley.

Murphy, P., Pritchard, M. and Smith, B. (2000) The destination product and its impact on traveller perception. *Tourism Management* 21 (1), 43–52.

Murray, M. (1997) Run with the pack. *Hospitality* (July–August), 20–21.

Naoum, S. (2003) An overview into the concept of partnering. *International Journal of Project Management* 21 (1), 71–76.

Narver, J. and Slater, S. (1990) The effect of a market orientation on business profitability. *Journal of Marketing* 54 (4), 20–35.

Newell, F. (1997) *The New Rules of Marketing: How to Use One-to-One Relationship Marketing to be the Leader in Your Industry*. New York: McGraw-Hill.

Nicholls, J. (1995) The MCC decision matrix: A tool for applying strategic logic to everyday activity. *Management Decision* 33 (6), 4–10.

Nielsen, R.P. (1988) Cooperative strategy. *Strategic Management Journal* 9 (5), 475–492.

Nissé, J. (2003a) British airways on a roll with Swiss. *The Independent on Sunday*, 24 August.

Nissé, J. (2003b) I've had a lot of luck . . . all of it bad. *The Independent on Sunday*, 24 August.

OECD (2000) *Airline Mergers and Alliances*. DAFFE/CLP(200)1, Organisation for Economic Cooperation and Development, Paris.

Ohmae, K. (1989) Managing in a borderless world. *Harvard Business Review* (May–June), 152–161.

Ohmae, K. (1991) *The Borderless World*. New York: Harper Perennial.

Oppermann, M. (1997) First time and repeat visitors to New Zealand. *Tourism Management* 18 (3), 177–181.

Oppermann, M. (1998) Destination theshold potential and the law of repeat visitation. *Journal of Travel Research* 37(2), 131–137.

Oppermann, M. (1999) Predicting destination choice: A discussion of destination loyalty. *Journal of Vacation Marketing* 5 (1), 52–62.

Oppermann, M. (2000) Tourism destination loyalty. *Journal of Travel Research* 39 (1), 78–84.

Osborn, R.N and Baughn, C.C. (1990) Forms of interorganizational governance for multinational alliances. *Academy of Management Journal* 33 (3), 503–519.

Osborne, D. and Gaebler, T. (1992) *Reinventing Government*. Reading: Addison-Wesley.

Oum. T.H. and Park, J.-H. (1997) Airline alliances: Current status, policy issues, and future directions. *Journal of Air Transport Management* 3 (3), 133–144.

Oum, T.H., Park, J.-H. and Zhang, A. (1996) The effects of airline codesharing agreements on firm conduct and international airfares. *Journal of Transport Economics and Policy* 30 (2), 187–202.

Oum, T.H., Park, J.-H. and Zhang, A. (2000) *Globalization and Strategic Alliances: The Case of the Airline Industry*. Oxford: Pergamon.

Palmer, A. (1996) Linking external and internal relationship building in networks of public and private sector organisations: A case study. *International Journal of Public Sector Management* 9 (3), 51–60.

Palmer, A. (1998a) *Principles of Services Marketing* (2nd edn). London: McGraw-Hill.

Palmer, A. (1998b) Evaluating the governance style of marketing groups. *Annals of Tourism Research* 25 (1), 185–201.

Palmer, A. (2002) Cooperative marketing association: An investigation into the causes of effectiveness. *Journal of Strategic Marketing* 10 (2), 135–156.

Palmer, A. and Bejou, D. (1995) Tourism destination marketing alliances. *Annals of Tourism Research* 22 (3), 616–629.

Palmer, A. and Mayer, R. (1996) Relationship marketing: A new paradigm for the travel and tourism sector. *Journal of Vacation Marketing* 2 (4), 326–333.

Papadopoulos, S. (1989a) A conceptual tourism marketing planning model: Part 1. *European Journal of Marketing* 23 (1), 31–40.

Papadopoulos, S. (1989b) Strategy development and implementation of tourism marketing plans: Part 2. *European Journal of Marketing* 23 (3), 37–47.

Park, J.-H. and Zhang, A. (1998) Airline alliances and partner firms' outputs. *Transportation Research E: Logistics and Transportation Review* 34 (4), 245–255.

Park, N.K. and Cho, D.-S. (1997) The effect of strategic alliance on performance: A study of international airline industry. *Journal of Air Transport Management* 3 (3), 155–164.

Payne, A., Christopher, M., Clarke, M. and Peck, H. (1996) *Relationship Marketing for Competitive Advantage*. Oxford: Butterworth-Heinemann.

Pearce, D. (1992) *Tourist Organisations*. Harlow: Longman.

Pekar, P., Jr and Allio, R. (1994) Making alliances work: Guidelines for success. *Long Range Planning* 27 (4), 54–65.

Pels, E. (2001) A note on airline alliances. *Journal of Air Transport Management* 7 (1), 3–7.

Perry, M.L., Sengupta, S. and Krapfel, R. (2002) Effectiveness of horizontal strategic alliances in technologically uncertain environments: Are trust and commitment enough? *Journal of Business Research* (forthcoming).

Piercy, N. (1997) *Market-led Strategic Change* (2nd edn). Oxford: Butterworth-Heinemann.

Poon, A. (1993) *Tourism, Technology and Competitive Strategies*. Wallingford: CABI Publications.

Porter, M. (1980) *Competitive Strategy*. New York: Free Press.

Pretty, J. (1995) The many interpretations of participation. *In Focus* 16, 4–5.

Prideaux, B. (2000) The resort development spectrum: A new approach to modelling resort development. *Tourism Management* 21 (3), 225–240.

Prideaux, B. and Cooper, C. (2002) Marketing and destination growth: A symbiotic relationship or simple coincidence? *Journal of Vacation Marketing* 9 (1), 35–51.

Prince, M. and Davies, M. (2002) Co-branding partners: What do they see in each other. *Business Horizons* 45 (5), 51–55.

Pyo, S., Song, J. and Chang, H. (1998) Implications of repeat visitor patterns: The Cheju Island case. *Tourism Analysis* 3 (3/4), 181–187.

Reid, L. and Reid, S. (1993) Communicating tourism supplier services: Building repeat visitor relationships. *Journal of Travel and Tourism Marketing* 2 (2/3), 3–19.

Rhoades, D.L. and Lush, H. (1997) A typology of strategic alliances in the airline industry: Propositions for stability and duration. *Journal of Air Transport Management* 3 (3), 109–114.

Riege, A.M. and Perry, C. (2000) National marketing strategies in international travel and tourism. *European Journal of Marketing* 34 (11/12), 1290–1305.

Riley, M., Niininen, O., Szivas, E. and Willis, T. (2001) The case for process approaches in loyalty research in tourism. *International Journal of Tourism Research* 3 (1), 23–32.

Ritchie, R.J.B. and Brent Ritchie, J.R. (2002) A framework for an industry supported destination marketing information system. *Tourism Management* 23 (5), 439–454.

Roberts, L. and Simpson, F. (2000) Developing partnership approaches to tourism in Central and Eastern Europe. In B. Bramwell and B. Lane (eds) *Tourism Collaboration and Partnerships: Politics, Practice and Sustainability* (pp. 230–246). Clevedon: Channel View.

Robson, J. and Robson, I. (1996) From shareholders to stakeholders: Critical issues for tourism marketers. *Tourism Management* 17 (7), 533–540.

Robson, M.J. and Dunk, M. (1999) Developing a pan-European co-marketing alliance: The case of BP-Mobil. *International Marketing Review* 16 (3), 216–230.

Roper, A. (1995) The emergence of hotel consortia as transorganizational forms. *International Journal of Contemporary Hospitality Management* 7 (1), 4–9.

Ross, G. (1993) Ideal and actual image of backpacker visitors to Northern Australia. *Journal of Travel Research* 32 (2), 54–57.

Ryan, C. (1991) Tourism marketing: A symbiotic relationship. *Tourism Management* 12 (2), 101–111.

Ryan, C. (2002) The politics of branding cities and regions: The case of New Zealand. In N. Morgan, A. Pritchard and R. Pride (eds) *Destination Branding: Creating a Unique Destination Proposition* (pp. 66–86). Oxford: Butterworth-Heinemann.

Sall, B. (1995) Strategic alliances. *Voice* 4 (3), 18–20.

SAS (2002) *Annual Report*. Stockholm: The SAS Group.

Satchell, A. (1995) Why Pride of Britain means business. *Voice* 4 (5), 12–13.

Sautter, E.T. and Leisen, B. (1999) Managing stakeholders: A tourism planning model. *Annals of Tourism Research* 26 (2), 312–328.

Schreiber, E.S. (2002) Brand strategy frameworks for diversified companies and partnerships. *Brand Management* 10 (2), 122–138.

Schuman, S.P. (1996) The role of facilitation in collaborative groups. In C. Huxham (ed.) *Creating Collaborative Advantage* (pp. 126–140). London: Sage.

Schweiterman, J. (1995) A hedonic price assessment of airline service quality in the US. *Transport Reviews* 15, 291–302.

Scott, N., Parfitt, N. and Laws, E. (2000) Destination management: Co-operative marketing, a case study of Port Douglas Brand. In B. Faulkner, G. Moscardo and E. Laws (eds) *Tourism in the 21st Century* (pp. 198–221). London: Continuum.

Seabright, M.A., Levinthal, D.A. and Fichman, M. (1992) Role of individual attachment in the dissolution of cooperative interorganizational relationships. *Academy of Management Review* 19 (1), 122–160.

Seaton, A.V. and Bennett, M.M. (1996) *The Marketing of Tourism Products: Concepts, Issues and Cases*. London: International Thomson Business Press.

Segil, L. (1996) *Intelligent Business Alliances*. London: Random House.

Selin, S. (1993) Collaborative alliances: New interorganizational forms in tourism. *Journal of Travel and Tourism Marketing* 2 (2/3), 217–227.

Selin, S. (1999) Developing a typology of sustainable tourism partnerships. *Journal of Sustainable Tourism* 7 (3/4), 260–273.

Selin, S. and Chavez, D. (1995) Developing an evolutionary tourism partnership model. *Annals of Tourism Research* 22 (4), 844–856.

Sharma, S. (1999) Trespass or symbiosis? Dissolving the boundaries between strategic marketing and strategic management. *Journal of Strategic Marketing* 7 (2), 73–88.

Sheth, J. and Parvatiyar, A. (2000) *Handbook of Relationship Marketing*. London: Sage.

Shundich, S. (1996) Consortia 25. *Hotels* 30 (7), 70.

Slater, S.F. and Narver, J.C. (1994) Does competitive environment moderate the market orientation–performance relationship? *Journal of Marketing* 58 (1), 46–55.

Slattery, P. (1992) Unaffiliated hotels in the UK. *Travel and Tourism Analyst*, 1, 90–102.

Slattery, P., Roper, A. and Boer, A. (1985) Hotel consortia: Their activities, structure and growth. *Service Industries Journal* 5 (2), 192–199.

Smith, S.L.J. (1994) The tourism product. *Annals of Tourism Research* 21 (3), 582–595.

Sonmez, S.F. and Apostolopoulos, Y. (2000) Conflict resolution through tourism cooperation? The case of the partitioned island-state of Cyprus. *Journal of Travel and Tourism Marketing* 9 (3), 35–48.

Spyriadis, A. (2002) Collaborative partnerships as strategic marketing tools of international hotel chains in pursuit of business development and competitive advantage in the global marketplace. Unpublished Masters thesis, Bournemouth University, UK.

Standeven, J. (1998) Sport tourism: Joint marketing – a starting point for beneficial synergies. *Journal of Vacation Marketing* 4 (1), 39–51.

TAI (2003a) *Sawasdee* (January). Bangkok: Thai Airways International.

TAI (2003b) *Sawasdee* (February). Bangkok: Thai Airways International.

Telfer, D.J. (2000) Tastes of Niagara: Building strategic alliances between tourism and agriculture. In J.C. Crotts, D. Buhalis and R. March (eds) *Global Alliances in Tourism and Hospitality Management* (pp. 71–88). New York: The Haworth Hospitality Press.

ten Have, S., ten Have, W. and Stevens, F. (2003) *Key Management Models*. London: Financial Times Prentice Hall.

Terpstra, V. and Simonin, B. (1993) Strategic alliances in the triad: An exploratory study. *Journal of International Marketing* 1 (1), 4–25.

Teye, V.B. (1988) Prospects for regional tourism cooperation in Africa. *Tourism Management* 9 (3), 221–234.

Thurlby, B. (1998) Competitive forces are also subject to change. *Management Decision* 36 (1), 19–24.

Timothy, D.J. (1998) Cooperative tourism planning in a developing destination. *Journal of Sustainable Tourism* 6 (1), 52–68.

Tribe, J. (1997) *Corporate Strategy for Tourism*. London: Thomson Learning.

Trist, E.L. (1977) A concept of organizational ecology. *Australian Journal of Management* 2 (2), 162–175.

Waddock, S.A. (1989) Understanding social partnerships: An evolutionary model of partnership organizations. *Administration & Society* 21 (1), 78–100.

Waddock, S.A. and Bannister, B.D. (1991) Correlates of effectiveness and partner satisfaction in social partnerships. *Journal of Organizational Change Management* 4 (2), 64–79.

Wahab, S. (1996) Tourism development in Egypt: Competitive strategies and implications. *Progress in Tourism and Hospitality Research* 2 (3/4), 351–364.

Wahab, S. and Cooper, C. (2001) *Tourism in the Age of Globalisation*. London: Routledge.

Walker, D.H.T. and Johannes, D.S. (2003) Construction industry joint venture behaviour in Hong King: Designed for collaborative results? *International Journal of Project Management* 21 (1), 39–49.

Wanhill, S. and Lundtorp, S. (2001) The resort life cycle theory: Generating processes and estimation. *Annals of Tourism Research* 28 (4), 947–964.

Webster, F. (1988) The rediscovery of the marketing concept. *Business Horizons* 31 (May–June), 29–39.

Webster, F. (1992) The changing role of marketing in the organisation. *Journal of Marketing* 56 (4), 1–17.

Weinstein, J. (2000) Where do we go from here? *Hotels* (January), 54–60.

Weinstein, J. (2001) Chains versus independents. *Hotels* (January), 5.

Wheeler, M. (1993) Tourism marketers in local government. *Annals of Tourism Research* 20 (2), 354–356.

Wheeler, M. (1995) Tourism marketing ethics: An introduction. *International Marketing Review* 12 (4), 38–49.

Williamson, O. (1975) *Markets and Hierarchies*. New York: Free Press.

Williamson, O. (1985) *The Economic Institutions of Capitalism*. New York: Free Press.

Wing, P. (1994) Multination marketing. In S. Witt and L. Moutinho (eds) *Tourism Marketing and Management Handbook* (pp. 395–398). New York: Prentice Hall.

Witt, S.F. and Moutinho, L. (1995) *Tourism Marketing and Management Handbook* (student edn). Hemel Hempstead: Prentice Hall.

Wood, D.J. and Gray, B. (1991) Towards a comprehensive theory of collaboration. *Journal of Applied Behavioral Science* 27 (2), 139–162.

WTO (2002) *Tourism in the Age of Alliances, Mergers and Acquisitions*. Madrid: World Tourism Organization.

WTO (2003) *World Tourism Highlights 2002*. Madrid: World Tourism Organization.

Yip, G.S. (1993) *Total Global Strategy: Managing for Worldwide Competitive Advantage*. London: Prentice Hall.

Yip, G.S. (1995) *Total Global Strategy*. London: Prentice Hall.

Zafar, U.A. (1991) The influence of the components of a state's tourist image on product positioning strategy. *Tourism Management* 12 (4), 331–340.

Online Sources

www.atwonline.com (accessed 23 May 2003).

www.aviationnow.com (accessed 15 September 2003).

www.bestwestern.com (accessed 21 October 2003).

www.economist.com (accessed 2 October 2003).

www.new.airwise.com (accessed 4 July 2003).

www.oneworldalliance.com (accessed 23 May 2003).

www.singaporeair.com (accessed 16 September 2003).

www.staralliance.com (accessed 11 September 2003).

www.visit-mekong.com (accessed 15 June 2003).

www.world-tourism.org (accessed 14 March 2003).

Index

KLM, 13, 236, 239, 241, 242, 243, 247, 251,
  257, 335, 353, 354
Korean Air, 227
KSS Consortium, 231

Lan Chile, 227
Laos, 295, 299, 300, 303, 330, 337, 339
Lastminute.com, 116
Lauda Air, 226, 243
LEADER, 17
Leading Hotels of the World, 117
Local authorities, 37, 44, 167, 168, 296, 297,
  298
Logis de France, 117
London Development Agency, 288
London Tourist Board, 288
London Tourism Action Group, 288
LOT Polish, 243
Loyalty reward schemes, 237
Lufthansa, 13, 225, 226, 236, 243, 246, 248,
  255, 256, 257, 258, 326, 351, 358,
Luxury Hotels of the World, 91, 270

m-technology, *see* technology
Macdonald Hotels, 274
Macro-environment, 25, 58-61, 317, 329-331,
  351
Malmaison Hotels, 261
m-commerce, 13
Maersk Air, 256
Management contracts, 234, 237
Marketing
– adversarial, 287, 311, 315, 316, 317, 327,
  353, 301
– audit, 22, 25, 58, 66-68, 318, 328-337
– competitive orientation, 29, 316
– components, 21-26
– concept, 19, 30, 32, 44, 45
– control, 23, 24, 25, 26, 29, 124-126, 358
– culture, 4, 17, 35, 39
– database, 120
– direct, 120–
– era, 20
– evaluation, 50, 124, 125, 325, 358
– focus, 162
– information system, 67, 318
– inward-looking orientation, 20, 21
– mix, 25, 105-121, 163, 164, 350-354
– myopia, 20, 39
– new, 29
– objectives, 96, 98, 99, 119, 319, 341-342
– one-to-one, 102
– orientation, *see* market orientation
– outward-looking orientation, 21, 22
– planning, 24, 25, 27, 35, 51, 52, 166-167,
  288
– production era, 20
– relational perspective, 22, 28, 29-34, 35, 38,
  44, 45, 52, 86, 138, 284, 315, 316, 317, 361

– relationship, 29, 32, 63, 107, 110, 216,
  304-309, 316, 333, 352
– research, 67
– sales orientation, 20, 21
– selling era, 20
– societal, 28, 38
– tactics, 22, 23, 24, 33
– transactional perspective, 24, 30, 31, 45
– undifferentiated, 92, 101, 102
Market
– attractiveness, 83, 102
– challengers, 92, 93
– concentration, *see* concentration
– development, 96, 97, 139-141
– diversification, 345
– environment, 25, 51, 58, 66-68, 138, 317,
  333-337
– followers, 92, 93, 339
– leaders, 92, 93
– nichers, 11, 92, 93, 339
– penetration, 96
– position framework, 93
– positioning, 25, 104, 319, 339
– orientation, 4, 20, 21, 26, 30, 32, 33, 34, 35,
  37-38, 44, 45, 67, 315
Marriott Hotels, 231
Media, 42
Meetings, incentives, conventions and
  exhibitions, 296
MERCOSUR, 9
Mergers, 8, 12, 134, 141, 148, 149, 157, 158,
  187, 229, 239, 329, 342
Mexicana, 226, 243, 246
MGC, *see* Museums and Galleries
  Commission
MICE, *see* meetings, incentives, conventions
  and exhibitions
Micro-businesses, 142
Micro-environment, 25, 58, 62-66, 331-333,
  341, 351, 352
MNC, *see* multinational companies
Monitoring, 25, 29, 50, 175, 179, 196, 199,
  201, 213, 322, 358
Multinational companies, 10, 11, 12, 142,
  218
Museums and Galleries Commission, 190
Mutual dependence, *see* interdependence
Myanmar, 295, 299, 300, 303

NAFTA, *see* North American Free Trade
  Agreement
National Lottery, 17
NATO, *see* North Atlantic Treaty
  Organisation
Networks, 10-11, 17, 31, 32, 52, 81, 131, 133,
  147, 153, 154, 179, 190, 216-218, 294, 316,
  333
New product development, *see* product
New tourists, 15

Middleton
el. a.